"It is a pleasure to see sanity and balance brought to a topic that is typically fraught with emotionality and simple-minded, wrong-headed diagnoses and solutions. Blumstein and Wallman have accomplished just that. They have done a beautiful job of sorting out and assessing the demographic, economic, and public-policy origins of the great fluctuations in American crime during the past two decades. Both the editors and authors are to be congratulated for their insistence on multiple causes, their methodological sophistication, and their prudent interpretations."

Neil Smelser, Director, *Center for Advanced Study in the Behavioral Sciences*

"At last, a scholarly, disinterested examination of the rapid decline in violence during the 1990s, a phenomenon as puzzling as it was unprecedented. Many have claimed credit, from police executives to prison advocates, yet these essays show that many forces were at work. Targeted policing, a strong economy, new gun policies, higher imprisonment rates, stabilized drug markets – all played a role. Yet the book offers sober reminders that broad social forces, including changes in youth culture and marriage patterns, contribute to our crime condition. For all who care about a safe and just society, this book is a required primer."

Jeremy Travis, Senior Fellow, *Urban Institute*,
former Director of the *National Institute of Justice* (1994–2000) and Deputy
Commissioner for Legal Matters of the *New York City Police Department* (1990–94)

"Pundits have been all too ready to assign credit for the recent near-miraculous reductions in violent crime. But before we commit to 1990s innovations in policing, sentencing, drug programs, and the like, it's necessary to take a careful look at the evidence. That's why this book is so important, and yet surely will irritate those who favor simple answers. The authors provide a patient and penetrating assessment of the contending explanations for the crime drop, nicely deflating the more strident claims and establishing a sound basis for moving forward."

Philip J. Cook, ITT Terry Sanford Distinguished Professor of
Public Policy Studies, *Sanford Institute of Public Policy, Duke University*,
coauthor, *Gun Violence: The Real Costs* (2000)

"This is the definitive examination of the crime drop. Every criminologist should read it ... before the crime rate starts to go up again. "

Jack Levin, Director, *The Brudnick Center on Violence and Conflict, Northeastern University*; coauthor, *The Will to Kill: Making Sense of Senseless Murder*

"Recent widespread declines in violence across the United States have puzzled criminologists and challenged traditional criminological theories. This volume, edited by Alfred Blumstein and Joel Wallman, assesses a wide variety of alleged causes of the decline. Criminologists interested in making sense of the puzzle will find the thematic collection of papers to be essential reading."

Robert J. Sampson, Lucy Flower Professor of Sociology and of the Social Sciences in the College, *The University of Chicago*

"A towering optimistic masterpiece in its clear, logical revelation that both the causes and answers to crime are many and complex, and don't lend themselves to the simplistic, one-solution-fits-all, bumper-sticker type slogans of politicians."

Peter Elikann, author of *Superpredators: The Demonization of our Children by the Law*; expert commentator, Court TV

"While politicians pounded their chests, the authors were doing it the right way: systematically mining for evidence of what led to the great drop in crime during the 90s. What they unearthed is both provocative and convincing, and they only give politicians some of the credit."

Wesley Skogan, Professor, *Institute for Policy Research, Northwestern University*

The Crime Drop in America

Violent crime in America shot up sharply in the mid-1980s and continued to climb until 1991, after which something remarkable and unprecedented occurred. For the next seven years it declined to a level not seen since the 1960s.

The puzzle of how and why this has happened, after decades of growing violence, has bedeviled criminologists, politicians, policy makers, and average citizens. Numerous explanations have been put forth, from improvements in policing to the decline in crack cocaine use. The authors of this timely and critical book explain and assess the plausible causes and competing claims of credit for the crime drop. Here some of America's top criminologists examine the role of guns and gun violence, the growing prison population, homicide patterns, drug markets, economic opportunity, changes in policing, and changing demographics.

As the authors point out, the trends that have contributed to the decline in violent crime-gun-control efforts (at both the local and federal levels), changes in drug markets (the decline of crack cocaine), and economic shifts (high employment in the flourishing economy of the late 1990s) cannot continue indefinitely. The control and prevention of crime will continue to challenge scholars and public policy makers. This book presents the most authoritative and intelligent discussion available on the rise and fall of American violence. The perspectives offered here will undoubtedly influence the public debate and the planning of future responses to crime.

Alfred Blumstein is J. Erik Jonsson University Professor of Urban Systems and Operations Research at Carnegie Mellon University and Director of the National Consortium on Violence Research.

Joel Wallman is Program Officer at The Harry Frank Guggenheim Foundation in New York.

Cambridge Studies in Criminology

Edited by
Alfred Blumstein, *H. John Heinz School of Public Policy and Management, Carnegie Mellon University* and David Farrington, *Institute of Criminology, University of Cambridge*

The Cambridge Studies in Criminology series aims to publish the highest quality research on criminology and criminal justice topics. Typical volumes report major quantitative, qualitative, and ethnographic research, or make a substantial theoretical contribution. There is a particular emphasis on research monographs, but edited collections may also be published if they make an unusually distinctive offering to the literature. All relevant areas of criminology and criminal justice are included, for example, the causes of offending, juvenile justice, the development of offenders, measurement and analysis of crime, victimization research, policing, crime prevention, sentencing, imprisonment, probation, and parole. The series is global in outlook, with an emphasis on work that is comparative or holds significant implications for theory or policy.

Other Books in the Series:

Life in the Gang: Family, Friends, and Violence, by Scott H. Decker and
    Barrik Van Winkle
Delinquency and Crime: Current Theories, edited by J. David Hawkins
Recriminalizing Delinquency: Violent Juvenile Crime and Juvenile Justice Reform,
    by Simon I. Singer
Mean Streets: Youth Crime and Homelessness, by John Hagan and Bill McCarthy
Criminality and Violence among the Mentally Disordered, by Sheilagh Hodgins
    and Carl-Gunnar Janson
*Crack Selling: The Political Economy, "Get Tough" Policies, and Marketing of Crack
    Cocaine,* by Bruce D. Johnson and Eloise Dunlap
The Framework of Judicial Sentencing: A Study in Legal Decision Making, by
    Austin Lovegrove
The Criminal Recidivism Process, by Edward Zamble and Vernon L. Quinsey
Judicial Policy Making and the Modern State: How the Courts Reformed America's Prisons
    by Malcom M. Feeley and Edward L. Rubin
Schools and Delinquency by Denise C. Gottfredson

The Crime Drop in America

Edited by

Alfred Blumstein
Carnegie Mellon University and National Consortium on Violence Research

Joel Wallman
The Harry Frank Guggenheim Foundation

CAMBRIDGE
UNIVERSITY PRESS

PUBLISHED BY THE PRESS SYNDICATE OF THE UNIVERSITY OF CAMBRIDGE
The Pitt Building, Trumpington Street, Cambridge, United Kingdom

CAMBRIDGE UNIVERSITY PRESS
The Edinburgh Building, Cambridge CB2 2RU, UK
http:www.cup.cam.ac.uk
40 West 20th Street, New York, NY 10011-4211, USA
http:www.cup.org
10 Stamford Road, Oakleigh, Melbourne 3166, Australia

First published 2000

Printed in the United States of America

Typeface New Baskerville 10/13 *System* QuarkXPress™   [HT]

A catalog record for this book is available from the British Library

Library of Congress Cataloging-in-Publication Data

The crime drop in America / edited by Alfred Blumstein, Joel Wallman.
p.   cm. – (Cambrige studies in criminology)
ISBN 0-521-79296-X
1. Crime – United States.   2. Violent crimes – United States.
I. Blumstein, Alfred.   II. Wallman, Joel.   III. Series.

HV6789.C6814   2000
364.973 – dc21

ISBN   0 521 79296 7 hardback
ISBN   0 521 79712 8 paperback

Contents

The research project for this book was sponsored
by the National Consortium on Violence Research
and the Harry Frank Guggenheim Foundation.

Contributors

Alfred Blumstein (Ph.D., Cornell) is a University Professor, the J. Erik Jonsson Professor of Urban Systems and Operations Research, and former Dean at the H. John Heinz III School of Public Policy and Management of Carnegie Mellon University. He is also director of the National Consortium on Violence Research (NCOVR), which is funded by a grant from the National Science Foundation. He has had extensive experience in both research and policy with the criminal justice system since serving the President's Commission on Law Enforcement and Administration of Justice in 1966–67 as Director of its Task Force on Science and Technology. Dr. Blumstein was a member of the National Academy of Sciences Committee on Research on Law Enforcement and the Administration of Justice. He is a member of the Academy's Commission on Behavioral and Social Sciences and Education. He is a member of the National Academy of Engineering and a fellow of the American Association for the Advancement of Science and the American Society of Criminology. He is past president of the Institute of Management Sciences, the Institute for Operations Research and the Management Sciences, and the American Society of Criminology. He was awarded the Kimball Medal and the President's Award by the Operations Research Society of America for "contributions to society" and the Sutherland Award and the Wolfgang Award for Distinguished Achievement in Criminology for his "contributions to research." Dr. Blumstein's research has covered many aspects of criminal-justice phenomena and policy, including crime measurement, criminal careers, sentencing, deterrence and incapacitation, prison populations, demographic trends, juvenile violence, and drug-enforcement policy.

Eloise Dunlap received her Ph.D. in sociology from the University of California-Berkeley. Her research has primarily examined the dynamics of African-American families and households, especially where drug abusers are present. Dr. Dunlap received advanced training in drug-abuse and treatment research as a Postdoctoral Fellow in the Behavioral Sciences Training in Drug Abuse Research program at National Development and Research Institutes, Inc. (NDRI), a private not-for-profit research institute in New York City. Since 1994, she has been a Principal Investigator at NDRI. She is currently researching the high levels of violence in inner-city households of crack users and sellers and writing a book on the conduct norms and behavior patterns in such households that lead to violence in relationships.

John E. Eck is Associate Professor in the Division of Criminal Justice at the University of Cincinnati. He received his Ph.D. from the University of Maryland (1994) and his Masters in Public Policy from the University of Michigan (1977). Dr. Eck was the Research Director at the Police Executive Research Forum and the Evaluation Coordinator for the Washington/Baltimore High Intensity Drug Trafficking Area. He is the author of numerous articles, chapters, and monographs on policing, drug markets, and crime patterns. With David Weisburd, he co-edited *Crime and Place* (1995).

James Alan Fox (Ph.D., University of Pennsylvania) is the Lipman Family Professor of Criminal Justice and a former dean at Northeastern University in Boston. He is the founding editor of the *Journal of Quantitative Criminology* and has published fourteen books, the most recent of which is *The Will to Kill: Making Sense of Senseless Murder* (2000). He has also published dozens of journal and magazine articles and newspaper columns, primarily in the areas of multiple murder, juvenile crime, school violence, workplace violence, and capital punishment. As an authority on homicide, Dr. Fox appears regularly on national television and radio programs and is frequently interviewed by the press. He has made over one hundred keynote or campus-wide addresses around the country and ten appearances before the United States Congress, has attended White House meetings on youth violence with the president and vice president, and has given briefings on violence trends to the attorney general and to Princess Anne of Great Britain. Dr. Fox is currently a visiting fellow with the Bureau of Justice Statistics of the U.S. Department of Justice.

Andrew Golub received his Ph.D. in public policy analysis from the Heinz School of Public Policy Analysis and Management at Carnegie Mellon. He is currently a Principal Investigator at National Development and Research Institutes, Inc. (NDRI). Dr. Golub's research examines social problems with an aim toward helping to develop more effective and cost-effective government programs. He is the author of *Decision Analysis: An Integrated Approach* (1997). Much of his recent research has been devoted to understanding drug abuse, especially drug epidemics, drug use by adolescents, and the association between drug use and criminality. He has directed or co-directed six research projects funded by the National Institute of Justice, the National Institute on Drug Abuse, and the Robert Wood Johnson Foundation. He is currently working on two books: an ethnographic examination of the impact of drug epidemics on New York's inner-city households, and an expanded analysis of the gateway model for understanding stages in adolescent substance use.

Jeffrey Grogger (Ph.D., University of California at San Diego) is an economist and Professor of Public Policy at UCLA. He is a fellow of the National Bureau of Economic Research (Cambridge, MA), the Center for Economic Policy Research (London), and the Institute for the Study of Labor (Bonn). He is the author of numerous scholarly articles on the link between crime and the labor market, including "The Effect of Arrests on the Employment and Earnings of Young Men" (1995, *Quarterly Journal of Economics*), "Market Wages and Youth Crime" (1998, *Journal of Labor Economics*), and "The Emergence of Crack Cocaine and the Rise in Urban Crime Rates" (2000, *Review of Economics and Statistics*). He is a co-editor of the *Journal of Human Resources* and sits on the editorial boards of the *Journal of Population Economics* and *Economic Inquiry*.

Bruce D. Johnson received his Ph.D. in Sociology from Columbia University. Since 1992, he has directed the Institute for Special Populations Research at National Development and Research Institutes, Inc. (NDRI). He has published over one hundred articles or book chapters and has authored or co-authored five books, including *Marihuana Users and Drug Subcultures* (1973), *Taking Care of Business: The Economics of Crime by Heroin Abusers* (1985), and *Kids, Drugs, and Crime* (1988). Dr. Johnson was honored in 1999 with the Senior Scholar Award by Drinking and Drugs Division of the Society for the Study of Social Problems and was chairperson of this division in 1994–96. He was a Woodrow Wilson Fellow at

Columbia University in 1965–66. During his 33-year career in drug-abuse research, he has been principal investigator or co-investigator on 25 research projects funded by the National Institute on Drug Abuse, National Institute of Justice, and other agencies. His current research includes ethnographic analysis of crack distribution, analysis of drug use among arrestees, estimation of the number of hard drug users and distributors, impacts of policing on criminal behaviors, an ethnography of heroin users and HIV in Brooklyn and Sydney, and analysis of new drug-detection technologies.

Edward R. Maguire is an Associate Professor of Administration of Justice at George Mason University. He has held research positions at the U.S. Department of Justice and the United Nations Crime Prevention and Criminal Justice Branch in Vienna. Dr. Maguire received his Ph.D. in 1997 from the School of Criminal Justice, University at Albany, SUNY. His primary professional interest is applying and testing organizational theories in police agencies. Professor Maguire serves on the Justice Department's National Community Policing Resource Board and is a principal investigator on three national studies of police organizational change (funded by NIJ and COPS). His most recent publication (with Craig Uchida), "Measurement and Explanation in the Comparative Study of American Police Organizations," appears in the National Institute of Justice's CJ2000 Volume, *Measurement and Explanation in Crime and Justice*. His book, *Context, Complexity and Control: Organizational Structure in Large Police Agencies*, will be published in 2000.

Richard Rosenfeld is Professor of Criminology at the University of Missouri-St. Louis. He received his Ph.D. in sociology from the University of Oregon. Professor Rosenfeld is a member of the steering committee of the National Consortium on Violence Research (NCOVR) and associate editor of the journal *Criminology*. His research focuses on the social sources of criminal violence. He is co-author with Steven Messner of *Crime and the American Dream* (1997, 2nd ed.), and his research articles have appeared in the *Journal of Criminal Law and Criminology, Social Forces, Criminology, Journal of Quantitative Criminology, Journal of Research in Crime and Delinquency*, and other leading journals.

William Spelman is Associate Professor at the Lyndon B. Johnson School of Public Affairs, University of Texas at Austin, where he teaches courses on applied mathematics and statistics, public management, and local government policy. He is author of *Criminal Incapacitation* (1994), *Repeat Offender Programs for Law Enforcement* (1990), and (with John E. Eck) *Problem Solving* (1987). He holds a Ph.D. in public policy from Harvard University. Between 1997 and 2000, Spelman served as a city councilmember in Austin, Texas.

Joel Wallman is Program Officer at the Harry Frank Guggenheim Foundation, which sponsors scholarly research on violence and aggression. He received the Ph.D. with Distinction from Columbia University and, before joining the HFG, taught at Hunter College, Rutgers University, and Columbia. His work has appeared in *Computer Applications in the Biosciences, Current Anthropology,* and the *Journal of Molecular Evolution,* and he is the author of *Aping Language* (1992). He is a member of the Academic Advisory Council of the National Campaign against Youth Violence.

Garen J. Wintemute is director of the Violence Prevention Research Program at the University of California, Davis. He attended medical school and completed his residency at U.C. Davis, and received his MPH degree from The Johns Hopkins University School of Hygiene and Public Health. He practices and teaches emergency medicine at U.C. Davis Medical Center, Sacramento (a Level I regional trauma center), and is Professor of Epidemiology and Preventive Medicine at the U.C. Davis School of Medicine. His research focuses on the nature and prevention of violence and on the development of effective violence-prevention measures. His most recent studies, published in the *Journal of the American Medical Association,* the *New England Journal of Medicine,* and the *American Journal of Public Health,* concern the effect of completed or denied handgun purchases on the risk of subsequent violence by prospective buyers. He is the author of *Ring of Fire* (1994), a study of the handgun makers of Southern California. Dr. Wintemute has testified on numerous occasions before committees of Congress and state and local legislatures as an expert on firearm violence and its prevention. In 1997 he was named a Hero of Medicine by *Time* magazine. He has served as a consultant for the National Institute of Justice; Bureau of Alcohol, Tobacco, and Firearms (as a member of the Youth Crime Gun Interdiction Initiative analysis group); World Health Organization; Centers for Disease Control and Prevention; and American Red Cross.

The Recent Rise and Fall of American Violence

Alfred Blumstein and Joel Wallman

AMERICANS' PRIDE IN THEIR NATION'S MATERIAL PROSPERITY, thriving democracy, and often admirable role in world affairs is tempered, for many, by concern and puzzlement over another American distinction – her perennial presence at the top of the list of the most violent industrial nations. Violence has been a major theme in public discussion for decades, and apprehension about it was intensified by the sharp rise in violence in the mid-1980s, a development most pronounced among inner-city minority youth. Despite the remarkable decline in violence that began in the early 1990s, a preoccupation with criminal violence persists among the citizenry as well as among scholars of violence, who are intent on understanding what has happened and predicting what will be.

Anxiety about violence was heightened considerably by the spate of school shootings in the late 1990s, which occurred after inner-city violence had declined appreciably. These incidents resonated in a broader constituency because, in contrast to what has come to be the standard image of American violence, they typically involved white, middle-class perpetrators and victims in rural or suburban settings. Thus, the late 1990s appeared to many to be a time of increasing suburban violence. In fact, however horrendous each of these school shootings was, fatal assaults in or around schools remain rare events, making up less than one percent of the violent deaths of school-age children. Lethal school violence is uncommon, and like criminal violence in general, is disproportionately an urban phenomenon. That is why this volume is properly focused on urban violence.

Urban violence is an issue of paramount concern to the two sponsors of this volume, the National Consortium on Violence Research (NCOVR), housed at the H. John Heinz III School of Public Policy and Management of Carnegie Mellon University, and the Harry Frank Guggenheim Foundation. The former is a research center sponsored by the National Science Foundation and the latter is a private foundation dedicated to research on the causes and control of violence and aggression. Both have been involved in efforts to understand the rise of violence in the United States in the late 1980s, and both are interested in explaining – and sorting out competing claims of credit for – the decline of violence in the 1990s.

The steady reduction in violence over eight years is unprecedented in contemporary crime statistics and has led to an effort on the part of many scholars and practitioners to explain it. Certainly there have been many claims for credit for the decline. William Bratton, former police commissioner of New York City, credits the police under his tenure for the decline in New York. President Clinton cited the federal investment in community policing. A number of observers have attributed the downward trend in crime since 1992 to the concurrent climb in imprisonment. Others ascribe it to changing demography, especially the aging of the baby boomers out of the high-crime ages.

Given the circulation of these competing claims and attributions in popular and academic forums, it seemed to us that the time was right to mobilize a scholarly effort to identify the plausible causes of the crime drop and to assess the contribution of each. Scholars with widely recognized expertise in a pertinent area were recruited to address the role of gun proliferation and gun control, incarceration, drug markets, policing, economic opportunity, and demography. Several chapters provide quantitative estimates of the magnitude of the effect of a given factor, although we have not tried to compare these estimates with each other, in part because their measurements are of quite different sorts. The number of very tenable explanations for the crime drop, none of which inherently excludes any of the others, leads to the conclusion that there is no single explanation but that a variety of factors, some independent and some interacting in a mutually supportive way, have been important.

In the remainder of this introduction, we present a precis of the various perspectives presented in this volume's careful analyses of the crime drop. Before doing so, we draw a thumbnail sketch of the crime backdrop against which the reduction is clearly visible. First, though, we should say something about the two main sources of information that studies of U.S. crime trends, including those in *The Crime Drop in America*, rely on.

Major Sources of Crime Data

The Uniform Crime Reports (UCR) is an annual compilation of data on U.S. crimes and arrests based upon information provided to the Federal Bureau of Investigation (FBI) by local law enforcement agencies. The Supplementary Homicide Reports (SHR), also part of the UCR program, contains detailed information on individual homicide incidents included in the aggregate figures sent to the FBI.

The National Crime Victimization Survey (NCVS), sponsored by the Department of Justice since 1973, is an annual telephone poll of over 40,000 U.S. households regarding residents' experience of victimization by various kinds of crime. The NCVS compensates for some of the shortcomings of the UCR, and vice versa. For example, the usefulness of the UCR data is limited by the extent to which UCR crime rates are a product of not just the actual frequency of crime but also of factors influencing the likelihood that various crimes will come to the attention of the police and by variation in police recording practices between agencies and within each over time. The NCVS is a survey of individuals and so is not vulnerable to failure of victims to report the crime to the police or to variation in police reporting. However, because it is a survey of limited size (under 100,000 respondents), the number of respondents in any particular place is limited, and the number reporting victimization of low-frequency crimes, such as forcible rape, tends to be small. Also, the NCVS does not collect data on homicide, so the UCR and the SHR are the main sources for analyses of this most serious of crimes, and the crime with which this volume is most concerned.

A Four-Decade Backdrop

Prior to 1965, the U.S. homicide rate was consistently under 5 per 100,000 population. Around 1965, it began a steady rise, and from 1970 it oscillated for twenty years in the range of 8 to 10 per 100,000. A decline from 1980 to 1985 was followed by a dramatic growth in youth violence during the period from 1985 to 1991, with arrest rates for homicide more than doubling for each age group of males under age 20; the rise for black youth was even steeper. Then, beginning in 1992, aggregate rates declined steadily to less than 6 per 100,000 in 1999, a level not seen since the 1960s, with no clear indication of when the decline would level off or reverse itself.

The Elements of the Crime Drop

Chapter 2, by Alfred Blumstein, provides an overview of the trends in violent crime, particularly homicide and robbery, and of the factors influencing these trends. The oscillatory nature of these trends might suggest merely random fluctuation, but there are indeed important causal factors contributing to upturns and downturns. The marked growth in violence between 1965 and the early 1970s may have been, at least in part, a result of the decline in perceived legitimacy of American social and governmental authority during this turbulent period, which contained the civil rights movement and the strident opposition to the war in Vietnam. The continuing uptrend from 1970 to 1980 and the decline to 1985 are largely attributable to the movement of the baby-boom generation into and then out of the high-crime ages of the late teens and early twenties; this is reflected in the general stability of violence rates within individual ages during that period. The rise following the 1985 trough should almost certainly be laid at the crack (smokable cocaine) epidemic and the contagion of violence spawned by its markets, which became a major factor in urban problems of the late 1980s. The decline in the 1990s is a much more complicated story, which involves the numerous factors addressed in the subsequent chapters of this volume.

Chapter 2 also highlights the necessity to partition the trends by key attributes of the problem. One critical dimension is the age of the offenders. We saw very different patterns across the different age groups, with the crime-rate rise of the late 1980s being caused almost entirely by offenders under age 25, whereas offending rates of older people displayed a steady decline. The sharpest decline in the 1990s has thus occurred among the young offenders. There were also important effects associated with weapons used, largely a growth in the use of handguns, with no comparable growth in other weapon types, and then a rapid decline in handgun use in the 1990s. Both the growth and the decline in violence occurred first in the largest cities, followed by smaller cities within one to three years.

It is somewhat ironic that the growth in violence with handguns was at least partly a consequence of the drug war's incarceration of many of the older drug sellers – the incarceration rate for drug offenses increased by a factor of 10 between 1980 and 1996. As older sellers were taken off the street, the drug market turned to younger individuals, particularly inner-city

African-Americans, partly to replace their incarcerated predecessors and partly just to meet the growing demand for crack. The reduction in age of workers in the crack trade entailed a predictable increase in violence, as the inclination to deliberate before acting is simply less developed in the young.

The Role of Handguns

Garen Wintemute, in Chapter 3, reviews the nature and scope of the problems associated with guns in the United States and the variety of efforts to address them. He discusses the independent contribution of guns to the spike in violence in the 1980s, a result of the intrinsic lethality of firearms as opposed to other weapons. Wintemute documents the increase in injury and death that resulted as gun manufacturers shifted handgun production to cheap medium- and high-caliber pistols.

Among the initial police responses to the burgeoning gun violence was a policy of aggressive stop-and-frisk. This occurred in a number of cities, most notably New York City. Boston focused its law-enforcement resources on youth gangs, as they were responsible for the great majority of its gun incidents. Federal law enforcement became involved in the early 1990s through serious efforts by the Bureau of Alcohol, Tobacco, and Firearms (ATF), which began tracing crime guns to identify their sources and focused on licensed dealers and "straw purchasers" – those buying guns for persons prohibited from doing so – who turned up in multiple traces. The Brady Bill, enacted in 1993 and effective in 1994, was intended to reduce access to guns by prohibited individuals, that is, those who had a high risk of using guns criminally, such as convicted felons and minors. Handgun violence took a sharp downturn at just about the time the Brady Bill became effective. To date, over 400,000 attempted handgun purchases have been denied, but it is not known how many of those customers eventually bought guns from an unregulated source. However, Wintemute presents evidence that denying handgun purchases to those with an elevated risk of dangerous behavior does prevent gun crime. He also discusses strategies to combat handgun violence that do not appear to be effective, ranging from gun-buyback programs to liberalized access to concealed-weapon permits.

The Role of Prisons

One crime-control factor whose effects are especially hard to sort out is incarceration. Following a fifty-year period of impressive stability, incarceration rates in the United States began an enormous increase in the mid-1970s, quadrupling by the end of the century. It would thus be surprising if prisons had not been a factor in the decline in violence. It is clear, however, that so simplistic an analysis as documenting the negative association between incarceration rate and crime rate in the 1990s cannot provide the basis for generating an estimate of its impact. After all, in the 1980s, during the period of the most prodigious growth in imprisonment, violence was increasing most markedly.

William Spelman considers the incarceration effect in Chapter 4. Drawing on the variety of studies that attempt to estimate the combined incapacitative and deterrent effects of incarceration, he derives estimates of the elasticity of crime due to incarceration, that is, the percentage change in crime associated with a one-percent change in prison population.

The radical expansion of the prison population occurred primarily because of expansion in the rate of commitment of offenders and an increase in time served, including time served after parole violation. Any crime-suppressing benefit of this augmentation process, however, would be attenuated somewhat by a diminishing-returns effect. Because the criminal justice system tends naturally to catch and imprison the highest-rate offenders, an increase in the system's inclination to imprison results in a decrease in the average offending rate of those being sentenced, thus diminishing the effectiveness of incarceration in reducing crime. Another factor that Spelman weighs in the balance is the ratio of adults to juveniles among those committing crime; the higher the ratio, the greater the crime-reduction leverage to be gained through imprisonment, since juveniles are still largely free of the risk of imprisonment. Varying these and other factors, Spelman derives a number of elasticity estimates, concluding that the prison buildup suppressed the yearly crime rate by 35 percent on average and that perhaps 25 percent of the crime drop is attributable to incarceration. Like Richard Rosenfeld in his own discussion of the incarceration effect (Chapter 5), Spelman raises the provocative question of whether the benefits of this reduction in crime outweigh the social and financial costs of such massive use of prisons.

The Steady Decline of Adult Violence

The violent crime pattern of adults above age 25 has been quite different from that of those younger. Adult homicide shows a steady decline through the 1980s, when the homicide rate of younger offenders was spiking, and all the way through the 1990s. This sustained reduction warrants its own investigation, the contribution of Richard Rosenfeld in Chapter 5. He focuses on two aspects of the adult homicide decline. One is its generality across both major racial groups, both sexes, and all offender – victim relationships – family member, acquaintance, and stranger. The second is that, for both men and women and blacks and whites, the greatest decline is seen in family homicides, a development that Rosenfeld attributes, in part – but only in part – to concurrent declines in marriage rates over the past two decades and to the emergence of a variety of support services intended to reduce domestic violence.

Regarding the general reduction in adult homicide, it is important to assess the contribution of incarceration, since the majority of prisoners are in this age category. Where Spelman derives his elasticity estimates through what he terms a "top-down" approach, statistically relating aggregate crime rates to aggregate incarceration rates, Rosenfeld employs what Spelman calls a "bottom-up" model, starting with an estimation of the offending rate of criminals and calculating how many crimes would be averted by locking the offenders up. This is a reasonably straightforward task for crimes, such as robbery, that offenders commit with some regularity. Deriving an individual "offending rate" for homicide, on the other hand, has no obvious algorithm. Rosenfeld's solution is to use the homicide *event* rate in our worst neighborhoods (100 to 125 per 100,000) as an estimate of the expected rate of homicide *involvement* (commission and victimization) of those being sentenced to prison. With this estimate in hand, he calculates that incarceration reduced the rate of murder at the hands of adults by 10 percent between 1980 and 1985, nearly 20 percent between 1985 and 1990, and some 25 percent between 1990 and 1995. Rosenfeld's estimates are lower than Spelman's for the earlier years but approach Spelman's for the 1990s.

Just as only a part of the overall decline in adult homicide can be ascribed to the ongoing acceleration in imprisonment, neither can the most pronounced component of that decline, family homicide, be accounted for by imprisonment. Some of this reduction can be credited to the growing availability of services for abused women. More important has been the decline in marriage rate – Rosenfeld calculates that roughly one-half of the domestic homicide drop for younger adults is attributable to this trend. The extent of the unexplained portion of the adult crime drop, however, prompts him to consider the possibility that we are witnessing a cultural sea change in the form of a growing aversion to interpersonal violence, a "civilizing" trend shared – variably, to be sure – across sex, class, and ethnicity.

The Role of Drugs

Whereas the adult-violence downtrend of the 1990s was a continuation of the previous decade's pattern, a significant fraction of the reduction in youth violence in the 1990s represented an undoing of the growth of youth violence in the late 1980s. Much of that growth resulted from the recruitment of young people into crack markets and the effect of those markets on youth more generally, effects that dominated much of inner-city life in the late 1980s and early 1990s. That the acquisition of firearms spread beyond those directly involved in the crack trade is attested to by youth surveys carried out during this period. These studies documented a rate of gun-carrying far higher than could be explained in terms of participation in drug sales. Geographic diffusion was evident as well – in the upswing in homicide (though of smaller magnitude) seen among white youth some three years after its occurrence in the inner cities, and in the upturn in violence in smaller cities some two years after it occurred in the larger ones. It is no accident that the time difference by city size in the surge in violence maps rather well, with a lag of one to three years, onto the time difference across cities in the beginning of juvenile involvement in crack markets.

Bruce Johnson, Andrew Golub, and Eloise Dunlap present a vivid picture in Chapter 6 of the origin of the devastating crack tidal wave and its ebbing in the early 1990s, placing crack in a historical profile of the major drug eras in New York City, from heroin to powdered cocaine and crack to marijuana "blunts." A focus on New York City is easily justified by its bellwether role in national drug and violence trends and its hugely disproportionate numeric weight in those trends. (For similar reasons, New York figures prominently in the discussion of police influences by John Eck and Edward Maguire, Chapter 7.) Johnson, Golub, and Dunlap credit the antidrug tactics of New York City's police department and its "quality-of-life" campaign with making life more difficult for participants on both sides of the crack market. But the major cause of the decline of crack was an attitude shift among inner-city youth consisting not just of loss of interest in crack but of a positive rejection of the drug and the violence and degenerate lifestyles it engendered. Marijuana, rolled in cigar wrappers as "blunts," has become this generation's illegal substance of preference, which is marketed in ways that seem to avoid the violence of the crack era.

The Role of Policing

Policing must be a major topic in any consideration of the crime drop, partly because the police are the first line of response to violent activity, but also because the period of the 1990s has been one of substantial innovation in policing. John Eck and Edward Maguire, both of whom have been close to police operations, systematically assess evidence for the efficacy of a wide variety of these innovations, including increases in the number of police officers on the street; community, problem-solving, and "zero-tolerance" policing; targeting of drugs and guns; and New York City's Compstat system, which uses geographic displays as a stimulus to interaction between department leadership and precinct commanders in order to hold the latter responsible for the crime in their precincts. Eck and Maguire, in Chapter 7, looked for differences between jurisdictions that implemented these changes and similar ones that did not. In general, they found that it is difficult to substantiate the often strong and enthusiastic claims made for particular policing strategies, either because the strategy was put in place after crime had already declined or because two or more innovations occurred simultaneously 'and thus cannot be causally partitioned. They conclude that the best case is to be made for the suite of tactics employed to combat the drug trade, because this campaign at least antedated the drop in crime.

Guns, drugs, prisons, and police – the subjects of the first chapters in this volume – are factors associated in a direct way with crime and the criminal justice system. It is not only variables intrinsic to crime and crime control, however, that inflect crime rates. The larger economy and demographic trends are widely – and correctly – regarded as important influences on crime, and each is the subject of a chapter.

The Role of Economic Opportunity

Jeffrey Grogger suggests in Chapter 8 that individuals weigh the tradeoff between the wages they can earn from crime and the wages they can earn in the legitimate economy and then choose the activity that maximizes their personal utility. This is most readily demonstrable for the case of property crime but can easily be extended to economic crime like drug dealing, and can then be linked to violent crime because of the instrumental role that violence can play in the pursuit of profit. This, he argues, was abundantly evident in the case of crack. For thousands of young men of limited job skills in the inner cities, the steady decline in wages in the legitimate economy in the 1980s, juxtaposed with the easy money possible in the emerging crack trade, forced a clear economic choice.

Forced to operate outside the civil dispute-resolution system, the crack business became a focus of violence. Dealers became a prime target for robbers, and in turn, retaliated whenever they could lest they gain a reputation for vulnerability. Dealers also employed violence to settle bad-debt disputes with customers and business partners, to discipline their employees, and to increase their market share by expanding their territorial dominion. But the violence that initially enhanced the profitability of this pursuit held the seeds of its own decline: the risks from the growing violence raised the cost to both buyers and sellers in the crack market. Grogger believes the increasingly deterrent effect of violence was an important part of the drying-up of the markets and their attendant carnage. That was the push away from illegal wages. The pull toward legitimate employment came with the upturn in the economy in the 1990s, which brought higher wages and more jobs, even for those with low skill levels.

The Role of Demography

Demography, another indirect but important factor in crime trends, asserts its influence through the sharp, patterned differences in criminality across age, sex, and ethnicity. The difference by gender is the largest, but it is the least important because gender composition is reasonably stable. Age and ethnic composition do change considerably, and these shifts can have a large effect on the aggregate violence rate. Demographic characteristics are of great interest also because they are one of the few crime-related factors that can be reliably projected into the future: every nonimmigrant of interest to the criminal justice system for the next eighteen years is already born.

James Alan Fox capitalizes on our knowledge of changing demography to interpret past patterns and consider future possibilities in Chapter 9. He conveys the usefulness of demographic analysis as well as its limitations. The rationale for the demographic approach is that, if all else were equal, crime rates would rise as the fraction of the population in the perennially crime-prone subgroups (young adult males) increased. Thus, Fox was able to predict correctly that violence would peak in 1980 and then decline on the basis of the movement of the baby-boom generation out of the high-crime age range. It is the "all else equal" proviso that limits the predictive value of demography, however. In particular, it is the assumption of stability in crime rates within demographic subgroups that is problematic. We saw this in the late 1980s, when, despite their declining numbers, the young male segment boosted the aggregate rate of violence because of the drastic spike in their per capita rate. This development could not have been – and was not – foreseen by those making predictions based solely on population trends. In recent years, within-segment changes for young males have been on the order of 10 percent per year, up or down, a fluctuation that tends to overwhelm the demographic shifts, which are only about one percent per year.

Rate changes aside, what do the demographic projections foretell? The good news is that the 50+ age segment, always relatively pacific, will be far-and-away the largest and fastest-growing part of the nation. The bad news is that the twenty-year decline in the size of the 18- to 24-year-old segment is now in reverse; they, too, are growing relative to the whole population, and they will continue to do so until around 2010 (although this bulge – the "baby-boomerang" generation – at only one percent per year, will not be nearly as consequential as that of their parents when they were the same age in the 1970s). The population segment with the highest rate of violent crime – 18- to 24-year-old black males – will be expanding at the even higher rate of about 2 percent per year, and will continue growing until at least 2020. Thus, if offending rates were to stabilize at about current values, the amount of youth violence would still increase somewhat.

The Past, Present, and Future of U.S. Violence

A careful reading of this volume will bring most readers, we believe, to concur with the observation that no single factor can be invoked as *the* cause of the crime decline of the 1990s. Rather, the explanation appears to lie with a number of factors, perhaps none of which alone would have been sufficient and some of which might not have been of noticeable efficacy without reinforcement from others. The decay of crack markets, due to some combination of police tactics, growing deterrence due to violence, and rejection of crack by a new generation, diminished the recruitment of young people to work in them, and fortunately, the strength of the economy has provided replacement job opportunities. Local and federal efforts to control crime guns appear to have made an important contribution to the general decline in violence, success that was complemented by the decline in the violence and in the diffusion of handguns associated with crack markets. The growth of incarceration has clearly contributed, but this would not have been an important factor among the younger offenders. Several of these elements – the decline of drug markets, reduction in gun-carrying, and growth of the economy – have been mutually supporting. Such interactions among these and the other factors discussed in this volume make it difficult to isolate the relative contribution of any one of them.

It would be unreasonable to expect the current downward trends to continue indefinitely, since crime cannot go negative. As the benefits of the current trends are exhausted, we will be left with residual levels of violence from forces immune to the ameliorative factors that have been driving the downturn. It is possible that, as Rosenfeld suggests, there has been a general cultural shift away from the use of violence, but we will have to see whether any such transformation persists when the other favorable factors are no longer at work.

Changing demography alone could well slow the turnaround. Various other factors could even reverse the steady decline in the within-group rates. We could see a revival of street drug markets, perhaps with the methamphetamines that have become prevalent in the Southwest and the western states but have not yet made major penetration in the East. A significant weakening in the economy that denied legitimate job opportunities to young people could lead to an upturn in crime and the violence often associated with criminal economic activity. The dropping of large numbers of people with no job skills from the welfare rolls could also move trends in this direction.

All of these possibilities suggest the need for strong efforts focused on crime prevention among young people, with an emphasis on enhancing their skills so that they continue to have options in the legitimate economy, even when it begins to narrow. It would also be prudent to develop a variety of early-warning signals of a reversal of the current decline, which would probably occur first in the larger cities, involve young people, and be associated with an emergence of new street markets for serious drugs. When those signals fire, it will be important to have at hand an array of strategic responses to the reversing trend. The perspectives presented in this volume will undoubtedly be important contributors to the planning of such responses.

Acknowledgment

The editors are grateful to Brian Slattery of the Harry Frank Guggenheim Foundation for superb editorial assistance in the production of this book.

Disaggregating the Violence Trends

Alfred Blumstein

The Changing Rates of Violence in the U.S.

THE PERIOD FROM 1980 TO 1998 has seen some sharp swings in the rate of violence in the United States.[1] The homicide rate in 1980 was at a peak value of 10.2 per 100,000 population, and by 1985 it had fallen to a trough of 7.9. It then climbed a full 24 percent to a peak of 9.8 in 1991, and has been declining markedly since then, reaching a level of 6.3 in 1998, a level that is lower than any annual rate since 1967. The rate of robbery has followed a very similar pattern, oscillating since 1972 between rates of 200 and 250 per 100,000 population, reaching its peaks and troughs within one year of the peaks and troughs of the murder trends. It has also displayed a steady decline since its 1991 peak, and its 1998 rate of 165.2 is lower than any experienced since 1969. These patterns are depicted in Figure 2.1.[2]

This chapter focuses primarily on homicide (the ultimate violent act) and secondarily on robbery (the taking of property by force or threat of force) as the principal indicators of violence. In homicide, there is usually a body to be explained, and homicides typically involve intensive police investigation. Robbery is also a relatively well-defined crime and is reported to the police by the victim over one-half the time.[3] The decline of homicide and robbery following their peak in 1991 has to be viewed in the context of the factors that contributed to their previous rise beginning in the late 1980s. This chapter concentrates primarily on crimes reported to the police that are, in turn, reported to the Federal Bureau of Investigation (FBI) and published annually in the FBI's Uniform Crime Reports (UCR).[4]

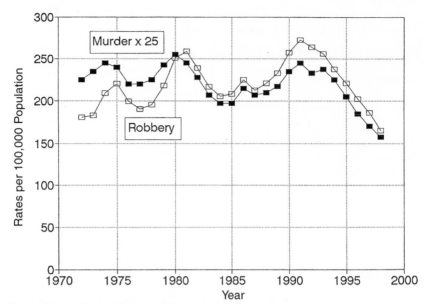

Figure 2.1. UCR murder and robbery rates.

The satisfaction with the recent decline in homicide and robbery is accompanied by widespread curiosity over the factors that are responsible for the decline.[5] This chapter explores some of those factors, focusing on those whose effects are reasonably measurable with special attention to factors where the aggregate picture may fail to capture some of the richness provided by examining the factors in a disaggregated form, or where the aggregate picture may even be misleading. Some ranges of a factor – age, for example – contribute to an increase in violence at the same time that other ranges contribute to a decrease.

Measuring Violence

The Mix of Violent Crime. The rate of violent crime in the United States is typically measured as the sum of the following crimes reported to and recorded by the police: murder and nonnegligent manslaughter, forcible rape, robbery, and aggravated assault. These rates are reported annually by the FBI in the UCR and combined into a *violent-crime index*.

These are very disparate offenses whose rates cover a very broad range. The absolute numbers recorded in a typical year, 1998,[6] display the large disparity across these categories:

Homicide	16,910
Forcible Rape	93,100
Robbery	446,630
Aggravated Assault	974,400

The ratio among these is approximately 1, 5, 25, and 50, that is, there are 50 times as many aggravated assaults and 25 times as many robberies as there are homicides. It is evident that even minor fluctuations in the reports of aggravated assault will overwhelm significant changes in the number of murders. For example, even if there is a doubling of the number of homicides, a relatively small 2 percent decrease in aggravated assault will counteract that doubling, and will lead to no change in the reported rate of *violent crime*. Thus, just as the total crime index[7] is dominated by larcenies (of which there were 7,373,900 reported in 1998),[8] the violent-crime index can be distorted by fluctuations in the reports of aggravated assault.

Because there tends to be a strong correlation among the various index offenses, these distinctions are often not serious. But there can be occasions when the distinction among them is of serious concern. This is especially true when there are shifts in reporting patterns rather than shifts in the underlying behavior. Thus, it is more appropriate to deal with the various violent-crime types individually in order to avoid the problem of distortions in the aggregate caused by changes in the numerically dominant offenses of robbery or aggravated assault.

Forcible rape has been the most difficult of the four violent offenses to measure. Because of stigma associated with rape and because police have often been insensitive to rape victims' emotions, the percentage of rapes reported to the police is about the lowest of the UCR index crimes, and so changes in reporting rates can be an important factor contributing to changes in the UCR rate of rape. Also, the National Crime Victimization Survey (NCVS), which samples over 40,000 households to ask about their victimization experiences, has discovered that typically there are too few cases of rape reported even to the NCVS to provide precise measures of the rate of that offense.[9] Thus, I do not deal further in this chapter with the serious offense of rape.

Aggravated Assault. The UCR rate of aggravated assault has displayed a pattern that is quite different from the generally flat trend displayed by homicide and robbery shown in Figure 2.1. The aggravated assault rate, shown in Figure 2.2, grew significantly – by 134 percent – during the

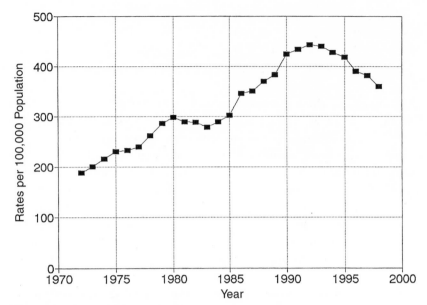

Figure 2.2. UCR aggravated assault rates.

twenty-year period from 1972 to 1992 before its more recent decline. But there are reasons to believe that this sharp trend is more artifactual than real. In contrast to murder and robbery, which are relatively well-defined offenses, "aggravated" assault requires discretion on the part of the police taking the report to distinguish it from "simple" assault.[10] Classification is an issue that is not absent from the other violent crimes noted (a murder could be misclassified as a suicide, or a street robbery as a larceny), but aggravated assaults leave much more room for the exercise of discretion. And perhaps most important in the current context, there is a good possibility that the nature of this distinction has been changing over time.

Support for this interpretation of the growth in aggravated assault is provided by evidence from the other principal source of crime data in the United States, the NCVS, which asks respondents whether they have been a victim of a crime over the past six months. One virtue of the survey is that the form of the questions has been largely stable over time,[11] and so responses to those questions are likely to be much more immune to the changes in discretion and classification that bedevil data from the police reports.

Figure 2.3 shows the responses to those victimization surveys for the twenty years until 1992.[12] Here, one sees aggravated assault and simple

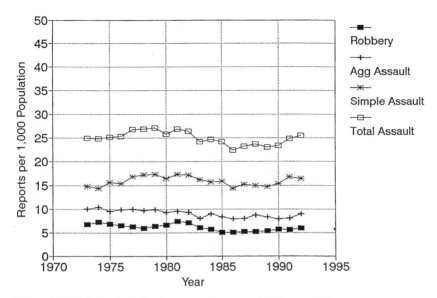

Figure 2.3. Violent victimization rates. Rates per 1,000 population.

assault with virtually no trend, and even with far less fluctuation than displayed in the police reports. Thus, there is a stark contrast between the rapidly rising trend in aggravated assault based on police reports and the very flat trend based on the victimization survey. The flat trend in the homicide series over this period is also consistent with the flat trend in the victimization survey. This suggests the reasonable possibility of a fairly stable ratio of aggravated assaults to homicides; if aggravated assaults were increasing while homicides were flat, we would require an explanation of that disparity.

The evidence from the victimization survey would appear to be the more compelling, and this calls for some investigation into why the growth in UCR aggravated assaults. It is possible that the chance that an aggravated assault turns into a homicide has been diminished somewhat because of the improved quality of emergency medical services in the United States over the past twenty years, but it would be surprising if that change could account for the doubling of the number of aggravated assaults relative to the number of homicides. Rather, it is much more likely that there has been a steady growth in the reporting of assaults that used to be ignored or dealt with as simple assaults. The principal candidates for this reporting shift are cases of domestic violence. Until relatively recently, police tended to downplay domestic assaults, largely because they were considered more

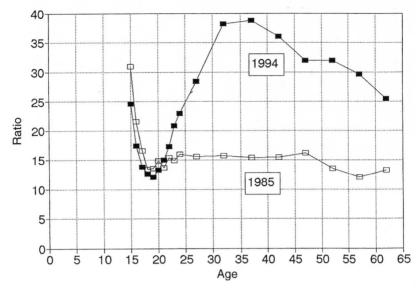

Figure 2.4. Ratio of aggressive assaults to murder rates by age. Arrest rates in 1985 and 1994.

private matters, and the police often chose not to record the crime in order to avoid the frustration of observing the victim recant after the immediate crisis had passed. Recent changes in public attitudes toward domestic assaults, in the attitudes of victims, and in the response by police suggest that these changes are likely to have been major contributors to the growth in the recording of aggravated assaults by the police.

This hypothesis is supported by Figure 2.4, which compares the ratios of the age-specific arrest rates for aggravated assault to those for murder in two years, 1985 and 1994. It is evident that in 1985, that ratio stayed very close to 15 for all ages except ages 15 and 16, where there were many aggravated assaults but relatively few of them resulted in homicides, a manifestation of teenage propensity for fighting, but with relatively low levels of lethality, at least in part because of the relatively low prevalence of firearms then available to teenagers.

The picture changed rather dramatically by 1994. The ratio continued to be close to 15 until age 23, when it began to grow appreciably. It increased to a maximum ratio of 39, and stayed at more than double the previous value of 15 for all the older ages prior to 60. But these are the ages when domestic relationships, and the potential for assault, are more salient in people's lives. It is also the case that the trend to arrest for domestic assault increased appreciably with the shift in policy that grew out of the Minneapolis Spouse Assault experiment conducted in the mid 1980s.[13] This change was reflected in many states adopting statutes mandating arrest for domestic violence; it also became policy in many police departments, even in the absence of a mandatory statute. Thus, we see this sharp growth in the rate of arrest for aggravated assault at the ages when domestic relationships are most likely. It seems most reasonable, then, to interpret the growth in the UCR rate of aggravated assault in the period between 1985 and 1994 predominantly as a reflection of a growing tendency of police to record incidents of domestic violence as aggravated assaults that would not have been so designated prior to 1985. This change in reporting practice is likely to have been the significant factor contributing to the perplexing growth in the UCR aggravated assault rate in the absence of comparable growth in the other indicators of serious assault, like homicide in the UCR or the NCVS assault-victimization rates.

Homicide and Robbery Rates. The two crimes that are best measured in the UCR are homicide and robbery, largely because these offenses are reasonably well defined and their definitions have been stable over time. Also, homicide tends to be very well reported to the police, and the rate at which victims have been reporting robberies to the police has been very stable over time.[14]

Although there have been sharp swings up and down, it is striking how trendless these two crimes are. The trend line for homicide is slightly negative, but is not statistically significant. For robbery, the trend line is slightly upward (at an annual trend of 0.87 percent of its mean rate of 223 per 100,000). This stability or relative trendlessness in crime rates is certainly at marked variance with the general view of the American public – and especially the rhetoric of its candidates for political office. Until the reporting of crime-rate declines in recent years finally sunk in, there was a widespread sense that crime rates were getting out of hand and that the crime problem was becoming an increasingly serious threat.

This is the case, for example, with age: During the late 1980s, homicides by young people were increasing whereas homicides by older people were decreasing. In other cases, there are important interactions – for example, between race and age. A large increase in homicide with handguns occurred among young African-Americans in the late 1980s, but we observe no such increase for older African-Americans. In such instances, demographic disaggregation is necessary to isolate the effects being examined. A general theme of this chapter is that it is not productive to think of homicide rates as a unitary phenomenon. Rather, recent change in the aggregate homicide rate is the product of several distinct subgroup trends. Any credible explanation – much less forecast – of the overall change in homicide rates, therefore, must address these multiple, interactive, and sometimes countervailing influences.

Many public figures and journalists have offered their own explanations for the recent decline in violence rates. There have been claims, most notably by New York City Mayor Rudolph Giuliani and by William Bratton when he was New York City's police commissioner, that virtually all of the homicide drop in New York resulted from smart and aggressive policing (Butterfield 1995; Kelling and Coles 1997; Krauss 1996; Mitchell 1994). Another view attributes the decline to a change in some of the factors that contributed to the growth, most importantly to a reduction in the high availability of firearms and their use in homicides or robberies by young people. Some of this turnaround may be the result of changes in policing, especially the use of aggressive stop-and-frisk tactics to remove guns from young people, but other factors could well be involved. These could include community efforts to mediate intergang disputes, a greater availability of jobs and income to low-skilled young people in the booming economy (Chapter 8), changing drug markets with diminished roles for young people (Chapter 6), and growing incapacitation effects through increases in the prison population of older offenders (Chapters 4 and 5). Looking across the nation, one finds that the effects of changes in the large cities have a dominant effect on the aggregate rates.

Differences Across Age Groups

A key factor providing important insight into the changes that have occurred since 1985 is the sharply differing trends in violence associated with different age groups, so this provides the initial departure point for the disaggregation.

Homicide. Elsewhere (Blumstein 1995), I discussed the striking changes between 1985 and 1992 in age-specific arrest rates for homicide. That article explained that, while the rates for persons age 18 and younger more than doubled, the rates for those age 30 and above declined by about 20 to 25 percent. I can now extend that analysis to 1998, and we see some striking changes in the opposite direction for the young people.

Figure 2.5 presents the age-specific arrest rate (known as the age-crime curve) for murder for the years 1985, which was the last year of a fifteen

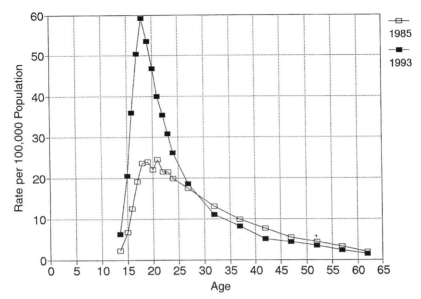

Figure 2.5. Murder arrest rate by age in 1985 and 1993.

year period of very stable age-specific rates, and 1993, which was the peak year of juvenile age-specific rates. Even though the rates for ages 20 and under had more than doubled over this interval, the rates for those over 30 had indeed declined.

Figure 2.6 depicts the same 1993 situation along with the figure for 1998, where we see the rates for all ages decline, with the steepest decline around age 18, where the growth since 1985 had reached the greatest level.

It is instructive to break out these changes in more detail by looking at the time trends for individual ages. Figure 2.7 depicts the trend for the ages traditionally displaying the peak homicide arrest rates – 18 through 24. We see how similar those rates were from 1970 through 1985, and then a divergence beginning in 1986. The rate for the 18 year olds more than doubled by 1991 (for an annual growth rate of 16 percent during this period), dropped in 1992, reached a new peak in 1993, and then continued down for the next five years. The pattern is similar for the other ages depicted in Figure 2.7, although the steepness of the rise in the late 1980s decreases with increasing age, and the decline after 1993 is correspondingly less for the older ages.

For youth 18 and under, depicted in Figure 2.8, the pattern is very similar to the pattern at age 18, although the stable base rate in the 1970–85

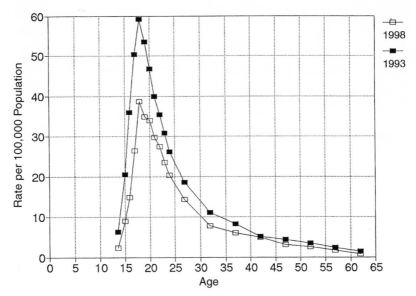

Figure 2.6. Murder arrest rate by age in 1993 and 1998.

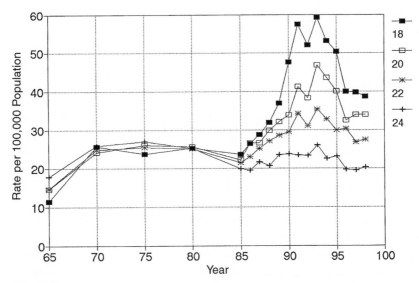

Figure 2.7. Trends in murder arrest rate by age (individual peak ages).

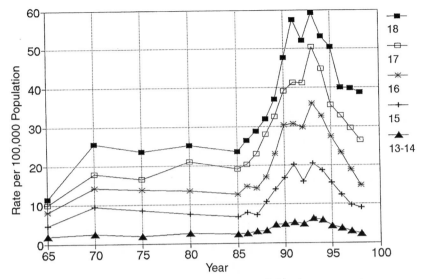

Figure 2.8. Trends in murder arrest rate by age (individual young ages).

period was lower. In all these cases of 18 and under, the rate more than doubled by 1993. The pattern for the ages above 24 generally declines after 1975.

These changes for the growth period, 1985 to 1993, and for the decline period, 1993 to 1998, are reflected in Figure 2.9, which depicts for each age the ratio of the age-specific arrest rate for murder to the rates that prevailed in 1985. Points above the heavy line (a ratio of 1.0) represent an increase in the rates, and points below that line represent a decrease. The upper graph portrays the ratio reached in the peak year, 1993, and the lower graph portrays the degree to which the ratio had declined by 1998.

The arrest rate for 15-year olds in 1993 was triple the rate that had prevailed in 1985. The growth to 1993 declined with age, but it was more than double the 1985 rate for all ages of 20 and below. In contrast, for the older ages of 30 and above, the 1993 rates were actually about 20 percent lower than the 1985 rates.

The graph of the 1998-to-1985 ratio is clearly below that for 1993, and the greatest decline occurred in the teenage years. But it is clear that the teenage rates in 1998 were still about 40 percent above the 1985 rates that had prevailed since 1970, and so there is still considerable room for improvement to get the teenage rates back down to the 1985 rates.

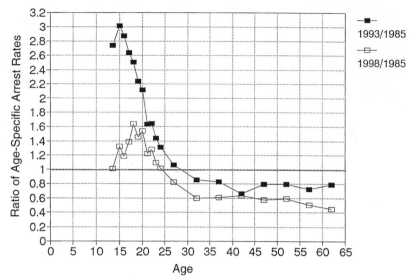

Figure 2.9. Ratios of recent age-specific murder rates (1993 and 1998 murder arrests versus 1985).

Also, there was a continuing decline in the homicide rates for the older ages. By 1998, the 25- to 30-year-old group had declined from the 1985 rates by about 20 percent, and the older groups had declined by about 40 percent.

These figures underscore the central importance of examining the different roles of the different age groups in explaining the trends in the aggregate homicide rate since 1985. The aggregate rate of Figure 2.1 grew to the 1991 peak solely because the rates of the younger people were increasing faster than the rates for the older people were declining. Between 1991 and 1993, the rates for younger people were generally flat (as reflected in the pattern for the 18 year olds in Figure 2.7), and so the decline by those in the older age groups dominated the aggregate, leading to the downturn that began in 1992. Since the rates of both young and old were decreasing after 1993, the aggregate rate continued to fall.

In sum, all of the increase in the level of homicide in the United States during the growth period of the late 1980s and early 1990s was due to the trends in the younger ages, because homicide rates for those 25 years old and older did not increase. However, the decrease during the decline period since 1993 is due to both the recent sharp drop in offending among young people and to the continuing decline in offending among older people.

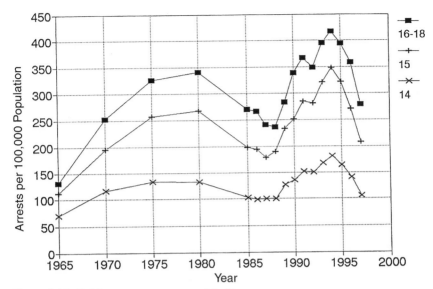

Figure 2.10. Robbery arrest rates ages 14–18.

Explanations of the homicide decline must differentiate between the factors that are responsible for the long-term fall in homicide among the older adults, and the ones causing the more recent drop in homicide offenses in the younger groups. Those two explanations are likely to be very different.

Robbery. The changes in levels of robbery have many similarities to those associated with homicide, but with some important differences. The time trends in the age-specific arrest rates for robbery based on UCR estimates are depicted in Figures 2.10 (for ages 14 to 18),[16] 2.11 (for ages 18 to 24), and 2.12 (for ages 24 and above).

Over the 1970–85 period, homicide arrest rates were fairly stable and also displayed a flat peak over the 18-to-24 age range as evidenced by the proximity of their trend lines in Figure 2.7. That period saw considerable change in robbery rates, most notably for the youngest age group: a rapid rise through 1975, a relatively flat period from 1975 to 1980, and a strong decline after 1980. In the period before 1985, the rise and the decline were strongest for the youngest group (Figure 2.10), more muted for the middle group (Figure 2.11), and even less pronounced for the oldest group (Figure 2.12), who had much lower rates generally.

The post-1985 period, which is the dominant period for homicide, also provides some interesting similarities and contrasts with the homicide situ-

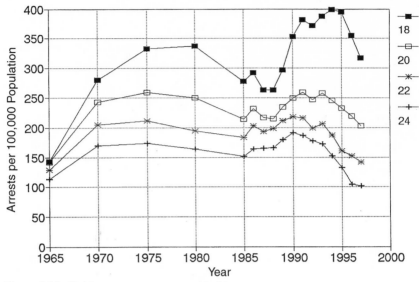

Figure 2.11. Robbery arrest rates ages 18–24.

ation. There was an important post-1985 increase in the robbery arrest rate, especially for the younger age group. For the young people (under age 20), the first noticeable uptick in robbery did not occur until 1989, three years after the increase for homicide (as seen in Figure 2.8). The

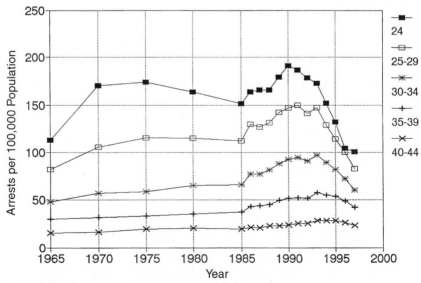

Figure 2.12. Robbery arrest rates age 24 and above.

peak in robbery occurred in 1994, one year after the homicide peak, and the downturn was comparably sharp. For all the ages of 18 and under, the growth in the five years between 1989 and the 1994 peak exceeded 70 percent.

As we examine older people (ages 24 and above in Figure 2.12), we find a rather different pattern: an earlier rise (starting in 1986 rather than 1989) and a much less sharp (at most half) rise than that displayed by the young people. But the decline after the peak (between 1990 and 1993) is comparably strong.

Methodological Considerations in Arrest Data. In discussing robbery and homicide trends, arrest data have been used to represent offending patterns by age. This approach is necessary because reports of crime could contain demographic information about the victim, but knowing the demographic characteristics of the offender is generally dependent on an arrest. In using this approach, it is important to recognize the possibility that arrest rates by age can differ from actual offending rates. That could be a consequence of differential vulnerability to arrest by different demographic groups. For example, it is possible that young offenders are more easily arrested because they are less skillful in avoiding arrest. Or, at least in the case of homicide, they may be less vulnerable to arrest because their victims are more often strangers, and finding the perpetrator in a stranger-homicide is much more difficult than in one involving intimates or other acquaintances (see Riedel 1993).

As one examines trends in arrests over time within a particular age group, any distortion in the trend pattern because of these differential vulnerabilities must be associated with a *change* in the vulnerability within any age group. Thus, if it were the case that younger people were more vulnerable to arrest than older people, then that difference could contribute to the higher absolute values of the arrest rates associated with the young people. But that difference could not be the cause of the rapid post-1985 rise in the arrest rate of the young people unless there was some reason why there would be a comparable increase in their arrest vulnerability, and there is no indication of any such change.

Another concern about using arrest rates as the proxy for offending rates is the possibility that there might be a greater tendency for multiple arrests in some demographic groups than in others. This might be a consequence of more aggressive police practices in dealing with some groups, leading to multiple arrests for a single homicide. Or it might result because homicide or robbery by some groups, and especially the younger groups, is, in fact, more likely to be committed by multiple offenders than single offenders. Then, a homicide or a robbery committed by a gang, for example, could well result in multiple members of the gang being arrested for the same offense, and that would contribute to a higher arrest rate in the age range typical of gang members.

These measurement problems are certainly real, but again, the concern over them is diminished somewhat in examining time trends. The time trends would be distorted only if there were time trends in the factors contributing to the differences across demographic groups. That could well be the case (e.g., if young people committing offenses today are more likely to be operating in gangs than was the case in the early 1980s), but the emphasis must then be on the shifts in those distorting factors. In view of the sharp shifts up and down observed among young offenders, it is reasonable to anticipate that the trends observed might be changed somewhat by these corrections, but that the basic thrust is not likely to be changed dramatically. In a preliminary examination of multiple arrests for homicides using the Supplementary Homicide Reports (SHR), we can account for at most 10 percent of the growth in the homicide arrest rate through increased incidence of multiple offenders in homicide incidents.

Changing Demographic Composition

Much of the speculation about the recent decline in homicide rates attributes the decline to changing demographics.[16] This may be a holdover from the realization that much of the decline that began in 1980 was attributable to a demographic shift, as the baby-boom generation aged out of the high-crime ages (Blumstein, Cohen, and Miller 1980; Steffensmeier and Harer 1991). But those same demographic effects were not still at work in the early 1990s, since demographic effects do not always have to work in the same direction.

The decline after 1980 was significantly affected by the shrinking size of the cohorts in the high-crime ages, but the United States in the late 1990s was in a period of growing cohort sizes in the late teens and early twenties. Figure 2.13 depicts the age distribution of the U.S. population in 1998.[17] It is evident that the smallest age cohort under 40 is about 23, the cohort born in 1976. Each of the younger cohorts is larger than its predecessor until the peak at age six. Thus, if teenage age-specific crime rates were to remain constant, then the aggregate crime rate would increase as a result of the larger cohort sizes. This possibility spurred the warnings of a demographic "crime bomb" set to go off during the 1990s (Dilulio 1996).

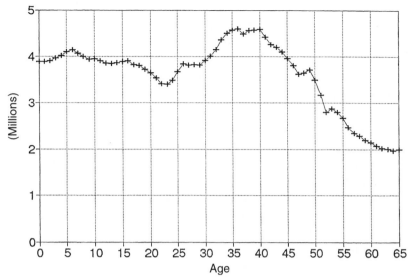

Figure 2.13. Age composition of U.S. population in 1998. Number of persons at each age.

Yet, it is important to recognize that these age-composition changes are relatively small, with cohort sizes growing at a rate of about one per-cent per year. In the face of much larger annual swings in the age-specific crime rates, as much as 10 to 20 percent per year up in the 1980s (16 per-cent per year for the 18 year olds from 1985 to 1991) as well as down in the 1990s, the one-percent change in demographic composition is a minor effect.

It is possible, finally, that changes in relative cohort size could alter the age-specific rates through mechanisms whereby larger cohort sizes tend to increase the criminality within a cohort, an effect described by Easterlin and others (Easterlin 1987; Smith 1986). However, the evidence suggests that, if changes in the relative size of age cohorts influence homicide rates, these cohort-size effects are minor compared to effects associated with vari-ation in age and changes over time or period effects (Maxim 1985; O'Brien 1989; Steffensmeier, Streifel, and Shihadeh 1992).

The Role of Handguns

There is widespread recognition of the changing role of weaponry in young people's hands. Over the last 15 years, the weapons involved in set-tling juveniles' disputes have changed dramatically, from fists or knives to handguns – and especially more recently to semiautomatic pistols with their much greater lethality. That growth in lethal weaponry is reflected in the changes in the weapons involved in homicides in different race and age groups (Blumstein and Cork 1996; and Cook 1996, more generally).

The FBI's Supplementary Homicide Reports (SHR) provide data to track such changes in homicides.[18] Those reports, filed by individual police departments, provide considerable detail on individual homicide incidents. I focus specifically on these reports from the cities over 100,000 population. Each report contains information on the victim and (where known) offender characteristics and the victim-offender relationship, the weapon involved in the homicide, and the circumstances leading up to the homicide, such as argument, drug involvement, or gang involvement. Unfortunately, only a single circumstance may be designated, and so time trends in the fashion with which police designate the single circumstance limits the reliability of that aspect.

The Growth Period, 1985–1993. Figures 2.14, 2.15, and 2.16[19] provide information on the time trends of the weaponry used in homicides by offenders[20] in three age categories: adults, 25 to 45 years old (Figure 2.14); youth, 18 to 24 (Figure 2.15); and juveniles or "kids," 17 and under (Figure 2.16). The weapons are classified into three groups:

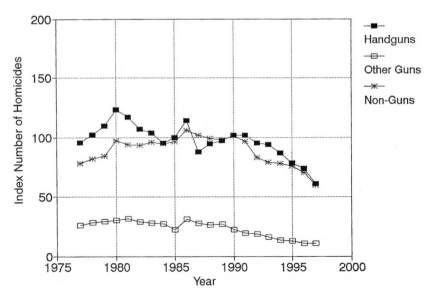

Figure 2.14. Homicide weapons by adults (ages 25–45). 1985 handguns equal 100.

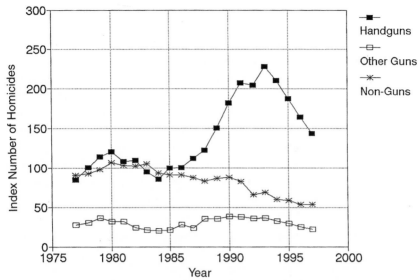

Figure 2.15. Homicide weapons by youth (ages 18–24). 1985 handguns equal 100.

handguns, other guns, and nonguns (which includes no weapon). We can see from Figure 2.14 that over the time period shown, 1977–97, there has been a general downward trend in total homicides by adults with all weapons and especially with handguns more recently; overall,

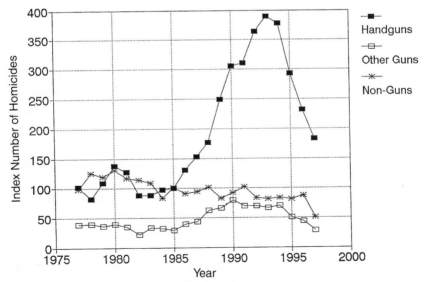

Figure 2.16. Homicide weapons by kids (under 18). 1985 handguns equal 100.

however, there has been only little change in the mix of weapons used by adults in homicide.

The situation for youth and juveniles is quite different, however. For both these groups, there was no clear trend until after 1985, and then a significant growth in handgun use began with no comparable growth in the other weapons. With 1985 as the base year, handgun homicide among youth increased by 1993 to an index value of 228 (an increase of 128 percent). The increase in juveniles' use of handguns was dramatically higher, to an index value of 389, almost quadruple the 1985 rate. In these groups, there is a sharp and steady decline following the 1993 peak. This decline is consistent with the decline in homicide arrest rates shown in Figures 2.7 and 2.8. I also note that, despite the sharp declines, the handgun indexes in 1997 were still well above the 1985 level for these groups, 43 percent above for youth and 83 percent for juveniles, an observation also consistent with the young people's arrest rates shown in Figure 2.9.

In all these figures, no appreciable increase has occurred in either the other-gun or the nongun categories. In fact, there has been a steady 40- to 50-percent decline from 1985 to 1997 in the nongun category for all three groups. Thus, there has been some degree of substitution of handguns for other weapons, but the absolute magnitude of non-handgun decline is still small compared to the dramatic growth in the use of handguns by youth and especially by juveniles. Thus, the observation based on Figures 2.5–2.9 that young people under age 25 accounted for all the growth in homicides in the post-1985 period is augmented with the recognition that that growth was accounted for totally by the growth in homicides committed with handguns. Clearly, the sharply increasing presence of handguns in youth and juvenile homicide must be considered of fundamental importance in any explanation of the aggregate homicide increase of the late 1980s and early 1990s. And the counterpart sharp decrease in the handgun homicides by these two groups is an important factor in the decline. But even though their handgun homicide rates are still well above the 1985 level, the continuing decline in homicides by adults, which, by 1997, reached a level almost half that of 1985, contributed to the aggregate decline since 1991.

Some important racial differences in the growth of handgun homicides can also be observed, with the dominant growth being among young African-Americans, as offenders and as victims. Figure 2.17 presents the index number of the weapons involved in homicides committed by black youth, ages 18 to 24. There is an even sharper growth in handgun use than for youth generally (Figure 2.15); the number of handgun homicides

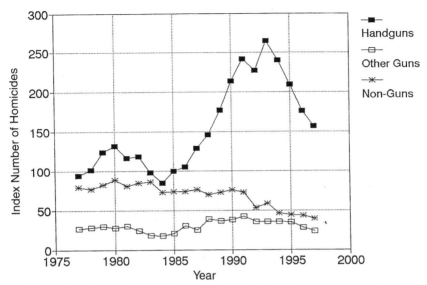

Figure 2.17. Homicide weapons by black youth (ages 18–24). 1985 handguns equal 100.

more than triples from the low in 1984 to the peak in 1993. There was no comparable growth in the role of the other weapon types.

Although some growth also occurred in handgun homicides by white youth, that growth was far less than among the black youth. The difference is depicted in Figure 2.18, which compares the two racial groups – blacks and a combined white and Hispanic group.[21] There is a strong growth in handgun prevalence for black youth, from a low in 1984 to a tripling by 1993. The rise for the white/Hispanic group does not start until 1989, four years after the start of the African-American climb. That growth reaches its peak in 1993, almost a doubling of the rate at the 1988 trough. That growth is attributable predominantly to a growth in handguns in homicides by Hispanics. We also note that the post-1993 decline is much steeper for the black youth than for the white/Hispanic youth.

Firearms have also played an important role in the growth in robberies. There is no incident-based data source for robberies comparable to the SHR for homicide. But there are aggregate statistics for the fraction of robberies that are committed with firearms, and there was indeed a large growth in the fraction committed with firearms during the 1989–91 period. During that time, which was precisely the time of the major increase in the involvement of young people in robbery, there was a 42-percent increase in the total rate of firearm robberies. Over that same period, there was only a 5-percent

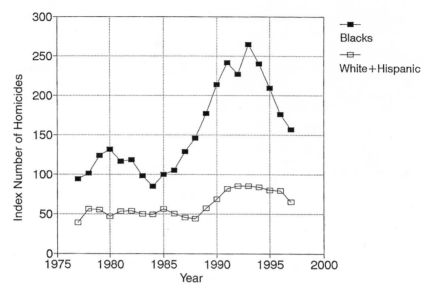

Figure 2.18. Handgun homicides by youth (ages 18–24). 1985 handguns by black youth equal 100.

increase in the rate of nonfirearm robberies. This shift suggests that young people carrying guns found uses for those guns outside the simple role of self-defense. This might help to account for the delay in the rise and the decline in robberies by the younger offenders compared to their older counterparts. For those age 24 and under, the first uptick in robbery did not occur until 1989, whereas for those in their late twenties and thirties, the upturn began three years earlier, in 1986. This may be an indication of the fact that the older people were more likely to include early crack users, and so their rise before the younger robbers may be explained less by their acquisition of guns (which were much less a novelty to them) and more by their use of robbery as means of getting the money to buy drugs. Exploring these issues will require analyses in individual cities, where more detailed information on demographic-specific arrest rates are available.

The Decline Period, 1993–1996. The steady decline in the handgun homicide rate after 1993 is clearly consistent with the decline in youth homicide rates shown in Figure 2.8, suggesting the importance of the decline in the use of handguns by young people in the decline of the aggregate homicide rate.

The pattern of growth and decline in handgun use is also reflected in Figures 2.19 and 2.20, which depict the time trend in the rate of weapons arrests at the various ages. The pattern here is very similar to the homicide patterns depicted in Figures 2.7 and 2.8, but there is a much more distinct peaking in 1993, with a clear decline subsequently. Changes in the rate of weapons arrests result from a combination of changes in the presence of illegal weapons in the relevant population group and changes in police aggressiveness in pursuing illegal weapons. It is clear from other data that there was considerable growth in weapon prevalence during the late 1980s, and also that police became more concerned about weapons, especially those in the hands of young people. That combination is reflected in the rise in weapons arrests until the peak in 1993. There is no indication that there was any diminution in police aggressiveness in pursuing young people's guns after 1993, and so it seems likely that the decline after 1993 is due much more to a reduction in the carrying of guns than to a slackening of police efforts to capture the guns. The reduction in gun-carrying seems to have been an important factor contributing to the decrease in homicide after 1993 and the decrease in robberies after 1994 by young people.

The Big Cities

The largest cities contribute disproportionately to patterns of serious violence for the nation as a whole. The prominent role of the large cities is

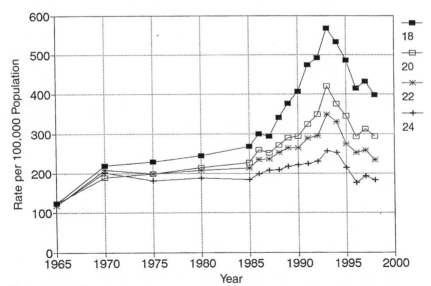

Figure 2.19. Trends: weapons arrest rate by age. Trends for individual ages 18–24.

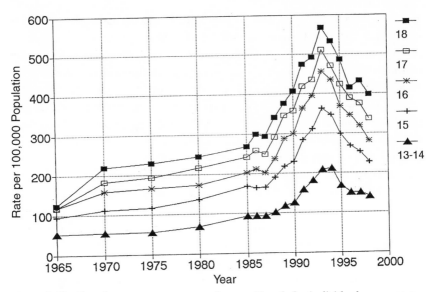

Figure 2.20. Trends: weapons arrest rate by age. Trends for individual young ages.

clearly evident in the trends in homicide. Based on UCR data for 1991, for example, the United States experienced 24,700 homicides. New York City alone provided 2,154 of them, or 9 percent of the total. Since New York City's homicide rate has declined faster than the national rate, its percentage contribution to the total has dropped to a value below 5 percent.

Although no other city has as large an effect as New York, the importance of the large cities is reflected in the relative contribution they make to the total homicide picture. In 1996, ten cities (New York, Chicago, Los Angeles, Detroit, Philadelphia, Washington, New Orleans, Baltimore, Houston, Dallas, in order of decreasing numbers of homicides) accounted for fully one-quarter of all the nation's homicides. In contrast, in 1991, when New York alone accounted for 9 percent of all U.S. homicides, only seven cities (New York, Los Angeles, Chicago, Detroit, Houston, Dallas, and Washington) were needed to account for a quarter of U.S. homicides.[22]

New York City has been a major contributor to the national decline since the early 1990s. In the national net decline in homicides from 1993 to 1994 (a reduction of 1,200 homicides), New York City's drop of 385 accounted for 32 percent of that change. In the net change from 1994 to 1995 (a national net drop of 1,720 homicides), New York City's drop of 384 accounted for 22 percent of the total decrease. New York City's contribution to the drop since 1995 has been closer to 10 percent, still very large, but smaller than in the earlier years, in part because the smaller cities are beginning to catch up. It is thus clear that what goes on in New York City, or the largest cities more generally, can have a very powerful effect on national statistics.

Examination of the trends over time offers a compelling picture of the saliency of the large cities, both in the rise of homicide in the 1980s and the decline during the 1990s. Figures 2.21 (for homicides with other than handguns) and 2.22 (for homicides with handguns) use the SHR to estimate the number (not the rate) of homicides in each of four groups of cities (those of one million or more, those in the range of 500,000 to one million, 250,000 to 500,000, and 100,000 to 250,000).[23]

Because each of the city-size groups other than the largest of over one million has a similar number of homicides in each year, we can contrast the large cities with the smaller cities.[24] There were six cities in the million-plus group: New York, Detroit, Philadelphia, Los Angeles, San Diego, and Dallas.[25] Such detailed analyses are not possible for robbery because of the lack of incident-based reports.

Figure 2.21 shows the limited variation associated with the non-handgun homicides. The change was relatively small in the smaller cities, but there was a rather steep and steady decline of almost 50 percent in the large

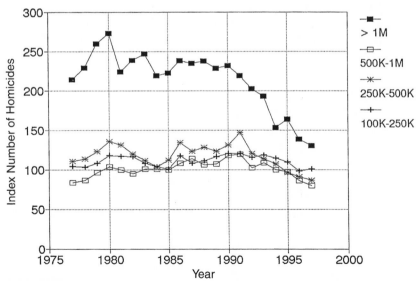

Figure 2.21. Nonhandgun homicides by city size. Cities of 500K-1 million in 1985 equal 100.

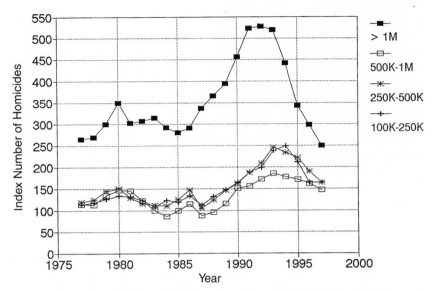

Figure 2.22. Handgun homicides by city size. Cities of 500k-1 million in 1985 equal 100.

cities from the peak in 1980 to the end of the series in 1997, with the decline accelerating after 1990.

These changes were much smaller than those in the handgun homicides. Figure 2.22 shows that the large cities had a major growth beginning in 1986, increasing 80 percent from 1985 to the flat 1991–93 peak, and then declining over 50 percent to the low in 1997, which was below the 1985 rate.

The smaller cities also had a distinct upturn in the handgun homicides, but that upturn did not begin until 1988, two years later than in the large cities. That upturn was even larger in percentage terms, increasing 110 to 130 percent from the trough in 1987 to the peak in 1993. The more recent downturn began one to two years later than in the large cities, and the drop from the respective peaks was still only about 20 to 30 percent by 1997.

Cork (1999) has shown the connection between the rise in the handgun homicides and the recruitment of juveniles into the crack markets. Using an epidemic model originally used in the marketing literature, he identified in individual cities the time when juvenile arrests for drugs began to accelerate and the corresponding point when juvenile homicides took off. He found most typically a one- to three-year lag between the two, a result consistent with the hypothesis- that the rise in juvenile homicides was attributable to the diffusion of guns from the kids recruited into drug markets to their friends and beyond. Cork also showed that crack markets generally emerged first in the largest cities, especially in New York and Los Angeles, and then diffused to the nation's center to smaller cities at a later time, again a result consistent with the lags shown in Figure 2.22. Thus, the observed patterns of handgun homicide are highly consistent with explanations that assign central importance to the rise and decline of crack markets in the United States.

Conclusion

It has been striking to note the sharp rise in violence by young people during the late 1980s and the correspondingly sharp decline in the 1990s. The increase in the aggregate homicide rate was due to escalating rates among juveniles and youth, predominantly (although not exclusively) by and against black males, particularly in the larger cities and exclusively involving handguns. By 1998, the youth decline was still well above the stable rate that prevailed for the fifteen years from 1970 through 1985. But we are still not necessarily at the end of the downturn of the cycle, and there is some reason to hope that the decline will continue. But, of course, because murder cannot become negative, that trend cannot continue indefinitely.

If the observed process of a rise, followed by a subsequent decline is cyclical with a reasonably well-defined cycle time, perhaps the difference between the larger and the smaller cities is merely one that reflects the lag in the initiation of this process: the large cities start first (as they do in many things both good and bad), and then the smaller ones follow. If the process is indeed cyclical, that opens the questions of the forces driving this cyclical process up and down, and of the factors contributing to the lag between the larger and the smaller cities. Again, I can only speculate. The evidence available so far is largely consistent with the earlier hypothesis (Blumstein 1995) of the sequence that created the rise phase: introduction of crack in the mid-1980s; recruitment of young minority males to sell the drugs in street markets; arming of the drug sellers with handguns for self-protection; diffusion of guns to peers; irresponsible and excessively casual use of guns by young people, leading to a "contagious" growth in homicide and possibly robbery also. Cork (1999) provides some strong evidence supporting this connection. There is still no comparably strong single hypothesis about the decline period. A variety of forces are likely implicated, and each is considered in detail in the following chapters.

A significant aspect of the improvement involved undoing some of the factors that contributed to the growth in the late 1980s – especially kids carrying and using guns and thereby stimulating others to do likewise. Efforts in that direction have been carried out by police and community groups. Much of the decline might be attributable to incapacitation associated with the doubling of the incarceration rate since 1985, but that effect shows itself predominantly in reductions in older individuals, since young people are only rarely candidates for incarceration. This observation emphasizes the importance of efforts to prevent violence by finding ways to socialize the young and train them with the skills necessary to function in a rapidly evolving economy. Current economic conditions seem to have provided legitimate economic opportunities at the same time that opportunities in the illicit drug markets are diminishing, but the cyclical nature of economic conditions makes their crime-reduction effects uncertain in the future. There is undoubtedly a connection between illicit drug markets – and particularly crack markets – and violence, but the nature of that connection is undoubtedly very complex and is not effectively addressed simply through prohibition of the drug or through cracking down on the participants in the markets. To the extent that addicts were treated medically, for example, the activity in the markets might decline, which could well diminish the violence as a result.

As we look to the future, we should be concerned about the possibility of a resurgence of active drug markets and any violence they may bring with them, a turndown in the economy and the impact it would have in the communities where violence is most likely to re-ignite, and the impact of welfare reform as the individuals least able to transition into the economy are dropped from the rolls. We cannot be certain when the next increase in violence will occur, but the current decline cannot continue indefinitely, and we should take advantage of the current opportunity to fashion criminal justice and community-based policies to forestall the next increase as long as possible.

Acknowledgments

The author would like to acknowledge assistance in data analysis by Mary Catherine Hult, Naomi Kleckner, Melissa Long, Sungsoo Sohn, and Carol Zierman while they were students at the H. John Heinz III School of Public Policy and Management of Carnegie Mellon University. Jacqueline Cohen has also provided important support in analysis of the SHR data. In view of our collaboration in the *JCLC* article mentioned in Note 1, Richard Rosenfeld has been a most important contributor to this chapter. My co-editor, Joel Wallman, has also made some important suggestions.

Notes

1. This chapter uses material that is included in two related articles: Alfred Blumstein, "Violence Certainly Is the Problem – and Especially with Hand Guns" in *Colorado University Law Review Symposium Edition*, vol. 69, no. 4 (Fall 1998), and Alfred Blumstein and Richard Rosenfeld, "Exploring Recent Trends in U.S. Homicide Rates" in *Journal of Criminal Law and Criminology*, vol. 88, no. 4 (Fall 1998).
2. On Figure 2.1, the rate for murder is scaled up by a factor of 25 to put it on the same scale as robbery in order to permit easy visual comparison of the two series.
3. Based on reports to the National Crime Victimization Survey (NCVS). U.S. Department of Justice, Bureau of Justice Statistics (BJS), *Criminal Victimization in the United States, 1995*, NCJ-171129 (Washington, 1998), Table 91.
4. U.S. Department of Justice, Federal Bureau of Investigation, *Crime in the United States: Uniform Crime Reports, 19xx*, Washington, DC. U.S. Government Printing Office. The UCR report for any year is usually published in the fall of the following year.
5. Even with the widespread reporting of the decline since 1991, it is not clear that those rates have contributed to a widespread feeling of greater safety. The frequency with which individual crimes are reported by the news media, and especially by television news, has certainly gone up, and fighting crime is still an important part of the political rhetoric every fall.
6. UCR 1998, p. 64, Table 1,
7. The total crime index is calculated as the sum of the of the seven *index crimes* of murder and nonnegligent manslaughter, forcible rape, robbery, aggravated assault (with these four designated collectively as the *violent crimes*), burglary, larceny-theft, and motor-vehicle theft (with these three designated collectively as the *property crimes*).
8. UCR 1998, p. 64, Table 1.
9. The National Crime Victimization Survey (NCVS), begun in 1973, is managed by the Bureau of Justice Statistics in the U.S. Department of Justice and carried out by the Census Bureau. Every six months, it interviews a probability-sample of households in a rotating panel (rotated after three years) involving about 100,000 individuals in about 40,000 households. The interview asks all household members at least 12 years old about their victimization experiences. For each such experience, they ask if the victimization was reported to the police. The NCVS does not measure homicides. See, for example, U.S. Department of Justice, Bureau of Justice Statistics, *Criminal Victimization in the United States, 1998*, A National Crime Victimization Survey Report 1 (Washington, DC, 1999), NCJ 176353.
10. The UCR defines aggravated assault as "an unlawful attack by one person upon another for the purpose of inflicting severe or aggravated bodily injury. This type of assault is usually accompanied by the use of a weapon or by means likely to produce death or great bodily harm. Attempts are included since it is not necessary that an injury result when a gun, knife, or other weapon is used which could and probably would result in serious personal injury if the crime were successfully completed." Subjective judgment is clearly required for the attribution of intent and for assessing the degree of bodily injury intended. Different police officers within a department – and certainly the standards of different police departments – can easily differ in those judgments.
11. There was a significant change in the design of the survey in 1993, and subsequent years have reflected a significant change in the number of events reported, requiring calibration to make the new survey's results consistent with the earlier years. See U.S. Dept of Justice, Bureau of Justice Statistics, *Criminal Victimization in the United States, 1993*, A National Crime Victimization Survey Report, 2, 2–3, (Washington, DC, 1996), NCJ 151658

12. In 1993, there was a significant change in the design of the survey, and the response rates changed significantly. During the period shown on Figure 3a, the survey instrument remained largely unchanged.

13. See Lawrence W. Sherman and Richard A. Berk, 1984, "The Specific Deterrent Effects of Arrest for Domestic Assault," *American Sociological Review* vol 49: pp. 261–72; also, Police Foundation Reports, No. 1, The Minneapolis Domestic Violence Experiment (1984) (available from the Police Foundation, Washington, DC).

14. For robbery, the rate of reporting to the police has been very stable at about 55 percent. See BJS, *Criminal Victimization in the United States.*

15. The robbery arrest rates for ages 16, 17, and 18 were all sufficiently close that they are combined into their collective average on Figure 2.3.

16. Writing in *The New York Times,* David Kocieniewski (1997) states that "some criminologists attribute the decline to demographic factors like a smaller number of teenagers." In an article on the "mystery" of the drop in crime, David Anderson (1997) notes that some analysts explain the drop as resulting from "random demographic changes" (p. 49).

17. The data in Figure 6 have been smoothed with three-point smoothing, so that the population at any age a is calculated as one-third the sum of the population at a, $a + 1$, and $a - 1$.

18. The number of incidents reported by an agency to the SHR is close to but not identical to the number of incidents reported to the UCR. The variation can result from differences in the reporting procedures when different segments of the police department handle the two reporting tasks. A number of jurisdictions have varied considerably over time in the number of incidents reported to the SHR, including years when they simply submitted no reports at all. Rather than misrepresent fluctuations in reporting as changes in homicides, those places that display such large fluctuations are omitted from the analyses. Because of these fluctuations in reporting to the SHR, the SHR data used here includes only those jurisdictions that submitted SHR reports consistently over the 1977 to 1997 period. Thus, states such as Florida, Illinois, and New Hampshire and cities such as Chicago are omitted. It also omits offenses that have not been consistently reported in the SHR, including "justifiable homicides" and voluntary manslaughter. These omissions are intended to avoid misinterpreting fluctuations associated with reporting as changes in the homicide patterns themselves.

19. In each of these figures for each age group, the data are presented as an index number representing the ratio of the number of homicides by each weapon in each year to the number of homicides committed with handguns in 1985. Thus, the index for handguns in 1985 is 100 in each figure.

20. These data are available only for those homicides in which the offender is known.

21. The two groups are combined because, in the SHR, Hispanics are treated as a distinct group in some years and combined with whites in other years. Thus, by combining the two groups, we avoid characterizing these reporting changes as changes in the homicide patterns.

22. Based on city-specific data from UCR 1991 and 1996.

23. Each individual city was assigned to a "city size" category based on its mean population over the period 1988 to 1992 in order to ensure that each category contains the same cities over the period shown. Without such a stabilizing assignment rule, this assignment would vary over time and would by itself affect the group rates whenever a change took place. Because the homicide rate is positively related to population, as cities grow and move from one class to a higher one, even if there were no change in any city's homicide rate, that movement alone would reduce the homicide rate in the group they left as well as in the group they moved up to. These effects would be negligible among the large numbers of smaller cities, but could be very influential among the smaller numbers of the largest cities.

24. This is partly a result of the fact that, as the population size approximately halves between groups, the number of cities approximately doubles, thereby keeping the number of homicides roughly stable.

25. Some cities, including Chicago and Houston, were not included here because their reporting to the SHR was sporadic, and I did not want to attribute these fluctuations in reporting to changes in the homicide patterns being observed.

References

Anderson, David C. 1997. "The Mystery of the Falling Crime Rate." *The American Prospect* (May-June):49–55.

Blumstein, Alfred. 1998. "Violence Certainly Is the Problem – and Especially with Hand Guns." *University of Colorado Law Review Symposium Issue* 69(4) (Fall):945–67.

Blumstein, Alfred, Jacqueline Cohen, and Harold Miller. 1980. "Demographically Disaggregated Projections of Prison Populations." *Journal of Criminal Justice* 8:1–25.

Blumstein, Alfred, and Daniel Cork. 1996. "Linking Gun Availability to Youth Gun Violence." *Law and Contemporary Problems* 59:5–24.

Blumstein, Alfred, and Richard Rosenfeld. 1998. "Exploring Recent Trends in U.S. Homicide Rates." *Journal of Criminal Law and Criminology* 88(4)(Fall):1175–1216.

Butterfield, Fox. 1995. "Many Cities in U.S. Show Sharp Drop in Homicide Rates." *The New York Times,* August 13, p. 1, 10.

Cook, Philip J., ed. 1996. "Kids, Guns, and Public Policy." *Law and Contemporary Problems* 59(1)(Winter).

Cork, Daniel. 1999. "Examining Space-Time Interaction in City-Level Homicide Data: Crack Markets and the Diffusion of Guns Among Youth." *Journal of Quantitative Criminology* 15:379–406.

DiIulio, John J. 1996. "Why Violent Crime Rates have Dropped." *The Wall Street Journal,* September 6.

Easterlin, Richard A. 1987. *Birth and Fortune: The Impact of Numbers on Personal Welfare,* 2nd edition Chicago: University of Chicago Press.

Hershey, Robert D. Jr. 1997. "Confidence of Consumers is Surging." *The New York Times* December 31, p. C1, C8.

Kelling, George L., and Catherine M. Coles. 1997. *Fixing Broken Windows: Restoring Order and Reducing Crime in Our Communities.* New York: The Free Press.

Kocieniewski, David. 1997. "New York City Murder Rate May Hit 30-Year Low." *The New York Times,* December 25, p. B1.

Krauss, Clifford. 1996. "Crime Rate Drops in New York City." *The New York Times,* December 20, p. A1, B23.

Maxim, Paul. 1985. "Cohort Size and Juvenile Delinquency: A Test of the Easterlin Hypothesis." *Social Forces* 63:661–79.

Mitchell, Alison. 1994. "Giuliani Points to Drop in Crime Rate Despite Other Problems." *The New York Times,* September 14, p. A13.

O'Brien, Robert M. 1989. "Relative Cohort Size and Age-Specific Crime Rates: An Age-Period-Relative Cohort Size Model." *Criminology* 27:57–78.

Police Foundation. 1984. *The Minneapolis Domestic Violence Experiment.* Police Foundation Reports, No. 1. Washington: Police Foundation.

Riedel, Marc. 1993. *Stranger Violence: A Theoretical Inquiry.* New York: Garland.

Sherman, Lawrence W., and Richard A. Berk. 1984. "The Specific Deterrent Effects of Arrest for Domestic Assault." *American Sociological Review* 261:261–72.

Smith, M. Dwayne. 1986. "The Era of Increased Violence in the United States: Age, Period, or Cohort Effect?" *Sociological Quarterly* 27:239–51.

Steffensmeier, Darrell, and Miles D. Harer. 1991. "Did Crime Rise or Fall During the Reagan Presidency? The Effects of an 'Aging' US Population on the Nation's Crime Rate." *Journal of Research in Crime and Delinquency* 28:330–59.

Steffensmeier, Darrell, Cathy Streifel, and Edward S. Shihadeh. 1992. "Cohort Size and Arrest Rates Over the Life Course: The Easterlin Hypothesis Reconsidered." *American Sociological Review* 57:306–14.

U.S. Department of Justice, Bureau of Justice Statistics (BJS). 1996. *Criminal Victimization in the United States, 1993.* A National Crime Victimization Survey Report 2, 2–3. Washington: U.S. Department of Justice.

U.S. Department of Justice, Bureau of Justice Statistics (BJS). 1997. *Criminal Victimization in the United States, 1994.* A National Crime Victimization Survey Report 1. Washington: U.S. Department of Justice.

U.S. Department of Justice, Bureau of Justice Statistics (BJS). 1998. *Criminal Victimization in the United States, 1995.* A National Crime Victimization Survey Report NCJ-171129. Washington: U.S. Department of Justice.

U.S. Department of Justice, Federal Bureau of Investigation. 19xx. *Crime in the United States: Uniform Crime Reports, 19xx.* Washington: USGPO. The UCR report for any year is usually published in the fall of the following year.

Guns and Gun Violence

Garen Wintemute

THE UNITED STATES IS EXPERIENCING A very rapid decline in rates of serious violence, and particularly firearm violence. As recently as 1993, America's homicide rate was at a near-historic high; by mid-1999 it was lower than at any time since the mid-1960s, and all indications are that it is continuing to fall. This chapter reviews some of the conditions that led to the increase in rates of firearm violence during the late 1980s and early 1990s and then focuses on some of the most important interventions that have helped reduce gun violence. My discussion is limited to interventions that targeted firearms and firearm violence directly, and mainly to interventions that have been formally evaluated. Many other promising but unexamined interventions are described in a recent report from the Department of Justice (Office of Juvenile Justice and Delinquency Prevention [OJJDP]: 1999).

The Importance of Guns in Violence

Why a chapter focused specifically on firearms? The answers are clear and compelling. The United States has experienced a true epidemic of firearm violence. As I explore later in detail, gun violence accounted for nearly the entire increase, and the more recent decrease, in overall rates of serious violence in the United States (Figure 3.1). Firearm violence remains very common; as recently as 1998, nearly 700,000 violent crimes were committed with firearms (Rennison 1999).

There are a great many firearms in the United States. American households contained 192 million firearms in 1994, of which 65 million were

45

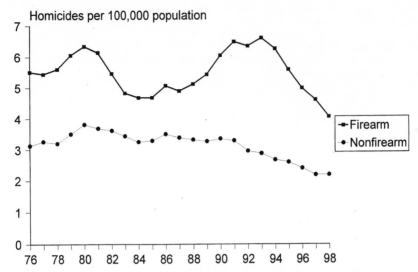

Figure 3.1. Homicide victimization in the United States from 1976–1998 by firearm involvement. Data from *Homicide Trends in the United States,* Bureau of Justice Statistics.

handguns (Cook and Ludwig 1996). Since 1994, an average of 3.9 million new firearms have been added annually to existing stocks through domestic production alone.

Not surprisingly, the more guns there are, the more gun crime there is. Many correlational studies, some geographic and some temporal, have established a close relationship between gun availability and rates of gun violence at the population level (Cook 1981, 1991; Hawkins 1997; Reiss and Roth 1993; Wintemute 1987; Zimring and Hawkins 1997). The equation works for individuals, too; keeping a firearm in the home more than doubles the risk that a member of the household will be killed in a firearm homicide (Bailey et al. 1997; Cummings, Koepsell et al. 1997; Kellermann, Rivara, Rushforth et al. 1993).

Access to firearms facilitates particular types of crimes, such as robbery against "harder" targets (Cook and Moore 1999; Kleck 1991). This is particularly the case when the person committing the crime is a stranger to the victim, and such crimes now constitute 44 percent of all violent crimes in the United States (Rennison 1999).

Firearms modify the consequences of crime. The use of a gun as opposed to some other weapon increases the likelihood that a violent crime will be completed, particularly in the cases of rape and robbery (Rand 1990, 1994).

In 1998, according to police data compiled by the Federal Bureau of Investigation (FBI) in its Uniform Crime Reports (UCR), assaults committed with a firearm were 4.6 times as likely as assaults committed with a knife or similar weapon to result in a fatality (Federal Bureau of Investigation [FBI] 1999a). Robberies and family and intimate assaults are three times as likely to result in death when a firearm is involved as when a knife or similar weapon is used (Cook 1987; Saltzman et al. 1992).

Firearm violence costs the United States dearly. The lifetime aggregate costs of firearm injuries sustained in 1990 (including suicides and unintentional injuries) were projected to be $20.4 billion, and the researchers who arrived at this figure considered it likely to "grossly underestimate" the actual costs (Max and Rice 1993). Lifetime medical care costs alone for the estimated 134,445 persons sustaining gunshot wounds in 1994 were estimated at $2.3 billion, about $17,000 per injured person (Cook et al. 1999). Between 50 and 80 percent of the medical care costs for firearm-related injuries are borne by the public, either through direct public expenditure or through uncompensated care provided by publicly supported hospitals (Cook et al. 1999; Wintemute and Wright 1992).

The cost of gun violence to the groups and individuals most directly affected cannot adequately be captured in financial terms. As recently as 1994, the year after the homicide rate reached its peak in the United States, more than one-half (53 percent) of *all* deaths among black males ages 15 to 24, and 12 percent of all deaths among white males of this same age, resulted from firearm homicide alone (Singh, Kochanek, and MacDorman 1996). Of homicides among women, 51 percent involved a firearm, and 34 percent were committed by a spouse or intimate partner; "more than twice as many women were shot and killed by their husband or intimate acquaintance than were murdered by strangers using guns, knives, or any other means" (p. 1) (Kellermann and Mercy 1992).

The 1980s to 1993: Rates of Gun Violence Increasing

Violence does not occur at random. With the acuity of hindsight this seems almost a truism. But perhaps the single most important characteristic of the epidemic of violence that began in the mid-1980s – one that has become clear only in retrospect – is how narrowly focused it was. Specific, easily identified populations, weapons, and places were all at much greater than average risk for involvement in serious or fatal violence. The recognition of this simple fact underlies much of the success in reducing rates of violence since 1993.

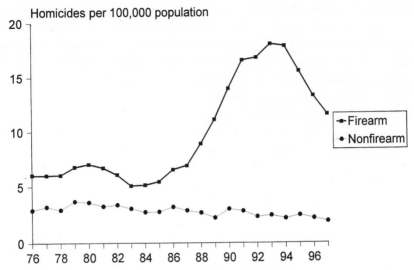

Figure 3.2. Homicide victimization in the United States from ages 15–19 in 1976–1997. Data from National Center for Health Statistics.

People

As Victims. The increase in risk for homicide from the mid-1980s through 1993 was largely limited to teenagers and young adults and was almost entirely due to rising rates of firearm homicide. The gun homicide rate for persons ages 15 to 19 increased more than threefold from 1984 to 1993, and that for persons ages 20 to 24 more than doubled, in both cases to levels far beyond anything seen before (Figures 3.2 and 3.3). Remarkably, rates of nonfirearm homicide for these groups decreased during the same time. By 1993, 90 percent of homicides among males ages 15 to 24 involved firearms, and the firearm homicide rate among black males ages 15 to 24 was 21 times that for the population as a whole. In many cities, a black male who turned 18 in 1989 had roughly a one in 20 chance of being murdered by 1995 (Cook and Laub 1998). Homicide rates for white males ages 15 to 24 increased as well, but not as dramatically.

Older and younger age groups were spared the worst of the epidemic. The firearm homicide rate for persons ages 25 to 34 showed no net upward trend, and that for persons ages 35 and older actually declined (Figures 3.4 and 3.5). Nonfirearm homicide decreased steadily in both groups. Children under age 14 experienced a small but steady rise in firearm homicide through 1993 and were the only age group for whom nonfirearm homicide also increased (Figure 3.6).

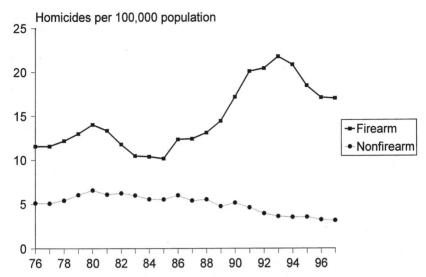

Figure 3.3. Homicide victimization in the United States from ages 20 to 24 in 1976–1997. Data from National Center for Health Statistics.

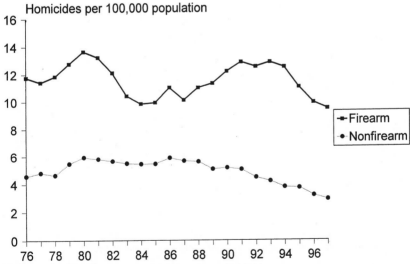

Figure 3.4. Homicide victimization in the United States from ages 25–34 in 1976–1997. Data from National Center for Health Statistics.

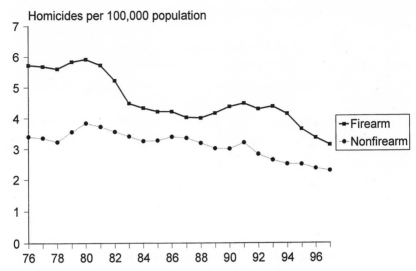

Figure 3.5. Homicide victimization in the United States, ages 54 and above, in 1976–1997. Data from National Center for Health Statistics.

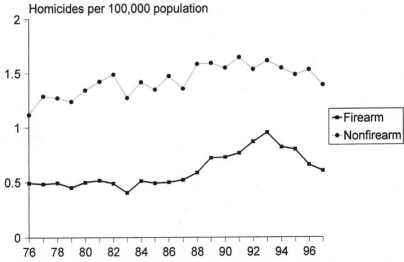

Figure 3.6. Homicide victimization in the United States from ages 0–14 in 1976–1997. Data from National Center for Health Statistics.

Nonfatal assaultive shootings followed a similar pattern. In the year ending May 1993, there were an estimated 99,000 nonfatal shootings in the United States. Of these, 71 percent were assaultive and 85 percent occurred among males. Of all shootings among males, 45 percent occurred among those ages 15 to 24. Nearly one-half (48 percent) of all nonfatal shootings were of blacks (Cherry et al. 1998).

As Perpetrators. The patterns of risk for committing a homicide were described in detail in Chapter 2, and are summarized here. Increases in homicide commission were also greatest among teenage and young adult males, particularly among minorities, and predominantly involved firearms. Weapon-related offenses among juveniles (age 17 or less) more than doubled from 1985 to 1993, whereas those among all adults taken together increased a relatively modest 33 percent (Greenfeld and Zawitz 1995).

A disproportionate number of weapon-related offenses were committed by persons who already had extensive criminal records. Of all felony weapons offenders in 1992, 34 percent had a prior felony conviction, and more than one-half of these had been convicted more than once (Greenfeld and Zawitz 1995). Many weapons offenders were already under active criminal justice supervision – 27 percent on probation or parole, 14 percent on pretrial release – a finding that would lend impetus to later interventions involving more restrictive parole and probation regimens. More than 95 percent were prosecuted in state courts; of those convicted of felony weapons offenses, only two-thirds were incarcerated and sentences were often light. Later efforts to federalize prosecutions for some weapons offenses would grow in part from such results.

Perpetrators as victims: "It's a War Out There". Those who were at greatest risk for firearm injury often had extensive criminal or substance abuse histories. In Philadelphia, for example, the percentage of gun homicide victims who had a prior criminal record increased from 44 to 67 percent between 1985 and 1990 (McGonigal et al. 1993). All those dying within twenty-four hours underwent toxicologic testing: The percentage of victims testing positive for cocaine rose from 9 to 39 percent, whereas positive results declined from 45 to 35 percent for alcohol and from 10 to 7 percent for other drugs.

In a nationwide survey of arrestees questioned in early 1995, 59 percent had been threatened with a gun, 40 percent had been shot at, and 16 percent had actually been shot (Decker, Pennell, and Caldwell 1997). One-fourth of detainees in Cook County Correctional Institutions in 1994 reported a prior gunshot wound (May et al. 1995). Among juvenile inmates, fully 84 percent reported that they had been threatened with a gun or shot at (Sheley and

Wright 1993). In Virginia, 13 percent of juvenile inmates had been shot and wounded at least once; researchers concluded that "the single best predictor of violent victimization may be involvement in the criminal justice system" (p. 751) (McLaughlin et al. 1996). In fact, these youthful offenders were more likely to have been shot and wounded than were American troops in any conflict since the Civil War.

Gang members were at remarkably high risk for sustaining gun violence. In the 1995 arrestee study just mentioned, 75 percent of gang members had been threatened with a gun, and 40 percent had been shot at (Decker et al. 1997). The homicide victimization rate for gang members was estimated to be 60 times higher than that in the general population (Bjerregaard and Lizotte 1995). In Los Angeles, the percentage of all gang-related homicides rose from 18 percent in 1979 to 43 percent in 1994–68 percent for children and adolescents – and the percentage committed with a firearm rose from 71 to 95 percent (Hutson et al. 1995). Among inner-city high school students, 34 percent of members of organized gangs and 19 percent of other gang affiliates reported having been shot at or injured with a weapon "many times" (Sheley, McGee, and Wright 1995).

High risk for being a victim of gun violence was not restricted to those actively involved in the criminal justice system. At the inner-city high schools studied by Sheley et al. (1995), 45 percent of all students had been threatened with a gun; 20 percent of males and 6 percent of females had been shot at, and 4 percent of students had been shot.

Place. As discussed in Chapter 2, the increase in gun homicide that occurred over the late 1980s and early 1990s was disproportionately a big-city phenomenon (Fox and Zawitz 1999). By 1993, one-half of all homicides in the United States occurred in sixty-six cities that contained just 16 percent of the nation's population; one-fourth occurred in just eight (Sherman 1997b). Within these high-risk cities homicide was concentrated in a small number of neighborhoods, where homicide rates were as much as 20 times the national average (Sherman 1997a). Chicago's entire increase in homicide was attributable to a rise in firearm homicide in a small number of neighborhoods (Block and Martin 1997). In Indianapolis, just 3 percent of the city's addresses accounted for 100 percent of its gun crime (Sherman and Rogan 1995).

Weapons. Firearms played a critical role in recent trends in violent crime. As Figure 3.1 illustrated, the entire increase in homicide in the United States through 1993 was attributable to firearm homicide. Firearm homi-

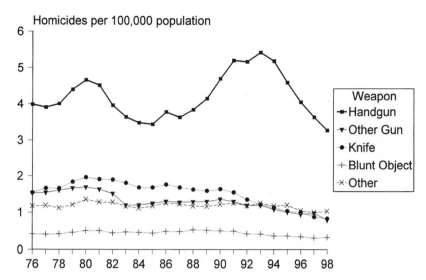

Figure 3.7. Homicides in the United States in 1976–1998 by weapon type. Data from *Homicide Trends in the United States,* Bureau of Justice Statistics.

cides increased by 53 percent from 1985 to 1993. During that same time nonfirearm homicides actually declined by 5 percent.

Recent trends in overall homicide rates were driven almost entirely by trends in handgun homicide. In the early 1990s handguns accounted for perhaps one-third of all firearms in civilian hands (Cook and Ludwig 1996) and 40 percent of firearm production, but were used in at least 80 percent of firearm homicides. Handgun homicides rose 71 percent from 1985 to 1993, whereas homicides by other firearms rose just 14 percent from 1985 to 1990 and fell thereafter (Figure 3.7).

As homicide rates rose, a rapid and significant transition occurred in the type of handgun most frequently used in homicide – from revolvers to semiautomatic pistols. (A revolver carries its ammunition in a cylinder that rotates – revolves – to bring each new cartridge into firing position; revolvers are the handguns in cowboy action films. A semiautomatic pistol typically carries its ammunition in a detachable magazine that fits in the grip of the gun, the part held by the shooter; think of "Miami Vice" or any recent police action program.)

In Chicago, almost the entire increase in handgun homicides was attributable to semiautomatic pistols (Figure 3.8) (Block and Martin 1997). Homicides committed with revolvers rose from 1987 to 1990 but then fell rapidly, while the overall number of gun homicides continued to increase

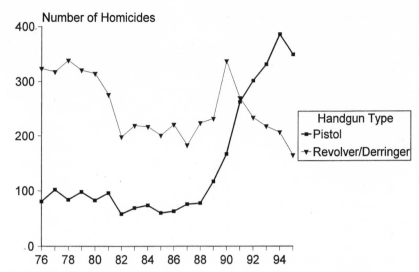

Figure 3.8. Handgun homicides by firearm type in Chicago from 1976–1995. Data from the Illinois Criminal Justice Information Authority, Chicago Homicide Dataset.

through 1993. The proportion of all firearm homicides in Chicago that were committed with semiautomatic pistols rose from 23 percent in 1985 to 60 percent in 1993 (Illinois Criminal Justice Information Authority et al. 1999).

The rapid increase in semiautomatic pistol use in homicide was documented in several other major cities. Pistols were used in 5 percent of gang homicides in Los Angeles in 1986 but 44 percent by 1994 (Hutson et al. 1995). In Philadelphia, the percentage of all firearm homicides involving 9mm or .380-caliber semiautomatic pistols rose from 4 percent in 1985 to 30 percent in 1990 (McGonigal et al. 1993). In Milwaukee, 9mm pistols were used in 7 percent of firearm homicides in 1990 but 23 percent in 1994 (Hargarten et al. 1996). Nationwide, more homicides were committed with 9mm pistols in 1992 alone than in the entire decade of the 1980s (Diaz 1999).

This transition from revolvers to semiautomatic pistols as homicide weapons was closely linked to trends in handgun production. The production of revolvers fell rapidly in the early 1980s, but pistol production mirrored handgun homicide rates (Figure 3.9).

In fact, nearly the entire increase in pistol production from the mid-1980s to 1993 involved the medium- and large-caliber pistols that increas-

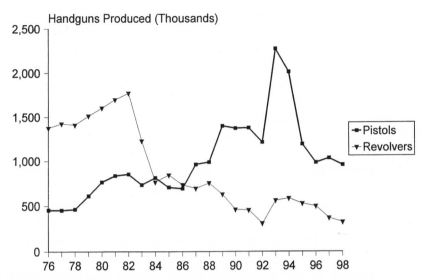

Figure 3.9. Handgun production in the United States from 1976–1998. Data from the Bureau of Alcohol, Tobacco, and Firearms.

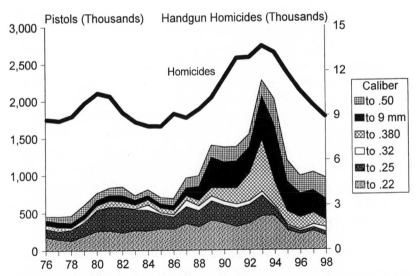

Figure 3.10. Handgun homicide and semiautomatic pistol production by caliber in the United States from 1976–1998. Data from *Homicide Trends in the United States,* Bureau of Justice Statistics, and the Bureau of Alcohol, Tobacco, and Firearms.

ingly became the weapons of choice for criminal use (Figure 3.10). Production of small-caliber pistols (.32 and smaller) increased by only 28 percent from 1984 to 1993, while production of medium- and large-caliber pistols (.380, 9mm, and larger) increased by more than sixfold over that same period. One observer, a former senior staff member to the House Judiciary Committee's Subcommittee on Crime, has argued that the firearms industry knowingly marketed increasingly lethal pistols in an effort to maximize sales to a customer base that was already saturated with less powerful weapons (Diaz 1999).

For several reasons, the replacement of revolvers by medium- to large-caliber semiautomatic pistols among street firearms contributed directly to the increase in firearm homicide rates. Pistols carry more ammunition. Revolvers typically carry six rounds, but in the "double-stack" magazine configuration that was very common until 1994 – and remains available today – conventional 9mm pistols carry as many as twenty rounds of ammunition and with special "after-market" magazines hold even more. Assault-type semiautomatic pistols have a still larger ammunition capacity (Wintemute 1996).

As the transition from revolvers to pistols progressed, handgun caliber increased with ammunition capacity. It has long been known that firearm caliber is an independent determinant of firearm lethality in civilian settings (Zimring 1972). One reasonably well accepted measure of the relative, if not absolute, wounding potential of a firearm is its "relative stopping power" (Hogg 1985). This measure takes into account the diameter, mass, shape, and muzzle velocity of bullets discharged from a specified firearm. The relative stopping power of a large-caliber handgun is many times that of a small-caliber handgun, as shown in Figure 3.11.

It was therefore of particular importance that relatively high capacity, medium-caliber semiautomatic pistols that were also very inexpensive became widely available for the first time in the late 1980s. These pistols, which typically sold new at retail for $100 to $150, were produced almost entirely by a small group of manufacturers in Southern California, the "Ring of Fire" companies (Wintemute 1994). During the late 1980s and early 1990s, pistol production by these companies increased at a rate of 20 percent or more per year; they produced nearly 900,000 handguns in 1993. In essence, these companies brought to market in large numbers a new generation of powerful "Saturday night special" handguns.

Buying these cheaply made, inexpensive, easily concealable handguns was a marker for future criminal activity, even for those who did not other-

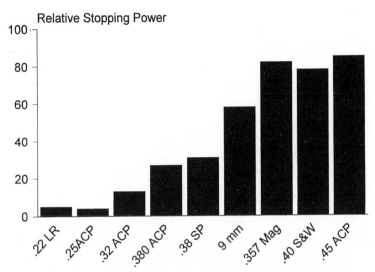

Figure 3.11. Relative stopping power of common handgun ammunition.

wise appear to be at high risk of committing crimes. Among young adults in California who purchased handguns legally in 1988 and who had no criminal record, those who bought such guns were 93 percent more likely than those who bought other handguns to be charged with new crimes involving guns or violence (Wintemute, Parham et al. 1998).

Medical studies documented the consequences of the appearance on the street of medium- and large-caliber semiautomatic pistols. In Philadelphia this occurred between 1985 and 1990. Emergency medical services improved during that time, and the percentage of those killed with revolvers who died at the scene of the shooting fell from 42 percent to 19 percent. However, the percentage of those killed with pistols who died at the scene rose from 5 percent to 34 percent (McGonigal et al. 1993). At one regional trauma center in Washington, DC, there was a substantial increase in the average number of gunshot wounds suffered by each gunshot victim admitted to the hospital from 1986 to 1990, at a time when the number of gunshot admissions also nearly quadrupled (Webster et al. 1992). The average caliber of bullets taken from patients in the operating room and at autopsy increased steadily (Caruso, Jara, and Swan 1999). In a comprehensive study of shootings in three cities with sophisticated trauma systems during 1992–94, 80 percent of those who died did so either at the shooting scene or shortly after reaching the hospital (Kellermann, Rivara, Lee et al. 1996).

The specific contribution of assault-type firearms to the rise in rates of gun violence was less clear. These high-capacity, generally semiautomatic handguns, rifles, and shotguns first came to widespread attention during the late 1980s and were involved in a number of widely publicized multiple-casualty and gang-related shootings.

Some evidence suggested assault-type firearms were of more than episodic importance. In a 1989 survey of law enforcement agencies in California, 63 percent noted a "significant increase" in the use of assault-type firearms (Rodman 1989). Among young adults who legally purchased handguns in California in 1988 and had any prior criminal record, those who bought an assault-type handgun were 70 percent more likely than those who bought other handguns to be charged with new crimes involving guns or violence (Wintemute, Wright, Parham et al. 1998).

But a national survey of state prison inmates in 1991 found that, while 8 percent of all inmates had owned a "military-type weapon such as an Uzi, AK-47, AR-15 or M-16," fewer than one percent of violent offenders had used such a firearm during the offense that led to their incarceration (Beck et al. 1993). Of 600 homicides in Virginia from 1989 to 1991, only 10 were known to have involved an assault-type firearm (Criminal Justice Research Center 1994).

Access to Firearms. In a comprehensive study of gun ownership and use in the early 1990s, Philip Cook and Jens Ludwig found that 35 to 40 percent of households had firearms, a decrease from approximately 50 percent in the 1970s (Cook and Ludwig 1996). The percentage of households keeping a handgun had increased modestly during that same time, however, from 20 percent to nearly 25 percent. Most gun-owning households had more than one firearm; 48 percent owned three or more. Remarkably, one-third of handguns in the United States – perhaps 20 million guns – were stored loaded and not locked away. These guns were obviously ready and accessible for other than their intended purposes.

Juveniles and young adults reported a remarkable degree of access to and use of firearms in several surveys. Sixty-two percent of urban middle and high school students in 1993 reported that they could get a firearm with little difficulty. One in six reported that they had actually carried a firearm in the prior month (Harris 1993). Nationwide in 1993, 8 percent of high school students had carried a gun in the prior thirty days; results for individual states ranged from 6 percent to 17 percent (Kann et al. 1995). Among high school students in Seattle in 1990–91, 11 percent of males reported that they owned a handgun, and of these handgun owners 33 percent had actually fired the gun at someone (Callahan and Rivara 1992).

Weapon-carrying and use were even more common among those at high risk for violence. Of high-risk students in Rochester, 37 percent of gang members and 8 percent of others owned at least one firearm for protection; 27 percent of gang members and 4 percent of others reported that they carried firearms (Bjerregaard and Lizotte 1995). Among inner-city high school students, 52 percent of gang members, 30 percent of drug sellers, and 22 percent of other students reported owning guns (Sheley and Wright 1993). Twelve percent of the students said they carried guns "all or most of the time," and another 23 percent carried "now and then" (Sheley et al. 1995).

Gun ownership and use were most common among those actively involved in the criminal justice system. Among juvenile inmates in Sheley and Wright's study, 83 percent owned guns and 65 percent owned at least three (Sheley and Wright 1993). More than one-half (55 percent) of these inmates carried firearms "all or most of the time," and 84 percent carried at least "now and then."

Two studies asked high-risk gun owners where they had actually acquired guns. Juvenile inmates and inner-city high school students had obtained guns from a wide variety of sources, and theft played a relatively unimportant role (Table 3.1A) (Sheley and Wright 1993). Gun store and pawnshop purchases were surprisingly frequent, given that all these subjects were below the legal age to purchase firearms. Beck and colleagues (1993) asked adult state prison inmates who had been incarcerated for an offense involving a handgun, where that handgun had been acquired. The guns were as likely to have come from a gun store as from an obviously illegal supplier, and theft again was a not a major source of supply (Table 3.1B).

Guns as Products. Many successful gun-oriented efforts to reduce rates of violence were based in part on our increasing knowledge of firearms themselves as consumer products and of how the markets in firearms furnished guns for illicit use. Some of the information presented here was gathered after rates of gun violence began to decline, but it describes the situation during the higher-violence years as well.

Making Guns. Although there are hundreds of licensed firearm manufacturers in the United States, data compiled by the Bureau of Alcohol, Tobacco, and Firearms (ATF) show that a relative few dominate the market. In 1998, the top ten producers of semiautomatic pistols accounted for 81 percent of all domestic manufacture; the top five revolver manufacturers accounted for 99 percent of all revolver production (ATF, 2000a). In the early 1990s, some 80 percent of Saturday night special handguns were produced by the six Ring of Fire manufacturers in Southern California

Table 3.1. Sources of Guns Used in Crime

A. Juvenile Inmates[a]
(Most recently acquired handgun)

Source	Percentage
Family or Friends	36
The Street	22
Drug Addict	12
Theft	12
Drug Dealer	9
Retail Outlet	7
Other	2

[a] From Sheley and Wright 1993.

B. State Prison Inmates[b]
(Handgun possessed in crime leading to incarceration)

Source	Percentage
Family or Friends	31
Black Market or Fence	28
Retail Outlet	27
Theft	9
Other	5

[b] From Beck et al. 1993.

(Wintemute 1994). The leading manufacturers of semiautomatic pistols in the 1990s are listed in Figure 3.12.

Manufacturers of firearms in the United States are largely exempt from regulation regarding the design and performance of their products. Firearms are unique among consumer products in this respect. Since the 1930s it has been illegal to manufacture machine guns or short-barreled shotguns or rifles without a special license, and since 1986 it has been illegal to manufacture machine guns for civilian use. Until 1994 there were essentially no other restrictions on the design or performance of firearms manufactured in the United States. ATF has only limited authority to oversee commerce in firearms, and has no jurisdiction over the design or safety of domestically produced guns. The Consumer Product Safety Commission, which regulates many other products, is forbidden by law from establishing regulations over firearms or ammunition.

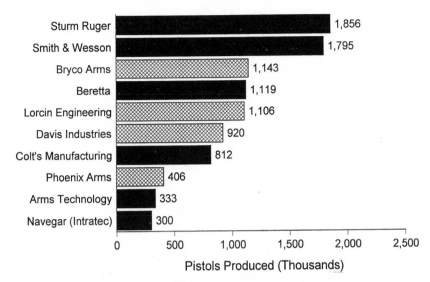

Figure 3.12. Top 10 producers of semiautomatic producers in the United States from 1990–1998. Companies with crosshatched bars are "Ring of Fire" manufacturers of so-called Saturday night special handguns. Data from the Bureau of Alcohol, Tobacco, and Firearms.

By contrast, the Gun Control Act of 1968 requires that firearms imported into the United States meet an array of tests designed to ensure that they are "particularly suitable for or readily adaptable to sporting purposes." At the time of the law's enactment, small, easily concealable, inexpensive, imported handguns were widely believed to be disproportionately involved in crime. Congress therefore set standards only for imported handguns; those produced in the United States were deliberately exempted. The widespread availability of inexpensive, domestically produced semiautomatic pistols is a direct result of this decision.

Selling Guns. The system of distribution of firearms in the United States operates in such a way as to make handguns readily accessible, including distribution to persons who are prohibited from possessing them. A former senior vice president of the nation's largest handgun manufacturer testified under oath that the industry was "fully aware of the extent of criminal misuse of firearms" but had decided to "take no independent action to insure responsible distribution practices" (Hass 1996, p. 6).

Major manufacturers sell firearms to regional distributors, of which there were approximately two hundred listed in a dealer resource book as of 1999 (Anonymous 1999). Little is known about these distributors. There are no good public data regarding their market share, region of coverage, or products sold. Records obtained in a 1999 court case, *Hamilton v. Accu-Tek*, established that some manufacturers require their distributors to certify that they sell only to reputable firearms dealers, but others do not.

These regional distributors sell to retail firearms dealers. Some distributors require their potential dealer customers to provide a copy of their current federal firearms license and also evidence of compliance with all relevant state and local laws and even a photograph of their store. Others require none of these things.

At the retail level it is more accurate to refer to firearms *markets,* than to a firearms market. There are, to begin with, both legal and illegal retail markets in firearms; direct diversion of guns from the former to the latter is an important source of guns used in crime. The legal firearms market has been subdivided into primary and secondary markets. As defined by ATF, the primary market consists of all transactions involving a firearm through its first retail sale. Any subsequent transfers of what is now a used gun constitute the secondary market. Another model, developed by Philip Cook, and colleagues, considers the primary market to consist of all transfers of firearms by mainstream sources such as licensed dealers, whether the guns involved are new or used. The secondary market consists of transfers involving less formal sources such as private parties, collectors, and vendors at gun shows (Cook, Molliconi, and Cole 1995).

By either definition the primary and secondary markets are of roughly comparable size. Annual sales of used guns are believed to equal those of new guns, and there is an approximately 60/40 split between retail sales by licensed dealers and sales by other sources (Cook et al. 1995; Cook and Ludwig 1996). Gun owners in a nationwide survey were asked where they had purchased firearms in the two years before the survey. Fifty-five percent had purchased firearms at a specialty gun store; 25 percent from a family member, friend, or acquaintance; 11 percent at a pawnshop or more diverse retailer, such as a sporting goods store or discount house; 4 percent at a gun show or flea market; and 5 percent from other sources (Cook and Ludwig 1996).

During the time that rates of gun violence were increasing, lack of regulation and oversight of licensed dealers contributed greatly to the availability of guns for criminal use. Prior to 1993, a three-year dealer's license could be obtained for just $30. With few exceptions, no effort was made to verify the information on the license application. ATF was prohibited from inspecting any dealer more often than once each year without a warrant.

By 1992, there were literally more gun dealers than gas stations in the United States (Sugarmann and Rand 1992). In some parts of the country there was at least one licensed firearms dealer for every 250 persons (Pierce, Briggs, and Carlson 1995). Nonetheless, ATF's inspection staff was shrinking; with just over two hundred field agents available they estimated that "it would take over 10 years to inspect each and every licensee" given the resources available at the time (ATF, 1993).

There was a truly remarkable concentration of risk among dealers for selling guns that were later used in crime. In 1990–94, just 145 dealers accounted for 26 percent of all 121,110 crime gun traces conducted by ATF (Pierce et al., 1995). There was no record of sales volume for individual dealers, however, as ATF was prohibited from collecting such information. It therefore remained possible, though highly improbable, that the high number of crime-gun traces involving these dealers simply reflected a high sales volume.

ATF conducted the first systematic study of licensed firearms dealers, Operation Snapshot, in 1993 (ATF, 1993). At that time there were about 244,000 dealers with active licenses, of which inspectors visited a random sample of 400. Seventy four percent were "kitchen-table" dealers who conducted their business out of their own homes. In the year prior to the survey, 46 percent had sold no guns, and only 20 percent had sold more than twenty guns. Only 35 percent of the dealers were subject to any state or local business requirements, and of these only 65 percent stated that they were in compliance. Nearly one-third were violating federal firearms laws; 12 percent surrendered their licenses on the spot.

Prior to 1993, no mechanism existed for ensuring that federally licensed dealers were actually engaged in the business of selling firearms or were in compliance with state and local laws regarding the operation of such a business. Among the noncomplying license holders were scofflaw dealers who purchased firearms – sometimes in large quantity – with their federal license and sold them outside any regulatory framework. California, for example, required that all handgun sales by licensed dealers be reported to its Department of Justice and that background checks be conducted on prospective purchasers. The forms were provided only to dealers who held required state licenses. A comprehensive study of more than 5,000 crime guns confiscated in Los Angeles from 1988 through 1995 found that, of 1,782 new guns shipped to California dealers, only 40 percent had a required record of sale on file with the state Justice Department (Wachtel 1998).

Scofflaw dealers were an important source of crime guns. In North Carolina, only 26 percent of federally licensed dealers had a required state license (Cook et al. 1995). One North Carolina dealer sold 1,200 guns primarily to convicted felons or juveniles. Another in Tennessee sold an average of 15,000 guns per year before being shut down by ATF. The Los Angeles study provided details on nearly thirty criminal trafficking cases involving 19,000 guns, more than 75 percent of which were associated with cases in which federally licensed dealers sold directly to illegal street dealers or traffickers (Wachtel 1998).

Undercover Chicago police officers compiled chilling evidence of how easily such transactions could be completed. In documents filed in support of that city's lawsuit against the firearms industry, details were provided of a dozen cases in which storefront firearms dealers in Chicago suburbs – selected because of the frequency with which guns they sold were used in crime in Chicago – willingly participated in sales that they knew to be illegal (City of Chicago and County of Cook 1998).

Firearms that were diverted into the illegal market were frequently bought and sold in bulk retail transactions known as multiple purchases. In Southern California in a nine-month period in 1994, there were 5,743 multiple purchases involving more than 13,000 guns (Wachtel 1998). ATF data showed that guns purchased in this way and later submitted for tracing as crime guns were particularly likely to have a partially or completely obliterated serial number – a clear indication of intent to use the gun for criminal purposes (ATF 1997, 1999b).

Such multiple purchases were an important source of firearms for traffickers. Among juvenile inmates in the Sheley and Wright study (1993), one in five stated that they had gone out of state in order to buy guns in quantity, and 45 percent of these had "bought, sold, or traded a *lot* of guns." Of young adults purchasing handguns in California in 1988, those buying multiple guns were more likely than others to be arrested for new crimes later (Wright et al. 1998).

But the importance of interstate trafficking may have been overestimated, notwithstanding Sheley and Wright's observation. In the mid-1990s, seventeen cities submitted data on all their confiscated crime guns to ATF for tracing. Guns that were first sold at retail in the state in which they were recovered made up a majority of all confiscated crime guns in twelve of these cities, and a plurality in three more. Not surprisingly, cities with tighter local regulations on firearms purchase and ownership had lower percentages of in-state guns among their confiscated crime guns (ATF, 1997).

Surrogate or "straw" purchasers – persons who purchased firearms for those who were prohibited from doing so – represented an important variant of trafficking. In the Sheley and Wright study, 32 percent of juvenile inmates, and perhaps even more surprising, 18 percent of high school students had asked someone to purchase a firearm for them from a retail outlet (Sheley and Wright 1993; Smith 1996).

And yet licensed dealers made up what was easily the most regulated, and probably also the cleanest, segment of the retail gun market. Federal law required those who were "engaged in the business" of selling guns to be licensed. But it did not require a license to buy and sell guns per se, and the law was deliberately ambiguous as to what "engaged in the business" meant. Unlicensed persons could buy and sell dozens or hundreds of guns each year and claim that they were pursuing a hobby.

This gave rise to what were in effect two parallel systems for the distribution of firearms, with clear implications for efforts to prevent the flow of guns into the illegal market. Licensed dealers were required (although enforcement was obviously problematic) to comply with federal, state, and local laws. They were required to keep records of all acquisitions and dispositions of guns and report all multiple sales. They were obligated to identify prospective purchasers, using a photo identification. They could not transfer guns to prohibited persons, and they were required to observe waiting periods and submit purchaser information for background checks. Unlicensed gun sellers, by contrast, could legally ignore the identification requirement and waiting period, could not conduct background checks, and were not required to keep records.

The problem was particularly acute at gun shows, the first systematic study of which was not conducted until 1998 (ATF, 1999a). There were more than 4,000 shows each year, typically with 2,000 to 5,000 attendees at each. ATF summarized the situation: "Under current law, large numbers of firearms at these public markets are sold anonymously; the seller has no idea and is under no obligation to find out whether he or she is selling a firearm to a felon or other prohibited person. If any of these firearms are later recovered at a crime scene, there is virtually no way to trace them" (ATF, 1999a, p. 1). As a result, "too often the shows provide a ready supply of firearms to prohibited persons, gangs, violent criminals, and illegal firearms traffickers" (ATF, 1999a, p. 6). The author has repeatedly observed straw purchases at gun shows that were conducted with the full knowledge of the seller.

Unlicensed vendors made up 25 to 50 percent of all persons who sold guns at gun shows. They marketed their exemption from the regulations that applied to licensed dealers. At one show, such a vendor posted a sign stating "No background checks required; we only need to know where you live and how old you are" (ATF, 1999a, p. 6).

Gun shows, swap meets, and flea markets were increasingly recognized as a free-for-all segment of the retail firearms market. ATF's report included data on 314 firearm investigations that involved gun shows. In one 1993 case, a licensed dealer in Tennessee sold more than 7,000 guns with altered serial numbers to unlicensed dealers who in turn sold them in gun shows and flea markets in North Carolina. In a 1994 California case, a licensed dealer sold 1,700 guns to unlicensed purchasers off the books over four years. Many of these appeared in swap meets in southern California and were sold to local gangs. The guns in this case were associated with a number of violent crimes, including homicide.

Given the wide-open channels for the diversion of guns directly from the legal to the illegal firearms market, reports that even serious criminals often bought rather than stole their guns gained credibility. A nationwide survey of inmates in state prisons in 1991 found that those incarcerated for a handgun offense were nearly as likely to have gotten the gun they used in that offense from a "retail outlet" (27 percent) as from the "black market, a drug dealer, or a fence" (28 percent) (Beck et al. 1993).

Theft remained a significant source of crime guns. The National Crime Victimization Survey suggested that there were approximately 340,000 instances of theft each year with an average of 1.5 guns stolen per theft, yielding an estimate of 500,000 stolen guns per year (Cook and Ludwig 1996). Nonetheless, the importance of theft may have been overestimated. When asked how they had acquired the handgun they used in the offense leading to their incarceration, just 9 percent of state prison inmates in 1991 said that they had stolen it (Beck et al. 1993). This may be because theft did not yield desirable guns. Guns stolen from residences, at any rate, tended to be older revolvers, not the semiautomatic pistols that had become the weapons of choice for criminal use (Kennedy, Piehl, and Braga 1996a).

Crime Guns. In the 1970s, Franklin Zimring had found that at least half of confiscated handguns that could be traced were five years of age or less (Zimring 1976). The importance of his finding went largely unrecognized until it was rediscovered in Boston in the early 1990s (Kennedy 1997; Kennedy et al. 1996a, 1996b). By the mid-1990s this "new guns hypothesis" had been confirmed. Across the seventeen cities that were providing comprehensive tracing data to ATF, the percentage of crime guns that were less than three years old at the time of their confiscation ranged from 22 to 43 percent for juveniles, from 30 to 54 percent for youth, and from 25 to 46 percent for adults (ATF, 1997). This meant that it might not be necessary, as had been commonly thought, to restrict the flow of the 200 million firearms already in civilian hands in order to lower gun-crime rates. Efforts could be focused instead on commerce in new guns.

A relatively small array of guns accounted for a substantial percentage of all those used in crime. In the seventeen comprehensive tracing cities, the top ten firearms accounted for 21 to 48 percent of all confiscated crime guns and for higher percentages of guns taken from juveniles and youth (ATF, 1997). Not surprisingly, pistols predominated, accounting for 58 percent of guns confiscated from juveniles, 61 percent of those taken from youth, and 47 percent of guns confiscated from adults.

Certain specific firearms predominated in gun crime year after year (Table 3.2). With the exception of the Raven Arms .25 caliber pistol, a firearm made in very large numbers until its manufacturer was destroyed by fire in 1991, these were generally medium-caliber handguns. Some guns were used often in crime largely because a great number of them were available. This was the case for the Smith and Wesson .38- and .357-caliber revolvers, of which more than 2.7 million were manufactured from 1984 to 1993.

Other handguns appeared to be on a fast track to criminal use. In an analysis that controlled for the number of guns recently manufactured, inexpensive handguns from the six Ring of Fire companies were 3.4 times as likely to appear in ATF's tracing data as were handguns from such manufacturers as Smith & Wesson, Ruger, and Colt (Wintemute 1994). The salient example was that of the Lorcin Engineering .380-caliber pistol, which was first manufactured in 1992. By 1993, the Lorcin .380 was among the most frequently traced firearms in the United States, and it maintained that status thereafter.

1993 to the Present: Rates of Gun Violence Decreasing

In 1998, the Centers for Disease Control and Prevention (CDC) published a detailed study of trends in gun violence in the United States. The rate of both fatal and nonfatal firearm injuries peaked in the third quarter of 1993. By the end of the second quarter of 1995, less than two years after the peak had been reached, there had been a 23 percent decrease in the rate of firearm injuries and a 10 percent drop in the fatality rate. Assaultive injuries among males ages 15 to 24 decreased 28 percent, and fatalities decreased 16.5 percent (Cherry et al. 1998).

From 1993 to 1998, the number of serious violent crimes in the United States declined substantially (Table 3.3). The single greatest percentage decline was seen in firearm robbery. Declines in firearm-related crime were greater than for crimes involving other weapons, so that the percentage of

*Table 3.2. The Ten Firearms Most Frequently Traced by the Bureau of Alcohol,
Tobacco, and Firearms, 1989–1998*[a]

1989	1992	1995	1998
Raven .25	**Raven .25**	S&W .38	S&W .38
S&W .38	S&W .38	**Lorcin .380**	**Lorcin .380**
S&W .357	**Davis .380**	**Raven .25**	Ruger 9mm
Mossberg 12G[b]	S&W .357	**Davis .380**	**Raven .25**
S&W 9mm	Mossberg 12G[b]	Norinco .762[c]	Norinco .762[c]
Marlin .22[c]	Marlin .22	S&W .357	Mossberg 12G[b]
Colt .45	S&W 9mm	Ruger 9mm	S&W 9mm
Intratec 9mm	Intratec 9mm	Mossberg 12G[b]	S&W .357
Remington 12G[b]	Remington 12G[b]	S&W 9mm	**Davis .380**
Ruger .357	**Jennings .22**	**Bryco .380**	Marlin .22[c]

[a] Some entries represent more than one specific firearm. For example, Smith & Wesson
produces many different .38-caliber revolvers, and ATF groups them together in establishing
its annual top-ten list. Lorcin Engineering, on the other hand, produced just one type of
.380-caliber pistol until it went out of business in late 1999. Inexpensive pistols manufactured
by the Southern California "Ring of Fire" companies are indicated in **bold font**.
[b] Shotgun
[c] Rifle

violent crimes that involved firearms also decreased. Among juveniles,
homicide arrests decreased 54 percent between 1993 and 1998 (FBI
1999a).

Provisional data for the first half of 1999 suggest that the decline in violent crime has continued; as compared to the first half of 1998, homicide
decreased a further 13 percent, robbery 10 percent, and aggravated assault
7 percent. All but homicide decreased in cities of all sizes and in rural areas
as well (FBI 1999b).

Reflecting again the close association between crime rates and gun availability, this downward trend in firearm violence was accompanied by a 58
percent drop in annual production of semiautomatic pistols between 1993
and 1998. The greatest declines were for .25- and .380-caliber guns (Figure
3.10).

Reported access to firearms remained easy, however, even for those for
whom it would be illegal. In 1996, 29 percent of male high school students
nationwide owned a firearm, and 4 percent owned an automatic or semiautomatic handgun (Sheley and Wright 1998). Six percent reported that
they carried firearms at least occasionally; those who were engaged in criminal activities were much more likely to carry. One-half said that getting a

Table 3.3. The Decrease in Violent Crime in the United States from 1993 to 1998, by Crime Type and Firearm Involvement[a]

Crime	Number of Events		% Decline 1993 to 1998	Involving Firearms	
	1993	1998		1993	1998
Homicide	24,526	16,914	31.0	69.6	64.9
Firearm	17,063	10,981	35.6		
Handgun	13,968	8,841	36.7		
Other/unspecified firearm	3,095	2,140	30.9		
Nonfirearm	7,463	5,933	20.5		
Aggravated assault	1,135,099	974,402	14.2	25.1	18.8
Firearm	284,910	183,188	35.7		
Nonfirearm	850,189	791,214	6.9		
Robbery	659,757	446,625	32.3	42.4	38.2
Firearm	279,737	170,611	39.0		
Nonfirearm	380,020	276,014	27.4		

[a] Data are from *Uniform Crime Reports,* 1993 and 1998 editions. Weapon-specific results are estimates based on data in those reports.

gun would be "little" or "no" trouble, and of particular interest given the age of the respondents, 35 percent of those who carried handguns said they had paid cash for them.

Gun ownership and use remain particularly prevalent among those involved in criminal activity. Among urban arrestees in 1995, 14 percent overall, 21 percent of juvenile males, and 31 percent of gang members reported that they carried a gun "all or most of the time" (Decker et al. 1997). More than one-half had paid cash for their most recent gun. Of arrestees who owned guns, 23 percent overall, 33 percent of juvenile males, and 50 percent of gang members had used guns in the commission of crimes. In a smaller study in Colorado and Florida, between 40 and 53 percent of gang members reported carrying a gun in school; 40 to 68 percent reported involvement in a drive-by shooting (Huff 1998).

Interventions

Beginning in the mid-1980s, medical and public health practitioners became increasingly involved in violence prevention. Perhaps their main contribution to the field was their emphasis on the importance of aggregating information on single instances of violence to seek underlying patterns. From cholera outbreaks in London in the eighteenth century to the advent of HIV/AIDS, they had grown used to the precept that such patterns were informative and frequently led to effective prevention measures (Kellermann et al. 1991; Teret and Wintemute 1993). Their arrival on the scene coincided with an already increasing interest on the part of criminologists and criminal justice practitioners in applying the lessons learned from such patterns – the "big picture" – at the street level.

In the case of gun violence, the big picture emerged with unexpected clarity. The distribution of gun violence was anything but random. It was highly concentrated in space. Relatively narrow subgroups of the population were at extremely high risk. A subset of weapons was disproportionately involved, and these weapons arrived in the hands of those who misused them by definable pathways. The criminal justice system could be surprisingly tolerant of criminal activity involving guns. Increasingly, interventions were designed with these specific findings in mind.

Focusing on Demand and Use

Changing Police Practices. In 1994, James Q. Wilson suggested that the best approach to preventing criminals from committing gun crime was to "just take away their guns" (Wilson 1994). The Kansas City Gun Experiment, a controlled experiment that fused science with practical law enforcement, sought to do just that (Sherman, Shaw, and Rogan 1995; also see Chapter 7). From July 1992 through January 1993, extra police patrols in a target area focused on gun-crime hot spots that had been identified by crime mapping. The widely publicized patrols were made up of officers working overtime; their mission was "to get guns off the street as cost-effectively as possible" (Sherman et al. 1995, p. 3). Gun seizures rose by 65 percent to a total of seventy-six, of which twenty-nine were seized by the additional patrols.

Gun crime in the target area decreased by 49 percent during the intervention, but it rose 4 percent in a comparison site where usual police practices were followed. There appeared to be no displacement of crime into neighborhoods surrounding the target area. The gun-crime rate returned toward its pre-intervention level when the intervention ended. It dropped again, although by a smaller amount, when the patrols were reinstituted.

The program's impact surprised all concerned. The evaluators believed that its effect was probably due more to the deterrence created by a highly visible police presence than by the incapacitative effect of the removal of firearms per se. They noted that these guns were probably at very high risk for use in crime, however, given the circumstances under which they were seized.

Efforts to repeat the Kansas City experience were widespread. Two variants of hot-spot policing were implemented in Indianapolis in the summer of 1997 (OJJDP 1999). In the first case, stops were made for any infraction, and in general, warnings were issued rather than citations. This approach failed; the incidence of both violent and property crimes increased in comparison to the summer of 1996.

The second trial, conducted elsewhere in Indianapolis, sought specifically to deter illegal gun-carrying and emphasized arrests rather than citations. This more-focused approach produced only an 8 percent increase in gun seizures in the target area, but homicides fell from eleven the prior summer to one during the intervention period while they increased by 53 percent citywide. Aggravated assault and armed robbery both decreased by 40 percent, and total gun crime decreased by 29 percent.

St. Louis experimented with a variation on this strategy in 1993 that is now being formally evaluated (Rosenfeld and Decker 1996). With permission from parents, police searched the homes of high-risk juveniles with the sole intent of confiscating firearms. As an element of obtaining consent to search, police certified that they would ignore evidence of other crimes and apparently made good on that promise. This Firearm Suppression Program, begun in 1993, seized 402 guns in 1994, 10 percent of all those seized by law enforcement. A formal evaluation is underway. The largest and best known application of gun-oriented policing has been in New York City. Beginning in 1994, the New York Police Department (NYPD) maintained a special Street Crime Unit charged with aggressive enforcement of gun laws (OJJDP 1999). The department targeted gun-crime hot spots and aggressively sought sources of crime guns. From 1994 to 1997, the NYPD made 46,198 gun arrests and confiscated 56,081 firearms. Nonfatal shootings fell by 62 percent from 1993 to 1997. In 1998, New York had just 633 homicides, fewer than in any year since 1964.

Fagan, Zimring, and Kim (1998) assessed the extent to which changes in police practice were responsible for New York's decline in violent crime. They found critical differences in time trends between firearm and nonfirearm violence. New York had experienced a rapid increase in firearm homicides from the mid-1980s through 1991 and a dramatic decrease thereafter. Firearm assaults followed essentially the same pattern. By contrast, nonfirearm homicides and assaults declined throughout the 1980s and early 1990s. Similar differences were seen between gun and nongun robbery. These divergent trends did not appear to result from a substitution of firearms for other weapons.

Fagan and colleagues argued that the rapid and specific decline in gun crime during the early 1990s could not simply be an instance of aberrantly high rates of violence returning to baseline, as rates fell to levels generally well below those of the mid-1980s. Nor did they find sufficient changes in drug use or the city's population structure in the 1990s to account for the decrease.

The decline in homicide began in 1991, when patrol strength began to increase and enforcement priorities were broadened to include "quality-of-life" offenses. Moreover, the decline in homicides was initially limited to those occurring on the street and therefore most likely to be deterred by an increased patrol presence. Other homicides began to decline only in 1994. They concluded that there was good circumstantial evidence, at least, that changes in police practices were partly responsible for the decline in violent crime in New York.

It is less clear that the aggressive policing tactics that characterized the newer Street Crime Unit were necessary. Nearly one-half of all felony gun court cases resulting from the unit's activities in 1997–98 were dismissed (Marzulli and Rashbaum 1999). Moreover, the decline in homicide began during a prior city administration that relied on community involvement and problem-oriented policing. The *New York Times* recently contrasted New York with San Diego, which also relied more heavily on community involvement. Although it took a very different approach to the problem, San Diego saw a 75 percent decrease in homicide after 1991, similar to New York's drop of 66 percent since 1990 (Butterfield 1999).

Increasing Criminal Justice Sanctions. Federalizing prosecution of some firearm-related crimes has recently received widespread attention. In many cases, federal penalties for possession of firearms by felons and for drug offenses involving the use of firearms are stiffer than those imposed at the state level.

In February 1997, Richmond, Virginia, initiated Project Exile, a practice of screening potential prosecutions and referring to the federal system those in which the potential penalties were tougher there (OJJDP 1999). By February 1999, there had been 404 federal indictments, and the conviction rate was 86 percent (Janovsky 1999). The average prison term was more than 4.5 years. Homicide decreased by 36 percent from 1997 to 1998. Richmond's experience has not been compared to that of cities without such programs, so it is impossible to know for certain that the change in prosecution tactics bears major responsibility for the decrease. No data on recidivism are available, but all of those incarcerated are presumably still in prison at the time of writing. Similar programs have since begun in Philadelphia, Rochester, San Francisco – Oakland, and elsewhere. Juveniles usually do not have formal felony records and are beyond the reach of such programs (Cook 1998).

Focusing on Supply

Tracing Crime Guns. ATF first began tracing the ownership of firearms in 1972. It was, and still is, a laborious process. When a trace request is received from a law enforcement agency, ATF contacts the gun's manufacturer to learn when and to whom it was sold – in most cases a wholesale distributor. ATF contacts the distributor, identifies the dealer who bought the gun, and then contacts the dealer to identify the first retail purchaser of the gun and the purchase date. Until 1994, dealers were not even required to provide this information.

In 1994, ATF began a series of valuable initiatives. Law enforcement agencies were asked to provide more complete information on confiscated guns, including the identity of the gun's possessor and of any associates, the date on which the gun was confiscated, and the nature of the crime involved. ATF merged this end-user information with the results of its own tracing investigations. As these reports were compiled and examined, patterns began to emerge. A small number of persons were identified as frequent first-purchasers of guns recovered in crime, sometimes over large regions of the country. They could be investigated as potential straw purchasers and could provide links to gun traffickers. Individual gun-crime cases could be linked by computer across common elements to provide new leads for field investigators.

In 1996, ATF began a program of comprehensive crime-gun tracing. Participating cities, of which there were thirty-seven by 1999, submitted tracing requests to ATF for all confiscated firearms. This helped to solve individual cases and yielded a much clearer picture of the dynamics of the illegal gun market. (Much of our earlier discussion of that topic is based on these comprehensive tracing data.) In 1993, ATF conducted just 54,195 traces. This rose to more than 205,000 by 1999, and several states had adopted requirements that data on all confiscated crime guns be submitted to ATF.

A 1999 ATF study documented that more than 3,000 firearms once owned by law enforcement agencies had been traced as crime guns since 1990 – 1,100 in 1998 alone (O'Connell and Barrett 1999a). The agencies had traded in hundreds of thousands of guns as they purchased more powerful weapons, and the guns were resold. By late 1999, the International Association of Chiefs of Police had recommended destroying old police guns rather than exchanging them, and cities were implementing the recommendations (O'Connell and Barrett 1999b).

The utility of gun-tracing as a tool for solving crimes and understanding the illegal firearms market will continue to grow. ATF's expanding program of comprehensive crime-gun tracing and a new ability to record each gun's ballistic "fingerprint" at the time of manufacture should help significantly.

Limiting the Number of Dealers. ATF began to tighten oversight of prospective and current dealers in January 1993, under a new National Firearms Program (General Accounting Office [GAO] 1996). Inspections were increased, and interviews were required for all new applications and selected renewals. More than 27,000 inspections were conducted in 1993, up from 11,800 in 1990; nearly 18,000 law enforcement referrals were made. These actions were reinforced by the Federal Firearms Licensee Reform Act, adopted in November, which increased licensing fees to $200 for an initial application and $90 for a renewal. New applicants were also required to submit a photograph and fingerprints; background checks were broadened and performed on renewing licensees as well. The 1994 Violent Crime Control and Law Enforcement Act required license holders to certify that they were in compliance with state and local laws and regulations.

The total number of federal firearms license holders (dealers, pawnbrokers, and manufacturers) fell from 287,000 at its peak in 1993 to just 86,180 by October, 1999, a 70 percent drop (ATF 1999c; Pierce, Briggs, and Carlton 1998). It is still falling. A 1996 survey by the General Accounting Office found that license holders who were engaged in the legitimate business of selling guns appeared to be relatively unaffected by the changes. Of eighty dealers who had let their licenses expire in late 1994 or early 1995, only two had sold more than 100 guns in an average year (GAO 1996).

Other interventions were taken at the state level. As mentioned previously, North Carolina found in 1993 that only 26 percent of dealers also possessed its required state license. Those in violation included large retail outlets such as Wal-Mart and Kmart. Noncomplying dealers were required either to obtain a state license or to forfeit their federal license. Alabama also identified federal firearms licensees who did not possess its required state license and notified each of them of the requirement. Nine hundred licensed dealers claimed to be ignorant of the requirement, obtained the license, and paid penalties. Another 900 said that they were not actively selling firearms, and 200 more could not be located; licenses for these 1,100 were slated for cancellation (Cook et al. 1995).

Many local jurisdictions went further. The Oakland, California police department worked with ATF to enforce a requirement that all holders of federal firearm licenses have a local police permit. Obtaining a permit meant a screening and background check. The number of license holders was reduced from fifty-seven before the program began to seven in 1997. New York City discovered that only 29 of its 950 license holders operated in compliance with local law. Under an agreement with ATF, all license applications were forwarded to NYPD, which undertook local screening and conducted inspections, often unannounced. The number of license holders in New York fell from 950 to 259 (Veen, Dunbar, and Ruland 1997).

Not all local interventions relied on police activities. In Sacramento County, California, few federal license holders possessed a required state license in 1995. Those who did not were sent a letter by the state's Franchise Tax Board advising them that they owed back taxes on any guns bought or sold. In Detroit, an existing zoning ordinance prohibited the operation of home businesses. Residential licensees were given thirty days to surrender their license or move to a commercial area; if they did not, they faced citation and prosecution.

Perhaps fortunately, in that it will help focus future intervention efforts, a very small fraction of licensed dealers still accounts for a very large share of crime guns, at least as reflected by ATF's tracing data. A recent study focused on nationwide traces for 1996–97 (Pierce et al. 1998). Of 89,771 dealers in all, just 89 – 0.1 percent of the total – had more than 100 traced guns linked to each and together accounted for 23 percent of all traced guns. Another 415 dealers, each involved in between 25 and 99 gun traces, accounted for another 23 percent of traces.

Given the increasing awareness of the importance of new guns among those used in crime, this study also focused on dealers with traced guns having a short average time from sale to crime-related confiscation, known as "time-to-crime." Just seventy-five dealers with an average time-to-crime of under three years for their traced guns accounted for 20 percent of all traces.

Future enforcement efforts are likely to focus on dealers who sell a disproportionately high number of guns that are later used in crime or who report frequent thefts. The number of dealers will also probably continue to decrease; there are only 15,000 to 20,000 gun stores in the United States, still far fewer than the number of licensed dealers (GAO, 1996;

Office of Technology Assessment [OTA] 1991). Several states have moved to eliminate the two-track system of firearms distribution by prohibiting direct sales of firearms by persons other than licensed dealers. Such private-party sales are then processed by licensed firearms dealers so that purchasers undergo a background check to establish their eligibility. Such a policy is supported by 72 percent of gun owners and 77 percent of the general public (Teret et al. 1998).

Limiting Gun Sales. Evidence that firearms acquired in multiple-purchase transactions were likely to be trafficked and used in crime led to restrictions on such purchases at the state level. Virginia adopted a law, effective in July 1993, that limited purchases of firearms by persons other than dealers to no more than one per month. Prior to that time, Virginia had been recognized as a major source of crime guns confiscated in other states, particularly in New England, that had more restrictive laws on gun purchase. Virginia was the source of 35 percent of crime guns confiscated in New England that were purchased before the effective date of the law, but just 16 percent of guns purchased later (Weil and Knox 1996). Maryland followed suit in 1996, and California in 1999.

A national one-gun-a-month policy would prevent the illegal firearms market from shifting to new sources of supply as individual states restrict or eliminate multiple purchases. Such a policy is supported by 81 percent of the general public and 53 percent of gun owners (Teret et al. 1998).

Restrictions on Buyers. Federal law has long prohibited felons, persons under felony indictment, controlled-substance users, and certain others from possessing firearms. The Gun Control Act of 1968 required prospective purchasers to certify that they were not a member of one of the prohibited classes, but did not require a background check to verify that these certifications were valid. A number of states instituted background checks on their own, and found that 1 to 2 percent of prospective handgun purchasers were prohibited persons (Regional Justice Information Service [RJIS] 1996).

Federal requirements changed in 1994 following the enactment of the Brady Handgun Violence Prevention Act. The Brady Act required a five-day waiting period prior to handgun purchase, and initially also required a designated state or local chief law enforcement officer to conduct a criminal records background check. The latter requirement was declared unconstitutional by the Supreme Court in June 1997. Most chief law enforcement officers continued to perform background checks on a voluntary basis.

By 1998, twenty-three states operated under the provisions of the Brady Act. The others, known as "Brady alternative" states, had screening requirements that were at least as restrictive as Brady and operated under their state statutes. Over the five years that Brady had been in operation, all states together had screened a total of 12.7 million applications to purchase guns and had issued 312,000 denials, including 207,000 for prior felony convictions or pending indictments (Manson, Gilliard, and Lauver 1999).

Procedures for screening handgun purchasers in the Brady states were reconfigured in November 1998. The waiting period and the background checks conducted by state or local law enforcement agencies were replaced by a National Instant Check System (NICS) administered by the FBI. During NICS's first year of operation, nearly 90 percent of background checks were completed within two hours of application; 72 percent were completed within thirty seconds. Difficult checks could take several days, however, and the law allowed dealers to release firearms to purchasers after three business days, whether or not the background checks were completed. By the end of 1999, 3,353 prohibited persons, most of them felons, had acquired firearms in this manner; just 442 had surrendered their guns. This problem would largely be eliminated if the waiting period for firearm purchases were lengthened (FBI 2000; GAO 2000).

Critics of programs to screen prospective purchasers of firearms suggested that they were unlikely to be effective. They argued that those with criminal intent who were prevented from buying firearms in the legal market would simply acquire them illegally. The provisions of the Brady Act were described as a "sop to the widespread fear of crime" (Jacobs and Potter 1995). But screening prospective handgun purchasers does work. It reduces risk for later criminal activity among felons whose applications to purchase handguns are denied. In a recent California study, 170 felons whose handgun purchases were denied were compared to 2,470 handgun buyers who had felony arrests but no felony convictions (Wright, Wintemute, and Rivara 1999). Over three years of follow-up, the felony arrestees whose purchases were approved were 21 percent more likely to be charged with a new gun offense, and 24 percent more likely to be charged with a new violent offense, than the convicted felons were. In Florida, a significant decrease in homicide rates followed that state's adoption of a mandatory waiting period and background check for handgun purchase (McDowall, Loftin, and Wiersema 1995).

Critics on the other side of the issue suggested that denying the purchase or possession of a firearm based on a prior felony conviction or indictment did not go far enough. The 1997 Omnibus Consolidated Appropriations Act banned the purchase or possession of firearms by persons convicted of a misdemeanor domestic-violence offense. Persons subject to active domestic-violence restraining orders had been prohibited from purchasing or possessing handguns since 1994.

Some eighteen states and Washington, DC now deny firearms to persons convicted of selected misdemeanors, typically crimes involving violence, alcohol, or drugs. New Jersey's statute is the most comprehensive, prohibiting the purchase of firearms by "any person who has been convicted of a crime" (ATF, 1998a). California expanded its denial criteria in 1991 to include persons convicted of selected violent misdemeanors. The newly added offenses included simple assault-and-battery and brandishing a firearm, among others. The prohibition remains in force for ten years following the conviction. Table 3.4 lists the reasons for which denials of handgun purchase were made in California in 1991. Table 3.5 presents more detailed information on the prior criminal histories of some of those felons and misdemeanants whose purchases were denied (Wintemute, Wright, Parham et al, 1999).

Among those who purchase firearms legally, misdemeanants are at substantially increased risk for committing crimes later. A California study compared handgun purchasers who had at least one prior misdemeanor conviction to purchasers who had no prior criminal history whatever (Wintemute, Drake et al. 1998). All members of both groups passed a criminal records background check. Over fifteen years of follow-up, 25 percent of misdemeanants, but only 4 percent of those with no prior criminal history, were charged with a new violent offense. After adjusting for demographic differences, misdemeanants were 6.1 times as likely as those with no prior criminal history to be charged with a new violent offense. Those who had two or more prior misdemeanor convictions involving violence were 15.1 times as likely to be charged with a violent-crime index offense.

But as with felons, making it more difficult for misdemeanants to acquire handguns appears to be effective. A California study of violent misdemeanants who sought to purchase handguns found that denying handgun purchase appeared to reduce their risk of committing new crimes involving guns or violence by 20 to 30 percent (Wintemute, Wright, Drake et al. 1999). A majority of firearms owners, let alone members of the general public, supports denying firearms purchases to persons who had been convicted of misdemeanors involving firearms, violence, or substance abuse (Teret et al. 1998).

Gun Bans

Assault-Type Firearms. Derived from designs originally intended for the military, assault-type firearms can be handguns, rifles, or shotguns. They

Table 3.4. Grounds for Denial of Handgun Purchase for 3,589 Prospective Handgun Purchasers, California, 1991[a]

Reason for Denial	Number	Percent
Misdemeanor Conviction		
Simple Assault	1,153	32.1
Aggravated Assault	334	9.3
Brandishing a Weapon	267	7.4
Discharging a Firearm	37	1.0
Other	11	0.3
Felony Conviction		
Drugs	408	11.4
Burglary	224	6.2
Theft	152	4.2
Assault	137	3.8
Forgery/Fraud	114	3.2
Robbery	65	1.8
Sex Crimes	62	1.7
Driving Under the Influence	41	1.1
Homicide/Manslaughter	21	0.6
Weapons	15	0.4
Other/Unspecified	170	4.7
Other Criminal Activity		
Juvenile Offenses	37	1.0
Restraining Order	24	0.7
Condition of Probation	4	0.1
Mental Health Impairment	67	1.9
Under 21 Years of Age	246	6.9
Total	3,589	100

[a] The data did not distinguish between persons denied because they themselves were illegal aliens and those denied because of felony convictions for alien smuggling.
Reprinted from Wintemute, Wright, Parham et al. *Denial of Handgun Purchase*, 1999.

share four fundamental characteristics: higher-than-average ammunition capacity, semiautomatic or fully automatic firing mechanisms, a rapid rate of fire, and an intimidating appearance.

Anecdotal evidence suggested a rapid rise in their use in street violence in the late 1980s, particularly in major cities. On January 17, 1989, Patrick Purdy brought an AK-47 rifle onto the grounds of the Cleveland School in Stockton, California. In two minutes he fired well over 100 rounds of ammunition, killing or wounding thirty-five school children and teachers before killing himself. Legislation to ban assault-type firearms in

Table 3.5. Criminal Histories at the Time of Application for Handgun Purchase of Selected Persons Whose Handgun Purchases Were Denied, California, 1991[a]

Case 1: 43 year old M. Convictions: felony theft, felony driving under the influence (DUI). Other charges not resulting in reported convictions: grand theft, battery, hit and run with death or injury, DUI with bodily injury.

Case 2: 31 year old M. Convictions: brandishing a firearm. Other charges not resulting in reported convictions: DUI (two), possession of controlled substance (four; entered drug diversion), assault with a deadly weapon, theft, assault with a firearm.

Case 3: 36 year old M. Convictions: assault with a deadly weapon. Other charges not resulting in reported convictions: trespassing, resisting arrest (convicted two months after purchase application), disturbing the peace (convicted two months after purchase application), check fraud.

Case 4: 22 year old M. Convictions: burglary, possession of dangerous weapon, contempt of court. Other charges not resulting in reported convictions: use of controlled substance (two; entered drug diversion), assault, battery.

Case 5: 37 year old M. Convictions: assault with a firearm, battery, robbery, aggravated mayhem, assault with a deadly weapon not a firearm, brandishing a firearm, attempted arson, vandalism, DUI (two), disobeying a court order.

Case 6: 34 year old F. Mandatory registration as controlled-substance offender. Convictions: carrying a concealed firearm, false impersonation. Other charges not resulting in reported convictions: carrying loaded firearm in a public place, transporting controlled substance (seven), conspiracy to transport narcotics, possessing controlled substance, possessing marijuana/hashish, selling marijuana/hashish, carrying concealed weapon, carrying loaded weapon in a public place, receiving stolen property, resisting arrest, furnishing false identification.

Case 7: 30 year old M. Convictions: robbery with a firearm. Other charges not resulting in reported convictions: robbery, spousal assault.

M, male; F, female.

[a] When more than one charge or conviction for a particular offense occurred, the number of occurrences is given in parentheses.

Reprinted from Wintemute, Wright, Parham et al. *Denial of Handgun Purchase*, 1999.

California, drafted before the Stockton shooting, was signed into law within months. The California ban was never formally evaluated, but a number of police agencies reported that, even before the ban became fully effective, affected weapons were being used less commonly in street crime.

A more comprehensive ban on specified assault-type firearms was enacted as part of the 1994 Crime Bill, and in 1998 the Clinton administration halted the manufacture and importation, but not sale, of large-capacity semiautomatic "copy cat" rifles that had been designed to avoid the prior bans on technical grounds (ATF, 1998b).

The ban imposed by the 1994 Crime Bill has been evaluated by researchers at the Urban Institute (Roth and Koper 1997, 1999). While the bill was being debated, the price of the targeted firearms rose by 50 percent. More important, production of those weapons doubled. After the ban's effective date these recently manufactured guns could still be sold legally, and prices fell nearly to their prelaw baseline.

In the short run the ban appeared to have beneficial, but modest, effects. In the first year and a half after the ban became effective, trace requests to ATF fell by 20 percent for banned weapons but just 11 percent for other guns. There was no such decrease in traces in this period in those states where assault-type firearms had been banned earlier. In St. Louis and Boston, where all confiscated firearms were traced, traces for banned weapons fell 29 percent and 24 percent, respectively. The ban may have contributed to a 7 percent drop in firearm homicide from 1994 to 1995, but it was not clear at that time whether the decrease represented a downward trend or simple year-to-year variation. A reevaluation over a longer time period is underway.

Saturday Night Specials. A number of jurisdictions acted to ban domestic production and sale of these poorly made, inexpensive handguns. By 1997, four states had established a minimum melting-point criterion for the metal used to produce gun frames; the inexpensive zinc alloy from which these guns are often made has a lower melting point than does high-grade steel. In California, more than forty cities and counties sought to eliminate Saturday night specials by outlawing the manufacture and sale of guns that failed to meet a series of design and materials criteria. Their approach was conceptually similar to that taken under federal law for imported handguns, but the criteria were different. Results varied, apparently as a result of variable monitoring and enforcement. In some cities sales of banned guns fell rapidly to zero; in others sales were not greatly affected (Wintemute 2000).

In 1989, Maryland created a Handgun Roster Board to develop a list of handguns that could legally be manufactured or sold in the state. The board was required to consider such characteristics as size, quality of materials, reliability, and suitability for sporting use, among others; no specific standards were set (Teret, Alexander, and Bailey 1990). A preliminary evaluation of the impact of the Maryland law has been completed. As with assault-type weapons, there was a substantial increase in sales of nonapproved guns prior to the law's effective date. Nonetheless, nonapproved guns accounted for a progressively smaller percentage of crime guns confiscated by law enforcement agencies (Vernick, Webster, and Huang 1998). The effect of the ban on crime was unclear; crime rates did not fall appreciably faster in Maryland than in neighboring states without similar legislation (Webster, Vernick, and Huang 1998).

In 1999, California adopted a rigorous set of design and performance standards for all handguns manufactured or sold in the state. Its provisions take effect on January 1, 2001. By the end of 1999, three of the state's six Ring of Fire handgun manufacturers were out of business and another had moved to South Dakota.

Handguns in General. Several major cities largely banned the purchase or possession of handguns, exempting those that were legally owned at the time the legislation became effective. The effectiveness of local bans is partly undermined by widespread trafficking in firearms: if guns are hard to purchase legally in a particular jurisdiction, they can simply be brought in from elsewhere. However, the new and more effective measures to disrupt gun trafficking may make local bans a more attractive option in the future.

In 1976, Washington, DC, banned the purchase and sale of handguns and the possession of all handguns that were not previously owned and registered. Violations of the law were misdemeanors. Passage of the law was followed by a 25 percent drop in firearm homicide (Loftin et al. 1991). There was no parallel decrease in homicide using other weapons, which would have suggested that the decrease in gun homicides was related to some external factor. Nor was there an increase in homicide by other means, suggesting that the law did not simply cause other weapons to be substituted for firearms. In addition, there was no change in either firearm or nonfirearm homicide in nearby areas of Maryland or Virginia. The effect persisted through 1987. Soon thereafter, as crack cocaine became common in the District, the effects of the law were overwhelmed by drug-related shootings.

New York City's Sullivan Law has largely banned the purchase of handguns since 1911. A controlled evaluation of the law has never been conducted, but for much of the twentieth century the city's homicide rate was substantially lower than that for the country's other largest cities. One of the major effects of the law was to alter the dynamics of the illegal firearms market. Nearly 85 percent of crime guns recovered by New York City law enforcement agencies are imported from outside the state (ATF 1999b).

Chicago also tightly restricted the purchase and possession of handguns. Recent events there illustrate the potential for synergy between local bans and interdiction efforts against gun trafficking. A small number of suburban dealers sold a large percentage of Chicago's crime guns, often bought by residents of Chicago who returned to the city with them. These dealers were targeted for investigation by the Chicago Police Department, as described earlier. They are now among the defendants in a $433 million civil lawsuit brought by the city for damages related to gun crime (City of Chicago and County of Cook 1998). Evidence gathered in the police investigations has also been referred to local and federal agencies for possible criminal prosecution.

The purchase of guns in the suburbs by Chicago residents has been widely publicized locally in the print and broadcast media. Elmwood Park, the location of at least one defendant dealer, has passed an ordinance banning the sale of handguns to residents of Chicago. Efforts are underway to encourage similar legislation in the other suburbs (personal communication, B.L. Crowe, City Attorney, City of Chicago, February 17, 1999).

Comprehensive Interventions. A rapidly growing number of cities have implemented comprehensive interventions focused on firearm violence. These interventions are organized around two principles. First, *go where the money is:* focus resources where the available evidence suggests they will do the most good. Second, *lots of things work:* implement several related interventions simultaneously to profit from synergy and reduce the possibility of adaptation.

The best-known of these is underway in Boston. In the early 1990s, Boston focused its efforts on juvenile and youth homicides, 72 percent of which involved firearms. Regular meetings were established among representatives from local and state police departments, corrections and probation agencies, prosecutors, federal agencies such as ATF, street-level gang workers, and researchers (Kennedy 1997).

The working group began by characterizing the problem. Gang members made up less than one percent of all youth in the city but accounted for 60 percent of youth homicide. Gang turf occupied less than 4 percent of the city but accounted for 25 percent of all serious crime and had particularly high rates of firearm-related offenses.

The research team studied youthful victims and perpetrators of homicide involving a knife or gun. Seventy-five percent of both groups had a criminal record involving on average more than nine prior offenses. Most (55 percent) had been on probation; 25 percent of the homicide offenders were on probation at the time of the offense (Kennedy 1997; Kennedy et al. 1996b).

Even though the purchase of handguns was tightly regulated in Massachusetts, one-third of the traceable crime guns confiscated in Boston had been purchased within the state. This suggested that straw purchasers played an important role.

Of guns confiscated from juveniles and youth, 52 percent were semiautomatic pistols, and 20 percent had partially or completely obliterated serial numbers. Pistols from just five companies, including four Ring of Fire firms, made up 40 percent of all guns confiscated from youth. New guns predominated; 25 percent were less than two years old, and nearly one-half of these were less than six months old. Almost all (90 percent) of the guns produced by Lorcin Engineering, 72 percent of guns made by Davis Industries, and 55 percent of guns made by Bryco Arms were confiscated within two years of their first retail sale. All these characteristics were very different from those of guns burgled from houses in Boston, indicating the lack of importance of theft as a source of crime guns in the city (Kennedy et al. 1996a).

The Boston Police Department had previously mounted highly publicized special enforcement campaigns. These were effective but short lived. They had included comprehensive street enforcement of even minor quality-of-life ordinances, intensive probation and parole supervision, service of outstanding warrants, and the like, along with gang mediation and other social services. Boston's new Youth Violence Strike Force adopted this approach on a sustained basis, with its interventions triggered by occurrences of weapon-related assaults. A new focus on firearms trafficking was added.

One early episode illustrates their approach:

> In one particularly violent gang neighborhood, they delivered a clear message to the effect that, unless the shootings stopped and guns were relinquished, gang members would be subject to an intense level of scrutiny and, for those on probation and parole, severe personal restrictions. Gang members were told the drug markets would shut down, warrants would be served, the streets would swarm with law enforcement officers (including a Federal presence), bed checks would be performed on probationers, rooms would be searched by parole officers, unregistered cars would be taken away, and disorder offenses such as drinking in public would be pursued. When one gang member with a 15-year history of violent felonies was found walking down the street with a single bullet in his possession, he was arrested. Taking into account his prior convictions, he was indicted as an

armed career criminal and sentenced to nearly 20 years in prison. Stunned gang members soon turned over their handguns, and the neighborhood became quiet. (Kennedy 1997)

This strategy was then pursued in other territories of the city.

Efforts to disrupt trafficking were triggered by confiscations of new guns of the most popular types, those on which an attempt had been made to obliterate the serial number, and those in the possession of gang members. Intensive efforts were made to identify the involved dealers and those who first purchased the guns at retail. Practitioners referred their investigations for federal prosecution when it was expected that federal penalties would be more severe.

No controlled evaluation of Boston's comprehensive intervention has been conducted, but there is strong circumstantial evidence that it has been effective. In the four years prior to the intervention, Boston averaged a steady forty-three youth homicides each year. The program was implemented over a relatively short period of time in late spring, 1996. There were eighteen youth homicides in the first year after implementation and ten in the second.

Data are now being collected in Minneapolis, where Boston's tactics have been adapted to local conditions (Kennedy and Braga 1998). Two-thirds of all homicides from 1994 to mid-1997 were committed with a gun; 64 percent of suspects and 40 percent of victims were ages 14 to 24. Large majorities of both suspects and victims were male and African-American. Forty-three percent of the victims and 72 percent of suspects had a criminal record; they had been arrested an average of more than seven times each. A plurality of homicides (45 percent) were gang related, although gang members made up only 4 percent of all youth in the city. Just eight of ninety-five neighborhoods in the city accounted for 59 percent of homicides.

The intervention proceeded along the lines described for Boston, beginning in June, 1997. In the summer of 1996, Minneapolis had experienced more than forty homicides. In the summer of 1997 there were five.

Interventions of Chiefly Symbolic Value

Gun Exchanges. Programs in which firearms are exchanged for cash or other material incentives are popular and widespread, but yield less than 2 percent of the firearms estimated to be in the participating communities. Several evaluations have not been encouraging. An exchange conducted in Seattle in 1992 recovered 1,172 guns, 95 percent of which were handguns, for a $50 cash incentive. However, 67 percent of the guns were more than five years old, and the mean age of the participants was fifty-one. There was no observable effect on either gun crime or firearm-related injury rates (Callahan, Rivara, and Koepsell 1994). Gun exchange programs in St. Louis in 1991 and 1994 were found to have no effect on rates of homicide or assault, but were considered to be a potentially effective vehicle for community mobilization (Rosenfeld 1996). A buy-back program during August, 1999, in Washington, DC obtained more than 2,900 guns by paying $100 each. Revolvers predominated, whereas semiautomatic pistols figured much more prominently in crime there. The average age of guns that could be traced was more than fifteen years (ATF, 2000b).

An evaluation of an exchange program in Sacramento focused on individual effects. Of participating households, 41 percent reported that there were no longer any firearms at home, and the prevalence of handgun ownership declined from 79 to 32 percent (Romero, Wintemute, and Vernick 1998). The program may have reduced the risk of violence for these participants, but their demographics suggested that they were at relatively low risk already.

Child Access Prevention Laws. States have passed laws imposing criminal penalties on adults whose negligence allows children to gain access to firearms with a resulting injury or death. An evaluation has been conducted of the effect of these laws in the twelve states adopting them by 1994 (Cummings, Grossman et al. 1997). Adoption of a child-access prevention law was associated with a 23 percent decrease in the rate of unintentional firearm death among children in affected states. However, this effect was limited to the three states where violations could be charged as felonies. In these three states shootings were reduced by approximately 40 percent; they rose by a statistically insignificant 14 percent in the nine misdemeanor states. Others have pointed out that, of the three felony states, only Florida actually experienced a decrease in unintentional shooting deaths. At this time there is no good evidence that the laws are effective (Teret and Webster 1999).

"Shall Issue" Mandates for Permits to Carry Concealed Firearms in Public. There has been much debate over the conditions under which permits to carry concealed firearms should be issued. In "may issue" states, local law enforcement agencies retain discretion over whether permits will be issued to eligible persons. In "shall issue" states, permits must be granted to all persons who request them and are legally able to possess concealable firearms. Beginning with Florida in 1987, more than one-half the states loosened their restrictions on carrying concealed firearms, most by adopting shall issue policies.

Individual evaluations yielded results that were frequently interpreted as contradictory but which in fact suggest that shall issue policies had little, if any, effect on crime rates. The first such study examined effects of shall issue policies on homicide rates in five metropolitan areas in Florida, Mississippi, and Oregon (McDowall et al. 1995). Homicides increased in four of the five sites and decreased in the other. One of the four increases and the one decrease were statistically significant. On average, homicides rose 25 percent after shall issue policies were adopted, but the authors cautioned that the variation between sites made this an unreliable result.

Another study, this one widely publicized, examined trends in county-level crime rates in ten states that adopted shall issue policies (Lott and Mustard 1997). There were decreases of 5 to 8 percent in most violent crimes and increases, which the authors considered to be compensatory, in property crimes. But when others examined data for individual states, they found neither consistent increases nor decreases. As with child-access prevention laws, many of the critical results could not be reproduced with Florida removed from the analysis (Black and Nagin 1998). Criminologist Gary Kleck concluded that most likely "the declines in crime coinciding with relaxation of carry laws were largely attributable to other factors," and not to the laws themselves (Kleck 1997, p. 376).

In a related study, Jens Ludwig determined that the decrease in homicide in the postlaw period in states that adopted shall issue policies consisted almost entirely of a decrease in juvenile homicides (Ludwig 1998). Homicide rates for adults may even have increased. The significance of this finding is that juveniles, who could not obtain concealed weapons permits under any circumstances, could not have been protected by more liberal access to these permits. He also found wide variation across individual states.

The reason for the lack of a clear effect is now emerging. About 7 percent of adults – 3.4 million persons – carry firearms in public on a regular basis and for reasons not related to their work (Cook and Ludwig 1996). Of these, 22 percent carry every day and 10 percent carry at least one-half the time; some 900,000 people may be carrying firearms on their person on a typical day. In states that adopted shall issue policies, typically no more than one or 2 percent of the eligible population requested a permit (Ludwig 1998), and a number of these new permittees probably carried firearms already. It is doubtful that the frequency of weapon-carrying was significantly affected by the adoption of shall issue statutes.

Building on Success

In the near future, many of these successful interventions will become more widespread. Other cities are seeking to replicate the "Boston miracle." Focused law enforcement and increased sanctions will raise the cost of doing gun crime. Other interventions will decrease the supply of firearms for criminal use. Firearms trafficking will become more difficult and dangerous. Dealers who furnish guns for crime will be the target of more aggressive identification and prosecution efforts. Manufacturers now face the real possibility that they will be held accountable in court for crimes arising in part from their manufacturing and distribution practices. In March, 2000, precisely to avoid such liability, Smith & Wesson, the country's largest handgun manufacturer, agreed to incorporate an array of safety features into its products and restructure its distribution procedures.

Much work remains to be done, and progress will not go uninterrupted. In 1999 a trend toward increasing homicide rates developed in the nation's largest cities: one percent overall and 9 percent in New York City (FBI 1999b; Flynn 1999). Nonetheless, while it would be foolish to make firm predictions, there is good reason to expect that overall rates of gun violence will continue to decrease.

References

Anonymous. 1999. "Distributors' Products and Business Requirements." *Shooting Industry* 44(12):206–17.

Bailey, James E., Arthur L. Kellermann, Grant W. Somes, Joyce G. Banton, Frederick P. Rivara, and Norman P. Rushforth. 1997. "Risk Factors for Violent Death of Women in the Home." *Archives of Internal Medicine* 157:777–82.

Beck, Allen, Darrell K. Gilliard, Lawrence Greenfeld, Caroline Harlow, Thomas Hester, Louis Jankowski, Tracy Snell, James Stephan, and Danielle Morton. 1993. *Survey of State Prison Inmates 1991.* NCJ-136949. Washington: U.S. Bureau of Justice Statistics.

Bjerregaard, Beth, and Alan J. Lizotte. 1995. "Gun Ownership and Gang Membership." *Journal of Criminal Law and Criminology* 86:37–58.

Black, Dan A., and Daniel S. Nagin. 1998. "Do Right-to-Carry Laws Deter Violent Crime?" *Journal of Legal Studies* 27:209–19.

Block, Carolyn Rebecca, and Christine Martin. 1997. *Major Trends in Chicago Homicide: 1965–1995.* Chicago: Illinois Criminal Justice Information Authority.

Bureau of Alcohol, Tobacco, and Firearms (ATF). 1993. *Operation Snapshot.* Washington: U.S. Bureau of Alcohol, Tobacco, and Firearms.

Bureau of Alcohol, Tobacco, and Firearms (ATF). 1997. *Youth Crime Gun Interdiction Initiative: Crime Gun Trace Analysis Reports: The Illegal Youth Firearms Market in 17 Communities.* Washington: U.S. Bureau of Alcohol, Tobacco, and Firearms.

Bureau of Alcohol, Tobacco, and Firearms (ATF). 1998a. *State Laws and Published Ordinances – Firearms, 1998.* ATF P 5300.5. Washington: U.S. Bureau of Alcohol, Tobacco, and Firearms.

Bureau of Alcohol, Tobacco, and Firearms (ATF). 1998b. *Study on the Sporting Utility of Modified Semiautomatic Assault Rifles.* Washington: U.S. Bureau of Alcohol, Tobacco, and Firearms.

Bureau of Alcohol, Tobacco, and Firearms (ATF). 1999a. *Gun Shows: Brady Checks and Crime Gun Traces.* Washington: U.S. Bureau of Alcohol, Tobacco, and Firearms.

Bureau of Alcohol, Tobacco, and Firearms (ATF). 1999b. *Youth Crime Gun Interdiction Initiative: Crime Gun Trace Analysis Reports: The Illegal Youth Firearms Market in 27 Communities.* Washington: U.S. Bureau of Alcohol, Tobacco, and Firearms.

Bureau of Alcohol, Tobacco, and Firearms (ATF). 1999c. *Federal Firearms Licensee List.* [Computer datafile.] Available through the U.S. Bureau of Alcohol, Tobacco, and Firearms.

Bureau of Alcohol, Tobacco, and Firearms (ATF). 2000a. *1998 Production and Exportation Report.* Washington: U.S. Bureau of Alcohol, Tobacco, and Firearms.

Bureau of Alcohol, Tobacco, and Firearms (ATF). 2000b. *Washington Metropolitan Police Departments' Gun Buy-Back Program.* Washington: U.S. Bureau of Alcohol, Tobacco, and Firearms.

Butterfield, Fox. 1999. "Citizens As Allies: Rethinking the Strong Arm of the Law." *The New York Times,* April 5. http://www.nytimes.com. Accessed 4/5/99.

Callahan, Charles M., and Frederick P. Rivara. 1992. "Urban High School Youth and Handguns: A School-Based Survey." *Journal of the American Medical Association* 267:3038–42.

Callahan, Charles M., Frederick P. Rivara, and Thomas D. Koepsell. 1994. "Money for Guns: Evaluation of the Seattle Gun Buy-Back Program." *Public Health Reports* 109:472–77.

Caruso, Robert P., Delma I. Jara, and Kenneth G. Swan. 1999. "Gunshot Wounds: Bullet Caliber Is Increasing." *Journal of Trauma* 46:462–65.

Cherry, Darci, Joseph L. Annest, James A. Mercy, Marcie-Jo Kresnow, and Daniel A. Pollock. 1998. "Trends in Nonfatal and Fatal Firearm-Related Injury Rates in the United States: 1985–1995." *Annals of Emergency Medicine* 32:51–59.

City of Chicago and County of Cook. 1998. Plaintiff's complaint. *City of Chicago and County of Cook v. Beretta USA Corp.,* et al. Chicago.

Cook, Philip J. 1981. "The Effect of Gun Availability on Violent Crime Patterns." *Annals of the American Academy of Political and Social Science* 445:63–79.

Cook, Philip J. 1987. "Robbery Violence." *Journal of Criminal Law and Criminology* 78:357–76.

Cook, Philip J. 1991. "The Technology of Personal Violence." In Michael Tonry, (Ed.). *Crime and Justice: A Review of Research Vol. 14* (pp. 1–71). Chicago: University of Chicago Press.

Cook, Philip J. 1998. "The Epidemic of Youth Gun Violence." In *Perspectives on Crime and Justice: 1997–1998.* Lecture Series. NCJ-172851. Washington: National Institute of Justice.

Cook, Philip J., and John H. Laub. 1998. "The Unprecedented Epidemic in Youth Violence." In Mark H. Moore and Michael Tonry (Eds.). *Crime and Justice: A Review of Research.* (pp. 101–38.) Chicago: University of Chicago Press.

Cook, Philip J., Bruce A. Lawrence, Jens A. Ludwig, and Ted R. Miller. 1999. "The Medical Costs of Gunshot Injuries in the United States." *Journal of the American Medical Association* 282:447–54.

Cook, Philip J., and Jens Ludwig. 1996. *Guns in America: Results of a Comprehensive National Survey on Firearms Ownership and Use.* Washington: The Police Foundation.

Cook, Philip J., Stephanie Molliconi, and Thomas B. Cole. 1995. "Regulating Gun Markets." *Journal of Criminal Law and Criminology* 86:59–92.

Cook, Philip J., and Mark H. Moore. 1999. "Guns, Gun Control, and Homicide." In M. Dwayne Smith and Margaret A. Zahn (Eds.). *Studying and Preventing Homicide: Issues and Challenges* (pp. 246–73). Thousand Oaks, CA: Sage.

Criminal Justice Research Center. 1994. *Guns and Violent Crime.* Richmond, VA: Department of Criminal Justice Services, Commonwealth of Virginia. Cited in Zawitz, Marianne W. 1995. *Guns Used in Crime:* NCJ-148201. Washington: U.S. Bureau of Justice Statistics.

Cummings, Peter, David C. Grossman, Frederick P. Rivara, and Thomas D. Koepsell. 1997. "State Gun Safe Storage Laws and Child Mortality Due to Firearms." *Journal of the American Medical Association* 278:1084–87.

Cummings, Peter, Thomas D. Koepsell, David C. Grossman, James Savarino, and Robert S. Thompson. 1997. "The Association Between the Purchase of a Handgun and Homicide or Suicide." *American Journal of Public Health* 87:974–78.

Decker, Scott H., Susan Pennell, and Ami Caldwell. 1997. *Illegal Firearms: Access and Use by Arrestees.* NCJ-163496. Washington: National Institute of Justice.

Diaz, Tom. 1999. *Making a Killing: The Business of Guns in America.* New York: The New Press.

Fagan, Jeffrey, Franklin E. Zimring, and June Kim. 1998. "Declining Homicide in New York City: A Tale of Two Trends." *Journal of Criminal Law and Criminology* 88:1277–1323.

Federal Bureau of Investigation (FBI). 1998. *Crime in the United States, 1997.* Washington: Federal Bureau of Investigation.

Federal Bureau of Investigation (FBI). 1999a. *Crime in the United States, 1998.* Washington: Federal Bureau of Investigation.

Federal Bureau of Investigation (FBI). 1999b. *Uniform Crime Reports: 1999 Preliminary Report.* Washington: Federal Bureau of Investigation. Available at http://www.fbi.gov/pressrm/pressrel/ucr0699.htm. Accessed November 22, 1999.

Federal Bureau of Investigation (FBI). 2000. *National Instant Criminal Background Check System Operations Report.* Washington: Federal Bureau of Investigation.

Flynn, Kevin. 1999. "Rebound in City Murder Rate Puzzling New York Officials." *The New York Times,* November 5. http://www.nytimes.com. Accessed 11/5/99.

Fox, James A., and Marianne W. Zawitz. 1999. *Homicide Trends in the United States.* NCJ-173956. Washington: U.S. Bureau of Justice Statistics. Available at http://www.ojp.usdoj.gov/bjs/homicide/homtred.htm. Accessed March 22, 1999.

General Accounting Office (GAO). 1996. *Federal Firearms Licensees. Various Factors Have Contributed to the Decline in the Number of Dealers.* GAO/GGD-96-78. Washington: General Accounting Office.

2000. *Implementation of the National Instant Criminal Background Check System.* GAO/GGD/AIMD-00-64. Washington: General Accounting Office.

Greenfeld, Lawrence A., and Marianne W. Zawitz. 1995. *Weapons Offenses and Offenders.* NCJ-155284. Washington: U.S. Bureau of Justice Statistics.

Hargarten, Stephen W., Trudy A. Karlson, Mallory O'Brien, Jerry Hancock, and Edward Quebbeman. 1996. "Characteristics of Firearms Involved in Fatalities." *Journal of the American Medical Association* 275:42–45.

Harris, Lou. 1993. "A Survey of Experiences, Perceptions, and Apprehensions About Guns Among Young People in America." Boston: Harvard University School of Public Health.

Hass, Robert I. 1996. Affidavit Before the United States District Court, Eastern District of New York, in *Hamilton v. Accu-Tek,* et al.

Hogg, Ian V. 1985. *Jane's Directory of Military Small Arms Ammunition.* London: Jane's Publishing Co., Ltd.

Huff, C. R. 1998. *Comparing the Criminal Behavior of Youth Gangs and At-Risk Youths.* NCJ-172852. Washington: National Institute of Justice.

Hutson, H. Range, Deirdre Anglin, Demetrios N. Kyriacou, Joel Hart, and Kelvin Spears. 1995. "The Epidemic of Gang-Related Homicides in Los Angeles County From 1975–1994." *Journal of the American Medical Association* 274:1031–36.

Illinois Criminal Justice Information Authority, Chicago Police Department, and Loyola University of Chicago. 1999. "Chicago Homicide Dataset." [Electronic Data File]. Available from the National Archive of Criminal Justice Data, Inter-University Consortium for Political and Social Research, University of Michigan. http://www.icpsr.umich.edu. Accessed 7/8/99.

Jacobs, James B., and Kimberly A. Potter. 1995. "Keeping Guns Out of the 'Wrong' Hands: The Brady Law and the Limits of Regulation." *Journal of Criminal Law and Criminology* 86:93–120.

Janovsky, Michael. 1999. "New Program in Richmond Is Credited with Getting Guns Off the Streets." *The New York Times,* February 10. Available at http://www.nytimes.com. Accessed 2/10/99.

Kann, Laura, Charles W. Warren, William A. Harris, Janet L. Collins, Kathy A. Douglas, Mary Elizabeth Collins, Barbara I. Williams, James Gross, and Lloyd

J. Kolbe. 1995. "Youth Risk Behavior Surveillance – United States, 1993."
    Morbidity and Mortality Weekly Report 44(SS-1):1–55, Table 4.

Kellermann Arthur L., Roberta K. Lee, James A. Mercy, and Joyce Banton.
    1991. "The Epidemiologic Basis for the Prevention of Firearm Injuries."
    Annual Review of Public Health 12:17–40.

Kellermann, Arthur L., and James A. Mercy. 1992. "Men, Women, and Murder:
    Gender-Specific Differences in Rates of Fatal Violence and Victimization."
    Journal of Trauma 33:1–5.

Kellermann, Arthur L., Frederick P. Rivara, Roberta K. Lee, Joyce G. Banton,
    Peter Cummings, Bela B. Hackman, and Grant Somes. 1996. "Injuries Due
    to Firearms in Three Cities." *New England Journal of Medicine* 335:1438–44.

Kellermann, Arthur L., Frederick P. Rivara, Norman B. Rushforth, Joyce G.
    Banton, Donald T. Reay, Jerry T. Francisco, Ana B. Locci, Janice Prodzinski,
    Bela B. Hackman, and Grant Somes. 1993. "Gun Ownership as a Risk Factor
    for Homicide in the Home." *New England Journal of Medicine* 329:1084–91.

Kennedy, David M. 1997. *Juvenile Gun Violence and Gun Markets in Boston.* NCJ-
    160766. Washington: National Institute of Justice.

Kennedy, David M., and Anthony A. Braga. 1998. "Homicide in Minneapolis:
    Research for Problem Solving." *Homicide Studies* 2:263–90.

Kennedy, David M., Anne E. Piehl, and Anthony A. Braga. 1996a. "Gun Buy-
    Backs: Where Do We Stand and Where Do We Go?" In Martha R.
    Plotkin (Ed.), *Under Fire: Gun Buy-Backs, Exchanges and Amnesty Programs,*
    pp. 141–171. Washington: Police Executive Research Forum.

Kennedy, David M., Anne E. Piehl, and Anthony A. Braga. 1996b. "Youth
    Violence in Boston: Gun Markets, Serious Youth Offenders, and a Use-
    Reduction Strategy." *Law and Contemporary Problems* 59:147–96.

Kleck, Gary. 1991. *Point Blank: Guns and Violence in America.* New York: Aldine
    de Gruyter.

Kleck, Gary. 1997. *Targeting Guns: Firearms and Their Control.* New York: Aldine
    de Gruyter.

Loftin, Colin, David McDowall, Brian Wiersema, and Talbert J. Cottey. 1991.
    "Effects of Restrictive Licensing of Handguns on Homicide and Suicide in
    the District of Columbia." *New England Journal of Medicine* 325:1615–20.

Lott, John R., and David B. Mustard. 1997. "Crime, Deterrence, and Right-to-
    Carry Concealed Handguns." *Journal of Legal Studies* 26:1–68.

Ludwig, Jens. 1998. "Concealed-Gun-Carrying Laws and Violent Crime:
    Evidence From State Panel Data." *International Review of Law and Economics*
    18:239–54.

Manson, Donald A., Darrell K. Gilliard, and Gene Lauver. 1999. *Presale
    Handgun Checks, the Brady Interim Period, 1994–98.* NCJ-175034. Washington:
    U.S. Bureau of Justice Statistics.

Marzulli, John, and William K. Rashburn. 1999. "Super Cops Blow Half Gun
    Cases." *The New York Daily News,* March 21. http://www.nydailynews.com.
    Accessed 9/4/99.

May, John P., Martha G. Ferguson, Richard Ferguson, and Karen Cronin. 1995. "Prior Nonfatal Firearm Injuries in Detainees of a Large Urban Jail." *Journal of Health Care for the Poor and Underserved* 6:162–75.

Max, Wendy, and Dorothy P. Rice. 1993. "Shooting in the Dark: Estimating the Cost of Firearm Injuries." *Health Affairs* 12(4):171–85.

McDowall, David, Colin Loftin, and Brian Wiersema. 1995. "Easing Concealed Firearms Laws: Effects on Homicide in Three States." *Journal of Criminal Law and Criminology* 86:193–206.

McGonigal, Michael D., John Schwab Cole, William See, Donald R. Kauder, Michael F. Rotando, and Peter B. Angood. 1993. "Urban Firearm Deaths: A Five-Year Perspective." *Journal of Trauma* 35:532–34.

McLaughlin, Colleen R., Scott M. Reiner, Benjamin W. Smith, Dennis E. Waite, Patricia N. Reams, Timothy F. Joost, and Alfred S. Gervin. 1996. "Firearm Injuries Among Virginia Juvenile Drug Traffickers, 1992 through 1994." *American Journal of Public Health* 86:751–52.

O'Connell, Vanessa, and Paul M. Barrett. 1999a. "Cities Suing Gun Firms Have a Weak Spot: They're Suppliers, Too." *The Wall Street Journal*, August 16.

O'Connell, Vanessa, and Paul M. Barrett. 1999b. "Trend in Unloading Old Police Guns Is Toward Banning Trade-Ins, Resales." *The Wall Street Journal*, November 10 (p. B1).

Office of Juvenile Justice and Delinquency Prevention (OJJDP). 1999. *Promising Strategies to Reduce Gun Violence*. NCJ-173950. Washington: Office of Juvenile Justice and Delinquency Prevention.

Office of Technology Assessment (OTA). 1991. *Automated Records Checks of Firearm Purchasers: Issues and Options*. Washington: U.S. Government Printing Office.

Pierce, Glenn L., LeBaron Briggs, and David A. Carlson. 1995. *The Identification of Patterns in Firearms Trafficking: Implications for Focused Enforcement Strategies*. Washington: U.S. Bureau of Alcohol, Tobacco, and Firearms.

Pierce, Glenn L., LeBaron Briggs, and David A. Carlson. 1998. *National Report on Firearm Trace Analysis for 1996–1997*. Boston: Northeastern University.

Rand, Michael R. 1990. *Handgun Crime Victims*. NCJ-123559. Washington: U.S. Bureau of Justice Statistics.

    1994. *Guns and Crime*. NCJ-147003. Washington: U.S. Bureau of Justice Statistics.

Regional Justice Information Service (RJIS). 1996. *Survey of State Procedures Related to Firearm Sales*. NCJ-160763. Washington: U.S. Bureau of Justice Statistics.

Reiss, A. J., and J. A., Roth. 1993. *Understanding and Preventing Violence*. Washington: National Academy Press.

Rennison, Callie Marie. 1999. *Criminal Victimization 1998: Changes 1997–98 with Trends 1993–98*. NCJ-176353. Washington: U.S. Bureau of Justice Statistics.

Rodman, C. 1989. *Assault Weapons Survey*. Sacramento, CA: Assembly Office of Research.

Romero, Michael P., Garen J. Wintemute, and Jon S. Vernick. 1998. "Characteristics of a Gun Exchange Program, and An Assessment of Potential Benefits." *Injury Prevention* 4:206–10.

Rosenfeld, Richard. 1996. "Gun Buy-Backs: Crime Control or Community Mobilization?" In Martha R. Plotkin (Ed.), *Under Fire: Gun Buy-Backs, Exchanges and Amnesty Programs,* p. 1–28. Washington: Police Executive Research Forum.

Rosenfeld, Richard, and Scott H. Decker. 1996. "Consent to Search and Seize: Evaluating an Innovative Youth Firearms Suppression Program." *Law and Contemporary Problems* 59:197–220.

Roth, Jeffrey A., and Christopher S. Koper. 1997. *Impact Evaluation of the Public Safety and Recreational Firearms Use Protection Act of 1994.* Washington: The Urban Institute.

1999. *Impacts of the 1994 Assault Weapons Ban: 1994–1996.* NCJ-173405. Washington: National Institute of Justice.

Saltzman, Linda E., James A. Mercy, Patrick W. O'Carroll, Mark L. Rosenberg, and P. A. Rhodes. 1992. "Weapons Involvement and Injury Outcomes in Family and Intimate Assaults." *Journal of the American Medical Association* 367:3043–47.

Sheley, Joseph F., Zina T. McGee, and James D. Wright. 1995. *Weapon-Related Victimization in Selected Inner-City High School Samples.* NCJ-151526. Washington: National Institute of Justice.

Sheley, Joseph F., and James D. Wright. 1993. *Gun Acquisition and Possession in Selected Juvenile Samples.* NCJ-145326. Washington: Office of Juvenile Justice and Delinquency Prevention.

1998. *High School Youths, Weapons, and Violence: A National Survey.* NCJ-172857. Washington: National Institute of Justice.

Sherman, Lawrence W. 1997a. "Communities and Crime Prevention." In Lawrence W., Sherman, Denise Gottfredson, Doris MacKenzie, John Eck, Peter Reuter, and Shawn Bushway, *Preventing Crime: What Works, What Doesn't, What's Promising?* (pp. 3–1–3–49). NCJ-165366. Washington: Office of Justice Programs.

Sherman, Lawrence W. 1997b. "Family Based Crime Prevention." In Lawrence W. Sherman, Denise Gottfredson, Doris MacKenzie, John Eck, Peter Reuter, and Shawn Bushway. *Preventing Crime: What Works, What Doesn't, What's Promising?* (pp. 4–1–4–42). NCJ-165366. Washington: Office of Justice Programs.

Sherman, Lawrence W., and D. P. Rogan. 1995. "Effects of Gun Seizure on Gun Violence: 'Hot Spots' Control in Kansas City." *Justice Quarterly* 12:673–93.

Sherman, Lawrence W., James W. Shaw, and Dennis P. Rogan. 1995. *The Kansas City Gun Experiment.* NCJ-150855. Washington: National Institute of Justice.

Singh, Gopal K., Kenneth D. Kochanek, and Marian F. MacDorman. 1996. "Advance Report of Final Mortality Statistics, 1994." *Mortality Vital Statistics Report* 45(3) Supplement:1–80.

Smith, M. Dwayne. 1996. "Sources of Firearm Acquisition among a Sample of Inner-City Youths: Research Results and Policy Implications." *Journal of Criminal Justice* 24:361–67.

Sugarmann, Josh, and Kristen Rand. 1992. *More Gun Dealers Than Gas Stations: A Study of Federally Licensed Firearms Dealers in America.* Washington: Violence Policy Center.

Teret, Stephen P., Greg R. Alexander, and Linda A. Bailey. 1990. "The Passage of Maryland's Gun Law: Data and Advocacy for Injury Prevention." *Journal of Public Health Policy* 11:26–38.

Teret, Stephen P., and Daniel W. Webster. 1999. *Reducing Gun Deaths in the United States. British Medical Journal* 318:1160–1.

Teret, Stephen P., Daniel W. Webster, Jon S. Vernick, Tom W. Smith, Deborah Leff, Garen J. Wintemute, Philip J. Cook, Darnell F. Hawkins, Arthur L. Kellermann, Susan B. Sorenson, and Susan DeFrancesco. 1998. "Support for New Policies to Regulate Firearms: Results of Two National Surveys." *New England Journal of Medicine* 339:813–18.

Teret Stephen P., and Garen J. Wintemute. 1993. "Policies to Prevent Firearm Injuries." *Health Affairs* 12(4):96–108.

Veen, John, Stacie Dunbar, and Melissa Stedman Ruland. 1997. *The BJA Firearms Trafficking Program: Demonstrating Effective Strategies to Control Violent Crime.* NCJ-166818. Washington: U.S. Bureau of Justice Assistance.

Vernick Jon S., Daniel W. Webster, and K. Huang. 1998. *Evaluation of Maryland's 1989 Law Banning Saturday Night Special Handguns: Intermediate Outcome Measures.* Paper presented at the 1998 annual meeting of the American Public Health Association November 15–18, Washington, DC.

Wachtel, Julius. 1998. "Sources of Crime Guns in Los Angeles, California." *Policing: An International Journal of Police Strategies & Management* 21:220–39.

Webster, Daniel W., Howard R. Champion, Patricia S. Gainer, and Leon Sykes. 1992. "Epidemiologic Changes in Gunshot Wounds in Washington, DC, 1983–1990." *Archives of Surgery* 127:694–98.

Webster, Daniel W., Jon S. Vernick, and K. Huang. 1998. *Evaluation of Maryland's Law Banning Saturday Night Specials: Effects on Violent Crimes.* Paper presented at the 1998 annual meeting of the American Public Health Association November 15–18, Washington, DC.

Weil, D. S., and Rebecca C. Knox. 1996. "Effects of Limiting Handgun Purchases on Interstate Transfer of Firearms." *Journal of the American Medical Association* 275:1759–61.

Wilson, James Q. 1994. "Just Take Away Their Guns: Forget Gun Control." *The New York Times Magazine,* March 20 (pp. 46–47).

Wintemute, Garen J. 1987. "Firearms as a Cause of Death in the United States, 1920–1982." *The Journal of Trauma* 27:532–36.

Wintemute, Garen J. 1994. *Ring of Fire: The Handgun Makers of Southern California.* Sacramento, CA: Violence Prevention Research Program.

Wintemute, Garen J. 1996. "The Relationship Between Firearm Design and Firearm Violence." *Journal of the American Medical Association* 275:1749–53.

Wintemute, Garen J. 2000. *The Effectiveness of Local Ordinances Banning the Sale of "Saturday Night Special" Handguns: A Preliminary Study*. Sacramento, CA: Violence Prevention Research Program.

Wintemute, Garen J., Christiana M. Drake, James J. Beaumont, Mona A. Wright, and Carrie A. Parham. 1998. "Prior Misdemeanor Convictions as a Risk Factor for Later Violent and Firearm-Related Criminal Activity Among Authorized Purchasers of Handguns." *Journal of the American Medical Association* 280:2083–87.

Wintemute, Garen J., Carrie A. Parham, Mona A. Wright, James J. Beaumont, and Christiana M. Drake. 1998. "Weapons of Choice: Previous Criminal History, Later Criminal Activity, and Firearm Preference Among Legally Authorized Young Adult Purchasers of Handguns." *Journal of Trauma* 44:155–60.

Wintemute, Garen J., and Mona A. Wright. 1992. "Initial and Subsequent Hospital Costs of Firearm Injuries." *Journal of Trauma* 33:556–60.

Wintemute, Garen J., Mona A. Wright, Christiana M. Drake, James J. Beaumont, and Carrie A. Parham. 1999. *Effectiveness of Expanded Criteria for Denial of Firearm Purchase*. Paper presented at the 1999 annual meeting of the American Society of Criminology November 17–20, Toronto.

Wintemute, Garen J., Mona A. Wright, Carrie A. Parham, Christiana M. Drake, and James J. Beaumont. 1998. "Criminal Activity and Assault-Type Handguns: A Study of Young Adults." *Annals of Emergency Medicine* 32:44–50.

Wintemute, Garen J., Mona A. Wright, Carrie A. Parham, Christiana M. Drake, and James J. Beaumont. 1999. "Denial of Handgun Purchase: A Description of the Affected Population and a Controlled Study of Their Handgun Preferences." *Journal of Criminal Justice* 27:21–31.

Wright, Mona A., Garen J. Wintemute, Carrie A. Parham, Christiana M. Drake, and James J. Beaumont. 1998. *The Effect of Multiple Handgun Purchase on the Risk for Subsequent Criminal Activity*. Paper presented at the 1998 annual meeting of the American Society of Criminology November 11–14, Washington.

Wright, Mona A., Garen J. Wintemute, and Frederick A. Rivara. 1999. "Effectiveness of Denial of Handgun Purchase to Persons Believed to Be at High Risk for Firearm Violence." *American Journal of Public Health* 89:88–90.

Zimring, Franklin E. 1972. "The Medium Is the Message: Firearm Caliber as a Determinant of Death from Assault." *Journal of Legal Studies* 1:97–123.

Zimring, Franklin E. 1976. "Street Crime and New Guns: Some Implications for Firearms Control." *Journal of Criminal Justice* 4:95–107.

Zimring, Franklin E., and Gordon Hawkins. 1997. *Crime is Not the Problem: Lethal Violence in America*. New York: Oxford University Press.

The Limited Importance of Prison Expansion

William Spelman

Introduction

OVER THE PAST TWENTY YEARS, the fifty American states have engaged in one of the great policy experiments of modern times. In an attempt to reduce intolerably high levels of reported crime, the states doubled their prison populations, then doubled them again, increasing their costs by more than $20 billion per year. The states and the Federal government have given up a lot to get to this point: That $20 billion could provide child care for every family that cannot afford it, or a college education to every high school graduate, or a living-wage job to every unemployed youth. But crime levels appear to have (at last) responded, dropping to their lowest level in years. Thus recent history provides a prima facie case for the effectiveness of prisons.

Not everyone has found this evidence persuasive. Some argue, quite convincingly, that the recent crime reductions had nothing to do with the prison buildup. Crime dropped because the job prospects of poverty-stricken youths have improved, or because police have become more effective at getting weapons off the street, or because neighbors are beginning to watch out for one another again. As usual, correlation does not guarantee causation. If we are to determine the role of the prison buildup in the recent crime reductions, we will need to take a more systematic approach.

There are two ways to measure the effects of prison expansion, corresponding to two, very different approaches to modeling the criminal justice system. *Bottom-up* researchers try to get inside the black box, combining survey information about criminal offenders, published reports on

criminal justice system operations, and complex probability models to simulate the detailed workings of the system (Greenwood 1982; Shinnar and
Shinnar 1975). Such details are the strength of this approach: Staying close
to the facts ensures frequent reality checks. As with any simulation, however, bottom-up prison studies demand an enormous amount of data,
some of which is of questionable validity. In addition, these studies only
measure the effects of incapacitation, not deterrence and rehabilitation.
Thus bottom-up or simulation studies are liable to underestimate the full
effects of prison expansion on crime rates.

In contrast, *top-down* researchers work around the black box, using
econometric methods and aggregate data on crime rates, prison populations, and other possible causes of crime to link inputs and outputs
(Devine, Sheley, and Smith 1988; Ehrlich 1973). Although these methods
cannot in general separate the effects of incapacitation from those of
deterrence and rehabilitation effects, they are much better suited than the
bottom-up methods to capturing the full effect of prisons. And the focus
on the behavior of the system, rather than its inner workings, is a strength,
in that top-down methods can be used to compare among competing
explanations. The fundamental weakness is the flip side of this strength:
Because it works around the black box, there are innumerable competing
explanations for the system's behavior at any given time. In the absence of
a controlled experiment, it is impossible to reject or even account for all
these explanations. Thus no matter how persuasive a top-down, econometric study is, it can never be definitive.

In the remainder of this chapter, I describe the principal results of studies
using these two approaches and use these results to estimate the extent to
which the prison buildup is responsible for the recent crime reductions. I
examine the principal threats to validity and limitations on each study's
applicability. Although one cannot be certain as to the role of prison expansion, one can use the available information to develop a reasonable estimate.

Previous Findings and the Crime Drop

The effectiveness of prisons at controlling crime has been an important
research issue since at least the late 1960s, when the current prison boom
began. Dozens of studies, mostly in the top-down, econometric tradition,
were conducted with increasing methodological sophistication (cf. Ehrlich
1973; Gibbs 1968; Logan 1975). The results of the 1970s were summarized
in a report commissioned by the National Research Council (NRC). In several essays (e.g., Cohen 1978; Nagin 1978; Vandaele 1978), researchers

reviewed the empirical studies and compared the results. One benefit of the NRC report was to draw researchers' attention to the critical role of the *elasticity* – the percentage change in the crime rate associated with a one-percent change in the prison population. The elasticity was easy to interpret and could be compared among different studies, places, and times. As an added bonus, the elasticity was exceptionally easy to calculate, at least for the econometric studies.

The primary role of the NRC report, however, was to point out the principal objections to the most popular analysis methods, and to show that they provided inaccurate or biased results. This had two effects:

- It raised the bar on econometric studies so high that, for a time, no one tried to jump it. Only in the last ten years have available data and statistical methods improved to the point that these objections can (perhaps) be overcome.
- It shifted attention from the econometric analyses, which had predominated during the 1970s, to bottom-up, simulation studies. The frailties of simulation were less clear at the time.

Recent studies using both approaches have succeeded in overcoming many of the objections to previous efforts. Whether these results are closer to the truth or not, they are certainly more defensible than the estimates of the 1960s and 1970s.

Simulation Studies. All simulation studies are based on a mathematical model developed by Avi-Itzhak and Shinnar (1973) and refined by Shinnar and Shinnar (1975). Briefly, this model combines estimates of the typical offender's

- offense rate per year (sometimes referred to as λ, the Greek letter "lambda"),
- probability of arrest, prosecution, and incarceration per crime committed, and
- average sentence served in jail or prison,

to estimate the likelihood that a typical offender will be incarcerated at any given time. When combined with information about the length of the typical criminal career, it is possible to estimate the proportion of that career that the typical offender spends behind bars. This proportion represents the reduction in the crime rate due to incapacitation. By plugging in different probabilities of arrest, prosecution, or incarceration, or different average sentence lengths, an analyst could estimate the effect of prison expansion, improved police and prosecution, or other criminal justice system improvements.

The NRC report suggested that the simulation model was promising but insufficiently developed to produce accurate estimates (Cohen 1978). For example, the initial model assumed that individual offense rates, arrest and incarceration probabilities, and criminal-career lengths were uncorrelated with one another and did not change over time. No empirical data were available to verify this assumption. Likewise, the model did not distinguish among offenders who committed crimes at different rates, and assumed that incapacitating one member of an offending group would eliminate all offenses committed by members of that group. These assumptions seemed patently untrue. Perhaps more important, data on the operations of the criminal justice system, and particularly on offense rates and career lengths among active offenders, were sorely lacking. In fact, Cohen estimated that the elasticity of crime rates with regard to time spent in prison per crime committed (roughly similar to the elasticity at issue here) could range anywhere from −.05 to −.70, given available data (Cohen 1978, pp. 219–21). That is, for every one-percent increase in the prison population, crime would decline by somewhere between .05 and .70 percent.

The model and the data on which it was based improved in bits and pieces throughout the 1980s. Greenwood (1982) showed how the model could be adapted to include a variety of offense rates. Reiss (1980) provided critical information on the size and behavior of offending groups. Most important, the Rand Corporation conducted a series of studies (Chaiken and Chaiken 1982; Petersilia, Greenwood, and Lavin 1978; Peterson, Braiker, and Polich 1980) that showed that tolerably accurate information on offense rates, arrest and incarceration probabilities, and other critical parameters could be obtained from surveys of incarcerated criminals. These surveys were successfully replicated (DiIulio 1990; Horney and Marshall 1991; Mande and English 1988), providing the knowledge base needed to support policy analysis.

Relying on these and further extensions of the model, DiIulio and Piehl (1991), Spelman (1994), and Piehl and DiIulio (1995) compared the benefits and costs of increased imprisonment. As shown in Table 4.1, these benefits and costs were derived from analysis of a variety of populations, and imply elasticities ranging from −.16 to −.26. Given the limited precision of any of these estimates, a more reasonable range might be anywhere between −.10 and −.30.

Econometric Studies. All econometric studies are based on the statistical method of *multiple regression* – sophisticated curve-fitting. Briefly, prison populations and crime rates for some population are plotted on an *X-Y* chart and the curve that best summarizes the relationship is found. Other variables that may affect crime rates, such as the age distribution of the population or the unemployment rate, can be controlled for statistically, according to a formula of the form,

$$C = \alpha + \beta\, P + \delta\, X, \tag{1}$$

where C is the crime rate, P is the prison population (somehow defined), and X consists of one or more control variables. The Greek letter α is an intercept and β and δ are slopes. Thus if P were to increase by one unit, C would increase by β units. A little algebra is sufficient to convert the unit-for-unit trade off given by β into a percentage-for-percentage elasticity.

Multiple regression was developed in the nineteenth century, but it was very difficult and time consuming to carry out until computers became readily available in the late 1960s. At that point, there was an explosion of studies, relying on a wide variety of found data. For a time, best practice in criminology was defined by Ehrlich's (1973) economic analysis of offender decision making. Ehrlich provided an economic framework for interpreting the results and set a new standard in mathematical sophistication. He also obtained a controversial result: A one-percent increase in prison population would reduce crime rates by anywhere from 0.99 to 1.12 percent. In theory, at least, doubling the prison population would completely eliminate crime.

Ehrlich, of course, made no such claims; no state had ever doubled its prison population in only one year, and diminishing returns would obviously accompany so large a shift. Nevertheless, skeptics took a close look at Ehrlich's data and methods and those of others who obtained similar results. By the late 1970s, some of the cracks in the edifice were showing clearly (Blumstein, Cohen, and Nagin 1978, pp. 22–53).

- For a variety of technical reasons, prison-effectiveness analysts must identify some variables that affect prison populations but *not* crime rates. Ehrlich and others used economic indicators, demographic characteristics, urbanism, region, and similar variables to fill the bill. It is hard to imagine how these variables could *not* be related to crime rates.
- Another to attempt to solve the same problem required the assumption that this year's police expenditures were unrelated to last year's

Table 4.1. Summary of Recent Prison Effectiveness Analyses

Simulation studies of incapacitation		
DiIulio and Piehl (1991)	−.22	Wisconsin, 1989
Spelman (1994)	−.16 ± .05	Approximates nationwide estimate, 1992
Piehl and DiIulio (1995)	−.26	New Jersey, 1993

Econometric studies of incapacitation and deterrence – national data		
Devine, Sheley, and Smith (1988)		
Violent Crimes	−2.84 ± 1.60	
Property Crimes	−1.99 ± 0.88	National time-series, 1948–85
All Index Crimes	−2.20	
Cappell and Sykes (1991)	−.91	National time-series, 1933–85
Marvell and Moody (1997, 1998)		
Violent Crimes	−.79 ± .29	
Property Crimes	−.95 ± .20	National time-series, 1958–95
All Index Crimes	−.93	

Econometric studies of incapacitation and deterrence – state data		
Marvell and Moody (1994)		
Violent Crimes	−.06 ± .11	
Property Crimes	−.17 ± .06	49 states, 1971–89
All Index Crimes	−.16	
Levitt (1996)		
Violent Crimes	−.38 ± .36	
Property Crimes	−.26 ± .24	50 states + DC, 1971–93
All Index Crimes	−.31	
Becsi (1999)		
Violent Crimes	−.05 ± .04	
Property Crimes	−.09 ± .03	50 states + DC, 1971–93
All Index Crimes	−.09 ± .03	

Note: Figures shown are elasticities of crime with respect to increases in prison population. Where available, 95 percent confidence intervals shown after "±".

expenditures. More generally, variables that change little from year to year – including crime rates, prison populations, and demographic and social variables – tell us less than they appear to about how one responds to the others.

- Many analysts used so-called ratio variables, such as crimes per population and arrests per crime. Though reasonable in theory, the fact that "crimes" appears in the numerator of one variable and the denominator of the other means that they will appear to be negatively correlated, even if there is no real correlation between them at all.

After reviewing these flaws, the NRC report argued that further studies of the same kind would not help to solve the problem. Instead, analysts should collect better data-sets and use improved statistical methods to identify more robust solutions.

Since the late 1970s, six econometric studies have appeared that respond in part to the NRC challenges. Three of the studies used national crime and prison statistics; because reliable data were not available until the early 1930s, use of national data puts a crimp on the number of cases available for analysis. The other three studies expanded on the national data-set by examining each state separately, in effect multiplying the number of cases by 50 or so. Results are shown in Table 4.1.

Clearly, the studies based on national data obtained results very different from those based on state data. In a separate analysis, Marvell and Moody (1998) found that the national-level elasticities are three times larger than the state-level elasticities. They provide a plausible explanation for some of the difference: Even if one state (say, Missouri) does not increase its prison population at all, increases elsewhere in the country will tend to reduce crime in Missouri because offenders who might have moved there are in prison. Thus Missouri is a "free rider," enjoying a crime reduction it hasn't paid for.[1]

Although this seems reasonable on its face, offenders do not appear to move often enough to account for these results. State arrest records show that the offenders active in the average state commit fully three-fourths of their crimes in that state, even though some of them also commit crimes elsewhere (Orsagh 1992). Thus we should expect that a one-percent increase in the Missouri prison population should reduce crime in Missouri by three times as much as a one-percent increase throughout the rest of the nation, not the other way around. Further, since the 1970s most states have increased their prison populations by about the same rate. Free riders are hard to find.

The most likely explanation for the much higher national-level elasticities is that the national prison population is a proxy for one or more as-yet unmeasured variables. For example, it may track an increase in support for aggressive policing, or the willingness of individuals to prevent crime on their own. More generally, it is dangerous to interpret the clear correlation between the national prison population and state crime rate as causation in the absence of a plausible explanation.

Accordingly, I focus attention on the three state-level studies (with the caveat that they may be underestimating the effect slightly due to a free rider phenomenon). These results cover a relatively narrow range, from $-.05$ to $-.38$. Of the three, the most accurate is probably the largest, produced by Levitt (1996). Levitt's model is the only one to account explicitly for the possibility that, just as prison population influences the crime rate, so can crime rates influence the prison population. For example, politicians may respond to rising crime rates by funding construction of more prison beds; likewise, if crime rates go up, more offenders are liable to be arrested and convicted, increasing the number available to be sentenced to prison. Thus higher crime rates can lead to higher prison populations, a positive relationship. Because more prison presumably leads to less crime (a negative relationship), failing to control for the effect of crime on prison population effectively mixes up two opposing effects, resulting in estimates of the effect of prisons that are systematically biased toward zero. Primarily because it separates these opposing effects, Levitt's model provides estimates of the elasticity that are larger (that is, more negative) than the others.

Although these estimates are generally larger than the elasticities obtained from the simulation studies, this is to be expected from a method designed to measure both incapacitation and deterrence effects. Nevertheless, some have argued that Levitt's estimates are systematically too high (Donohue and Siegelman 1998). Hence a second reason for relying on these results: If estimates based on his elasticities suggest that the prison buildup is still a relatively minor cause of the crime drop, one can be fairly sure that alternative estimates would show the prison buildup to be even less important.

Although all of the studies estimated elasticities separately for violent and for property crimes, none of the differences were statistically significant. In addition, none of the results shown in Table 4.1 are very precise. Thus we should not be very surprised to find that the true elasticity for violent crime was anywhere between $-.10$ and $-.50$. Combined with the results of the simulation studies and the possibility of out-of-state effects, we tentatively conclude that the elasticity is probably in the neighborhood of $-.30$.

Interpreting the Elasticities. To help make sense of these elasticities, I put them to use in answering the following question: What would have happened, had the state and Federal governments *not* made an enormous investment in prisons over the last twenty-five years?

Perhaps surprisingly, all that is needed to answer this question are actual changes in prison and crime rates and an estimate of the elasticity. Briefly, one can apply the elasticity estimates to each year's prison expansion and calculate what the crime rate would have been, had that year's expansion not taken place. If one continues these calculations, year after year, one eventually comes up with an estimate of what today's crime rate would have been, had *none* of the previous year's expansions taken place.

An example will show how this works. In 1974, the imprisonment rate (that is, sentenced prisoners per 100,000 population) increased from 97.8 to 103.6 – an increase of 5.9 percent. If the elasticity of violent crime with respect to prison is –.30, then the effect of this increase on the crime rate was

$$\Delta\ VC = -.3 \times 5.9\% = -1.8\%. \tag{2}$$

Holding everything else constant, this first step in our twenty-five year prison expansion reduced the violent-crime rate by 1.8 percent. Alternatively, the 1974 violent-crime rate should be 98.2 percent what it was in 1973.

In reality, of course, everything else is never constant. The social, economic, and public policy changes considered elsewhere in this volume act on their own to increase or decrease crime each year. In general, we can separate the effects of prison expansion from the rest of these factors by recognizing that the total percentage change in crime rates will be equal to

$$\Delta VC = \text{prison effect} \times \text{all other effects}, \tag{3}$$

and that the effect of all other factors taken together will be

$$\Delta VC/\text{prison effect} = \text{all other effects}. \tag{4}$$

In 1974, the reported violent crime rate went from 417.4 crimes per 100,000 population to 461.1, an increase of 10.5 percent nationwide. Thus the net effect of all nonprison factors must be

$$1.105/0.982 = 1.125, \tag{5}$$

or a net increase in the violent-crime rate of 12.5 percent. Had the 1974 prison expansion never taken place, then, the violent-crime rate would have increased by 12.5 percent – somewhat more than it actually did. If the elasticity was in fact –.30, the prison expansion put a damper on what would have been a larger increase in crime rates. If the elasticity were higher or lower, the dampening effect would increase or decrease proportionately.

Similar results are obtained for most years since 1974. Crime rates went up in most of these years, but they would have gone up by more

Table 4.2. Estimated Changes in Violent Crime Rates in Absence of Prison Expansion[d]

	Percent Change in Rates of		Percent Change in Violent-Crime Rates Due to Nonprison Factors at Elasticity of		
Year	Violent Crime	Prison	–.15	–.30	–.45
1974	10.5	5.9	11.5	12.5	13.5
1975	5.8	9.1	7.3	8.8	10.3
1976	–4.1	8.8	–2.8	–1.5	–.1
1977	1.7	4.9	2.5	3.2	4.0
1978	4.6	4.7	5.3	6.1	6.8
1979	10.3	.7	10.4	10.5	10.6
1980	8.7	2.2	9.1	9.4	9.8
1981	–.4	10.1	1.1	2.7	4.3
1982	–3.9	11.1	–2.3	–.6	1.2
1983	–5.8	5.3	–5.1	–4.3	–3.6
1984	.3	5.0	1.0	1.8	2.6
1985	3.2	6.4	4.2	5.2	6.3
1986	11.0	8.0	12.3	13.7	15.1
1987	–1.3	5.6	–.5	.4	1.2
1988	4.5	7.0	5.6	6.8	7.9
1989	4.2	11.1	5.9	7.7	9.6
1990	10.3	7.7	11.6	12.9	14.2
1991	3.6	6.2	4.6	5.5	6.5
1992	–.1	6.5	.9	1.9	2.9
1993	–1.4	6.1	–.5	.4	1.4
1994	–4.4	11.1	–2.8	–1.1	.6
1995	–4.1	5.7	–3.2	–2.4	–1.6
1996	–7.0	3.9	–6.5	–5.9	–5.4
1997	–4.0	5.2	–3.3	–2.5	–1.8

[a] U.S. Department of Justice, Federal Bureau of Investigation (annual); U.S. Department of Justice, Bureau of Justice Statistics (annual); author's calculations.

than they did, had prison populations not expanded as they did. Table 4.2 compares the actual change in violent crime to the change due to nonprison factors – roughly, the change in violent-crime rates that *would* have occurred, had prison populations remained constant – for elasticities of –.15, –.30, and –.45.

Now that we have factored out the effects of the prison expansion on an annual basis, it is easy to estimate the cumulative effect. Assuming an elasticity of –.30, Table 4.2 shows that violent-crime rates would have increased by 12.5 percent in 1974, by 8.8 percent in 1975, and so on. In the absence of any prison expansion, the 1975 violent crime rate would have been

$$VC(1975) = 1.125 \times 1.088 = 1.224 \qquad (6)$$

or 22.4 percent higher than it was in 1973; the 1976 violent-crime rate would have been

$$VC(1976) = 1.125 \times 1.088 \times 0.985 = 1.206 \qquad (7)$$

or 20.6 percent higher than in 1973; and so on. Figure 4.1 shows the actual reported violent-crime rate and three hypothetical violent-crime rates for each year since 1974.

The simplest way to read Figure 4.1 – and the simplest way to interpret the effects of the prison expansion – is to compare the endpoints of the

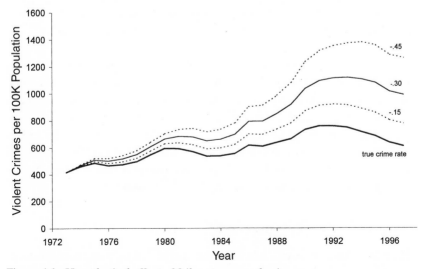

Figure 4.1. Hypothetical effect of failure to expand prisons.

four lines, the actual and predicted values of today's violent-crime rate. In 1997 the violent-crime rate was 610.8 per 100,000 population. If the prison expansion of the last twenty-five years had never taken place, the violent-crime rate would have been somewhere between 775 and 1,260. Thus the prison expansion is responsible for reducing the violent-crime rate by 20 to 50 percent, with a best guess of roughly 35 percent.

Such an effect is more than large enough to account for the recent downturn in violent-crime rates. Can we then claim that the prison buildup is responsible for this downturn? As a careful examination of Figure 4.1 shows, probably not. Consider the experience of the 1990s: Prison populations went up and violent crime went down. So far, so good. But, as shown on the three hypothetical lines on Figure 4.1, violent-crime rates would have gone down in the 1990s even if prison populations had *not* gone up.[2] Further, the hypothetical lines show that the drop would have come at almost exactly the same time, and been almost exactly the same size, as the actual drop. These projections suggest that prison expansion was not responsible for the crime drop.

In fact, violent crime dropped by a little bit more than I have projected that it would have in the absence of a prison buildup – between 4 and 21 percent more. Thus prison expansion during the 1990s increased the size of the crime drop slightly. Nevertheless, the basic result remains: Even had the United States *not* spent $20 billion per year in jails and prisons, violent-crime rates would have gone down, anyway. Between 79 and 96 percent of the violent-crime drop cannot be explained by prison expansion.[3]

In retrospect, this should not be too surprising. The prison boom has been remarkably steady, with the prison population increasing by roughly 6 percent per year, nationwide, for a quarter century. The prison increases of the late 1980s and early 1990s were no larger than they had been at earlier times during the buildup. Unless these prison increases were somehow more effective than previous increases, one should not have expected to see a downturn in crime rates. Any such downturn must be largely the result of other forces.

Of course, this begs the question of whether prisons are somehow more effective at reducing crime today than they were in the 1970s and 1980s. Has the elasticity increased over time? To find out, I take a closer look at some critical assumptions underlying these conclusions.

Why Prisons May Have Become More Effective

There are three reasons to believe that prisons may have become more effective over time.

1. *Scale* – Even in the face of diminishing marginal returns, one can expect the incapacitation elasticity to increase. Increases in the scale of incarceration can also change the prospects for deterrence.
2. *The age structure of crime* – Prisons are almost certainly more effective at preventing adult crimes than juvenile crimes. For most of the last twenty-five years, the proportion of violent crimes committed by adults has been increasing.
3. *Selective incapacitation* – The War on Drugs, combined with increasing use of "three strikes you're out" laws and repeat-offender programs, might have created (or destroyed) selective incapacitation effects.

In this section, I consider how these factors should affect the elasticities and the probable size of each effect.

The Unexpected Effects of Scale. Lots of people commit crimes. According to some estimates, as many as 30 percent of the American population commit a serious crime at some point in their lives (Visher and Roth 1986). On the other hand, only about 16 percent are ever arrested (Tillman 1987), and only about 5 percent ever go to jail or prison (Langan 1985). Thus many offenders escape incapacitation; put another way, the criminal justice system acts as a filter, keeping most offenders out.

Even if the criminal justice system is not explicitly attempting to do so, one can be fairly certain that the offenders who are kept out are, by and large, the least offensive. This is because offenders who run repeated risks of getting caught are more likely to be caught. Consider a simple example. Suppose the criminal population can be divided into two types: amateurs, who commit only five crimes each year but account for 75 percent of the population, and professionals, who commit twenty-five crimes each year but account for only 25 percent of all criminals. If all criminals run a constant 10 percent chance of being arrested for each crime they commit, then it is not hard to show that

- The average arrest rate among amateurs will be $.10 \times 5 = .5$ per year, while the average arrest rate among professionals will be $.10 \times 25 = 2.5$;
- A few amateurs will be arrested two or more times, but most (59 percent) will not be arrested at all in a given year; on the other hand, only 7 percent of professionals will escape detection;
- The average offense rate for the whole criminal population is ten crimes per year, climbing to fourteen for the once-arrested population, and to twenty for the twice-arrested population.

In general, so long as offense rates differ among offenders, one can expect these rates to be higher for arrestees than nonarrestees, higher still for repeat arrestees than one-time arrestees, and highest for those who are ultimately incarcerated.

More rigorous estimates of this phenomenon, sometimes called "stochastic selectivity," show that it is even more important than this simple example suggests. Blumstein, Canela-Cacho, and Cohen (1993) applied a probability model to the 1978 Rand inmate data, and found that the average robber who went to prison committed robberies eleven to fourteen times as often as the average among all robbers. In a similar analysis, Canela-Cacho, Blumstein, and Cohen (1997) found that only one to 4 percent of free robbers commit more than ten robberies per year, but 24 to 48 percent of imprisoned robbers do.

These estimates are based on the logic of probability models, but they are borne out by studies of offense rates conducted at various levels of the criminal justice system. Figure 4.2 shows the average offense rate for several studies conducted of one-time arrestees, two-time arrestees, "active offenders" (roughly corresponding to offenders who stand a reasonable chance of going to prison; Chaiken 1980), and a cohort of offenders entering prison in any given year. The offense rate gradually increases as one gets deeper into the system. Simply put, it takes more work to get imprisoned than to get arrested.

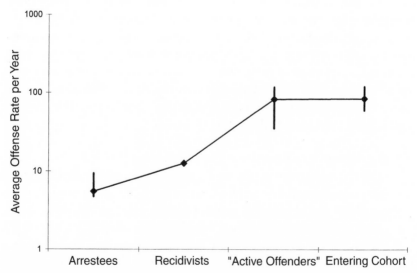

Figure 4.2. Offense rates highest for prisoners.

In some times and places, it takes less work to get imprisoned than in others. If the likelihood of going to prison per crime committed is high, then a relatively large proportion of offenders should be behind bars at any given time, and the offense rates of imprisoned offenders should be relatively low. The self-report studies of imprisoned offenders provide direct evidence that this is true: Among the eight states for which data are available, the correlation between preincarceration violent-offense rates of inmates and prison commitments per 1,000 population is −.95; it is also negative, though less so, for property crimes and all crimes. The deeper you dip into the pool, then, the lower the offense rate. As the probability models show, this phenomenon of diminishing marginal returns occurs even if every offender runs exactly the same chances of arrest, prosecution, and incarceration per crime committed.

In fact, criminal justice agencies work hard to create diminishing marginal returns, by reserving scarce resources for those offenses and offenders who deserve them most. Police respond faster to more serious crimes and investigate them more carefully; through their plea-negotiation procedures, prosecutors effectively forgive the first few arrests; judicial sentencing and parole-release guidelines provide shorter sentences for first-time offenders. As a result, we would expect marginal returns to diminish even more than they would through natural filtering, because the system is trying to force the worst offenders through the system. Although the worst offenders are, not surprisingly, trying to keep themselves out, available evidence suggests that they do not succeed well enough to overcome the effects of natural filtering (Spelman 1994, pp. 172–95).

This, then, suggests that as the prison population increases, the offense rate of the average prisoner – and thus, more or less, the effectiveness of the prison at reducing crime – should go down. Mapping this effect requires a tremendous number of assumptions about the distribution of offense rates, career lengths, and arrest probabilities among offenders, and about the operations of the criminal justice system. Given the number of possible assumptions, many of them equally credible, it makes sense to simulate a wide range of alternatives and report the limits. Following a previous analysis (Spelman 1994, pp. 216–21), I simulated sixty-two combinations of possible assumptions to create the results shown in Figure 4.3. As expected, the average offense rate – roughly equivalent to the social benefits per prison bed – drops as the prison population climbs. If the prison population were to double, the system would dig deeper enough into the pool that the average offense rate among those imprisoned would drop by 14 to 22 percent. If the population were to quadruple (as it did over the

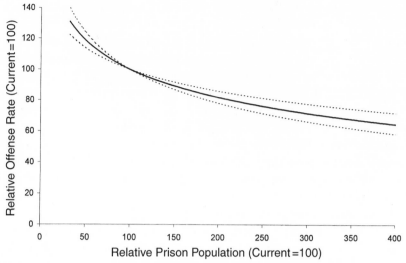

Figure 4.3. Average offense rate drops as prison population increases.

previous twenty-five years), the average offense rate would drop by 28 to 42 percent. Cutting the prison population in half, on the other hand, would increase the average offense rate by about 18 percent.

Bed for bed, prisons become less effective as they fill up. On the other hand, the effects of prison expansion are usually measured not in terms of beds or cells, but in terms of percentages. Because a one-percent increase in prison population is a lot more prisoners after twenty-five years of expansion than before, an apples-to-apples comparison requires that we examine the elasticity (which depends on the percentage increase) rather than the offense rate (which depends on the numerical increase).

A short example will illustrate the problem. Say a small state operates a prison with one thousand beds. A one-percent increase in this system will therefore be ten beds. If the typical criminal commits, say, twenty crimes per year, the effect of this one-percent increase is to reduce crime by roughly $10 \times 20 = 200$ crimes per year.

Now suppose the prison system is doubled, to two thousand beds. A one-percent increase is now twenty beds. The typical criminal may be less dangerous than before – that criminal might commit only fifteen crimes per year, for example – but the effect of a one-percent increase is now to reduce crime by about $15 \times 20 = 300$ crimes per year. Thus diminishing marginal returns can be consistent with an increasing elasticity as prisons are built and filled.

Figure 4.4 shows what happens when the findings of Figure 4.3 are converted to elasticity terms. Despite the moderate reduction in average offense rate described previously, the elasticity increases steadily as the prison population increases. If the elasticity began at around –.15 in 1973, after one doubling it would increase to –.28 or so, and after a second doubling – more or less, today's prison population – it would increase to anywhere from –.35 to –.7. Thus a one-bed increase would have less effect on the crime rate in 2000 than in 1973, but a one-percent increase would be much more effective in 2000, because it represents far more additional beds.[4]

These results assume that prisons reduce crime only through incapacitation. It is uncertain how changes in prison populations will affect deterrence. Percentage increases are more likely to be noticeable when they are also large in absolute terms; this suggests that a one-percent increase can be a more effective deterrent when prison populations are large. On the other hand, small changes in probability have their greatest effect on behavior when the probability itself is small (Kahnemann and Tversky 1979), suggesting that the deterrence elasticity may actually go down as prison population climbs. The theory of deterrence is too imprecise to provide much guidance. Nevertheless, the size of the prison boom and the clarity of its theoretical effect on the incapacitation elasticity suggests rather strongly that net elasticity must have increased over the past twenty-five years. Whether the increase is sufficient to account for much of the crime drop remains to be seen.

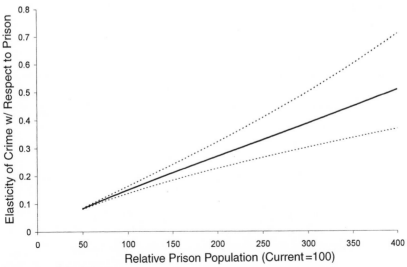

Figure 4.4. Elasticity increases steadily as prison population expands.

The Changing Role of Juvenile Crime. Prisons, like dirty movies, are supposed to be for adults only. This is not always true: Every year, some twelve thousand juveniles are transferred to adult courts, and roughly one-half of them are sentenced to terms in adult prisons. Nevertheless, at fewer than 2 percent of all prisoners, this is almost trivial. From an incapacitation viewpoint, prisons are unlikely to affect juvenile crime noticeably.

As usual, the deterrence picture is somewhat more complex. On the one hand, youths may be deterred from committing crimes if they see that their older friends and big brothers spend a lot of time behind bars. Although temporarily immune to adult prosecution, juvenile criminals are presumably smart enough to know this will not always be true. It is also possible that youthful offenders – relative novices, presumably less inculcated in a criminal subculture – respond more readily to changes in punishment than adults. Some have even argued that deterrence (among juveniles, not adults) is responsible for the downturn in violent crime (Kocieniewski 1997). On the other hand, drug rings and gangs may take advantage of relatively lenient juvenile penalties by assigning especially risky tasks to their youngest members. For well-organized units, at least, an increase in adult prison population may thus cause crime to increase among youths. On balance, it probably makes most sense to expect that prisons are more effective at controlling crime among adults and thus will be more effective when the proportion of crimes committed by adults is high than when it is low.

If this is true, then there are reasons to suspect that prison effectiveness peaked in the late 1980s. In 1974, fewer than 70 percent of all arrestees were adults; this percentage increased steadily through the 1970s and 1980s, peaking at 82 percent in 1989; over the last decade, the percentage has stayed around 80 percent. Although the cycle has been more pronounced for property crimes than for violent crimes, the two trends are almost identical.[5] The reason for the increasing predominance of adults is mostly demographic. The baby boom was followed by a baby bust. Because the incidence of crime peaks in the late teens, the boomers dominated the crime problem as juveniles in the late 1960s to mid-1970s and have since continued to dominate it as adults. Only very recently have the children of the boomers – the "baby boomerangs" – begun to enter the most crime-prone years.

The decrease in juvenile arrestees may also be due in part to a reduced incidence of criminal activity among successive cohorts. Marijuana and alcohol use among 12 to 17 year olds appears to have peaked in the 1970s (Maguire and Pastore 1995, p. 294). The number of high school seniors that report using harder drugs dropped from 1982 to 1988, and has changed little since. On the other hand, a slightly higher percentage of high school seniors reported committing assaults, robberies, and some property crimes during the mid-1990s than during the early 1980s (Johnston, O'Malley, and Bachman 1995).

Although a gradual reduction in the proportion of juvenile arrestees suggests a similar decrease in the proportion of juvenile crimes, there are caveats. On the one hand, adults are probably more skilled than juveniles at avoiding arrest and therefore less likely to be arrested for each crime they commit than are juveniles (Spelman 1994). Thus the proportion of all crimes committed by adults is liable to be even greater than the proportion of adult arrests, suggesting that the increase in the adult fraction of arrestees does indeed reflect a decrease in the relative offense rate of juveniles. On the other hand, it is plausible that the population of juvenile offenders is becoming more or less skilled at avoiding arrest. If, for example, the youthful criminal population is becoming more and more a group of relatively unskilled "losers" who are not much good at crime, the overall likelihood of arrest among juvenile offenders may be increasing. As a result, the gradual reduction in juvenile arrests may mask a larger reduction in juvenile criminality. Alternatively, if "losers" are turning away from crime (perhaps because of better opportunities in the legitimate economy), the overall likelihood of arrest among juveniles may be going down, and the reduction in arrests may overstate the reduction in criminality. It is even conceivable that juveniles may be committing a larger, not smaller, share of violent crimes. There is as yet no evidence either way.

Caveats notwithstanding, it seems most likely that juveniles are a smaller part of the crime problem today than they were in the 1970s. The practical upshot is that this probably changes the overall elasticity over time. Changes in the prison population have one effect among adults and another among juveniles. If the effect is larger among adults, which seems very probable, then the elasticity should be increasing somewhat over time, particularly for property crimes. Whether the effect is large enough to matter, or even to be measurable, is a matter taken up shortly.

Changes in the Selectivity of the Criminal Justice System. A general increase in prison population is only the most visible change in the criminal justice system over the past twenty-five years. Other changes could conceivably have reduced the crime rate by shifts in the kind of offenders who are put in prison, thus improving the effectiveness of imprisonment. Several of the most widely touted innovations are considered here.

The most familiar innovation emerges from the War on Drugs: About one-fourth of all prison beds are now occupied by offenders convicted, not of violent or property crimes, but of drug possession and dealing. The usual justification for this is that incarcerating drug dealers causes them to charge higher prices to cover their risks; this is intended to reduce the amount of drugs sold, in turn reducing the number of crimes committed to pay for those drugs (Reuter and Kleiman 1986).

It is conceivable that incarcerating drug dealers has a substantial deterrent effect on those offenders, or on would-be drug offenders. Because the simulation model deals with incapacitation, it cannot be used to evaluate such effects. The logic of the model is helpful in evaluating the incapacitation aspects of the argument, however, and the results are unambiguous: Incapacitation of drug dealers is not only ineffective, it may be counterproductive.

Briefly, the argument is this. Imprisonment does not cause replacement of violent and property offenders, because such crimes are not typically organized as a business where individuals fill necessary roles. Not so with drug dealing. Removal of one dealer opens up an opportunity for another to enter; conceivably, replacement is 100 percent and incapacitation is not effective at all.

Now, it is unlikely that 100 percent of the offenders removed will be replaced in any criminal organization; to extend the business metaphor, recruitment and training are time consuming and expensive, and higher-ups will want to minimize such costs. Nevertheless, it is still possible that dealer-incapacitation strategies will backfire. Both heavy drug users and drug dealers commit serious crimes at higher rates than others (Chaiken and Chaiken 1982); newly recruited dealers are thus liable to increase their offense rates for other crimes, as they move deeper into the criminal subculture. It seems unlikely that they will go back to their straight jobs when their predecessors return from prison. Neither is it reasonable to presume that the released offenders will spontaneously quit committing burglaries and robberies when they return from prison and find their dealing jobs filled. Thus the number of offenders – and the number of (non-drug) offenses committed – will tend to increase, so long as the chances of replacement are higher than the percentage of the criminal career the typical dealer spends in prison. (When they are equal, replacement is just sufficient to keep the total number of offenders constant.)

Estimating the chances that an individual drug dealer will be incapacitated, for drug dealing or anything else, is difficult. However, simulation results reported by Spelman (1994) suggest that between 6 and 12 percent of offenders are in jail or prison at any given time. Because replacement is almost certainly greater than that, the War on Drugs may have had the unintended side effect of increasing, not reducing, the crime rate. Certainly there is no argument for it having reduced the number of criminals or crimes through incapacitation.

Another celebrated change in criminal justice system operations is the notion of selective incapacitation, which has been discussed (and from time to time, implemented in one form or another) for decades. In general, the term refers to any program or policy that puts the most frequent and dangerous offenders in prison at higher rates. So-called three strikes, you're out laws, predictive sentencing and parole decision making, and law enforcement repeat-offender programs, are all examples of selective incapacitation strategies.

The best-known of these strategies are the three strikes, you're out laws, which increase prison terms for convicted offenders with a certain number of prior convictions. Such programs in fact depend on the filtering of the criminal justice system for their effects. Because three-time convicts are fairly sure to commit crimes at higher rates than one- and two-time losers of the same age, the result should be higher average offense rates among prisoners. As described above, limited evidence suggests that this is true. Two- and three-time losers commit crimes two to three times more often, on average, than offenders with no or one prior conviction (Spelman 1994, p. 214).

The effectiveness of such programs may be enhanced or offset by the effects of aging on offender behavior. Offenders tend to burn out in the same way that electronic circuit boards do. A lot of them quit committing crimes within a year or two; presumably they find they can't take the stress, or aren't any good at it. If they do not drop out in the first few years, however, criminals appear to settle into crime and stay with it until they near age 40. At this point, the risks of burnout begin to increase again (Blumstein, Cohen, and Hsieh 1982). The practical effect of this is that programs that focus attention on older offenders, as three strikes laws doubtless do, may be more or less effective depending on the age of the offenders they target. If they focus on offenders in their late twenties and early thirties, they are probably more effective than not. If they focus on offenders in their late thirties or beyond, they risk imprisoning offenders who would have quit committing crimes had they simply been left alone.

Explicit selective-sentencing programs are a somewhat more sophisticated (and effective) means of accomplishing the same objective. A statistical yardstick is developed that predicts future criminal behavior. Judges or parole boards then use these yardsticks to determine how long a prison sentence to give or whether to release an offender on parole. Such programs are controversial. Some argue that sentences should be based entirely on the offense committed (Fletcher 1982), or to a very limited extent on the number of prior convictions only (von Hirsch 1985). Others would balance the constraints of just deserts against the benefits of crime control; the balance could be struck in various places depends on the accuracy of the selection technique, the disparity of the sanctions between predicted high- and low-rate offenders, and the effectiveness of the program (Monahan 1982; Morris 1982).

Simulation results suggest that the most effective programs are those that really throw the book at predicted frequent offenders, giving those predicted to be in the high-rate offending group (about 12 percent of the total) sentences that are about 20 times longer than those given to the low-rate group. The ethical dilemmas here are tremendous: Because none of the predictive instruments are very accurate, the predicted high-rate offenders only commit crimes 2 or 3 times more often than predicted low-rate offenders. If, in response, we are only willing to give out sentences that are 2 or 3 times as long (Monahan 1982), this cuts into the effectiveness of the program considerably. Nevertheless, simulation results suggest that implementing such an ethically constrained program increases the offense rate of the marginal offender and the elasticity by about 5 percent.

More promising is the recent movement to increase the arrest, conviction, and incarceration rate among the most frequent and dangerous offenders. Through surveillance, stakeouts, selective warrant service, and MO analysis, repeat-offender programs attempt to focus scarce resources on the worst offenders (Martin and Sherman 1985; Pate, Bowers, and Parks 1976; Spelman 1990). Like selective sentencing, this tends to increase the offense rate of the average prisoner, and thus the effectiveness of incarceration.

As with selective sentencing, the effect depends on the number of offenders targeted and the effectiveness of the program. There is evidence that the most effective feasible program would focus intensive resources on about 4 percent of active offenders, increasingly the elasticity of prison by about 25 percent. Limited evidence from current programs suggests that they are about half as effective as that (Spelman 1994).

Now suppose a given jurisdiction implements both Monahan's modified just deserts sentencing and the best of the current selective police and prosecution programs. It is not hard to show that the result will be an increase in the elasticity of about 20 percent. Thus, if such repeat-offender programs were widely adopted between the early 1970s and late 1990s, they might have increased the elasticity by that amount over this period.

A lot of jurisdictions adopted one of these selective schemes, and a few adopted both. Most adopted neither. Nevertheless, suppose *all* jurisdictions in the entire country adopted *both* schemes and succeeded in increasing the elasticity of prison over the twenty-five year period by 20 percent. Such an increase is, in theory, just the smoking gun one seeks: that improvement in practice responsible for improving the effectiveness of imprisonment and not just suppressing the violent-crime rate but turning it down. Would it have been sufficient to turn the violent-crime rate down?

As it happens, probably not. If one conducts a similar thought-experiment to the one described earlier, but allows the elasticity to increase over time by 20 percent, the results are almost identical to those shown in Figure 4.1. As before, violent-crime rates would have gone down, even had the prison buildup never taken place. Prison expansion during the 1990s would now be responsible for increasing the violent-crime drop by 10 to 24 percent, somewhat larger than the 7 to 20 percent estimated earlier. Thus one can conclude that selective police, prosecution, and prison programs might have helped to reduce the crime rate. Even had these programs been universal, however, they would not have been nearly effective enough to account for the crime reductions of the 1990s.

Did Prisons Become More Effective?

Increases in the scale of incarceration, in the proportion of crimes committed by adults, and in the selectivity of the criminal justice system all suggest that the crime-control effectiveness of prisons, as measured by the elasticity, has increased over the past twenty-five years. As a result, the prison buildup is probably responsible for a larger percentage of the crime drop than estimated earlier. It is difficult to estimate how much larger using bottom-up thought experiments, however. The assumptions required about how offenders commit crimes and are arrested, imprisoned, and ultimately released, and in particular the assumption that prisons only control crime through incapacitation and not through deterrence, are difficult to justify. A more direct means of measuring changes in the elasticity over time would surely be preferable.

The top-down, econometric studies suggest just such a direct measurement. Although previous top-down studies have assumed that the elasticity for a particular crime type is the same for all states and time periods, it is not difficult to relax this assumption. More specifically, one can examine whether the elasticity responds to the shifts over time described previously. If it does, then one must estimate the approximate elasticity at work during each year over the past twenty-five years, apply that time-specific elasticity to our problem, and reevaluate the effects of the prison buildup on the crime drop.

The best of the top-down studies rely on a panel data-set collected by Marvell and Moody (1994) and improved by Levitt (1996). It covers all fifty U.S. states and the District of Columbia for the period from 1971 to 1997.[6] One important benefit of this data-set is that it contains a wide variety of control variables that can be expected to influence crime rates. By controlling explicitly for the effects of income, unemployment, age structure, and other characteristics, the effect of prisons on crime can be isolated.

At least three sets of results have been obtained from this data-set, corresponding to the specific statistical models used by Becsi (1999), Levitt (1996), and Marvell and Moody (1994). The analysis that follows relies primarily on Levitt's model. As described previously, it is the only model that deals explicitly with the possibility that crime rates affect prison population, and it may provide conservative results by systematically overstating the effect of prisons on crime.

As with most top-down models, the Levitt model controls for a variety of social and economic characteristics. In addition, the model was altered to account for scale, juvenile, and trend effects.[7] Table 4.3 shows the results of four, increasingly complex models.

> Model 1 replicates Levitt's findings, showing the effect of a variety of factors on the violent-crime rate under the assumption that elasticity is a constant;
>
> Model 2 replaces the constant-elasticity term with one that depends on the scale of imprisonment;
>
> Model 3 also includes a term measuring the proportion of violent crimes committed by adults;
>
> Model 4 also includes terms measuring other changes in elasticity over time.

Note first that all four models are virtually identical in most respects. The coefficients on social and economic indicators vary little from one model to the next. In addition, they all predict the average elasticity to be in the vicinity of −.40 – toward the high end of the expected range, but well within that range. Model 2 is slightly more accurate than Model 1 (as measured by the standard error of the estimate and the adjusted R^2); the statistical significance of the scale-flexible coefficient in Model 2 is also greater than that of the constant-elasticity coefficient in Model 1. This alone sug-

Table 4.3. Estimates of the Crime Function

	Model 1	Model 2	Model 3	Model 4
Control Variables				
Per Capita Income	*.362*	*.356*	*.352*	*.344*
	(.126)	(.126)	(.126)	(.132)
% Unemployment	.430	.422	.432	.460
	(.298)	(.298)	(.298)	(.304)
% Black	−.028	−.032	−.038	−.046
	(.025)	(.025)	(.026)	(.027)
Police Per Capita	.081	.082	.083	.083
	(.046)	(.046)	(.046)	(.047)
% Urban	.006	.006	.008	.006
	(.012)	(.012)	(.012)	(.012)
% Aged 0–14	−.176	−.170	−.207	−.139
	(.408)	(.407)	(.409)	(.419)
% Aged 15–17	.233	.214	.195	.107
	(.213)	(.214)	(.215)	(.221)
% Aged 18–24	.309	.310	.295	.316
	(.246)	(.245)	(.246)	(.251)
% Aged 25–34	*.724*	*.729*	*.706*	.596
	(.344)	(.342)	(.343)	(.350)
Prison Elasticity Variables				
Prison Rate (constant)	*−.401*			
	(.150)			
Prison Rate (variable)		*−.082*	*−.089*	−.064
		(.028)	(.029)	(.069)
Prison Rate × Percent Adult Crimes			−.442	−.684
			(.489)	(.543)
Prison Rate Annual Differences				−1.827 to + 1.055
(range of values)				(.866) (.648)
Summary Statistics				
R^2	.3058	.3069	.3075	.3190
adjusted R^2	.2864	.2875	.2874	.2855
std Error of Estimate	.07204	.07198	.07199	.07208
ΔF			0.818	0.861
$p(\Delta F)$			.366	.638
mean η	−.401	−.428	−.391	−.488
std dev of η	−	.045	.054	.614

Note: In variable sections, first value shown is coefficient; standard error is shown in (parentheses).
Statistically significant coefficients ($p < .05$) are shown in *italics*.
Source: Author's calculations, based on data provided by Steven Levitt, University of Chicago, updated to 1997.

gests that the assumption of constant elasticity is inappropriate. The differences between Model 2 and Model 3 are not statistically significant, but the adult-proportion coefficient is of the expected sign, and adding the new term at least does little harm to predictive accuracy. Not so with Model 4: It is the least accurate predictor, the new terms are not statistically significant, and perhaps most important, there is no clear pattern in the changes in elasticity over time. On balance, then, Model 3 (or, perhaps, Model 2) is the most successful of the four.

The elasticity implied by Model 3 differs among states and over time, and can be expressed as

$$\text{elasticity} = -.089 \log \text{prison rate} -.442 \log p(\text{adult}).$$

As expected, for violent crimes, at least, the elasticity increases (that is, it becomes more negative) as the scale of imprisonment (here measured by the log of the prison rate per 100,000 residents) increases. The elasticity also responds to the extent of juvenile involvement: The elasticity is most negative in the times and places where the vast majority of crimes were committed by adults. Perhaps most important, elasticity does not change significantly or consistently over time, once changes in scale and juvenile involvement have been taken into account. This suggests that any nationwide increases in selectivity are too slight to be identified using these data.

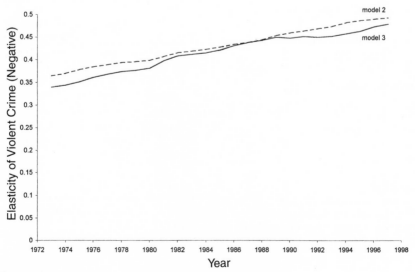

Figure 4.5. Elasticity has risen gradually over time.

Finally, the equation has no intercept; this is because, at very low values of the prison rate, one can expect that the elasticity is very close to zero.

When this formula is applied to the panel data, the resulting estimates are as shown in Figure 4.5. The elasticity has clearly increased over time, from a low point of –.34 in 1973 to a high of –.48 in 1997. Even without a specific selectivity effect, it is clear that changes in the scale of imprisonment and the incidence of juvenile violent crime have helped to make prisons more effective (at least on a percentage basis) over time.

Conclusion

Armed with direct evidence of increasing elasticity, I return to the original problem. What effect did the prison buildup have on the crime drop? Figure 4.6 shows what happens when the elasticities of Figure 4.5 are applied to the violent-crime and prison data of the last twenty-five years.

The results are very similar to the hypothetical cases of Figure 4.1:

- The violent-crime rate would have dropped, anyway, at almost the same time, but
- The crime drop would have been 27 percent smaller than it actually was, had the prison buildup never taken place.[8]

In short, the prison buildup was responsible for about one-fourth of the crime drop. Other factors are responsible for the vast majority of the drop.

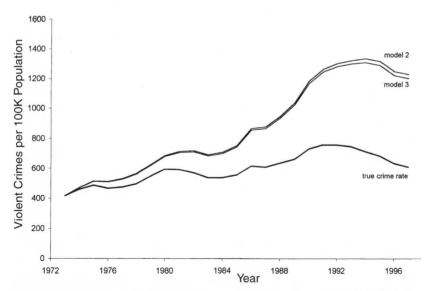

Figure 4.6. Hypothetical effect of failure to expand prisons assuming changing elasticity over time.

Some will find this estimate disturbingly low; others, astonishingly high. The threshold question is, Does it make any sense? I think it does, for three reasons.

First, keep in mind that crime has been among the most persistent public problems over the past twenty-five years, and that prison construction has been our principal response to this problem. About as many police officers per capita are employed today as were employed twenty-five years ago; only a tiny fraction of probationers and parolees are assigned to intensive-supervision programs; the courts behave about the same as they did in the early 1970s. But four times as many people are in prison. Even if imprisonment were an incredibly inefficient means of reducing crime – and there are strong arguments that it is exactly that – it could hardly have helped but have a substantial effect on the crime rate, given the enormous scale of the difference.

Second, these estimates are consistent with everything else known about the effects of prisons on crime. The elasticities are within the range established by previous estimates. As expected, they are higher than the bottom-up estimates, which measure only the effects of incapacitation; although they are also a bit higher than most top-down estimates, most of these estimates are biased toward zero. In the broader context of economic research, an elasticity of −.4 or thereabouts is entirely unexceptional.

Finally, this estimate is based on the best-available methods. It controls explicitly for economic indicators and the most important demographic characteristic – the age structure of the population. It controls implicitly for other nationwide shifts in culture, economics, and politics over the past twenty-five years. Most important, it separates the effects of prisons on crime from the effects of crime on prisons, and does so using a method that is theoretically justifiable and an improvement over the best, previous estimates.

Nevertheless, it is hardly the last word on the subject. Over the next few years, researchers should consider making a variety of improvements in this model. Although it allows for random shifts from year to year, the model explicitly considers only scale and juvenile involvement as reasons for changes in elasticity. There may be others, and the methods demonstrated here can be applied to these variables as they are identified. Persistent differences in elasticities among states are beyond the scope of this chapter, but they may be substantial and are of obvious policy relevance. Again, state differences can be included in the model through a straightforward expansion. Finally, the whole question of policy implications is beyond the scope of this analysis. Given the likelihood of changing elasticities over time and the probability of differences among states, the most appropriate policy implications would be very time- and place-specific. Some states could very well benefit from further prison expansion today; others may have expanded too much as it is. Although I don't go there, somebody needs to, and soon.

One may conclude, with considerable conviction, that the prison buildup was an important contributing factor to the violent-crime drop of the past few years. America would be a much more violent place had billions of dollars not been invested in prison beds over the past two decades; violent crime would not have dropped as far and as fast as it has. Nevertheless, violent crime *would* have dropped a lot, anyway. Most of the responsibility for the crime drop rests with improvements in the economy, changes in the age structure, or other social factors. Whether the key to further reductions lies in further prison expansions, or (more likely) in further improvements in these other factors remains an open question.

Notes

1. Rosenfeld (Chapter 5) implicitly relies on this explanation in using the national-level studies of the effect of prison expansion on homicide rates. Although what evidence is available suggests that murderers are much like other criminals in their movement patterns, the low rate of homicides makes any such estimates imprecise. Thus it is possible that most homicides are committed by people who commit murder in more than one state. As a result, the national-level studies might be more appropriate for homicide than for other violent crimes.
2. Columns 4, 5, and 6 on Table 4.2 show that same thing in slightly different form.
3. Although three hypothetical crime rates are provided, corresponding to three reasonable estimates of the elasticity, this general conclusion holds equally for any estimate of the elasticity between −10 and −.50. Thus the size of the elasticity is relatively unimportant, so long as it does not change over time. Almost identical results are obtained if this analysis is applied to property-crime rates.
4. This is a reasonable place to mention an important caveat. If the aim is to determine whether or not to increase the prison population, the proper metric is the social benefit per prison bed, and more or less, the offense rate of the marginal prisoner. If, instead, the aim is just to determine the extent to which prisons have reduced crime, the proper metric is the elasticity. Even if we find that crime has been reduced by a lot as a result of the prison buildup, it may be that it was not cost effective to have done so, and that the money could have been better spent elsewhere. That is an issue for another study, and need not be considered here.
5. The trend for murder, described in Chapters 2, 5, and 9, is similar.
6. Levitt's version of the data-set extended to 1993. I used published sources to extend it to 1997.
7. Because there is no direct way to measure the selectivity of a state's criminal justice operations, one can let a time trend stand in for any time-varying effects, among them shifts in selectivity. Table 4.2 only shows results for violent crime; property crime results were very similar, though the elasticity for all models was considerably closer to zero, averaging to about −.28.
8. This result was obtained by using the elasticities implied by Model 3. Similar results were obtained by using Model 2 (28 percent of the crime drop can be attributed to the prison buildup) and Model 4 (34 percent).

References

Avi-Itzhak, Benjamin, and Reuel Shinnar. 1973. "Quantitative Models in Crime Control." *Journal of Criminal Justice* 1:185–217.

Becsi, Zsolt. 1999. "Economics and Crime in the United States." *Economic Review of the Federal Reserve Bank of Atlanta* 84 (First quarter):38–56.

Blumstein, Alfred, José A. Canela-Cacho, and Jacqueline Cohen. 1993. "Filtered Sampling from Populations with Heterogeneous Event Frequencies." *Management Science* 39:886–99.

Blumstein, Alfred, Jacqueline Cohen, and Paul Hsieh. 1982. *The Duration of Adult Criminal Careers.* Final report to the National Institute of Justice. Pittsburgh: Carnegie-Mellon University, School of Urban and Public Affairs.

Blumstein, Alfred, Jacqueline Cohen, and Daniel Nagin. 1978. *Deterrence and Incapacitation: Estimating the Effects of Criminal Sanctions on Crime Rates.* Report of the Panel on Research on Deterrent and Incapacitative Effects. Washington: National Academy of Sciences.

Canela-Cacho, José A., Alfred Blumstein, and Jacqueline Cohen. 1997. "Relationship between the Offending Frequency (λ) of Imprisoned and Free Offenders." *Criminology* 35:133–75.

Cappell, Charles L., and Gresham Sykes. 1991. "Prison Commitments, Crime, and Unemployment: A Theoretical and Empirical Specification for the United States, 1933–1985." *Journal of Quantitative Criminology* 7:155–99.

Chaiken, Jan M. 1980. "Models Used for Estimating Crime Rates." In Mark A. Peterson, Harriet B. Braiker, and Suzanne M. Polich (Eds.), *Doing Crime: A Survey of California Prison Inmates* (pp. 224–52). Santa Monica: Rand.

Chaiken, Jan M., and Marcia R. Chaiken. 1982. *Varieties of Criminal Behavior.* Santa Monica: Rand.

Cohen, Jacqueline. 1978. "The Incapacitative Effect of Imprisonment: A Critical Review of the Literature." In Alfred Blumstein, Jacqueline Cohen, and Daniel Nagin (Eds.), *Deterrence and Incapacitation: Estimating the Effects of Criminal Sanctions on Crime Rates* (pp. 187–243). Washington: National Academy of Sciences.

Devine, Joel A., Joseph F. Sheley, and M. Dwayne Smith. 1988. "Macroeconomic and Social-control Policy Influences on Crime Rate Changes, 1948–1985." *American Sociological Review* 53:407–20.

DiIulio, John J., Jr. 1990. *Crime and Punishment in Wisconsin.* Wisconsin Policy Research Institute Report, Volume 3, No. 7. Milwaukee: Wisconsin Policy Research Institute.

DiIulio, John J., Jr., and Anne Morrison Piehl. 1991. "Does prison pay?" *Brookings Review* (Fall): 28–35.

Donohue, John J., III, and Peter Siegelman. 1998. "Allocating Resources among Prisons and Social Programs in the Battle Against Crime. *Journal of Legal Studies* 27:1–43.

Ehrlich, Isaac. 1973. "Participation in Illegitimate Activities: A Theoretical and Empirical Investigation." *Journal of Political Economy* 81:521–65.

Federal Bureau of Investigation. Annual. *Crime in the United States.* Washington: U. S. Government Printing Office.

Fletcher, George. 1982. "The Recidivist Premium." *Criminal Justice Ethics* 2:54–59.

Gibbs, Jack P. 1968. "Crime, Punishment, and Deterrence." *Southwestern Social Science Quarterly* 48:515–30.

Greenwood, Peter W. 1982. *Selective Incapacitation.* Santa Monica: Rand.

Horney, Julie, and Ineke Marshall. 1991. "Measuring Lambda through Self-Reports." *Criminology* 29:401–25.

Johnston, Lloyd D., Patrick M. O'Malley, and Jerald G. Bachman. 1995. *Monitoring the Future 1995.* Ann Arbor: Institute for Social Research, University of Michigan.

Kahnemann, Daniel, and Amos Tversky. 1979. "Prospect Theory: An Analysis of Decision under Risk." *Econometrica* 47:263–91.

Kocieniewski, David. 1997. "Mayor Gets Credit for Safer City, But Wider Trends Play a Role." *The New York Times* (October 28, p. 1).

Langan, Patrick A. 1985. *The Prevalence of Imprisonment.* Special Report. Washington: U.S. Bureau of Justice Statistics.

Levitt, Steven D. 1996. "The Effect of Prison Population Size on Crime Rates: Evidence from Prison Overcrowding Litigation." *Quarterly Journal of Economics* 111:319–51.

Logan, C. H. 1975. "Arrest Rates and Deterrence." *Social Science Quarterly* 56:376–89.

Maguire, Kathleen, and Ann L. Pastore. 1995. *Sourcebook of Criminal Justice Statistics – 1994.* Washington: U.S. Government Printing Office.

Mande, M. J., and Kim English. 1988. *Individual Crime Rates of Colorado Prisoners: Final Report. 1988.* Denver: Colorado Division of Criminal Justice, Research Unit.

Martin, Susan E., and Lawrence W. Sherman. 1985. *Catching Career Criminals: A Study of the Repeat Offender Project: Technical Report.* Washington: Police Foundation.

Marvell, Thomas B., and Carlisle E. Moody, Jr. 1994. "Prison Population Growth and Crime Reduction." *Journal of Quantitative Criminology* 10:109–40.

Marvell, Thomas B., and Carlisle E. Moody, Jr. 1997. "The Impact of Prison Growth on Homicide." *Homicide Studies* 1:205–33.

Marvell, Thomas B., and Carlisle E. Moody, Jr. 1998. "The Impact of Out-of-State Prison Population on State Homicide Rates: Displacement and Free-Rider Effects." *Criminology* 36:513–35.

Monahan, John. 1982. "The Case for Prediction in the Modified Desert Model of Criminal Sentencing." *International Journal of Law and Psychiatry* 5:103–13.

Morris, Norval. 1982. *Madness and the Criminal Law.* Chicago: University of Chicago Press.

Nagin, Daniel. 1978. "General Deterrence: A Review of the Empirical Evidence." In Alfred Blumstein, Jacqueline Cohen, and Daniel Nagin (Eds.), *Deterrence and Incapacitation: Estimating the Effects of Criminal Sanctions on Crime Rates* (pp. 95–139). Washington: National Academy of Sciences.

Orsagh, Thomas. 1992. *The Multi-State Offender: A Report on State Prisoners Who Were Criminally Active in More Than One State*. Washington: U.S. Bureau of Justice Statistics.

Pate, Tony, Robert A. Bowers, and Richard Parks. 1976. *Three Approaches to Criminal Apprehension in Kansas City: An Evaluation Report*. Washington: Police Foundation.

Petersilia, Joan, Peter W. Greenwood, and Marvin Lavin. 1978. *Criminal Careers of Habitual Felons*. Santa Monica: Rand.

Peterson, Mark A., Harriet B. Braiker, and Suzanne M. Polich. 1980. *Doing Crime: A Survey of California Prison Inmates*. Santa Monica: Rand.

Piehl, Anne Morrison, and John J. DiIulio, Jr. 1995. "'Does Prison Pay?' Revisited: Returning to the Crime Scene." *Brookings Review* (Winter 1995): 21–25.

Reiss, Albert J., Jr. 1980. "Understanding Changes in Crime Rates." In Stephen E. Fienberg and Albert J. Reiss, Jr. (Eds.), *Indicators of Crime and Criminal Justice: Quantitative Studies* (pp. 11–17). Washington: U.S. Government Printing Office.

Reuter, Peter, and Mark A. R. Kleiman. 1986. "Risks and Prices: An Economic Analysis of Drug Enforcement." In Michael Tonry and Norval Morris (Eds.), *Crime and Justice: A Review of Research* (pp. 289–340). Chicago: University of Chicago Press.

Shinnar, Shlomo, and Reuel Shinnar. 1975. "The Effects of the Criminal Justice System on the Control of Crime: A Quantitative Approach." *Law and Society Review* 9:581–611.

Spelman, William. 1990. *Repeat Offender Programs for Law Enforcement*. Washington: Police Executive Research Forum.

Spelman, William. 1994. *Criminal Incapacitation*. New York: Plenum.

Tillman, Robert. 1987. "The Size of the 'Criminal Population': The Prevalence and Incidence of Adult Arrest." *Criminology* 25:561–79.

U. S. Bureau of Justice Statistics, Annual. *Correctional Populations in the United States*. Washington: U. S. Department of Justice.

Vandaele, Walter. 1978. "Participation in Illegitimate Activities: Ehrlich Revisited." In Alfred Blumstein, Jacqueline Cohen, and Daniel Nagin (Eds.), *Deterrence and Incapacitation: Estimating the Effects of Criminal Sanctions on Crime Rates* (pp. 270–335). Washington: National Academy of Sciences.

Visher, Christy A., and Jeffrey A. Roth. 1986. "Participation in Criminal Careers." In Alfred Blumstein, Jacqueline Cohen, Jeffrey A. Roth, and

Christy A. Visher (Eds.), *Criminal Careers and "Career Criminals"* (Vol. 2, pp. 211–91). Washington: National Academy Press.

Von Hirsch, Andrew. 1985. *Past and Future Crimes: Deservedness and Dangerousness in the Sentencing of Criminals*. New Brunswick, NJ: Rutgers University Press.

Patterns in Adult Homicide: 1980–1995

Richard Rosenfeld

> There is a prediction implicit in any discussion of age structure and crime.
> It is that the generation that made the crime wave can break it, too.
>
> Landon Y. Jones, *Great Expectations: America and the Baby Boom Generation*

ADULT HOMICIDE RATES have fallen continuously for over twenty years. Although it has not gone completely unnoticed, the decline in adult homicide has not figured prominently in recent scholarly attention devoted to violent-crime trends in the United States, which has been dominated by the issue of youth violence. The result is that little is known about patterns of adult violence – a notable exception being domestic or "intimate partner" violence – and we have neither the theory nor requisite research for understanding the decline in adult homicide, including the drop in intimate partner killings. That would not be a big problem for homicide research if adults contributed little to the overall homicide rate. Yet persons 25 years old or older make up over 60 percent of all homicide victims and nearly one-half of the offenders.[1] Moreover, with the aging of the baby boomers, adults are not only the largest but also the fastest growing segment of the U.S. population (U.S. Bureau of the Census 1996a, p. 24, Table 23). An accurate, comprehensive, and policy-relevant portrayal of the recent violence – the goal of this volume – must, therefore, include a description of the patterns among adults, and should offer some assessment of alternative explanations for the two-decade-long decline in adult homicide.

The drop in adult homicide is both pronounced and pervasive. It has taken place among men as well as women, blacks as well as whites. It cuts across differing victim-offender relationships and manifests itself in declining rates of adult offending as well as victimization. After documenting these subgroup patterns, I inspect them for insights they may provide into the social changes responsible for the falling adult rates, especially in the rate for the 25- to 49-year-old group, whose sharply growing numbers otherwise would have exerted enormous upward pressure on the total homicide rate. I assess the contributions of two institutional shifts in particular: the dramatic increase in incarceration that began in the late 1970s and the equally striking, but less remarked on, changes in the living arrangements of young adults brought about by their falling marriage rates. Although both of these factors undoubtedly have helped to lower the level of adult homicide, in my estimation they do not account fully for the decline. Future research on U.S. homicide trends also must address broader cultural shifts that have reduced the tolerance for and participation in serious interpersonal violence by adults.

Age Structure and Homicide

Since 1980 about 400,000 persons have been the victims of criminal homicide in the United States, an average of 20,000 victims per year, the great majority of whom were over the age of 24. Figure 5.1 graphically depicts the dominance of the nation's yearly homicide count by adults. About two-thirds of the victims in recent years have been in their mid-twenties or older, and fully one-half are in the 25- to 49-year-old age group dominated by the baby boomers. About one-quarter of homicide victims are between the ages of 18 and 24, and roughly 10 percent are age 17 or younger.

Because these figures are multiyear averages, they mask important changes during the period in the proportion of victims in the different age groups, such as the rough doubling of teenage victims ages 12 to 17 since the mid-1980s. Because they are absolute counts, they obscure the age differences in the relative risk of victimization and the changes over time in age-specific risk. Figure 5.2 presents these now-familiar differences in age-specific homicide rates, revealing the sharp growth in risk beginning in the 1980s for teenagers and young adults ages 18 to 24 (for detailed discussions of these trends see Blumstein 1995 and Chapter 2 this volume; Blumstein and Rosenfeld 1998; Fox Chapter 9 this volume). In contrast, little change occurred in the risk for children under age 12, and the adult rates display appreciable declines.

The diminishing risk in the 25- to 49-year-old group, from sixteen to about eleven victims per 100,000 population, is especially impressive –

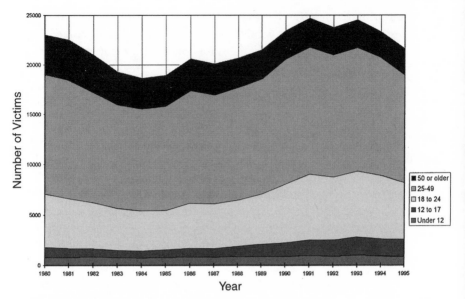

Figure 5.1. U.S. homicide victims by age from 1980–1995. Source SHR (Snyder and Finnegan, 1997).

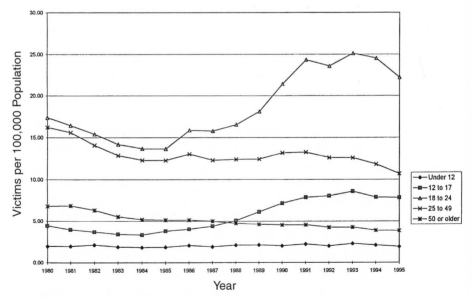

Figure 5.2. Age-specific homicide victimization rates from 1980–1995. Source SHR (Snyder and Finnegan, 1997) and the U.S. Bureau of the Census.

and fortunate – given the huge growth in their numbers as the baby boomers joined the ranks of the middle aged in the 1980s.[2] The first baby-boom cohorts born in the late 1940s and early 1950s turned 30 around 1980. The latter cohorts, born in the early 1960s, passed 30 in the 1990s. The result has been a dramatic increase over the past twenty years in the number of adults in their late twenties, thirties, and forties. The population between the ages of 25 and 49 grew by 37 percent between 1980 and 1995, from about 74 million to 101 million, while the teenage and young adult cohorts shrank in relative and absolute size. The growth rate in the African-American adult population since 1980 has been especially striking, exceeding 50 percent for both men and women (see Table 5.1).

The importance of these population increases for the nation's homicide problem is highlighted by asking what would have happened to the total homicide rate had the adult rate not fallen during the 1980s and 1990s. In 1980, 11,969 persons between the ages of 25 and 49 were victims of criminal homicide, a rate of 16.2 victims per 100,000. In 1995, that rate would have produced 16,352 homicide victims, 5,568 more than the 10,784 25–49-year-old victims recorded in the FBI's Supplementary Homicide Reports (SHR) for 1995.[3] The 5,568 additional victims, in turn, would have resulted in an overall U.S. homicide rate in 1995 of 10.3 per 100,000 population, substantially greater than actual rate of 8.2 per 100,000, and higher even than the record rate of 10.2 for 1980 (Maguire and Pastore 1998, p. 261, Table 3.111). Of course, confining attention to the extra homicides that would have occurred in 1995 had the 1980 rate remained unchanged, and ignoring those for the years 1981 to 1994, understates the full impact of the adult-homicide decline. But the point of the exercise should be clear. Adults have contributed importantly to the nation's falling homicide rate. Without that contribution, reporters and policy makers would not be pressing crime researchers to provide explanations for the decrease; they would be asking why the homicide rate was continuing at record levels in spite of declines in youth homicide.

Part of the explanation for the adults' contribution to the overall decline is relatively straightforward. As the huge baby-boom cohorts moved into adulthood, they brought down the total rate of homicide and other crimes, just as they had exerted upward pressure on crime rates when they were young, because of the sheer weight of their numbers and the well-known (if poorly understood) age difference in predatory offending and victimization (Blumstein 1995; Fox Chapter 9 this volume; Hirschi and Gottfredson 1983). But changes in the age composition of

Table 5.1. Total Population by Age and Population Ages 25–49 by Race and Sex: 1980–1995

	Population (000s)			Percent Change 1980–95
	1980	1990	1995	
Age				
Under 12	40,345	43,562	46,378	15.0
12–17	23,410	20,042	22,365	−4.5
18–24	30,022	26,738	24,926	−17.0
25–49	73,806	94,627	100,832	36.6
Over 49	58,962	63,740	68,319	15.9
Race and Sex,				
Ages 25–49				
White Males	30,624	38,250	41,971	37.0
Black Males	3,700	5,137	5,831	57.6
White Females	31,049	38,214	41,667	34.2
Black Females	4,362	5,908	6,632	52.0

Source: U.S. Bureau of the Census.

the population do not explain the observed changes in age-specific homicide rates. Adding more adults to the population does not necessarily alter the rate at which adults are killed or kill others, and why should it have *lowered* those rates? If anything, one ought to have seen constant or even increasing adult rates over time, reflecting the continuing economic disadvantage and social dislocations of the aging baby-boom cohorts. Despite their plausibility, arguments linking the youth-crime increases of the 1960s and 1970s to changes in cohort size have garnered only limited empirical support (Messner and Rosenfeld 1999, pp. 36–37). There is even less reason to assume they would be successful in explaining the adult declines of the 1980s and 1990s.[4]

Credible explanations for the decline in adult homicide, then, must be able to account for sizable decreases among younger as well as older adults. They also must account for decreases among both African-Americans and whites, both males and females, and across differing victim-offender relationships. Although adult homicide rates have fallen in nearly every race-by-sex by victim-offender category, the sharpest declines have occurred in the rate wives kill their husbands. Close inspection of these patterns is necessary for assessing the adequacy of explanations for the overall decline in adult homicide.

Sex, Race, and Victim-Offender Relationship

At every age beyond infancy, males are more likely than females to be victims of homicide, and for both sexes, the risk of homicide among African-Americans is far greater than among whites.[5] Black males between the ages of 25 and 49 were nearly 5 times more likely than black females of the same age to be a homicide victim during the period 1980–95. Homicide risk among 25- to 49-year-old black females, in turn, was 1.5 times that for white males, and almost 5 times the risk for white females (see Table 5.2).

Table 5.2. Homicide Victims per 100,000 Persons Ages 25–49 by Race, Sex, and Relationship to Offender: 1980–1995

	M	Sd	Trend[a]	
			AdjR^2	b
Black Male	92.309	13.813	.367	−1.856**
Family	8.589	3.188	.959	−.657**
Acquaintance	38.784	8.552	.806	−1.625**
Stranger	11.210	2.351	.272	−.280**
Unknown	33.727	6.704	.198	.706**
White Male	12.195	1.711	.785	−.321**
Family	1.205	.342	.907	−.069**
Acquaintance	4.668	.664	.842	−.129**
Stranger	2.246	.341	.552	−.055**
Unknown	4.076	.750	.136	−.069*
Black Female	18.998	1.587	.045	−.110
Family	4.337	1.136	.817	−.217**
Acquaintance	7.660	.804	.337	−.104**
Stranger	1.182	.235	.059	.005
Unknown	5.821	1.216	.630	.207**
White Female	3.892	.278	.702	−.050**
Family	1.326	.194	.876	−.038**
Acquaintance	1.266	.120	.066	−.002
Stranger	.338	.059	.112	−.005*
Unknown	.962	.119	.045	−.004

[a] Yearly rate regressed on time where 1980 = 0, 1981 = 1, ..., 1995 = 15.

* Coefficient one and a-half times its standard error.

** Coefficient twice its standard error.

Source: Supplementary Homicide Reports (Snyder and Finnegan 1997); U.S. Bureau of the Census.

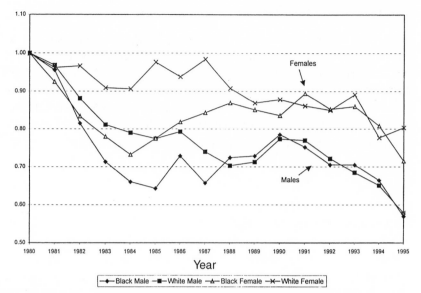

Figure 5.3. Proportional change in homicide victimization rates for persons ages 24–49 by race and sex from 1980–1995. Yearly rates are expressed as proportion of the rate in 1980. Source SHR (Snyder and Finnegan, 1997) and the U.S. Bureau of the Census.

Adult homicide rates have fallen within each race-sex group since 1980, although the declines generally have been greater and more consistent for the males. Figure 5.3 shows the changes in the victimization rates for each group. To more clearly compare the group trends, scale differences have been removed by expressing each group's yearly rates as a fraction of its rate in 1980.[6] The rates for the males dropped sharply during the first half of the 1980s, were fairly flat from the mid-1980s to 1990, and then fell again through 1995. The patterns for the females differed from one another as well as from those for the males. Until 1988, white-female victimization was reasonably stationary, at or above 90 percent of the rate in 1980, and fell modestly thereafter to about 80 percent of the 1980 rate. In contrast, the rate for black females dropped to about 75 percent of their 1980 rate during the first half of the 1980s, rose for several years, and then headed down again in the early 1990s.

Even though the group-specific rates have been somewhat erratic, especially for black females, all have trended downward since 1980, as shown by the negative slope coefficients in the last column of Table 5.2. The linear trends for the males and the white females are statistically significant.

Given their extremely high base rate of 125 homicides per 100,000 population, the downward trend for the 25- to 49-year-old black males is an especially important contributor to the overall homicide decline. If adult black males had the same victimization rate in 1995 that they had in 1980, the number of U.S. homicide deaths in 1995 would have increased by more than 3,000.[7]

Table 5.2 breaks out the race- and sex-specific time trends for adults by the relationship between the victim and offender (family, acquaintance, stranger, and unknown relationship). Figures 5.4 through 5.7 present the year-to-year changes in those trends between 1980 and 1995.

Male Victimization and Offending. Looking first at the males, one sees that the modal victim-offender relationship for both blacks and whites consists of nonfamily acquaintances. Roughly 40 percent of adult male victims were killed by acquaintances during the period. About one-third of the males were killed in incidents for which the victim-offender relationship is classified in the SHR as "unknown." That does not necessarily mean that the victim did not know the offender, only that the police were unable to classify their relationship. Some of those cases very likely do involve strangers, but many others involve offenders who knew the victim but were not arrested, or who were arrested after the police submitted the SHR report to the FBI (Riedel 1998; 1999, pp. 81–82). About 12 percent of the black male victims were killed in incidents that the police were able to classify for the SHR as stranger-homicides. A somewhat larger percentage of the white males were killed by strangers (18 percent). Finally, about one of every ten male homicide victims was killed by a family member. Given the age of the victims, the great majority of these cases involve husbands killed by their wives.[8]

For the period as a whole, then, we see little difference by race in the *relative* victimization rates of adult males according to the relationship between the victim and offender (there are, of course, very large *absolute* differences by race in all victim-offender categories). Males of either race are, on average, most likely to be killed by a nonfamily acquaintance and least likely to be killed by a family member. The year-to-year changes in victimization by victim-offender relationship also are similar for black and white males, as revealed by the trend coefficients in Table 5.2. With a single exception, the slopes on the linear trends in male victimization by victim-offender relationship are negative and statistically significant. The exception is the rate for the unknown category among black males, which trends upward after 1985 (see Figure 5.4). The sharpest declines are observed in the family category, followed by acquaintances, and then strangers.

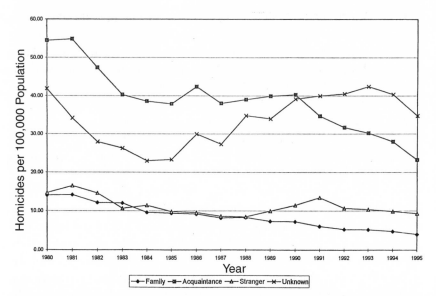

Figure 5.4. Homicide victimization rate for persons ages 25–49 by victim-offender relationship from 1980–1995. Black males. Source SHR (Snyder and Finnegan, 1997) and the U.S. Bureau of the Census.

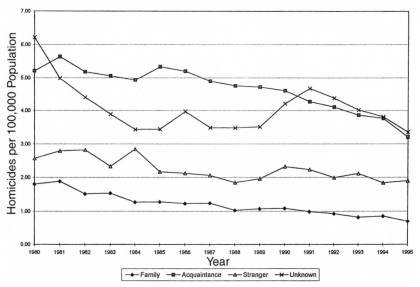

Figure 5.5. Homicide victimization rate for persons ages 25–49 by victim-offender relationship from 1980–1995. White males. Source Supplementary Homicide Reports.

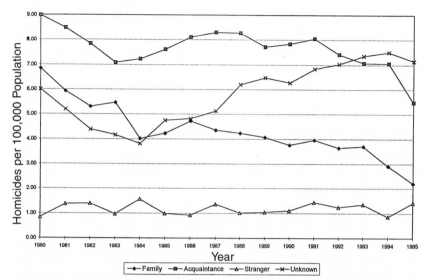

Figure 5.6. Homicide victimization rates for persons ages 25–49 by victim-offender relationship from 1980–1995. Black females. Source Supplementary Homicide Reports.

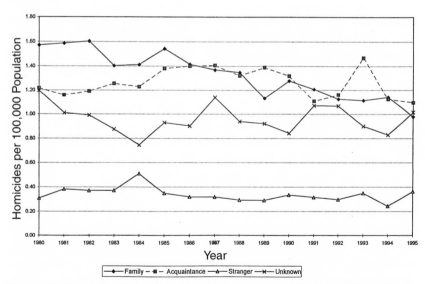

Figure 5.7. Homicide victimization rate for persons ages 25–49 by victim- offender relationship from 1980–1995. White females. Source Supplementary Homicide Reports.

The downturn in family homicide among the males is impressive. Recall that only 10 percent of adult male victims on average are killed by a family member. However, 22 percent of the total decline in the white-male victimization rate occurred in the family category. Fully 35 percent of the total decline observed for black males is attributable to the falling rate of family homicide (if the upturn in the unknown category is ignored, that figure drops to 26 percent).

The disproportionate contribution of the decline in family homicide to the overall decrease in adult-male victimization also is revealed by comparing the average annual percentage change in victimization rates across the various victim-offender categories. The family victimization rate for white males fell by 5.7 percent per year between 1980 and 1995; the comparable yearly decrease for black males was 7.6 percent.[9] The rate of victimization by acquaintances fell by 2.8 percent per year for the white males and 4.2 percent for black-males. The stranger-homicide rates decreased by 2.4 percent and 2.5 percent each year for white and black males, respectively. In general, then, male family-homicide victimization declined at twice the rate observed for the other victim-offender categories.

The time trends in adult male offending within specific victim-offender relationships are similar to those for victimization, especially for the black males (see Table 5.3). Their rate of family offending dropped by 5.6 percent per year between 1980 and 1985 and by 3.9 percent and 3.0 percent, respectively, in the acquaintance and stranger categories. No significant change over the period occurred in the rate black males killed persons with whom their relationship was officially unknown. There was, however, a significant increase in victims in the unknown category, resulting in a much larger fraction of victims than offenders in this category (34 percent of victims v. 9 percent of offenders). This difference implies that the growth in the unknowns observed for the victims is due primarily to an increase in the rate younger persons were killing adults.

The offending patterns for the white males are comparable, although the differences across the victim-offender categories are not as large as those seen for the white male victims or the black male offenders. The rate at which white males kill family members dropped by 3.4 percent per year, compared with a 2.5 percent yearly decline in the acquaintance category, a 3.8 percent decline in stranger offending, and a 3.5 percent decrease in the unknown category. Compared with the victimization patterns, then, the time trend in family offending is not as dominant. On the other hand, the average *level* of family offending among white males (2.1 per 100,000)

Table 5.3. *Male Homicide Offenders Per 100,000 Persons Ages 25–49 by Race and Relationship to Victim: 1980–1995*

| | M | Sd | Trend[a] | |
			AdjR²	b
Black	73.052	13.593	.776	−2.539**
Family	9.771	2.705	.904	−.542**
Acquaintance	41.106	8.387	.833	−1.619**
Stranger	13.318	2.914	.394	−.403**
Unknown	8.860	1.808	.067	.025
White	10.272	1.541	.906	−.309**
Family	2.072	.346	.920	−.070**
Acquaintance	5.382	.721	.773	−.135**
Stranger	1.756	.355	.801	−.067**
Unknown	1.062	.310	.277	−.037**

[a] Yearly rate regressed on time where 1980 = 0, 1981 = 1, ..., 1995 = 15.
* Coefficient one and one-half times its standard error.
** Coefficient twice its standard error.
Source: Supplementary Homicide Reports (Snyder and Finnegan 1997); U.S. Bureau of the Census.

is almost twice as large as their level of family victimization (1.2 per 100,000). Twenty percent of white-male homicide offenses between 1980 and 1995 involved a family member, compared with less than 10 percent of victimizations.

In summary, for the males, family homicide, which in most cases means spousal homicide, comprises a comparatively small fraction of all homicides, whether one looks at victimization or at offending patterns. However, the downturn in family homicides has contributed disproportionately to the overall decline in male victimization, and to a lesser extent, offending. Whatever factors are associated with the general homicide decline for adult males, therefore, seem to have been especially important in the category of family and marital relationships. Alternatively, the factors responsible for the downturn in family homicide differ from those operating in other victim-offender relationships. One such factor is the marked decrease over the past twenty years in the fraction of young adults who are married (Rosenfeld 1997). Before assessing the role of this and other changes in explaining the adult homicide decline, one needs to consider the homicide trends by victim-offender relationship for adult women.

Female Victimization. Women are more likely than men to be killed by a family member. Between 1980 and 1995, 23 percent of adult black female-homicide victims and 34 percent of white female victims were killed by a family member, typically their husband (see Table 5.2). Family homicide is not the most prevalent form of victimization for black women, who are more likely to be killed by a nonfamily acquaintance or by an unknown offender (again, not always or necessarily a stranger) than by a family member. For white women, on the other hand, victimization by a family member is a little more common than by a nonfamily acquaintance, and far more likely than by a stranger or unknown offender.

For black and white women, the downward trend in homicide between 1980 and 1995 is dominated by the decrease in family victimization (see Figures 5.6–5.7). Fully three-quarters of the total decline for the whites is attributable to the drop in family homicide. Family homicides declined by 2.9 percent per year, compared with decreases of .15 percent, 1.5 percent and .42 percent in the acquaintance-, stranger-, and unknown-offender categories. The total victimization rate for black women fell only slightly over the period, at a rate of about .5 percent per year. However, the stationary total rate observed for black women represents the combination of contrasting trends within the different victim-offender relationships. Black women's risk of being killed by a family member fell by 5 percent per year between 1980 and 1995. Their risk of being killed by a nonfamily acquaintance decreased by 1.4 percent. Little change occurred in the probability of stranger victimization (.42 percent), while black women's risk of victimization by an unknown offender increased at an annual rate of 3.6 percent.[10]

Taken together, the time trends in adult-homicide rates tell a fairly consistent story across the differing victim-offender categories, for blacks and whites, males and females. With few exceptions, the within-race trends are negative, and in all cases the declines are greater in the family category than in the other victim-offender relationships. These patterns suggest that the conditions responsible for the decline in adult homicide rates are both pervasive – they affect all victim-offender relationships – and specific – the more pronounced declines are in the family category. A comprehensive assessment of the sources of the decline in adult homicide is beyond the scope of this chapter. Instead, I focus on two factors that appear to be strongly implicated in the general decrease in adult homicide and the specific drop in intimate killings: the explosive growth in incarceration rates in recent decades and the changing living arrangements among young adults associated with declining rates of marriage. Although the influence of increasing rates of incarceration pervades differing homicide circumstances and victim-offender relationships, it is reasonable to assume somewhat stronger incarceration effects for homicides resulting from other criminal activity, such as robbery or drug trafficking, than for those associated with arguments between acquaintances or intimates. If that is true, then the sharper declines observed for the family homicides compared with stranger homicides, which are more likely to involve a concurrent felony, imply that other factors also are associated with the drop in the family events. I begin my assessment with an analysis of incarceration effects on the general decline in adult homicides and then turn to the specific effects of falling marriage rates on the downward trend in intimate-partner homicide.

The Effect of Incarceration Growth on the Homicide Decline

The rate of imprisonment in the United States has risen sharply over the past two decades, tripling from 1980 to the mid-1990s (Blumstein and Beck 1999). It seems difficult to believe that an increase of this magnitude in the prison population would have no impact on the crime rate, including the rate of homicide. Prisoners are not randomly drawn from the population; by definition, they are drawn from the ranks of criminal offenders, indeed the most serious of offenders. Barring full and instantaneous replacement of imprisoned offenders with new recruits, as the ranks of offenders are drawn down through increasing imprisonment, the level of offending (outside the prisons) should drop. As long as criminal offenders are more likely to commit homicide than nonoffenders, then even though persons convicted of homicide comprise only a small fraction of imprisoned offenders, the level of homicide should decline as the rate of imprisonment increases. All else equal.

That is the catch, of course. Sharp disagreement exists regarding the impact of incarceration on crime rates, and much of the debate centers on the influence of other factors that, taken together, may counterbalance the crime-reduction effects of the rise in incarceration. A simple model predicts that increases in imprisonment should result in decreases in crime, because prisons incapacitate offenders, preventing them from victimizing the general public, or because would-be offenders view imprisonment as an intolerable risk and are deterred from committing crimes. In practice, however, it has proven difficult to separate the incapacitation effects from the deterrent effects of imprisonment (Blumstein, Cohen, and Nagin

1978). In addition, decreases in homicide linked to imprisonment could be offset by increases associated with other forces discussed in this volume (e.g., demographic changes, economic swings, drug markets) or the criminogenic effects of incarceration itself (Blumstein and Rosenfeld 1998; Miller 1996).

The small number of studies of the influence of incarceration rates on changes in the level of homicide typically combine incapacitation and deterrence in a single measure and do not attempt to isolate their separate effects. Those studies have produced disparate results, some showing small or nonsignificant effects (Levitt 1996; Marvell and Moody 1994; Zimring and Hawkins 1995), others showing stronger impacts (Devine, Sheley, and Smith 1988; Marvell and Moody 1997). The latter studies are of particular interest, not because they conclude that increases in incarceration result in homicide declines, but because, consistent with the present investigation, their conclusions are based on national-level time-series analyses of incarceration and homicide trends. They also meet the ceteris paribus criterion for assessing the effects of incarceration. Both are based on multiple-regression analyses of homicide trends that, in principle, permit assessments of incarceration effects controlling for other determinants of homicide.

The two studies produce similar estimates of the effect of incarceration growth on homicide rates, and those estimates imply a sizeable impact. Devine et al. (1988) find that growth in imprisonment is associated with drops in the homicide rate ranging from –1.5 to –1.9, depending on the particular model specification. Because these coefficients are elasticities, they can be interpreted as the percentage change in homicide associated with a one-percent change in the prison population. The results imply that a 10 percent increase in the number of prisoners produces a 15 to 20 percent decline in homicide.

Marvell and Moody (1997) replicate the Devine et al. analysis on a longer time series (1930–94), incorporate additional controls (including a 1985–91 trend indicator to capture the rise in crack markets), and subject their models to multiple sensitivity tests. For the full series, they find an elasticity associated with growth in the prison population of –1.3. For the more recent period of 1962–94, the incarceration effect is somewhat larger and equal to the lower-bound estimate from Devine et al. (1988) of –1.5. A 10 percent increase in the number of prisoners, in other words, is associated with a 15 percent decline in homicide.

These are impressively large estimates of the effect of incarceration on homicide, so large, as Marvell and Moody (1997, p. 207) point out, they may seem implausible. The fact that two independent investigations produced highly similar results is encouraging, but neither is it terribly surprising given that they utilize similar methods and data. Confidence in these regression-based estimates of incarceration effects on homicide would be heightened were they confirmed by the results of a distinct estimation procedure. I employ a very different method for estimating the impact of recent growth in incarceration on yearly change in homicides. The method assumes incarceration averts homicides only through incapacitation (i.e., assumes no deterrence effects), makes no assumptions about other conditions affecting homicide, and requires measurements of only three quantities: yearly change in homicides, yearly change in prisoners, and the number of homicides those prisoners would have committed had they remained free. Nonetheless, it produces results strikingly close to those from the two previous investigations.

The estimation procedure is based on a simple question: Given a net increase in imprisoned offenders from one year to the next, how many homicides would they have committed had they remained free, and therefore, how many homicides were averted by their incarceration? Assume, for example, that in year t the number of inmates increased by 50,000 and the number of homicides decreased by 500. Assume, further, a homicide rate for those offenders of .0015 (i.e., 150 homicides per 100,000 population). Had they not gone to prison, then, they would have produced an additional 75 homicides (50,000 × .0015), reducing the size of the decline for the year to 425. Incarceration growth in year t, therefore, averted 75 homicides, 15 percent of the observed decline ([75/500] × 100).

Even though this example relates declines in homicide to increases in incarceration, the procedure requires no assumptions about the direction of the year-to-year change in either prisoners or homicides. If the number of homicides had increased by 500 in year t, it still would be possible to calculate the effect of incarceration growth on that increase. If the number of prisoners had not changed, 575 homicides would have occurred in year t, 15 percent above the observed increase of 500 ([75/500] × 100).[11]

The critical unknown in this estimation procedure, of course, is the offender homicide rate. Prior studies of the incapacitation effects of incarceration on other types of criminal offending have relied on arrest records or offender self-reports to estimate the number of crimes averted by imprisonment (see Blumstein, Cohen, Roth et al. 1986, for a review). Whatever the merits of such approaches with respect to other offense types, they are of doubtful reliability for estimating the effects of incarceration on homicide. Offenders are likely to underreport homicides even in confidential surveys, and neither arrest records nor self-reports can provide information about events that have not yet occurred. For high-frequency offenses such as assault, burglary, or robbery, records of past behavior, in principle, can be used to gauge the frequency of the same behavior in the future. But for a low-probability event such as homicide, there is no past record in most cases, and therefore little basis for estimating the counterfactual of the number of events averted through incarceration.

In the absence of reliable data for *individuals,* an alternative is to use data for the *populations* from which imprisoned offenders are drawn as the basis for estimating their homicide rate. Prison inmates are drawn disproportionately from high-risk urban communities. A reasonable basis for estimating their homicide rate is the rate for those communities.[12] That is the approach taken here. Using microdata from police case files, I computed the homicide rates for the top decile of census tracts in the cities of St. Louis and Chicago for the period 1980–94, the most recent year for which the Chicago data were available.[13] To allow for change over time in the level of homicide, the rates were computed for three subperiods: 1980–84, during which the total homicide rate in both cities declined; 1985–89, during which homicide rates increased; and 1990–94, when homicide rates peaked and began to decline. Homicide trends in St. Louis and Chicago not only parallel one another during this fifteen-year period but also closely track changes in the national rate. It seems reasonable, therefore, to use data from these cities to estimate national-level trends in urban homicide risk.

Little change was observed in either city in the homicide rates for the top decile of tracts over the period 1980–89. Throughout the decade of the 1980s, the yearly rates for St. Louis averaged 1.4 per 1,000 tract population, and those for Chicago were 1.15 per 1,000 population. During the 1990–94 period, the rates for the highest risk tracts rose in both cities, to 1.8 in St. Louis and 1.25 in Chicago. Based on these results, I estimated the homicide rates for imprisoned offenders to be .00125 for the period 1980–89 and .0015 for 1990–95.

These levels of homicide – 125 to 150 deaths per 100,000 population – are nearly 20 times higher than those recorded for the nation as a whole during the 1980s and early 1990s (Maguire and Pastore 1998, p. 261, Table 3.111). The highest-risk communities in two large cities will have above-average homicide rates by construction, but it is fair to ask whether the use of rates of this magnitude will result in exaggerated estimates of the number of homicides averted through incarceration. Although that possibility exists, there is good reason to suppose that the homicide rate from high-risk urban areas actually understates the true rate for offender populations and consequently will lead to low estimates of incarceration effects. Offenders may be highly concentrated in high-risk areas, however most residents in those areas are not criminal offenders and do not have an appreciable imprisonment risk. The denominators used to create the estimated homicide rate for prison-bound offenders, therefore, will be inflated by the inclusion of nonoffenders with little risk for imprisonment. The resulting "offender" homicide rate is thereby reduced, and the estimated impact of incarceration on homicide will be biased downward.[14]

The other two values needed to estimate incarceration effects on homicide, the yearly change in homicides and the yearly change in state and federal prisoners, are taken from, respectively, the SHR (Snyder and Finnegan 1997) and the Bureau of Justice Statistics (reported in Maguire and Pastore 1998, p. 464, Table 6.1). These data are presented in Table 5.4 as multiyear averages for the three subperiods 1980–85, 1985–90, and 1990–95. For each subperiod, the figures represent the average year-to-year change in the number of homicides and the number of prisoners in the United States.[15] The multiyear averages provide a more reliable basis for estimating time trends in incarceration effects than single-year changes in the number of homicide victims or incarcerated persons. The SHR counts may be inexact for a single year (e.g., if the incident occurs in one year but the victim does not die until the next year), and we cannot be certain that persons admitted to prison during a given year otherwise would have been in the community (some may have been incarcerated in a local jail).

Finally, two homicide counts are used to estimate incarceration effects, the total number of victims and the number killed by adults between 18 and 49 years old (based on the age of the oldest offender). The latter is the more accurate gauge of the incapacitation effect of incarceration on homicide because only one percent of imprisoned offenders are under the age of 18 (Bureau of Justice Statistics 1993, p. 3). However, to facilitate comparison with the regression-based studies of incarceration effects, which do not incorporate such an age restriction, I have produced separate estimates based on total victims and those killed by adults.

Reflecting the national trends reviewed earlier, the average yearly change in homicide victims was negative during the early 1980s, turned up during the late 1980s, and then turned down again during the first half of the 1990s. By contrast, no such break in trend characterizes the yearly change in the prisoner population. As shown in Table 5.4, during an average year in the early 1980s, 33,000 to 34,000 offenders were added to the nation's state and federal prisons. A decade later, the annual growth in prisoners had increased to 67,000. Given the growth in imprisoned offenders that prevailed during the early 1980s and an estimated homicide rate of .00125 for those offenders, on average, 42 homicides were averted by incarceration each year (33,599 × .00125). Total homicides declined by 812 per year during the first half of the 1980s. Therefore, 5.2 percent of that decline is attributable to the growth in prisoners ([42/812] × 100). Victims of adult offenders declined by 420 per year during the period, and 10 percent of that reduction is associated with the increase in incarceration (see Table 5.4).

The estimated effects of incarceration on homicides during the growth period of the late 1980s are somewhat larger than those for the earlier period, especially for homicides committed by adults. The 51,158 additional prisoners each year between 1985 and 1990 averted 64 homicides per year, or 7.2 percent and 18.9 percent of total victims and victims of adults (see Table 5.4). Because the number of victims was growing during this period, these percentages reflect the *additional* growth in homicides averted by the growth in prisoners. In the absence of the incarceration increase, in other words, there would have been 7 percent more total victims, on average, and 19 percent more victims of adults per year during the late 1980s.

The growth in incarceration contributed importantly to the homicide decline of the early 1990s, accounting for more than one-fourth of the drop in total victims and victims of adults. The sizable incarceration effects

Table 5.4. Estimated Effects of Incarceration Growth on Yearly Change in Homicide, 1980–1995

	1980–85	1985–90	1990–95
Yearly Change in Total Victims	−812	892	−369
Yearly Change in Victims of Adults[a]	−420	338	−377
Yearly Change in Prisoners	33,599	51,158	67,032
Homicides Averted[b]	42	64	100
Percent Impact			
Total Victims	5.2	7.2	27.1
Victims of Adults	10.0	18.9	26.5

[a] Oldest offender between 18 and 49 years old.

[b] Based on estimated per capita rates of .00125 (1980–89) and .0015 (1990–95).

Source: Victim data from *Supplementory Homicide Reports* (Snyder and Finnegan 1997); prisoner data from Maguire and Pastore (1998, p. 464, Table 6.1).

observed during this period were due both to the continuing growth in prisoners and to the higher estimated rate of homicide among them had they remained free (.0015 homicides per capita compared with .00125 during the 1980s). However, it is important to note that, when expressed as percentages as in Table 5.4, the size of the incarceration effects also is influenced by whatever other factors are contributing to homicide trends. When the impact of those other factors is weak, resulting in small year-to-year changes in homicide, the *relative* effect of incarceration on those changes will increase. When other factors are more important, larger homicide swings will occur, and the relative effect of incarceration on those changes will be diminished.

Such changes in the relative impact of incarceration are apparent in the data reported in Table 5.4. Compare, for example, the incarceration effect on total victims during the late 1980s with the much larger effect in the early 1990s. During the late 1980s, homicide offending rates of youths rose sharply, and much of that increase was driven by the firearm violence associated with the growth in urban crack markets (Blumstein 1995). The escalation in youth homicide was largely responsible for the increase in total victims observed in Table 5.4, and the impact of incarceration on that increase was relatively small. Youth-homicide rates peaked in 1993 and then began to fall (see Figure 5.2), resulting in a much smaller net change in total homicides and a larger incarceration impact.

Because youth under the age of 18 have a very small incarceration risk, it can be misleading to use fluctuations in total victims as the basis for conclusions about the effect of incarceration on homicide. The time trends observed for victims of adults are much more consistent with an "incarceration story." The year-to-year fluctuation in victims of adult offenders is considerably smaller than the fluctuation in total victims through the end of the 1980s, resulting in correspondingly larger incarceration effects. The growth in the relative impact of incarceration on the year-to-year changes in victims of adults, from 10 percent in the early 1980s to 26 percent during the first half of the 1990s, closely reflects the increase in what might be termed the absolute incarceration effect, which grew from 42 homicides averted per year in the early 1980s to 100 averted a decade later. By contrast, the relative impact of incarceration on total victims grew much more rapidly than what would be expected strictly on the basis of the increase in homicides averted by incarceration. The more volatile fluctuations in the total victim trends reflect the operation of several factors, none more important than the epidemic-like outbreak of youth firearm violence in the mid-1980s (Blumstein and Rosenfeld 1998).

Those factors had much less influence on adult offending. The smoother trajectory of adult homicide is more consistent with the monotonic increase in incarceration. That increase, it appears from this analysis, has had an appreciable and growing effect on the decline in adult homicide since 1980.

It remains to be determined whether the incarceration effects produced by the estimation procedure employed here are in line with the regression-based estimates reviewed earlier. To compare the alternative estimates, it is necessary to transform the effects reported in this investigation to elasticities (i.e., the percentage change in homicides associated with a one-percent change in prisoners). We also must average the effects over the entire 1980–95 period for comparison, because the previous research does not report separate estimates for smaller subperiods. The closest comparison period from that research is 1962–94, for which Marvell and Moody (1997) estimated an incarceration effect of –1.5 percent. In other words, a one-percent increase in the number of prisoners is associated with a 1.5 percent decrease in the number of homicides.

The number of inmates in state and federal prisons grew 8.7 percent per year between 1980 and 1995 (Bureau of Justice Statistics 1995, 1996). That growth, in turn, reduced the total number of homicide victims by 13.2 percent and victims of adults by 18.5 percent each year (the simple average of the subgroup percentages presented in Table 5.4). Converting these changes to elasticities, we observe that a one-percent increase in prisoners is associated with a –1.5 percent change in total homicides and a –2.1 percent change in victims of adults. These results are virtually identical to those reported by Marvell and Moody (1997).

The strong convergence between the results produced by two very different analytical approaches increases confidence in the assumptions underlying each of them. Increases in incarceration appear to reduce the number of homicides in the United States. Those reductions have grown in recent years with the escalation in incarceration rates, and are now sizeable, accounting for declines of 15 to 20 percent in homicide for each 10 percent increase in the number of prisoners. To my mind that must be counted as good news, but it comes with a huge price tag and perhaps confounding effects that, factored in, would dampen enthusiasm for incarceration as the nation's main crime-control policy.

The United States has embarked on what one analyst has termed "a massive 'experiment' in incarceration unprecedented in this country or in any other advanced society" (Currie 1998, p. 95; see also Spelman, Chapter 4). There is no question that the experiment is costly. The nation's corrections budget is approaching $40 billion annually. A fiscal commitment of this scale, even during periods of economic expansion, inevitably reduces the resources available for education, health, child welfare, and other forms of state spending that conceivably have crime-reduction effects of their own (Mauer 1999, pp. 81, 180–81). Are the gains in homicides averted worth the cost?

That is essentially a political and moral question, not a scientific one, and therefore it cannot be answered by the results of the analysis presented here or by any research on the impact of incarceration on crime. True, one can calculate, at least roughly, the cost of averting homicides through incarceration, but one cannot say whether that cost is justifiable. It costs approximately $20,000 to keep an offender in prison for a year. Given the estimates of homicide risk employed in this study, averting a single homicide during the early 1990s required a net increase of 670 prisoners at a total cost of $13.4 million per year (exclusive of other legal costs or the savings from averting other crimes).[16] At that price, the 100 homicides averted annually through incarceration from 1990 to 1995 cost the nation over $1 billion a year (see Table 5.4). Even if I have considerably underestimated the homicide risk for imprisoned offenders, the cost of reducing homicide by increasing incarceration would remain very high. Doubling the number of homicides averted through incarceration would reduce the cost by half, to $6.7 million for each victim saved per year. Is $13.4 million too much to spend to avert a single homicide? Is $6.7 million? Would we be better off if the $1 billion were spent on preschool programs, parent training, vocational training, drug treatment, and other promising prevention programs (see Sherman et al. 1998)?

Although research cannot answer such questions, it can and should inform the public debate over the benefits and costs of the nation's increasing reliance on incarceration to reduce crime and violence. The need for such research is critical. If we are just beginning to learn the extent to which incarceration might reduce homicide, we know next to nothing about the effects of imprisonment on the conditions that *produce* homicide. Critics of current corrections policy insist that the massive increase in incarceration over the past two decades has reduced the job prospects of former inmates, depleted marriage markets, destabilized families, and increased street-gang activity – all factors associated with high levels of crime and violence, particularly in the inner-city communities affected most by the incarceration boom (Mauer 1999; Miller 1996; Vera Institute of Justice 1996). If the critics are correct, the growth in prisoners has indirectly contributed to the annual homicide totals that are then muted by the incapacitation effects of incarceration.

Much speculation but little systematic research underlies the criminogenic hypothesis regarding the effects on individuals and communities of the incarceration experiment of the past two decades. Without such evidence, the significance of the incapacitation effects reported here and elsewhere remains uncertain, and it would be unwise to use those results to justify the cost of current policy or future increases in incarceration.

Declining Domesticity and the Drop in Intimate Partner Homicide

Even if future research discloses no criminogenic effects of incarceration and replicates the incapacitation effects found in this study, other factors in addition to the escalation in imprisonment must be responsible for the observed decline in adult homicide since 1980. At most, incarceration explains 15 to 20 percent of that decline. The variation in homicide trends according to the relationship between the victim and offender also suggests that we look beyond incarceration for additional explanatory factors. The decrease in adult homicide rates has been extensive, cutting across all victim-offender relationships, but it has been especially sharp in the family category. For reasons noted earlier, it is not obvious why the incapacitation effects of incarceration should be stronger for victims and offenders who are related to one another than for those less intimately acquainted. Although the incarceration boom may have played a part, prior research indicates that the decrease in family and intimate-partner homicide over the past two decades also is associated with improvements in the status of women, the rise of domestic violence prevention services, and changes in the living arrangements of young men and women associated with declining marriage rates (Browne and Williams 1993; Dugan, Nagin, and Rosenfeld 1999; Rosenfeld 1997).

My focus here is on the decline in marriage. Falling marriage rates reduce intimate-partner homicides through a simple mechanism: opportunity. To become the victim of an intimate-partner homicide, you have to be married to or otherwise intimately involved with your killer. To my knowledge, reliable trend data on the number of boyfriends and girlfriends in the population do not exist, and so it is difficult to determine whether the *rate* of nonmarital intimate homicide is rising or falling. The *number* of such killings has risen slightly over the last twenty years, but not nearly enough to offset the decline in spousal murders. Even so, married persons continue to account for most intimate-partner homicides, 60 percent in 1995, down from about 75 percent in 1980 (Greenfield et al. 1998). For these reasons, it seems fair to assume that the decline in the spousal-homicide rates dominates the trends in intimate-partner homicide more generally, and therefore, reasonable to ask how much the falling rate of marriage might have to do with that decline.

Marriage rates have plummeted among young adults in the United States. In 1980 about one-half of women between the ages of 20 and 24 had never been married. By 1996 that fraction increased to 70 percent. Over the same period, the percentage of women between 25 and 29 who had never been married grew from approximately 20 to 40 percent. Although considerably smaller, the fraction of 30- to 34-year-old single women also doubled, from 10 percent in 1980 to 20 percent in 1996 (U.S. Bureau of the Census 1984, 1998). These sharp declines in the propensity to marry have occurred in the young-adult age groups with the highest levels of risk for intimate-partner violence. How much has the drop in marriage contributed to the decline in spousal killings?

I address this question by estimating the change in the number of married intimate-partner homicide victims that would have occurred between 1980 and 1995 had the rate of spousal homicide remained constant and only the number of married persons (the denominator of the rate) changed. This "expected" change in the number of victims assuming no change in the rate of victimization is then compared to the observed change in victims. That comparison permits an assessment of the extent to which the change in the number of married victims is attributable to the change in the number of married persons.

As an example, consider the decrease in the number of 20- to 29-year-old black men murdered by their wives or ex-wives. The number of such killings fell by 88, to 24 in 1995 from 112 in 1980.[17] There were 906,000 married or divorced black men in this age group in 1980, yielding a victimization rate of 12.4 per 100,000. By 1995, the number of married or divorced black men in their twenties had fallen to 537,000. At the rate they were killed by their wives or ex-wives in 1980, 67 black men in their twenties would have been victims of spousal homicide in 1995 (.000124 × 537,000). The expected change between 1980 and 1995 in 20- to 29-year-old black male victims, then, is −45 (67 − 112), compared to the observed change of −88. Therefore, the expected change in victims accounts for roughly one-half of the observed change.

Tables 5.5 and 5.6 present the victimization rates and compare the observed and expected changes between 1980 and 1995 in spousal homicide for 20- to 44-year-old blacks and whites. Given the difference in their marriage rates, the results are broken out separately for the younger-adult age group between the ages of 20 and 29 and the older group between 30 and 44. Table 5.5 presents the results for males and Table 5.6 reports those for females.

The results reproduce the substantial declines in spousal killings reported earlier in the trends for family homicide. The sharpest decreases

Table 5.5. Male Spousal Homicide Victimization by Race and Age: 1980–1995[a]

	1980	1995	Observed Change	Expected Change[b]
Black				
Ages 20–29				
Cases[c]	112	24	−88	−45
Population[d]	906	537		
Rate[e]	12.4	4.47		
Ages 30–44				
Cases[c]	211	66	−145	73
Population[d]	1,723	2,329		
Rate[e]	12.2	2.83		
White				
Ages 20–29				
Cases[c]	65	18	−47	−20
Population[d]	8,446	5,807		
Rate[e]	.77	.31		
Ages 30–44				
Cases[c]	176	76	−100	57
Population[d]	16,277	21,595		
Rate[e]	1.08	.35		
Total Males				
Cases[c]	564	184	−380	60
Population[d]	27,352	30,268		
Rate[e]	2.06	.61		

[a] Victim counts and rates based on three-year averages (1979–1981, 1994–1996).

[b] See text for calculation of expected change.

[c] Common-law and ex-spouses included.

[d] Currently married and divorced males (in 000s).

[e] Per 100,000 population.

Source: Supplementary Homicide Reports; U.S. Bureau of the Census.

Table 5.6. Female Spousal Homicide Victimization by Race and Age: 1980–1995[a]

	1980	1995	Observed Change	Expected Change[b]
Black				
Ages 20–29				
Cases[c]	131	46	–85	–43
Population[d]	1,223	822		
Rate[e]	10.7	5.60		
Ages 30–44				
Cases[c]	152	86	–66	67
Population[d]	2,002	2,890		
Rate[e]	7.59	2.98		
White				
Ages 20–29				
Cases[c]	200	118	–82	–53
Population[d]	10,838	7,970		
Rate[e]	1.84	1.48		
Ages 30–44				
Cases[c]	258	240	–18	101
Population[d]	16,878	23,482		
Rate[e]	1.53	1.02		
Total Females				
Cases[c]	741	490	–251	101
Population[d]	30,941	35,164		
Rate[e]	2.40	1.39		

[a] Victim counts and rates based on three-year averages (1979–1981, 1994–1996).
[b] See text for calculation of expected change.
[c] Common-law and ex-spouses included.
[d] Currently married and divorced females (in 000s).
[e] Per 100,000 population.
Source: Supplementary Homicide Reports; U.S. Bureau of the Census.

in victimization rates, on the order of 50 to 75 percent, are observed for the black males, white males, and black females. The white females, by comparison, exhibit more modest decreases of 20 to 33 percent. The results in Tables 5.5 and 5.6 also reveal sizable effects on the spousal-homicide trends of the changes in marriage rates – but only for the younger-adult groups. I have already shown that the drop in marriage explains about one-half of the decline in spousal homicide for black men in their twenties. Generally the same is true for the younger white men, black women, and white women. Changes in marriage rates explain 43 percent, 51 percent and 65 percent, respectively, of the observed declines in spousal homicides for these groups. However, the number of spousal homicides also drops between 1980 and 1995 for the older-adult groups, and none of these declines is explained by changes in the number of married persons. Changes in the number of married persons would lead us to expect *increases* in spousal killings for the older groups.

Differential population growth by age helps to explain why changes in marriage account for much of the decrease in spousal homicide in the younger group and none of it in the older group. As in the younger group, marriage rates have declined over the past twenty years by more than one-half for adults in their thirties and early forties (U.S. Bureau of the Census 1984, 1998), but those declines have not been sufficient to offset increases in the *number* of married middle-aged adults brought about by the huge growth in size of the baby-boom cohorts documented at the beginning of this chapter. Nevertheless, as shown in Tables 5.5 and 5.6, spousal homicides have decreased in the older groups. If declining "domesticity" cannot explain these changes, then what does?

Some of the drop in intimate-partner homicide among the baby boomers might be due to the influence of domestic violence services and improvements in women's status. The expansion in incarceration also might have played a role, by removing violent men from families and by reducing marriage and family formation in the most violent communities. Declining marriage rates, by this logic, reduce domestic violence not simply through diminished opportunity, but also through a selection process that results in a lower propensity to violence on the part of those who do marry (Rosenfeld 1997).

Additional research is needed to test such speculations about the demographic, social, and policy changes associated with the decline in intimate-partner homicide. Researchers also should consider the possibility that *cultural* transformations have, in effect, reduced the tolerance for domestic violence in the United States. Straus (1995) reports a substantial drop since the late 1960s in the proportion of the population approving of a husband slapping his wife's face (no change occurred in public support for a wife slapping her husband). Straus argues that reduced tolerance for domestic violence is responsible in part for decreases in the rate husbands assault their wives. But changes in cultural norms may have contributed to the decline in adult violence more generally. It is possible that American adults are becoming, in a word, civilized.

The Civilizing Process and the Decline in Adult Homicide

The decline in adult homicide in the United States has been substantial, widespread, and enduring. Although such predictions are always hazardous, it does not appear to be part of a cyclical process that is likely to turn up soon – if anything, it is countercyclical. The adult rates dropped during periods of high and low unemployment, falling and rising income levels, and during both the growth and the decline phase of the youth-firearm-violence epidemic (Blumstein and Rosenfeld 1998). It follows that the conditions responsible for the downward trend in adult homicide themselves must be relatively enduring features of the social and political order. We have examined two such conditions, the decline in marriage and the increase in imprisonment. Neither shows signs of reversing in the near future, although their rate of change might slow, as marriage rates for young adults approach zero, and if some critics are correct, the marginal costs of future incarceration growth begin to increase. Alterations in the living arrangements of young adults and the incarceration experiment of the last quarter of the twentieth century are, at most, contributing causes of the decline in adult homicide. Neither alone nor in combination do they fully explain the breadth, depth, or length of the decline. Nor are alternative accounts based on standard economic or criminological theories readily apparent. It has proven less difficult, in retrospect, to explain the abrupt and unexpected youth-homicide epidemic of the late 1980s and early 1990s than the long and steady decline in adult homicide.

If church is the last refuge of scoundrels, "culture" is the final recourse of social scientists in search of explanations when existing economic, social, and political theories have been exhausted. Culture consists of the values, norms, beliefs, and sensibilities of a people. Cultural theories are not unknown in criminology, but they are usually invoked to explain high or increasing levels of violence. A recent example is Nisbett's explanation of the Southern subculture of violence (Nisbett and Cohen 1996; see also Butterfield 1995). An important exception is Norbert Elias's (1994) theory of the *civilizing process*.[18]

Elias sought to explain the general decline in interpersonal violence in Western societies in terms of evolving cultural sensibilities that define displays of aggressive behavior as distasteful, unsightly, uncouth, and "animalistic." The key psychological aspect of the civilizing process is *self-control*. As Garland (1990, p. 222) writes, "the civilizing process produces individuals of heightened sensibilities whose psychological structures are heavily loaded with restraints, self-controls, and inhibitions." The corollary at the social level is the expansion of formal institutions of social control and monopolization of the means of violence by the state. The result is reduced tolerance for violence as a means of settling disputes or acquiring status in everyday life.

Elias's thesis has been invoked to explain the centuries-long decline in interpersonal aggression in European societies. Some debate exists regarding its application to the United States, where traditions of self-help and resistance to centralized state power persisted well into the twentieth century (see Gurr 1989). However, a modified version of his argument does seem consistent with what Zimring and Hawkins (1997, pp. 213–14) suggest is a growing intolerance for interpersonal violence, lethal violence in particular, in the United States. Americans have enjoyed steady declines in traumatic injury and death in recent decades, on the job, on the roads, and in their homes. Those declines, in turn, have created heightened "social expectations of progress in public safety" (p. 60). In such a climate, it would not be surprising to observe elevated levels of fear even as overall rates of crime decline or the application of "zero tolerance" policies in schools where levels of violence are already at or near zero (Glassner 1999). Nor is the expanded use of incarceration as a means of social control inconsistent with a growing intolerance for violence in everyday life. The modern prison substitutes for more visible and disorderly forms of violent punishment, and in fact, is one of the major achievements of the civilizing process (Garland 1990, pp. 234–37). Even capital punishment is compatible with the requirements of a civilized society, as long as it is executed behind the scenes as a painless quasi-medical procedure (p. 244). The civilizing process, it should be noted, does not reduce the quantity of *evil* in society, only the unauthorized and unregulated use of violence.

Finally, we should expect a society with strong democratic traditions that is undergoing the civilizing process to elevate freedom from interpersonal violence to the status of a *right*. The victims' rights movement can be understood as the final step in the full institutionalization of the criminal justice system through the creation of a formal role, with explicit privileges and prerogatives, for crime victims as well as offenders. The domestic violence movement arguably has been even more successful in gaining formal recognition for the rights of a special class of victims, because it is able to embed the procedural guarantees of the victims' rights movement within a powerful liberationist ideology. The movement sends a clear and potent cultural signal that women have a right to be free from male violence. The full effects of that message on levels of intimate-partner violence may extend well beyond the specific reductions associated with the hotlines, shelters, restraining orders, and other protective mechanisms the movement has spawned. According to recent ethnographic research, the cultural message that women are entitled to nonviolent relationships with men is not limited to the middle-class and may have important consequences for marriage and family formation. Working-class and poor women interviewed in one study rank the risk of physical abuse as a major motive for avoiding marriage (Edin 2000; see also Wilson 1996, pp. 87–110).

With rights come responsibilities. If something like the civilizing process is finally at work in the United States, we should expect it to influence the behavior of adults before it affects youth. The baby-boom generation has enjoyed the benefits of declining levels of lethal violence since attaining adulthood in the 1980s. It now must extend those benefits to the next generation. The challenge for adults is to find ways of insulating themselves from violence that do not compound the problem or shift its burden to their children. Massive incarceration may avert homicides in the short run, but at the expense of diverting resources from longer-term prevention efforts. Avoiding marriage may reduce the risk of intimate violence for adults only to increase it for children who grow up in communities devoid of stable two-parent families. More prisons and fewer families are at best temporary, limited, and negative remedies for violence. The baby boomers must leave a larger legacy of nonviolence that befits a genuinely civilized society.

Notes

1. These figures are from the FBI's Supplementary Homicide Reports (SHR) for 1995, compiled by Snyder and Finnegan (1997).
2. The decline in adult victimization continued through 1997 (the most recent year available as of this writing) and is mirrored by decreasing adult offending rates (Blumstein and Rosenfeld 1998; Fox and Zawitz 1999). Between 1980 and 1995, the number of homicide offenders ages 25 to 49 fell from just under 13 to 7 offenders per 100,000 population. The age-specific rates were calculated using yearly SHR victim and offender counts from Snyder and Finnegan (1997) and population figures for 1980, 1990, and 1995 from U.S. Bureau of the Census (1983, 1996b) and at http://www.census.gov (figures for 1981–89 and 1991–94 are interpolated).
3. The SHR victim counts are from Snyder and Finnegan (1997). The hypothetical count for 1995 is obtained by applying the 1980 per capita rate of .000162 to the 25- to 49-year-old population of 100,832,000 in 1995.
4. Compositional changes could explain some of the decline in the adult rates as a simple function of the age effect. As homicide decreases with increasing age, then the movement of the large baby-boom cohorts through their twenties, thirties, and forties should result in lower overall adult rates over time. Although such changes should not be discounted, their influence is limited for two reasons. First, the age effect diminishes considerably after the early thirties: 49-year olds resemble 35-year olds more than 34-year olds resemble 25-year olds (Blumstein 1995, p. 17, Figure 3b). Second, the younger adult cohort of

25- to 34-year olds experienced significant decreases in offending and victimization over the past twenty years, although not as large as those for the older cohort of 35- to 49-year olds (Fox Chapter 9; Tables 5.1 and 5.2).

5. Racial comparisons are limited to blacks and whites. Persons of other races comprised only 2.1 percent of all 25- to 49-year-old homicide victims during the period 1980–95 (Snyder and Finnegan 1997). Hispanics may be of any race.

6. The 1980 rates per 100,000 25- to 49-year olds in each group were as follows: black males, 125.04; black females, 22.69, white males, 15.79; and white females, 4.30. The homicide data are from Snyder and Finnegan (1997). The population data are from U.S. Bureau of the Census (see n. 2).

7. In 1980, 4,626 25- to 49-year-old black males died from homicide, for a rate of 125 per 100,000 population. Applying that rate to the 25- to 49-year-old black male population in 1995 yields 7,289 estimated victims (.125 × 5,831,000). The SHR recorded 4,158 25- to 49-year-old black male victims in 1995, a difference of 3,131. The population totals are from Table 5.1; the SHR data are from Snyder and Finnegan (1997).

8. In addition, the offenders in the family category are restricted to the 25- to 49-year-old age range. The same age constraint is placed on the victims of family homicide in the analysis of offending patterns presented later.

9. The average yearly percentage changes are obtained by dividing the mean victimization rates presented in Table 5.2 into the slope coefficients (and multiplying by 100).

10. The adult-female trends in homicide offending by victim-offender relationship are not shown here. Inspection of those trends shows declines in all relationship categories for black and white women. Results available from the author by request.

11. The more intriguing consideration perhaps is the effect of a net *decrease* in incarceration on the yearly change in homicide. In that case, during years when the number of homicides fell, the expected decrease given no change in the number of prisoners would exceed the observed decrease; in years when the number of homicides rose, the observed change would exceed the expected change. Although the calculations are straightforward, they seem rather academic in light of the fact that the prisoner population has not declined in a single year for over twenty-five years.

12. Indeed, it is not stretching matters too much to suggest that criminal offenders with the greatest incarceration risk are largely responsible for the homicides in their communities.

13. The Chicago data are from the Chicago Homicide Dataset, a collaborative project of the Chicago Police Department, the Illinois Criminal Justice Information Authority, and Loyola University (co-investigators Carolyn Rebecca Block and Richard L. Block). The St. Louis data are from the St. Louis Homicide Project (co-investigators Scott H. Decker, Carol Kohfeld, Richard Rosenfeld, and John Sprague).

14. Spelman (Chapter 4) points out that, by widening the net of offenders brought into the system, escalations in incarceration will have diminishing incapacitation effects over time as persons with lower offending propensities comprise an increasing fraction of prisoners. To the degree that is so, the estimation procedure used here will overstate the marginal returns to incarceration.

15. Although it appears from the table as though the beginning and end points of the subperiods overlap, they actually represent adjacent year-to-year changes. For example, the year 1985 ends the first subperiod and begins the second. In the first case, it represents the change in the number of homicides and prisoners between 1984 and 1985, and in the second the corresponding changes between 1985 and 1986.

16. At a per capita rate of .0015 homicides per offender, a net increase of 670 inmates is necessary to avert one homicide (.0015 × 670 = 1). If each additional prisoner costs $20,000, the total cost of averting one homicide equals $13.4 million (670 × $20,000).

17. To induce stability in the sometimes small single-year homicide counts, the values for 1980 and 1995 are the three-year averages of the SHR victim counts for 1979, 1980, 1981, and 1994, 1995, and 1996, respectively. Married persons include spouses, exspouses, and common law. The small number of same-sex intimate homicides in the SHR data has been excluded. The results presented here are based on unpublished SHR data retrieved from the National Archive of Criminal Justice Data (http://www.icpsr.umich.edu/NACJD/SDA/shr96.html).

18. Elias's two-volume account of the civilizing process was originally published in 1939. The discussion here is based on the excellent summary and assessment in Garland (1990, pp. 213–47).

References

Blumstein, Alfred. 1995. "Youth Violence, Guns and the Illicit Drug Industry." *Journal of Criminal Law and Criminology* 86:10–36.

Blumstein, Alfred, and Allen J. Beck. 1999. "Factors Contributing to the Growth in U.S. Prison Populations." In Michael Tonry and Joan Petersilia, (Eds.), *Crime and Justice: A Review of Research* (pp. 17–61). Chicago: University of Chicago Press.

Blumstein, Alfred, and Richard Rosenfeld. 1998. "Explaining Recent Trends in U.S. Homicide Rates." *Journal of Criminal Law and Criminology* 88:1175–1216.

Blumstein, Alfred, Jacqueline Cohen, and Daniel Nagin. 1978. *Deterrence and Incapacitation: Estimating the Effects of Criminal Sanctions on Crime Rates.* Washington: National Academy Press.

Blumstein, Alfred, Jacqueline Cohen, Jeffrey A. Roth, and Christy A. Visher. 1986. *Criminal Careers and "Career Criminals."* Washington: National Academy Press.

Browne, Angela, and Kirk R. Williams. 1993. "Gender, Intimacy, and Lethal Violence: Trends from 1976 through 1987." *Gender and Society* 7:75–94.

Bureau of Justice Statistics. 1993. *Survey of State Prison Inmates, 1991.* Washington: U.S. Department of Justice.

Bureau of Justice Statistics. 1995. *Prisoners in 1994.* Washington: U.S. Department of Justice.

Bureau of Justice Statistics. 1996. *Prison and Jail Inmates, 1995.* Washington: U.S. Department of Justice.

Butterfield, Fox. 1995. *All God's Children: The Bosket Family and the American Tradition of Violence.* New York: Knopf.

Currie, Elliott. 1998. "Race, Violence, and Justice Since Kerner." In Fred R. Harris and Lynn A. Curtis (Eds.), *Locked in the Poorhouse: Cities, Race, and Poverty in the United States* (pp. 95–115). Lanham, MD: Rowman & Littlefield.

Devine, Joel A., Joseph F. Sheley, and M. Dwayne Smith. 1988. "Macroeconomic and Social Control Policy Influences on Crime Rate Changes, 1948–1985." *American Sociological Review* 53:407–20.

Dugan, Laura, Daniel S. Nagin, and Richard Rosenfeld. 1999. "Explaining the Decline in Intimate Partner Homicide: The Effects of Changing Domesticity, Women's Status, and Domestic Violence Resources." *Homicide Studies* 3:187–214.

Edin, Kathryn. 2000. "Few Good Men: Why Poor Mothers Don't Marry or Remarry." *American Prospect* (January 3):26–31.

Elias, Norbert. 1994. *The Civilizing Process.* New York: Blackwell.

Fox, James Alan, and Marianne W. Zawitz. 1999. *Homicide Trends in the United States.* Washington, DC: Bureau of Justice Statistics. http://www.ojp.usdoj.gov/bjs/homicide/homtrnd.htm. Accessed 11/23/99.

Garland, David. 1990. *Punishment and Society: A Study in Social Theory.* Chicago: University of Chicago Press.

Glassner, Barry. 1999. "School Violence: The Fears, The Facts." *The New York Times,* August 13, A19.

Greenfield, Lawrence A., Michael R. Rand, Diane Craven, Patsy A. Klaus, Craig A. Perkins, Cheryl Ringel, Greg Warchol, Cathy Maston, and James Alan Fox. *Violence by Intimates: Analysis of Data on Crimes by Current or Former Spouses, Boyfriends, and Girlfriends.* US Department of Justice, Office of Justice Programs, Bureau of Justice Statistics, March 1998. NCJ 167237

Gurr, Ted Robert. 1989. "Historical Trends in Violent Crime: Europe and the United States." In T. R. Gurr (Ed.), *Violence in America.* Vol. 1, *The History of Crime* (pp. 21–54). Newbury Park, CA: Sage.

Hirschi, Travis, and Michael Gottfredson. 1983. "Age and the Explanation of Crime." *American Journal of Sociology* 89:552–84.

Jones, Landon Y. 1980. *Great Expectations: America and the Baby Boom Generation.* New York: Ballantine.

Levitt, Steven D. 1996. "The Effect of Prison Population Size on Crime Rates: Evidence From Prison Overcrowding Litigation." *Quarterly Journal of Economics* (May):319–51.

Maguire, Kathleen, and Ann L. Pastore. 1998. *Sourcebook of Criminal Justice Statistics – 1997.* Washington: U.S. Government Printing Office.

Marvell, Thomas B., and Carlisle E. Moody. 1994. "Prison Population and Crime Reduction." *Journal of Quantitative Criminology* 7:237–73.

Marvell, Thomas B., and Carlisle E. Moody. 1997. "The Impact of Prison Growth on Homicide." *Homicide Studies* 1:205–33.

Mauer, Marc. 1999. *Race to Incarcerate.* New York: Norton.

Messner, Steven F., and Richard Rosenfeld. 1999. "Social Structure and Homicide: Theory and Research." In M. D. Smith and M. A. Zahn (Eds.), *Homicide: A Sourcebook of Social Research* (pp. 27–41). Thousand Oaks, CA: Sage.

Miller, Jerome. 1996. *Search and Destroy: African-American Males in the Criminal Justice System.* New York: Cambridge University Press.

Nisbett, Richard E., and Dov Cohen. 1996. *Culture of Honor: The Psychology of Violence in the South.* Boulder, CO: Westview.

Riedel, Marc. 1998. "Counting Stranger Homicides: A Case Study of Statistical Prestidigitation." *Homicide Studies* 2:206–19.

Riedel, Marc. 1999. "Sources of Homicide Data: A Review and Comparison." In M. D. Smith and M. A. Zahn (Eds.), *Homicide: A Sourcebook of Social Research* (pp. 75–95). Thousand Oaks, CA: Sage.

Rosenfeld, Richard. 1997. "Changing Relationships Between Men and Women: A Note on the Decline in Intimate Partner Homicide." *Homicide Studies* 1:72–83.

Sherman, Lawrence W., Denise C. Gottfredson, Doris L. MacKenzie, John Eck, Peter Reuter, and Shawn D. Bushway. 1998. *Preventing Crime: What Works, What Doesn't, What's Promising.* National Institute of Justice, *Research in Brief.* Washington: U.S. Department of Justice.

Snyder, Howard N., and Terrance A. Finnegan. 1997. *Easy Access to the FBI's Supplementary Homicide Reports: 1980–1995.* Washington: Office of Juvenile Justice and Delinquency Prevention.

Straus, Murray A. 1995. "Trends in Cultural Norms and Rates of Partner Violence: An Update to 1992." In S. A. Stith and M. A. Straus (Eds.), *Understanding Partner Violence: Prevalence, Causes, Consequences, and Solutions* (pp. 30–33). Minneapolis, MN: National Council on Family Relations.

U.S. Bureau of the Census. 1983. *1980 Census of the Population: General Population Characteristics.* Washington: US Government Printing Office.

U.S. Bureau of the Census. 1984. *1980 Census of Population.* Volume 1: *Characteristics of the Population.* Washington: US Government Printing Office.

U.S. Bureau of the Census. 1996a. *Statistical Abstract of the United States: 1996.* Springfield, VA: National Technical Information Service.

U.S. Bureau of the Census. 1996b. *Current Population Reports. Population Projections of the United States by Age, Sex, Race, and Hispanic Origin: 1995–2050.* Washington: US Government Printing Office.

U.S. Bureau of the Census. 1998. "Marital Status and Living Arrangements: March 1996." *Current Population Reports* (pp. 20–496). Washington: U.S. Department of Commerce.

Vera Institute of Justice. 1996. *The Unintended Consequences of Incarceration.* New York: Vera Institute of Justice.

Wilson, William Julius. 1996. *When Work Disappears: The World of the New Urban Poor.* New York: Knopf.

Zimring, Franklin E., and Gordon Hawkins. 1995. *Incapacitation: Penal Confinement and the Restraint of Crime.* New York: Oxford University Press.

Zimring, Franklin E., and Gordon Hawkins. 1997. *Crime is Not the Problem: Lethal Violence in America.* New York: Oxford University Press.

The Rise and Decline of Hard Drugs, Drug Markets, and Violence in Inner-City New York

Bruce D. Johnson, Andrew Golub, and Eloise Dunlap

Introduction

IN THE MID- TO LATE 1990s, violent crime plummeted nationwide. The Uniform Crime Report (UCR 1998) program documented a 28 percent decline in homicides recorded by the police from 1993 to 1997 and similar or larger declines in robbery and aggravated assault. The National Crime Victimization Survey (NCVS) also identified a 21 percent decline in reported victimization for violent crimes (U.S. Dept. of Justice 1998). These statistics are discussed in detail in Chapters 2 and 9.

This chapter examines the cultural changes behind the statistical trends. Violence is the outgrowth of personal interactions. The violence statistics thus reflect a propensity based on the way people are organized and interact. We suggest that the recent decline in violence reflects fundamental transformations in drug use and sales. This chapter focuses in detail on inner-city New York, our geographic area of greatest expertise. New York City has historically had the nation's largest number of heroin users and crack users, the largest and most diverse market for illegal drugs, and a disproportionate share of crime, violence, and disorder in public places (Musto 1973, 2000). Golub and Johnson (1997) found evidence to suggest that similar changes in recent drug use prevailed across much of the nation; this observation provides limited evidence to suggest that comparable subcultural transformations might have occurred in other locations.

Since World War II, inner-city New York has experienced three major drug eras with distinct conduct norms: the *Heroin Injection Era* (which peaked 1960–73), the *Cocaine/Crack Era* (which peaked 1984–89), and the

Marijuana/Blunts Era (which started in 1990). The latest drug of choice among youths is the blunt, made by placing marijuana in the wrapper of a cheap cigar. The new conduct norms associated with the Marijuana/Blunts Era explain the social context behind the observed decline in violence.

This social history draws on the senior author's direct observations from thirty years of study and more than fifteen major research projects (summarized in Lipton and Johnson 1998) covering the following: 1. Epidemiology of heroin (Johnson 1978; Johnson et al. 1985), cocaine/crack (Golub and Johnson 1996, 1997, 1999b; Sanchez and Johnson 1987), and marijuana (Johnson 1973; Johnson and Uppal 1980); 2. Drug Markets (Dunlap and Johnson 1992, 1996a; Dunlap, Johnson, and Maher 1997; Johnson, Dunlap et al. 1998; Johnson, Golub, and Fagan 1995; Johnson, Hamid, and Sanabria 1992); 3. The Distressed Inner-City: (Austin et al. 1977; Dunlap and Johnson 1992; Johnson, Williams et al. 1990; Johnson and Muffler 1992, 1997); and 4. Violence (Dunlap, Johnson, and Rath 1996; Johnson, Dunlap, and Maher 1998).

Much of this work focused on documenting drug subcultures. This chapter first describes the concept of a subculture, explores potential links between drugs and violence, and describes the severely distressed inner-city households often heavily involved and affected by drugs. Next, the chapter presents a quantitative analysis that identifies the timing of each drug era. With this information as preamble, the remainder of the chapter describes the subcultures governing illegal drug use, drug sales, and violence in each drug era.

Subcultures. The use and sale of many drugs are proscribed by the mainstream culture in the United States, as is violence. These prohibitions are codified as laws that define specific penalties for noncompliance. However, there are much more intricate sets of rules governing human behavior in any place and time that sociologists call "conduct norms" (Johnson 1973, 1980; Johnson, Dunlap, and Maher 1998; Johnson and Manwar 1991; Wolfgang 1967; Wolfgang and Ferracuti 1967). Conduct norms may also be conceptualized as the specific rules persons internalize (Sellin 1938) that allow them to function as if on "automatic pilot." A subculture of drug use and drug sales consists of the related conduct norms organized around a specific behavior that prescribe what participants must do, proscribe what they must not do, and define sanctions for noncompliance. These subcultures have an existence independent of their participants. Individuals may cease their personal involvement, but the subculture continues as long as others participate. Subcultures can change over time due to internal influences such as the rising popularity of different drugs or as a result of external efforts aimed at social control.

Drugs and Crime. The strong association between drugs and crime has been well documented (Ball et al. 1981; Ball, Shaffer, and Nurco 1983; Johnson et al. 1985; Nurco 1998; Tonry and Wilson 1990). Goldstein (1985) presents an elegant model that identifies three potential causal mechanisms for this linkage, which we have adapted to potentially explain the connection between drugs and violence: 1) The distinct *psychopharmacology* of a drug can lead an individual to act out in violent ways toward others; 2) In order to support their expensive drug consumption, many users turn to income-producing crimes such as robbery, resulting in *economic-compulsive* violence; and 3) The sale of illegal drugs takes place outside the mainstream economy where the legal system is not available to resolve disagreements leading to *systemic violence* over turf or as a means of punishing subordinates.

Severely Distressed Households in the Inner-City. Starting in 1890 and accelerating after World War II, a stream of African-Americans moved north in what has come to be called the "Great Migration." Simultaneously, waves of immigrants from Puerto Rico and the Caribbean arrived in New York City. These hopeful pilgrims were met with housing discrimination, high rents, and low-wage jobs. Life in inner-city New York during the 1960s was far from easy, especially for minority youths (Brown 1965, Butterfield 1995). From the 1960s to the mid-1980s, the situation became even worse as hundreds of thousands of low-wage manufacturing jobs moved from New York City to the Sun Belt or other countries (Kasarda 1992; Wilson, W. J. 1996). Most inner-city youths lacked the skills needed for the new high-tech jobs that were developing. Consequently, during the 1970s and 1980s, unemployment among African-American and Hispanic youths in communities like Harlem, South Bronx, and Bedford-Stuyvesant often exceeded 50 percent (Gibbs 1988; Sullivan 1989). This economic pressure severely distressed inner-city households and devastated the lives of many children (Dunlap 1992, 1995; Dunlap and Johnson 1992). The late twentieth century experienced the rise of the single-parent and then no-parent household.

The following portrait is a collage – not a description of every inner-city household nor of any one particular household. This portrait describes typical experiences characterizing the struggles of inner-city households, especially African-American and Hispanic households, during this period.

These circumstances led (and continue to lead) many inner-city youths to be socialized into subcultures of drug use, drug sales, and violent behavior (Bourgois 1995; Duncan and Brooks-Gunn 1997; also see Wilson, W. J. 1987, 1993).

A typical distressed household might be headed by a single mother (or often a grandmother) living on welfare, without a legal job and having no prospects for legal jobs due to poor jobs skills and a heavy burden of child care responsibilities. Sometimes the household head's chances of employment are further restricted by the demands of regular drug use. Children growing up in such households often do not know anyone who works at a legal job (Johnson, Dunlap, and Maher 1998). They rarely complete high school and do not learn the basic skills (literacy, numeracy, punctuality, ability to take directions, and mainstream norms of interaction) needed to find and keep legal employment as adults. As a result, they rarely obtain or retain steady employment, even at the minimum wage.

Children growing up in such households typically have several relatives (often including parents) who survive in the street and drug economies, sometimes with welfare support. Many of these children develop excellent skills in selling or helping to sell drugs, performing a variety of income-producing hustles, and avoiding police (Dunlap and Johnson 1996a, 1996b, 1998; Johnson, Dunlap, and Maher 1998; Dunlap, Johnson, and Rath 1996). If current conditions continue, many will never obtain regular legal employment.

Despite their exclusion from legal employment, and often from welfare support, and despite the imposition of severe penal sanctions on some, these excluded inner-city young adults must be given substantial recognition for creating, maintaining, and expanding the subcultures described later. Most remarkably, they quite literally created whole new economic systems, albeit illegal, that rivaled in economic importance the legal enterprises of inner-city communities. Illegal drug markets provided large numbers of inner-city youths with jobs, money, drugs, social meaning, status, and a way of life that is often transmitted across generations.

The Timing of Drug Eras. Starting in 1987, the National Institute of Justice initiated the Arrestee Drug Abuse Monitoring Program (ADAM, formerly Drug Use Forecasting) to track changes in drug use among arrestees (National Institute of Justice [NIJ] 1998). Analyses of urine test results and survey responses from over 13,000 ADAM-Manhattan arrestees interviewed from 1987–97 have documented three major drug eras in inner-city Manhattan over the last forty years (Golub, and Johnson 1994a,

1994b, 1996, 1997, 1999a, 1999b, 2000; Johnson and Golub 2000; Johnson, Golub, and Fagan 1995; Johnson, Thomas, and Golub 1998). Each era has been characterized by a single substance dominating use among persistent drug-abusing criminal offenders. During the Heroin Injection Era (1960s and early 1970s) that substance was heroin and it was mostly consumed by injection. During the Cocaine/Crack Era (1980s), the drug of choice was cocaine. In the early 1980s, users primarily snorted cocaine but from 1985 to 1989 most of them smoked cocaine as crack. During the Marijuana/Blunts Era starting around 1990s, inner-city youths favored marijuana smoked primarily as blunts, but avoided heroin and cocaine.

In the mid-1970s, the Heroin Injection Era entered a decline as fewer youths became regular users (Boyle and Brunswick 1980; Clayton and Voss 1981; Hunt and Chambers 1976; Johnson, Thomas, and Golub 1998). Similarly, the Cocaine/Crack Era entered a decline around 1990 (Golub and Johnson 1997). However, many adult users persisted in their habits long after the peak of each era. Consequently, the variation in drug of choice across arrestees of different ages roughly identifies the timing of each drug eras (Golub and Johnson 1999b).

Figure 6.1 tracks each drug era's influence on successive birth years through three key measures: any lifetime self-reported injection of heroin, any lifetime self-reported use of crack, and recent marijuana use as detected by urinalysis. The Heroin Injection Generation (or *HeroinGen*) was identified as the birth years from 1945 to 1954, for which the reported lifetime injection drug use among ADAM-Manhattan arrestees ranged from 30 to 52 percent.

The percentage reporting lifetime heroin use was much lower among arrestees born before 1945 and declined rapidly among arrestees born after 1954.

Crack use was highest (50 to 55 percent) among persons born 1948 to 1969. Interestingly, the rate of self-reported crack use was also quite high among individuals born before 1948. Indeed, the data strongly indicate that cocaine and crack became just as popular among arrestees from the HeroinGen as heroin itself. Most of these arrestees, however, were heroin injectors who added crack when it became widely available in the late 1980s (Golub and Johnson 1994a, 1994b, 1997; Johnson, Lewis, and Golub 1992). The Cocaine/Crack Generation (or *CrackGen*) was identified as the birth years from 1955 to 1969; the rate of crack use plummeted after the 1969 birth cohort.

Manhattan arrestees born in the 1970s were distinguished by their low rates of reported heroin injection and crack use, as compared to their pre-

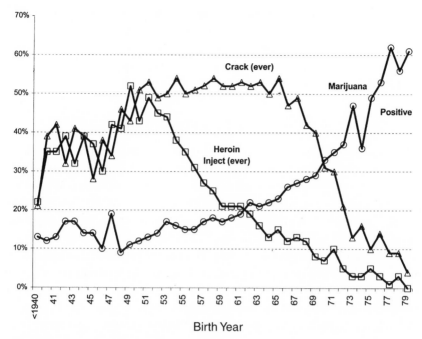

Figure 6.1. Key drug use indicators by birth year (ADAM-Manhattan age 18 plus from 1987–1997, $n = 13,084$).

decessors, accompanied by increasing rates of detected marijuana use. The majority of arrestees in every birth year self-reported lifetime use of marijuana. However, the rate of detected marijuana use among older birth cohorts (born before 1970) remained generally low, typically in the 10 to 20 percent range. The data suggest that many older arrestees had tried or used marijuana when younger, but they were not currently using marijuana or used it infrequently (less than once a month). Among arrestees born since 1970, the rate of detected marijuana use increased from a substantial 33 percent (1970 cohort) to as much as 62 percent (1977 cohort). These 1970s birth cohorts were detected as using marijuana in their twenties much more frequently than were members of previous birth cohorts, who were more likely to have progressed to use of crack or heroin by this age (Golub and Johnson, 1999b). Thus, it was not their youthfulness at the time of the interview but a distinct avoidance of cocaine, crack, and heroin – combined with increased rate of detected marijuana use – that characterized this birth cohort's illicit substance use. The Marijuana/Blunt Generation (*or BluntGen*) was identified as including all birth years from 1970 through at least 1979, the last birth year included in the analysis.

Some statistical data suggest that similar changes in drug of choice prevailed across the nation.[1] The rate of lifetime cocaine use reported by high school seniors declined from 17 percent in 1985 down to 6 percent by 1992 (Johnston, O'Malley, and Bachman 1998). Subsequently, lifetime marijuana use increased from 33 percent in 1992 up to 50 percent in 1997.

A Social History of Drug Use, Drug Markets, and Violence

The following sections describe the subcultures that had become established as part of New York City's "street scenes" in primarily 1968, 1988, and 1998, near the peak of each successive drug era (Golub and Johnson 1999b). Each section briefly describes: the economic, social, and political context in which each generation grew up; subcultures regarding drug use, drug sales, and violence; the ensuing criminal justice response; and concludes with a status report as of 1998. The conduct norms described represent "typical" subcultural patterns. Not all inner-city residents participated in these drug-related subcultures, nor did all drug users and sellers adhere strictly to these patterns. However, these norms were observed frequently enough to suggest that they were characteristic of the time and place.

The Heroin Injection Era in New York Around 1968. Much of the pool of eventual drug users came from poor Puerto Rican and African-American families who had migrated to New York before or during World War II. Due to language barriers, lack of money, and housing discrimination, these families often ended up in New York's inner-city neighborhoods. Many of these poor inner-city households were technically "intact," with both a mother and father (or stepfather) present. The father (and sometimes mother) expected to and did hold steady, low-wage work in a variety of manufacturing or domestic jobs (Dunlap 1992, 1995; Dunlap and Johnson 1992, 1996a).

This appearance of mainstream "normality," however, did not mean that life was harmonious. Quite often one or both parents were heavy alcohol consumers, if not alcoholic. As children, the HeroinGen often observed their father heavily intoxicated, and sometimes hitting his spouse and children. Yelling, cursing, and aggressive language were commonplace. These households transmitted violent conduct norms to the HeroinGen, which effectively prescribed use of loud, aggressive, and threatening language and physical assault of loved ones to dominate them (Dunlap 1996, 1997a; Dunlap and Johnson 1992, Dunlap, Johnson, and Rath 1996).

Many individuals who became drug users had experienced difficulty with formal schooling, often acting out as class clowns or bullies, and subsequently becoming social isolates and poor performers. They were often suspended from school and encouraged to drop out. Most did so before age 16. As a result, the HeroinGen typically left school with few skills that would serve them in finding and retaining a job. By contrast, they routinely hung out on the streets in their early teen years, learning conduct norms of the street subculture: evade subway and bus fares, drop litter and food on the street, shoplift food and clothing, employ loud language, intimidate passersby with a looming physical presence, engage in a variety of hustles, and give and attend parties where heavy consumption of alcohol and drugs occur (Dunlap 1996, 1997a, 1997b, 1997c; Dunlap and Johnson 1996a, 1996b, 1997, 1998).

Subculture of Alcohol Abuse. Quite often, parents provided the HeroinGen with alcohol during childhood (by age 13) and even expected them to consume full drinks and become daily tobacco smokers. A substantial proportion of the HeroinGen became heavy alcohol consumers during adulthood as they adapted and adopted their parents' norms for alcohol abuse:

> Drink to intoxication, excuse excessive behavior upon inebriation, blame alcohol for the harms that occur.

Other members of the HeroinGen reacted against their parents' alcohol abuse, perceived alcohol negatively, preferred not to use it, and avoided heavy alcohol use (Dunlap and Johnson 1992).

Subculture of Marijuana Use. In mid-adolescence (around age 15), members of the HeroinGen were "turned on" to marijuana and marijuana subcultures developed (Johnson 1973):

> Pot makes you feel great. A mellow high. Share with others. Correct ways to roll a joint. Where and how to purchase marijuana. How to evade police and arrest while using and buying.

Subculture of Heroin Use and Injection. In 1964–65, the New York streets were buzzing about heroin. The HeroinGen was promised that it was the greatest "high," definitely better than marijuana and alcohol. Many youths eagerly accepted their first samples typically offered by a somewhat more experienced peer and started the process of inculcation into heroin use (Malcolm X and Haley 1965; Brown 1965; Preble and Casey 1969). As use spread subcultures developed:

> Heroin is the greatest high, continue using it again and again.

Early users were careful to avoid the frequent use that leads to addiction. However, they soon found that snorting doesn't provide a good high any longer and progressed to the more effective techniques of skin-popping (injection under skin) and intravenous injection. In becoming a user, they took on additional conduct norms:

> Get the most from every precious bag of heroin. Speedballs (cocaine mixed with heroin) are a great way to go "fast then slow." Learn a variety of needle-injection practices and rituals. Share heroin and needles when you don't have enough heroin. Go to a shooting gallery to inject heroin. Rent works for injection. "Pay" the gallery owner by giving him a taste of your heroin. Borrow and engage in various hustles to raise money to purchase heroin. Locate the seller with the best bag of heroin. Engage in various crimes to generate income to purchase heroin. Sell heroin to make good money, and maintain a large habit. If wholesale quantities of heroin can't be acquired, help sellers by performing various roles. Avoid cash expenditures for basic necessities (food, shelter, clothing) if others can be persuaded to provide them. Learn various strategies for avoiding police and lengthy penal sanctions. Learn how to avoid those who would rob or steal your drugs or money.

By 1968, a great many young adults (ages 15 to 25 in 1968) were using heroin regularly (Boyle and Brunswick 1980). On average, typical users injected heroin twice per day, but often had days with no heroin use (Johnson 1984; Johnson et al. 1985). For many, daily lives became organized around their habit and consisted of a variety of quasi-legal hustles, nondrug crimes, a variety of drug sales/distribution roles, chasing the best bag of heroin, locating a safe place to inject, conning others into sharing drugs or needles, avoiding police, and finding free food, shelter, and clothing. This compulsive lifestyle did not typically cause them to despair. For the HeroinGen, "taking care of business" provided a sense of purpose and meaning that was denied to them in conventional society (Preble and Casey 1969).

Subculture of Heroin Sales. Prior to 1965, Heroin selling was highly privatized. Buyers had to be referred to a seller, and transactions took place in secluded locations like apartments (Brown 1965; Malcolm X and Haley 1965). As the number of heroin users expanded, however, sales became more public often taking place in bars. In 1965, almost every corner in Harlem had a bar that served as a social gathering place. As drug sales became more commonplace from 1965–73, bars became viewed as dangerous, their publike congeniality was lost, conventional citizens stopped coming by, and many of them were pressured into closing by the police or closed on their own. In contrast, by 1968 the HeroinGen's energy and competence had created a multimillion dollar market in illicit drugs.

Subculture of Robbery. About one-fourth of the HeroinGen became involved with robbery on a regular basis, primarily to support their habits (Johnson, Goldstein et al. 1985). The robbery conduct norms included:

> Locate ordinary citizens who are apt to carry a lot of cash. Try to identify persons leaving banks on paydays. Target working-class and pink-collar workers who typically cash their payroll checks. Hold up businesses with other robbers. Don't rob banks. Don't attempt to rob someone when stoned on alcohol or heroin.

Subculture of Assault. The need for money to purchase led many of the HeroinGen to assault mainstream society as robbers. Heroin is a depressant. Psychopharmacological violence rarely resulted from its use. Rather, most robberies were committed when users were temporarily "straight" but beginning to experience withdrawal and in need of money. While robbers sometimes targeted drug sellers, they were only occasionally robbed, because sellers carried knives (but rarely guns in 1968). At least in Harlem, most robbers avoided robbing heroin sellers for fear of retaliation from Nicky Barnes's organization, which controlled most of the heroin trade until about 1972. This central control over heroin markets minimized the kind of systemic violence that would characterize later drug markets.

Heroin use actually reduced much of the street violence that had been occurring. During the early 1960s, many of the HeroinGen had been active in gangs in which violent behavior often brought prestige and honor. Preble and Casey (1969) reported that as gang members began "nodding out" on heroin, hustling for money, and seeking the best bag, their interest and involvement in gangs, gang activity, fights, and assault disappeared. Many gangs dissolved. Heroin users soon discovered that sharing money or heroin was vitally important to maintaining habits. They argued and sometimes physically fought over money or drugs – but no longer over turf and gang honor.

Subculture of Handguns. The HeroinGen rarely obtained, carried, or used handguns. Most of them neither knew much about how to get handguns nor felt a strong need to have them. Knives and blunt instruments were the weapons of choice among those who felt them necessary.

Policing Practices. In response to growing concern about drug use, the city, state, and federal governments launched a variety of initiatives between 1968 and 1974 designed to control heroin abusers and sellers (Massing 1998). Nelson Rockefeller (New York Governor 1958–74) initiated three major programs, two of which have been judged to be failures.

First, the Narcotic Addiction Control Commission established criminal and civil-commitment treatment facilities where users could be sent even without having committed a crime. They were closed in 1976 (Waldorf 1973; 1998). Second, the Rockefeller Drug Law of 1973 established mandatory life sentences for minor drug sellers and contributed to growth in prison population. Recent efforts to repeal these laws have failed (*The New York Times* 1998a). And third, New York State helped establish various drug treatment programs, which have proven effective.

National (under President Nixon), state, and local funding for a variety of drug treatment programs has endured for over twenty-five years (Massing 1998). New York City (under Mayor Lindsay) established the largest methadone maintenance program in the world, as well as numerous other outpatient drug-free programs. Therapeutic communities (like Synanon and Phoenix House) were established as an important, albeit expensive, option for helping addicts develop a drug-free lifestyle. Much research has established the efficacy of these programs for keeping drug users out of the criminal justice system and helping them become drug free (Anglin and Perrochet 1998; Government Accounting Office [GAO] 1998b).

The epidemic of heroin use was actually only one of several major crises facing New York City in the 1960s and 1970s. The civil rights movement, black power, Vietnam war protests, and threat of riots all drew police away from drug law enforcement (National Advisory Commission on Civil Disorders 1968). New York City experienced a near bankruptcy in the 1970s, and thousands of police officers, school teachers, and city officials were laid off. To maximize their impact, police concentrated their limited resources on high-level sellers. At the same time, the rise of "professional policing" discouraged regular contact between police and criminals in order to prevent corruption (Kelling and Coles 1996; Wilson, O. W. 1963).

The Rise of Street Markets. Social protests, factory closings, civil rights actions, and the flight of the middle-class to the suburbs all contributed to the decay of the inner-city – especially in northern and midwestern industrial cities like New York. A lack of street-level enforcement allowed the HeroinGen to create lively and very public markets for illicit drugs. One well-known market, at Eighth Avenue and 116th Street in Harlem, survived for nearly twenty-five years. Virtually every park in New York City and many street locations were transformed into wide-open drug supermarkets, where upwards of 100 users and sellers often congregated at a single location, milling about and just hanging out. "Loose joints" and bags of marijuana were available for $1 to $5. Bags of cocaine and heroin for $10. Most passersby, even the most conventional, were approached by low-income minority youths eager to sell them illegal drugs.

The conduct norms of the street markets were as follows:

> Sell illegal drugs in public places. Sell drugs from buildings. Police will rarely arrest you. Look out for and warn others of police and undercover officers. Worry more about competition. Try to control good selling locations. Control crowds of buyers. Hire addicts to help sell drugs and reduce the personal risk of arrest and jail. Try to control the competition in your turf. Conduct drug sales mainly during the most profitable times.

The swarms of drug sellers and distributors in inner-city neighborhoods had effectively reached accommodation with the beleaguered citizenry of the inner city (Kelling and Coles 1996). Citizens did not call the police. In return, heroin and cocaine sellers did not rob, burglarize, or steal from citizens on the block. Many drug sellers also "gave back" to the community by providing parents with money for kids' clothes or for personal crises, by throwing block parties, and so forth.

By 1982, wide agreement existed among public officials and community leaders that drug sellers effectively controlled many New York streets and most parks. Looking back, it seems easy to cast blame upon many parts of the city's government, police, business elite, and leadership in inner-city communities (see Kelling and Coles 1996). However, these were tumultuous times. To be fair, research colleagues Edward Preble and Paul Goldstein, along with Bruce Johnson, did not clearly see or document what was happening concerning cocaine use during this period.

Taking Back the Streets. Starting in the 1980s, policing underwent a philosophical reformation. The new mantra of community leaders became "take back the streets," which effectively refocused enforcement against low-level drug sellers and their crews instead of drug kingpins. A 1982 *Atlantic Monthly* essay by James Q. Wilson and George Kelling argued that reducing social disorder by "fixing broken windows" and aggressively policing highly visible infractions regardless of their apparent seriousness would militate against more serious criminality.

The Koch administration launched Operation Pressure Point in which all major agencies were directed to cooperate with the New York Police Department (NYPD) in a comprehensive initiative. The police would move in and make buy-busts; the building and fire departments would condemn abandoned buildings, which would be bulldozed to eliminate drug-selling locations. By mid-1985, Operation Pressure Point had essentially suppressed the heroin and cocaine supermarkets (but not all drug selling) on the Lower East Side and reduced traffic in Harlem's heroin supermarket at Eighth Avenue and 116th Street as well (Zimmer 1987).

The Heroin Generation in 1998. In 1998, many of the HeroinGen started to reach their fifties. Many continued to follow the conduct norms institutionalized in the late 1960s. They comprise a disproportionate share of the extant injectors of heroin and cocaine. These remaining injectors withstood extensive efforts at social controls from police, drug treatment programs, penal sanctions, and pressure from family and friends (GAO 1997, 1998a,b; Maher 1997; Waldorf 1973, 1998; Waterston 1993). Many others, however, died from AIDS as the practice of sharing needles served as a central vector for transmission of HIV in the 1970s and 1980s (Des Jarlais 1998; Des Jarlais et al. 1994, 1998). In 1998, the remainder of the HeroinGen, older and less active, constituted a declining pool of those committing robberies, assaults, and domestic violence.

The Cocaine/Crack Era in New York City around 1988. During the 1970s, snorting cocaine grew into a major leisure-time activity in many segments of New York City and of the nation as a whole. Around 1980, the innovative practice of "freebasing" emerged in which cocaine powder and ether were mixed over an open flame (Hamid 1992b). Inhaling the vapors given off by this process led to a faster and more intense cocaine high. The difficulty and expense of this practice effectively limited its use to drug dealers and other wealthy customers who met at after-hours clubs.

Around 1984, "crack" cocaine began to be distributed in vials meant for perfume samples. Simply heating these specially prepared crystals allowed individuals with limited money, limited technical expertise, and limited equipment to smoke cocaine vapors. During 1985–86, crack use and abuse exploded in New York as well as in other major cities. The media also exploded with concern about crack (Hartman and Golub 1999; Reinarman and Levine 1997). The extensive population of cocaine snorters and heroin injectors had the opportunity to try this new product. Many became frequent users (Golub and Johnson 1994a, 1994b; 1996; Johnson, Golub, and Fagan 1995; Johnson, Lewis, and Golub 1992; Johnson, Natarajan et al. 1994).

Persons born between 1955 and 1969, the CrackGen, came of age during the peak of the Cocaine/Crack Era (1985–89). Some were offspring of the HeroinGen and experienced many serious deprivations during childhood as they became well socialized into street culture and the drug business (Dunlap, Johnson, and Maher 1998; Dunlap, Johnson, and Rath

1996). During the crack era, the inner-city experienced substantial increases in violence, including robbery, aggression/assault, domestic violence, and homicide. Official statistics identify an overall doubling of homicides for New York City from 1985 to 1992 (Chapters 2 and 7). Ethnographic evidence suggests that the expansion of violence among the inner-city African-American and Hispanic populations may have been even more extensive. Most of this increase was not reflected accurately in police and official statistics, because nonfatal violence involving inner-city drug users and sellers is typically not reported to the police.

Subculture of Crack Use and Abuse. Crack use was characterized by intensive binges known as "runs" or "missions," jargon derived from *Star Trek* (Waldorf, Reinarman, and Murphy 1991; Williams 1989). A very common cyclical pattern emerged. The crack user would commit a small crime that would generate a few dollars (e.g., $10 to $20), the entire amount would be expended for crack almost immediately (as soon as a crack seller could be located), and the crack would be rapidly smoked up. The cycle would be repeated within the next hour or two, and so on, often leading to a continuous multiday binge even during hours when most conventional persons were sleeping. About two-thirds of regular crack users in 1988 reported four or more episodes a day (Johnson, Natarajan et al. 1994). In contrast, daily heroin users typically injected once or twice a day and a regular cocaine snorter used one or two bags at a time.

This hyperactivity resulted from several psychopharmacology effects combined with various conduct norms. First, several studies have documented that smoking of cocaine freebase causes rapid elevation of blood level of cocaine creating euphoria within one to five minutes of consumption (Gold and Miller 1997; Van Dyke and Byck 1982). Shortly thereafter, a dramatic drop in cocaine level ensues, often causing severe dysphoria (a temporary but intense depression). During the dysphoric period, the consumption of another "hit" or vial of crack alleviates the dysphoria and provides another euphoric episode. Second, cocaine and crack use often leads to paranoia leading to accusations, arguments, and fights. And third, crack binges cause heavy stimulation, which keeps users wide awake and very active – even when very sleep-deprived.

The conduct norms associated with crack use fed the expectations of hyperactivity:

> Crack is pure cocaine (or impurities are removed). Crack gives the greatest highs. Everyone is smoking crack. Expend all your income on crack. Devote all your labor and skills to obtaining crack. Trade labor or skills (including

sex) for small amounts of crack. Spend time mainly with other crack users. Abandon friends and family for crack use. Go on "missions" and "runs" of crack use. Continuously obtain money and crack without sleep or much food, until extremely exhausted. Purchase small amounts of crack as soon as money is available. The purchase and use of crack comes before all other needs (e.g. food, shelter, clothes, family). (Johnson, Golub, and Fagan 1995).

Through communication among a variety of high-risk subgroups, these conduct norms became effectively institutionalized, creating an entirely new "subculture of crack use" that was quite different from the subculture of cocaine snorting, even though the same substance (cocaine) was ultimately being consumed in each.

Subculture of Crack Distribution. Crack sales was so lucrative that by 1988 nearly the entire labor force of the illicit drug distribution industry was attracted to it (Johnson, Dunlap et al. 1998; Johnson, Dunlap, and Tourigny 2000; Johnson, Kaplan, and Schmeidler 1990; Johnson, Natarajan et al. 1994). By 1988, the following conduct norms had evolved:

Crack is the hot drug to sell. Crack makes "crazy money." Sell during the best hours (weekend evenings). Be your own boss. Work your own hours. Claim a location and regularly sell from it. Maintain good relations with competition. Don't sell to police and undercover officers. Maintain good relations with nonusers living in the community. Protect against robbery or theft of drugs.

Structure of the Crack Industry. As in any business, the key factor organizing the entire crack industry was "keeping the money and product straight." Those who paid wholesale prices for cocaine (or crack) and sold most of the product for cash (rather than consume it) could quickly establish "good street reputations" and make money (Dunlap, Johnson, and Manwar 1994). Such persons had careers as sellers, crew lieutenants, dealers, and wholesalers. By contrast, the vast majority of potential sellers were "always late and short." This was especially true of those who consumed most of the product entrusted to them. They rapidly achieved a street reputation as very unreliable; most of them were not trusted as sellers and were fortunate to occasionally perform low-level distribution roles. (Furst, Curtis et al. 1997; Hamid 1992a, 1992b; Johnson, Hamid, and Sanabria 1992; Johnson, Kaplan, and Schmeidler 1990; Williams 1989).

From 1984–87, crack was often sold freelance by a "juggler" who purchased (or was advanced on credit) ten to twenty-five vials of crack ("a bundle"). If the juggler sold all these vials for a standard retail price ($10 average at the time), he would double the investment and be allowed to "re-up" (obtain more vials). During several cycles, the freelance seller would make up to fifty transactions a day. The vast majority of freelance sellers did not make much money, however, because of competition, paying others to help sell, discounted sales, and most important, because perhaps as many as 90 percent of them used too much of the product themselves (Caulkins et al. 1999). Probably fewer than one in ten freelancers had multiyear careers.

Some of the early successes eventually developed their own small business groups, sometimes called "crews," "posses," or "yellow tops" (after a brand marking of some kind). The dealer would obtained wholesale supplies, oversee the creation of several bundles, and hire a crew boss or lieutenant to manage street sales (Bourgois 1995; Williams 1989). The crew boss would hire people to perform very specific low-level distribution roles (counter of customer's money; pitcher, who would hand crack to the buyer; holder of wholesale supplies; lookout for police or business rivals, etc.). When well organized and managed, such crews were able to sell over 1,000 vials of crack during one hundred to three hundred transactions a day. Low-level distributors were most often paid in crack, which they subsequently consumed. In contrast, the dealer and crew boss who limited or controlled their personal use brought in "crazy money," often several hundred to over one thousand dollars every day (Williams 1989). However, direct costs (payments to staff, rent, food, entertainment) as well as training and supervision of a constantly changing staff, competition from other sellers, avoidance of police, arrest, and incarceration rendered true profits elusive to all but the most systematic crack sellers (Reuter, MacCoun, and Murphy 1990).

Crack sellers were active on virtually every block in inner-city New York City and at some locations in many middle-class and suburban neighborhoods as well. Potential buyers often had to ward off simultaneous offers from several sellers. Aggressive sellers often approached total strangers, including those in cars. Some blocks in inner-city New York became crack street markets, with over 100 crack sellers and even more crack buyers simultaneously active. Such markets would often be open "24/7," twenty-four hours a day, seven days a week to serve users' binges.

By the mid-1980s, cocaine selling was already a serious felony, and enforcement was increasing. Sales of crack came to be penalized even more heavily than cocaine powder with the passage of the Anti-Drug Abuse Act of 1988 (Belenko 1993). Nonetheless, police and criminal penalties were perceived by crack sellers as only a minor concern. So many people were striving to make "crazy money" or to support their crack consumption that competition among sellers was the major problem. The price of a retail crack vial declined from $20 for a "jumbo" (1985) to about $5 for a "small" vial (1988) of crack; occasionally the price would drop to $2 to $3 for a small chunk in tiny vial (Caulkins 1997; Caulkins and Padman 1993) to provide the binger with a small hit who had only two dollars. The more-organized crack sellers introduced a variety of violent innovations to control competition and increase their profits. Crew leaders started to hire a "protector" to defend turf and enforce sanctions against operatives. Many of these "muscle men" were perceived as "crazy," or unpredictably violent, which enhanced their image, instilled fear in others, and increased their worth.

Juveniles were expressly sought for distribution roles in crack-selling crews, because they accepted lower pay, faced less stringent penal sentences (if arrested) than adults, and had not yet developed compulsive patterns of cocaine or crack use, so they were often reliable workers. Although initially hired as lookouts, touts, and drug carriers by crew bosses, they quickly learned of enhanced job opportunities associated with acting crazy. Many juveniles who had experienced violence in their homes took to the job with alacrity. One of the most effective tactics toward this end was to talk about, display, or use guns.

Subculture of Handguns. The burgeoning interest in guns was supported by a vigorous gray market. Handguns would often be purchased in southern states (having few or no controls over sales) and resold in New York City to drug sellers and robbers (Butterfield 1998). This increase in systemic crack-market-related violence accounts for much of the increase in violence in the late 1980s as well as its association with juveniles and guns.

Most of the drug-related violence during the crack epidemic was systemic, and not psychopharmacological or economic compulsive. Goldstein, Brownstein et al. (1997; Goldstein 1998) examined the circumstances of 218 drug-related homicides investigated by the NYPD in 1988. They determined that nearly three-fourths of these drug-related homicides were systemic in nature. Only 14 percent were judged to have been psychopharmacological, and less than 5 percent were economic-compulsive. Homicides have been well studied because they are the only crime type reasonably well recorded by police. (Dead bodies can rarely be hidden from police for long.) Other violent acts, such as assaulting a subordinate or shooting him in the kneecap, were mostly unrecorded in official statistics. However, the number of crippled young men wheeling themselves around the inner-city provides ample testament to this brutality.

Subculture of Assault. Aggravated assault increased substantially as crack crews brutally "disciplined" workers who violated group norms including the following:

> Never accept "shorts." Day workers who accepted shorts or used while selling would not be rehired. Sometimes they were beaten. Always repay your debts with the first money you earn. Never use crack while selling for this crew. Workers who didn't repay sizable drug debts (used two or more bundles instead of selling them) could expect to be severely beaten and possibly crippled. Always show respect to the crew boss. Never give information to police. Don't sell to undercover officers or persons you don't know. Workers who helped competitors could be shot.

Violence also permeated the way sellers did their job through additional norms for sellers:

> Be aggressive and threatening to avoid robbery or being taken advantage of. Stand up to and argue loudly with those who threaten. Fight back if someone physically attacks you. Carry weapons for protection. Engage in fist or knife fights. Disparage and belittle your opposition. Threaten or assault those who attempt to sell crack in your territory. Maintain your reputation as dangerous, tough, and "crazy," regardless of the physical harm inflicted or suffered.

These norms resulted in a constantly edgy street culture where one's actions could easily be construed as disrespecting another's reputation and result in a fight (Dunlap 1997a, 1997c; Dunlap and Johnson 1996b; Dunlap, Johnson, and Rath 1996).

Violence was also commonly used to settle disputes between crack crews for control of a given sales area. Such intercrew conflicts were among the most dangerous for the local citizenry, who might get caught in the middle of a fight or drive-by shooting.

Subculture of Robbery. Crack markets fundamentally transformed the conduct norms of robbery. During the Heroin Injection Era, robbers preyed on citizens and businesses. During the Cocaine/Crack Era, drug sellers became the preferred target. Robbers would closely observe one or more drug sellers, carefully noting where they stashed their money or drugs, and then rob them when they were not well protected. A robber would typically use a gun to threaten the seller to "give it up." Occasionally the robber would shoot the victim if there was substantial resistance. Sometimes the victim was also armed and a shoot-out might occur. But robbers who systematically targeted drug sellers or members of crack crews would eventually become known and thus subject to execution. A robber was viewed as a threat to the existing crack distribution system and the reputation of the drug seller or crew. Thus, dealers felt compelled to protect themselves.

Subculture of Domestic Violence. The crack distribution industry and crack use transformed the nature of violence in household settings. In inner-city minority communities, especially where one or more partners in a household was a crack user, long-term male–female relationships nearly became extinct. Marriage rarely occurred, and the few marriages quickly ended in separation (although rarely a legal divorce). The most common form of male–female relationship might be called *transient domesticity*, in which a man, typically unemployed, moves in with a woman who often has children from another relationship (Dunlap 1998; O'Sullivan 1999). They might live together as sexual partners for one to several months, after which the man might be put out for any of several reasons or leave on his own. Each would often find another partner within six months. While living as a couple, the man and (less frequently) woman would have sexual relations with other partners as well. Children sometimes resulted from these unions, but the biological father rarely remained in the household after the child was born and had almost no role in raising it (Dunlap 1998; Johnson, Dunlap, and Maher 1998).

A primary reason that crack-using or crack-selling males sought out a woman was to have a free place to live, sleep, and eat. The man expected the woman to share her bed and sexual favors, to feed him, and give him spending money from her welfare check or job. Although the woman occasionally expected the man to give her money for "expenses," such income support was rarely provided, except as gifts of crack or other drugs. In a similar fashion, crack-using women would seek out an older male with housing and income support. The woman would move in, providing sex and some domestic services in exchange for a rent-free place to sleep, bathe, and occasionally steal some spending money (Hamid 1992a; Maher et al. 1996; Williams 1991).

The transient man also brought his entire background and often his participation in the drug industry into the woman's household. If the man had been maltreated in childhood, he was often surly and violent toward the female household head and her children. Numerous arguments and physical fights would occur, often precipitated by smoking crack or running out of crack, but very few serious assaults ever came to police attention (Dunlap, Johnson, and Rath 1996). In addition, male sellers often took over the female's household as a crack-selling location, which was subsequently targeted by robbers, police, or other crack sellers.

An important ancillary form of domestic violence involved neglect or abuse of children. Especially when the female household head became a crack user, her children were often neglected, with food and supervision woefully inadequate. Indeed, many female crack users effectively gave their children to other relatives to raise, or child protective services removed the children to foster care (Johnson, Dunlap, and Maher 1998). In other households the primary caregiver changed frequently, so that no psychological continuity was provided to the children. The woman's partner would often physically abuse male children. Female children, especially recently pubescent girls, were often sexually abused by the partner (Dunlap 1997a, 1997c), which sometimes resulted in transmission of STDs to the girl (Dunlap, Johnson, Randolph et al. 1998).

Violence in domestic settings was somewhat alleviated by domestic violence legislation, and especially by the policy of arresting and prosecuting males who assault their intimate partners or others in the household, even in these severely distressed inner-city households (O'Sullivan 1999). In the heat of a domestic dispute, a woman might say, "If you fuck with me, I'll call the cops." Although women rarely did so, males were somewhat deterred from beating their partners.

Policing Practices. The dramatic expansion of crack selling brought about major changes in public and governmental responses to crack and other hard drugs (Belenko 1993; Hartman and Golub 1999; Reinarman and Levine 1997). When crack use exploded in the mid-1980s, policy makers did not have clear ideas about how to prevent or intervene in its use (GAO 1998a). No drug treatment (like methadone) was available to stop the repetitive and compulsive cycle of crack consumption. Political leaders perceived that the American public and journalists were demanding swift introduction of a tough and punitive response.

The policing initiative of Operation Pressure Point (underway since 1983) was inadequate in 1986 to contain the flood of crack sellers who had appeared in New York City. In 1988, about one-fourth of the NYPD was reassigned to newly launched Tactical Narcotics Teams (TNT) further focused on "taking back the streets." TNT proved fairly effective in regaining control of selected blocks, although many crack sellers and users simply moved to other locations (Sviridoff et al. 1992). Meanwhile, the criminal justice system expanded to handle a doubling of its caseload (Belenko 1993).

At the federal level, Congress passed legislation that mandated lengthy penal sanctions for possession or sale of small amounts of crack.

Predicate felony legislation also lengthened sentences of those convicted in state courts. Most crack-specific legislation went into effect in 1989–90. Between 1980 and 1990, the prison population in New York State doubled (as did the national prison population), with most of the new inmates sentenced on charges of possession or sale of narcotic drugs, primarily crack (Bureau of Justice Statistics [BJS] 1999a, 1999b; Johnson and Muffler 1997). Overall, governmental policies and policing practices were focused upon crack sellers and distributors. Thousands were arrested, processed, and sentenced, and many additional persons were lodged in New York City and state correctional facilities at the end of the 1980s. Nationally, the proportion of African-American males in jail or prison, on probation or parole or some other form of criminal justice supervision increased from 25 percent to 33 percent between 1989 and 1994 (Mauer 1995). By the end of 1999, about 2 million will be in jail or prison nationwide, and over 5 million will be on probation or parole (BJS 1999b; Johnson and Muffler 1997, p. 113).

The Cocaine/Crack Generation in 1998. As members of the CrackGen pass through their thirties, many have persisted in their habits. However, they have become very isolated as they constantly conceal their compulsive behaviors from police, mainstream society, and, as described shortly, from the BluntGen. Crack markets have contracted and transformed. Persons who may have been effective crew leaders, dealers, or freelance sellers in the 1980s have become largely unable to sustain lucrative sales roles. Many sellers have been jailed or incarcerated. More importantly, most members of the CrackGen have acquired a reputation among crack suppliers as untrustworthy, primarily due to their compulsive use. They have had to accept low-level distribution roles (Furst, Curtis et al. 1997) as the frequency of their transactions and income from crack distribution have diminished (Caulkins et al. 1999).

Despite these changes, many of the CrackGen appear likely to continue using crack regularly during their forties, in the first decade of 2000. The remainder of the CrackGen effectively settled into more controlled consumption patterns, using about as frequently as long-term heroin injectors tend to use their drugs of choice, perhaps twice a day, and often interspersed with several days of nonuse. These persistent users seem somewhat less eager, less likely to sustain multiday "missions," and more likely to wait a few days between binges. The conduct norms have thus shifted:

> Use crack when you can get the money. Live with the ups and downs of crack use. Avoid or ignore denigration from others. Share crack with others.

Seek help only among small groups of other crack users. Socialize mainly with a few similar crack users.

The Marijuana/Blunts Era in New York City Around 1998. A most remarkable transformation occurred among inner-city youths born in the 1970s and reaching adulthood in the 1990s: the BluntGen developed very strong avoidance norms regarding crack smoking and heroin injection, in particular, but even against snorting of heroin and cocaine:

> Don't use crack. Crackheads are shit! Heroin injection causes AIDS. Addicts are scum of the earth. Stay safe, stay alive. Don't mix cocaine or heroin with my marijuana. Shun and exclude heroin and crack users from peer groups (Furst, Johnson et al. 1999).

Indeed, this anti-hard-drug peer pressure could become quite physical. One group of youths who determined that a peer had been using crack beat him up on the spot (Randolph, Dunlap, and Johnson 1998).

As compared to the HeroinGen in 1968, who were busy "taking care of business," and the CrackGen in 1988, who were "on a mission," the BluntGen in 1998 were not so consumed by their drug habit. Consequently, they had a lot of idle time during a typical day. The BluntGen's avoidance of hard drugs is in one sense quite remarkable, given that they grew up in severely distressed households where one or more adults were near daily users of heroin or crack or both (Golub and Johnson 1999b; Hamid et al. 1997). In another sense, though, it is not surprising: The primary reason that the BluntGen gives for avoiding crack and heroin is the *negative* role models in their lives. They clearly do not want to emulate their parents, older siblings, close relatives, or acquaintances who were ensnared by crack or heroin. Indeed, the BluntGen typically blame much of the poverty and other difficulties of their predecessors on heroin and crack.

Subculture of Blunt and Alcohol Use. Inner-city youths born in the 1970s, however, have not adopted conventional society's condemnation of illicit drugs. Their illegal drug of choice is the blunt. The conduct norms associated with the blunt subculture include:

> Smoke marijuana in a cigar. Enjoy the preparation ritual. Share with friends. Use with beer or alcohol. Spend a lengthy period of time after consumption enjoying the euphoric effect and slowly coming down. Define marijuana as "not a drug." Combine funds in peer group to purchase marijuana. Be willing to occasionally commit a crime to get money to buy mari-

juana. Maintain good contacts with marijuana sellers. Sell marijuana to friends occasionally to be able to "smoke free" (Sifaneck and Kaplan 1996; Sifaneck and Small 1997).

The BluntGen also appears to be transforming the conduct norms of disinhibition associated with alcohol consumption. A typical blunt-using episode will involve two to five peers in their twenties sharing a half ounce of marijuana and two or three quarts of malt beer over two to five hours. While passing the marijuana blunt around, each person will also sip beer or malt liquor so that everyone enjoys a modest high while talking and listening to rap music. As everyone's euphoria diminishes about an hour later, the ritual may be repeated. The BluntGen has effectively promoted conduct norms of controlled alcohol intake among high-risk youths. These conduct norms also discourage rapid ingestion of alcohol and displays of drunken comportment, including aggressive language and threatening or violent behavior. If one consistently and rapidly consumes large quantities of alcohol, acts drunk, or is violent towards others, that person will be sanctioned and if necessary excluded from the blunt-sharing group at future times.

Subculture of Illicit Drug Sales. The BluntGen are very aware that they face a dilemma when considering whether to sell drugs. A substantial majority of this generation quite literally see young men in wheelchairs (from kneecappings or other violence), know several persons in jail or prison, or know those who died in drug-related violence. They are also aware that few sellers actually make much money. For all of these reasons, most avoid becoming involved in drug sales as a career activity. Selling marijuana does not appear to be much of an alternative either; profit margins are low and wholesale quantities of marijuana are difficult to obtain without a substantial advance payment, in cash.

Subculture of Robbery. Robbery has declined in the 1990s for a variety of reasons. For one, fewer citizens carry substantial amounts of cash, people who have money use credit cards instead. Drug dealers as well keep less money on them and keep it in a hidden stash. Perhaps most important, the BluntGen lifestyle does not require large quantities of money. The funds required to purchase marijuana are sufficiently small that less serious crimes (e.g., shoplifting, steering customers) will often provide enough. The marijuana market has historically had little systemic violence; organized crews of sellers have not engaged in turf wars or assaults for control of marijuana-selling territory. Nor is marijuana typically associated with any psychopharmacological violence.

Subculture of Assault. The BluntGen also appears less involved in aggravated assaults than the CrackGen. The BluntGen do come from households with high levels of family assault and violence, and do occasionally become involved in fights. Yet, the types of drug-related conflicts and disagreements of the CrackGen and HeroinGen occur less often among the BluntGen. The crack-induced paranoia of the CrackGen or withdrawal anxiety of the HeroinGen are seldom present among those who only smoke marijuana or blunts. If anything, the BluntGen conduct norms of sharing blunts ("puff, puff, and pass") are associated with sociable relations. While some bickering may occur among marijuana smokers over the duration that each smokes a shared blunt, this seldom leads to physical violence. The conduct norms dictate that participants be sociable and pleasant while smoking blunts and avoid arguments or fights. In addition, the modest euphoria from marijuana appears to reduce the hostility and aggressiveness of even very angry and frustrated persons, so that aggression is rare before, during, or soon after marijuana consumption – even among persons who engage in assaultive behavior on other occasions.

Subculture of Domestic Violence. Many in the BluntGen were assaulted, raped, or physically victimized as children or young adults. They perceive their violent parents and other violent adults as negative role models, the kind of people the BluntGen do not wish to become. In some households, the BluntGen (in early adulthood) have become dispute mediators among aggressive adults. When BluntGen initiate a sexual cohabitation relationship, the conduct norms associated with shared marijuana use enjoin cordiality, sexual enjoyment, and harmony in domestic affairs. Indeed, a pleasant surprise emerging from ongoing studies of drug-abusing households is that some unemployed high-risk men in their early twenties who primarily smoke blunts are forming compatible common-law relationships with women who have steady (although low-income) jobs that support the household (Dunlap, Johnson, Randolph et al. 1998; Randolph, Dunlap, and Johnson 1998). The men provide some housekeeping services and often care for the woman's children, irrespective of whether they are the father. The women often provide enough funds to support the man's marijuana consumption, as well as her own. When domestic disputes do arise, they often involve the failure of the man to obtain a job or to contribute financially to the household. But such disputes rarely lead to violent behavior.

Subculture of Handguns. The BluntGen are largely gun free, for two reasons. The federal Brady Bill and New York City laws ban handguns and require significant sanctions for illegal possession. But more important, the BluntGen are "doing nothing wrong," as they see it, nothing that would necessitate having a handgun. Most of their criminality involves such low-level offenses (shoplifting, helping steer customers, selling or sharing marijuana with their friends) that a handgun is not needed. Only the small proportion of the BluntGen engaged in robbery, sales of cocaine or heroin, or both feel a need for "protection." Some drug sellers who feel a need for protection from robbers now keep pitbulls or other aggressive dogs instead of guns.

Policing Policies and Quality-of-life Enforcement. In the 1990s, the number of police officers was substantially increased and the effecetiveness of the NYPD was enhanced. Most important, the department has successfully achieved integrated management (via Compstat meetings) of its numerous precincts, created special squads (detectives, narcotics, gangs, vice), and employed statistical information to suppress crime and disorder throughout the city (Silverman and O'Connell 1999). In large measure, the police (and cooperating agencies) have successfully "taken back the streets" from drug sellers and other disorderly persons in the 1990s.

Two policing policies appear to have been especially successful in eliminating handguns and in reducing the public visibility of street-level criminality: handgun checks, and quality-of-life enforcement. Both uniformed and undercover police routinely approach persons whom they observe with a "suspicious bulge" for a "handgun check." The police will ask them to open their coat, explain the bulge, and possibly, show the contents of pockets. If suspicions remain, they may pat down the person. If a gun is found, the person will be arrested, and if convicted, will face a jail sentence of a year or longer. Such gun checks are routinely performed in the course of general quality-of-life enforcement. In the 1990s, police routinely stop persons observed committing any of a wide range of minor offenses, ask them for photo identification, and conduct a radio check for warrants, parole/probation, or other criminal justice status. If the person has adequate identification and no current criminal charges but has committed an illegal act, the offender may be given a desk appearance ticket (DAT). The offender subsequently pays a fine or provides a community service (Anderson 1996). If the person lacks photo ID or has an outstanding warrant, that person is arrested and spends the better part of a day going through the booking process, awaiting arraignment.

Quality-of-life enforcement and handgun-check policies have been implemented across the city, but especially in major drug-selling areas. These two policies resulted in over 300,000 arrests in 1998 (NYPD 1998).

By the middle of 1998, police policy made it more difficult for a violator to qualify for a mere DAT. Police now arrest most quality-of-life violators and conduct a full record check based on fingerprints. This increase in quality-of-life policing has challenged the BluntGen's pattern of buying and smoking marijuana in public locations. Marijuana possession, smoking, and small sales have been decriminalized in New York since 1972, but not in public locations. For nearly twenty-five years, the police have written a DAT to public smokers, and released them. If the offenders showed up at court, they typically paid a fine.

Since July 1998, persons observed by police to be smoking, possessing, attempting to purchase, or selling marijuana (including blunts) in public locations are now arrested and processed through the city's central booking facilities (*The New York Times* 1998c). In the four largest boroughs, this means that inner-city youths (and some Wall Street marijuana consumers) smoking blunts outdoors are arrested, handcuffed, taken to a central booking facility, and made to wait for up to a full day in crowded holding cells while awaiting arraignment. The onerousness of the booking process itself serves as sanction for marijuana use in public locations. In this manner, the police are sending a message to offenders about appropriate conduct in public places. Whether such arrests will have a substantial impact upon the BluntGen's pattern of marijuana smoking in public remains to be documented. It seems unlikely that the policy can discourage youth from marijuana smoking altogether.

Quality-of-life policies have clearly reduced social disorder within inner-city neighborhoods (Kelling and Coles 1996). These policies have been very popular with working- and middle-class voters. Reducing disorder has contributed to the boom in the city's economy. Tourists from the United States and foreign countries in great numbers are paying premium prices for the city's hotels and entertainment. Tourists are feeling safe again, as they are less likely to observe the blatant drug selling, hear gun shots, experience violence, or view other disorderly behaviors. The appearance of reduced crime and disorder has been enhanced by the Giuliani administration's policy of withholding information, so that "crime stories" are less evident in the New York City press (*The New York Times* 1998b). Thus, the amount of crime and the amount of media attention per crime are dramatically down, both of which increase the perception of safety on city streets.

The preceding social histories of the HeroinGen, CrackGen, and BluntGen occurred in parallel to many other relevant activities. Tables 6.1, 6.2, and 6.3 very briefly summarize the subcultures of each drug era in sev-

Table 6.1. *Drug Subcultures: Shifts and Changes in Inner-City New York*

Drug Subcultures	Heroin Era (1966–73)	Cocaine Powder Era (1973–83)
Main Birth Years	1946–55	1956–65
	Heroin Subculture	*Cocaine Powder Subculture*
	Many teens initiate heroin	Cocaine more available
	Become regular injectors	Mainly snorted, some smoking
	Speedballing with cocaine	Only heroin users inject cocaine
	Use/share works & heroin	Many cocaine users try freebase
	Shooting galleries popular	Cocaine sales more than heroin
	Needles illegal/shared often	Cocaine sales in many locales
	Heroin selling common	
Marijuana	Explosion of marijuana use	High rates of youth marijuana use
	Consumed as "joints"	Make & sell "loose joints"
	Common in all classes	Widespread marijuana use
	"Hippie" era (Psychedelics)	LSD rare in inner-city markets
	Used/sold by inner-city youth	Marijuana sellers dominate park markets and streets
Drug-Selling		
Dominant Drugs	Heroin and marijuana	Cocaine powder and marijuana
Major Retail Unit	$10 bags (heroin), 2% purity	$10 bags (cocaine), good purity
Seller Style	Street sellers and galleries	Freelance and private
	Nicky Barnes controls Harlem	Colombians control cocaine market

Crack Era (1984–89)	Post-Crack Era (1990s)
1966–69	1970–79
Crack Subculture	*Blunts Subculture*
Crack vials explode in NYC	Marijuana use increase among youths
Crack use dominates all drugs	Smoke as a blunt, in a cigar wrapper
Youths initiate crack heavily	Avoid crack, heroin, injection
Basehouses become crack	Disrespect "crackheads" & "junkies"
Street crews and freelancers	Marijuana selling increases
Crack major drug sold by users	Mainly private networks, phones
Hard drug users limit marijuana	Marijuana and cigars used
Joints preferred use	Blunts replace joints
Crack users reduce marijuana	Marijuana/blunts very common
Few inner-city psychedelic users	Few psychedelic users
Marijuana selling suppressed in public places	Marijuana sellers arrested/booked
	Private sales most common
Crack	Crack and marijuana dominate
$2–5 crack vials, good quality	$5 crack vial, $10–20 marijuana
Street crews, freelancers	Freelancers, phone, delivery service
Dominicans major cocaine/crack wholesalers	Multiple suppliers of marijuana

Table 6.2. *Nondrug Criminal Subcultures: Shifts and Changes in Inner-City New York*

Nondrug Criminal Subcultures	Heroin Era (1966–73)	Cocaine Powder Era (1973–83)
Main Birth Years	1946–55	1956–65
Handgun	Few handguns available Most sellers, no guns Knives most common	Handguns widely available Sellers seek handguns Knives commonly carried
Robbery	Citizens with money Usually no guns employed Some robbery of sellers	Seek citizens with money Guns increasingly employed Other drug sellers targeted
Assaultive	Fight & argue common Domestic assault common Alcohol involved in assaults Gang fights diminish	Cocaine paranoia increase fights Domestic assault increases Cocaine plus alcohol in assault Gang fights disappear
Burglary	Mostly against homes Some burglary of business	Home burglary continues Business burglary increases
Shoplift/Larceny	Lift from stores, trucks Parts from cars Little auto theft	Decline of stores in inner-city "Popping shorts" very common Few inner-city New Yorkers drive
Street	Hang out on streets Fare evasion common Open alcohol use & sale Police ignore many violations	Streets major locale of activity Few inner-city youth pay fare Drinking common violation Police ignore many violations
Stolen Goods Market	Many low-income buyers Way to "shop" Buyers place orders with drug user-thieves	Fewer have cash to purchase Stolen goods hard to afford Orders decline in inner-city

Crack Era (1984–89)	Post-Crack Era (1990s)
1966–69	1970–79
Guns needed for "protection"	Gun use reduced by police stops
Crack seller & users carry guns	Sellers rarely carry guns
Knives commonly carried	Knives commonly carried
Citizens decline as targets	Citizens avoided as targets
Guns used in citizen robbery	Guns rarely used in citizen robbery
Most robbers target sellers	Most robbers target sellers
Crack creates arguments	Less fights and arguments
High levels of domestic assault	Less crack use, less assault
Crack plus alcohol in assault	Crack crews less common
Crack crews have much assault	Gangs/wanabees emerge
Home burglary about the same	Burglary declines modestly
Targets harden, burglary down	Business burglary down
Few stores to steal from	Few stores to steal from
Thefts from autos continue	Crackdown on auto part buyers
Anti-theft devices cut auto theft	Low rates of auto theft
Major activities on streets	Major activities on streets
Few inner-city youth pay fare	New turnstiles, police arrest
Police fare-beating campaign	Farebeating reduced
Police enforce many regulations	Quality-of-life violations down
Limited purchase of stolen good	Limited purchase of stolen goods
Few buyers for expensive stolen goods	Few buyers for expensive stolen goods
Few direct orders for goods	Few direct orders for goods

Table 6.3. Social Control Efforts by the Government in New York

Social Control Efforts	Heroin Era (1966–73)	Cocaine Powder Era (1973–83)
NYS Governor NYC Mayor Police Chief	Rockefeller Lindsey Brodrick, Leary, Murphy	Rockefeller, Carey Beame, Koch Codd, McGuire, Devine
Low-Wage Job Market	Several manufacturing jobs Service jobs few Odd jobs common SROs major housing for poor No public shelters	Decline in manufacturing jobs Increase in service jobs Minimum/below wage jobs only SROs converted to residences Growing public shelters
Policing of Drug Sellers	Get big dealers Patrolmen avoid street sellers Heroin primary target Some undercover officers Quality-of-life offenses ignored	Take back the streets Operation Pressure Point Cocaine and heroin Expand narcotic police force Quality-of-life offenses ignored
Penal sanctions for Drug Offenses	Heroin sales sanctions increased Marijuana decriminalized Cocaine powder not changed Prisons not expanded	Rockefeller law sentences several sellers to life terms Marijuana arrests decline Cocaine powder remains same Prison population grows
Drug Treatment	Few before 1968 Prison-like treatment facilities begun for criminal addicts Methadone maintenance for blocking heroin begins Therapeutic communities begin NY State begins funding of community programs	Expansion of drug treatment NACC failure; closed in 1976 became state prisons
Welfare System	AFDC become entitlement Welfare pays better than jobs Few homeless, no shelters	Drug users get welfare, SSI Welfare benefits decline Homelessness grows

Crack Era (1984–89)	Post-Crack Era (1990s)
Carey, Cuomo	Cuomo, Pataki
Koch, Dinkins	Dinkins, Giuliani
Ward, Condon, Brown	Kelley, Bratton, Safir
Few jobs for HS dropouts	Few jobs for HS dropouts
Few service jobs for dropouts	Some service jobs for dropouts
Minimum wage jobs only	Some above minimum wage jobs
SROs converted by nonprofit agencies	SROs become tourist hotels
Major shelter system	Declines in shelter system
Buy-bust large numbers	Remove seller from streets/parks
Tactical Narcotics Teams	Quality-of-life policing
Crack seller primary target	Crack and marijuana seller
Major expansion-quarter of force	Major squads and all police
Suppression of fare evasion	Quality-of-life policing major policy
Heroin selling not emphasized	Heroin selling secondary focus
Crack selling severely punished	Crack selling severely punished
Marijuana fines only, no jail	Marijuana possession booked
Cocaine powder enforced	Cocaine selling secondary focus
Big increase in prison population	Prison populations stable in NY
Treatment slots stable	Stable treatment slots stable
Prisons contain most drug abusers, limited treatment	Prison drug treatment cutback; Bootcamps become popular
Methadone slots stable	Mayor seeks to end methadone but backs away
Stable slots, mainly treat crack abusers	Stable slots, mainly treat crack and criminal justice referrals
Outpatient slots large, clients mainly crack users	Community treatment funding has modest cutbacks
Major source of legal income	Workfare, not entitlement
Buying power declines	Poor pressured off welfare rolls
Large public shelters	Cutback on shelters

eral domains (drug and criminal subcultures, and social control efforts). Many of the dimensions described in these tables have not been discussed in the text, but are relevant to a more in-depth understanding of the transformations occurring across the three drug eras delineated.

Conclusion

The rise and fall of violence in New York City, particularly homicide, clearly coincides with the succession of drug subcultures in the inner-city. Different drugs have been popular at different times. From 1960 to 1975, heroin injection was the drug practice of choice among hard-core drug users and abusers. Subsequently, the popularity of heroin waned and cocaine became the drug of choice. In the mid-1980s, the practice of smoking crack emerged. Crack involved intensive use, which led to highly competitive drug markets and increasing violence in the late 1980s. The subculture of crack use and sales calmed down in the 1990s leading to a decline in violence. This decline was enhanced by growing intolerance in inner-city communities of crack sellers' public behavior and by aggressive policing. But the decline was primarily due to the BluntGen's sustained avoidance of hard drugs and their attendant violent lifestyle. Instead, the BluntGen's subcultural norms stress sharing marijuana and alcohol in a cooperative and unobtrusive manner.

Official records document major declines in both homicide (which is generally accurately counted by the police) and robbery. The subcultural transformations described in this chapter suggest that all forms of interpersonal violence, including domestic assault and street fights, are probably also down, at least in New York's inner-city neighborhoods.

The ebb in violence has clearly been influenced by changes in policing practices especially the aggressive targeting of guns and street-level drug markets. No data will ever definitively identify how much of the decline in violence was the result of subcultural changes and how much is the result of policing initiatives; the two are clearly confounded. The BluntGen's norm against carrying a gun was influenced by increased penalties and increased enforcement (Taylor, Johnson, and Caulkins 1999). Members of the BluntGen report that it is the ravages that befell the HeroinGen and CrackGen that led them to avoid hard drugs. Those ravages include both deteriorating health as well as increased encounters with police and long prison terms. Thus, stepped-up policing efforts may have hastened the transformation of the inner-city subcultures of drug use.

It is not clear how much additional benefit is to be derived from continuing or expanding this intensified policing. The current programs have already been criticized by many inner-city residents as harassment of minorities – an antagonism that may prove counterproductive to other efforts at social reform. Moreover, the calm of the inner-city may be temporary and superficial. Intensified policing and criminal justice solutions will not address the continued exclusion of inner-city residents from legal labor markets. Hundreds of thousands of residents of inner-city communities in New York are not in the formal labor market, and many of them are being systematically excluded from welfare and other income transfers. Additionally, a large number of inner-city residents with legal jobs are trapped by low wages, part-time hours, and irregular work schedules. This large pool of surplus labor constitutes a persistent threat of a new epidemic of discontent, despair, drug abuse, crime, and violence.

The authors strongly feel that the low rates of violence and nondrug criminality and the marginal involvement in hard-drug sales of the BluntGen (those born in 1970s), combined with their eagerness to enter the legal workforce, combined with the expansion of the U.S. economy, provide an unparalleled opportunity. Clearly, the BluntGen has avoided the destructive lifestyles associated with hard-drug use and sales. However, they still face many life challenges; it is unclear how long their nonviolence will continue in the face of continued economic difficulties. Well-formulated policies in the new century could shrink the labor supply available to illicit-drug markets and systematically incorporate thousands of inner-city residents. Most inner-city youths, especially those reared in seriously distressed households, are extraordinarily isolated from mainstream American society. They are quite unclear about how to interact with whites, employed persons, middle-class authority figures, or the banking system. They need training and support to gain legal jobs, keep jobs, develop skills, and increase their income. But, most important, policies are needed to encourage employers, large and small, to create jobs and to hire inner-city youths and young adults. As the pool of unemployed and out-of-labor-market young adults from the inner-city declines, the potential for illegal-drug markets would shrink accordingly. Moreover, the extensive cost of bringing youths from the Blunt and subsequent generations into steady legal jobs with above-poverty wages would result in enormous reductions in welfare, policing, and social disorder – as well as converting them into taxpayers. Eventually the violence, drug use, and drug sales evident in the late 1980s might recede into distant memories. The time to begin is now.

Notes

1. Analyses of the National Household Survey of Drug Use and Monitoring the Future (high school seniors) reveal trends similar to those documented among ADAM-NYC arrestees, but with much lower prevalence of cocaine, herion, and marijuana use. Likewise, analyses in twenty-three major cities in the United States (ADAM sites in 1997) document trends for heroin, cocaine, and marijuana very much parallel to those in Manhattan, as depicted in Figure 1; various differences in the prevalence and the years that specific birth cohorts became heavily involved with or began avoiding the specific drugs are evident for these cities (Golub and Johnson 2000).

References

Anderson, D. C. 1996. *New York City, a "Community Court" and a New Legal Culture.* NCJ 158613. Washington: National Institute of Justice.

Anglin, M. D., and B. Perrochet. 1998. "Drug Use and Crime: A Historical Review of Research Conducted by the UCLA Drug Abuse Research Center." *Substance Use and Misuse* 33(9):1871–1941.

Austin, G. A., B. D. Johnson, E. E. Carroll, and D. J. Lettieri. 1977. *Drugs and Minorities.* Research Issues 21. Rockville, MD: National Institute on Drug Abuse.

Ball, J. C., L. Rosen, J. A. Flueck, and D. N. Nurco. 1981. "The Criminality of Heroin Addicts When Addicted and When Off Opiates." In J. A. Inciardi (Ed.), *The Drugs-Crime Connection.* Beverly Hills, CA: Sage.

Ball, J. C., J. W. Shaffer, and D. N. Nurco. 1983. "The Day-to-Day Criminality of Heroin Addicts in Baltimore: A Study in the Continuity of Offense Rates." *Drug and Alcohol Dependence* 12:119–42.

Belenko, S. 1993. *Crack and the Evolution of Anti-Drug Policies.* Westport, CT: Greenwood.

Bourgois, P. 1995. *In Search of Respect: Selling Crack in El Barrio.* New York: Cambridge University Press.

Boyle, J., and A. F. Brunswick. 1980. "What Happened in Harlem? Analysis of a Decline in Heroin Use Among a Generational Unit of Urban Black Youth." *Journal of Drug Issues* 10:109–30.

Brown, C. 1965. *Manchild in the Promised Land.* New York: Macmillan.

Bureau of Justice Statistics. 1999a. *Prisoners in 1997.* Washington: U.S. Bureau of Justice Statistics, NCJ 170014.

    1999b. *Prison and Jail Inmates at Midyear 1998.* Washington: U.S. Bureau of Justice Statistics, NCJ 173414.

Butterfield, F. 1995. *All God's Children: The Bosket Family and the American Tradition of Violence.* New York: Knopf.

Butterfield, F. 1998. "New Data Point Blame at Gun Makers." *The New York Times,* November, 28, p. A9.

Caulkins, J. P. 1997. "Is Crack Cheaper Than (Powder) Cocaine? *Addiction* 92(11):1437–43.

Caulkins, J. P., B. D. Johnson, A. Taylor, and L. Taylor. 1999. "What Drug Dealers Tell Us About Their Costs of Doing Business." *Journal of Drug Issues* 29(2):323–40.

Caulkins, J. P., and R. Padman. 1993. "Quantity Discounts and Quality Premia for Illicit Drugs." *Journal of the American Statistical Association* 88(423):748–57.

Clayton, R. R., and H. L. Voss. 1981. *Young Men and Drugs in Manhattan: A Causal Analysis*. Research Monograph 39. Rockville, MD: National Institute on Drug Abuse.

Des Jarlais, D. C. 1998. "Understanding the Long-term Course of HIV Epidemics." *AIDS* 12(6):669–70.

Des Jarlais, D. C., K. Choopanya, P. Millson, P. Friedmann, and S. R. Friedman. 1998. "The Structure of Stable Seroprevalence HIV-1 Epidemics Among Injecting Drug Users." In G. Stimson, D. C. Des Jarlais, and A. Ball (Eds.), *Drug Injecting and HIV Infection: Global Dimensions and Local Responses*. London: World Health Organization, UCLA Press.

Des Jarlais, D. C., S. R. Friedman, J. L. Sotheran, J. Wenston, J. Marmor, S. R. Yankovitz, B. Frank, S. T. Beatrice, and D. Mildvan. 1994. "Continuity and Change Within an HIV Epidemic: Injection Drug Users in New York City, 1984 through 1992." *Journal of the American Medical Association* 27:121–27.

Duncan, G. J., and J. Brooks-Gunn (Eds.). 1997. *Consequences of Growing Up Poor*. New York: Russell Sage Foundation.

Dunlap, E. 1992. "Impact of Drugs on Family Life and Kin Networks in the Inner-City African-American Single Parent Household." In Adele Harrell and George Peterson (Eds.), *Drugs, Crime, and Social Isolation: Barriers to Urban Opportunity*. Washington: Urban Institute Press.

Dunlap, E. 1995. "Inner-City Crisis and Drug Dealing: Portrait of a Drug Dealer and His Household." In Suzanne MacGregor and Arthur Lipow (Eds.), *The Other City: People and Politics in New York and London*. Totowa, NJ: Humanities Press.

Dunlap, E. 1996. *Violence and Self-Image of Drug Dealers: Surviving in Street Life/Drug Industry*. Paper presented at The Society for the Study of Social Problems, August, New York City.

Dunlap, E. 1997a. *Let the People Speak: An Episodic Approach to Understanding Violence*. Paper presented at the American Society of Criminology, November, San Diego.

Dunlap, E. 1997b. *Street Life–Women and Drugs: Where Do They Go from Here?* Paper presented at the Society for the Study of Social Problems in Canada, August, Toronto.

Dunlap, E. 1997c. *Impact of Crack Use/Sales on Household and Family Interaction Patterns and Violence*. Paper presented at the Western Society of Criminology, February, Honolulu.

Dunlap, E. 1998. *Transient Fathering among Inner-city Black Men.* Application to National Institute on Drug Abuse. New York: National Development and Research Institutes.

Dunlap, E., and B. D. Johnson. 1992. "The Setting for the Crack Era: Macro Forces, Micro Consequences (1960–92)." *Journal of Psychoactive Drugs* 24(3):307–21.

Dunlap, E., and B. D. Johnson. 1996a. "Family and Human Resources in the Development of a Female Crack Seller Career: Case Study of a Hidden Population." *Journal of Drug Issues* 26(1):175–98.

Dunlap, E., and B. D. Johnson. 1996b. *Household and Family Interaction Patterns and Violence: Conduct Norms When Drug Use and or Sales Are Present.* Paper presented at the Society for the Study of Social Problems in August, New York City.

Dunlap, E., and B. D. Johnson. 1997. *Treatment Unreadiness: Gleaning Insights About the Social Construction of Drug Treatment Among Street-Level Crack and Injection Drug Users in Manhattan.* Paper presented at Society for Applied Anthropology in March, Seattle.

Dunlap, E., and B. D. Johnson. 1998. *Drugs, Socialization and the Mortification of Self: Case Study of Intergenerational Behavior Patterns and Conduct Norms.* Paper presented at the American Society of Anthropology in April, San Juan.

Dunlap, E., B. D. Johnson, and L. Maher. 1997. "Female Crack Dealers in New York City: Who They Are and What They Do." *Women and Criminal Justice* 8(4):25–55.

Dunlap, E., B. D. Johnson, and A. Manwar. 1994. "A Successful Female Crack Dealer: Case Study of a Deviant Career." *Deviant Behavior* 15:1–25.

Dunlap, E., B. D. Johnson, D. Randolph, and D. Murray. 1998. *Reproductive Practices and Sexual Learning in Drug-Abusing Households: Implications for HIV and STDs.* Paper presented at the American Society of Criminology in November, Washington, DC.

Dunlap, E., B. D. Johnson, and J. Rath. 1996. "Aggression and Violence in Households of Crack Sellers/Abusers." *Applied Behavioral Science Review* 4(2):191–217.

Furst, R. T., R. Curtis, B. D. Johnson, and D. Goldsmith. 1997. "The Rise of the Street Middleman/Woman in a Declining Drug Market." *Addiction Research* 5(4):1–26.

Furst, R. T., B. D. Johnson, E. Dunlap, and R. Curtis. 1999. "The Stigmatized Image of the Crack Head: A Sociocultural Exploration of a Barrier to Cocaine Smoking Among a Cohort of Youth in New York City." *Deviant Behavior* 20:153–81.

Gibbs, J. T. 1988. *Young, Black and Male in America: An Endangered Species.* Dover, MA: Auburn House.

Gold, M. S., and N. Miller. 1997. "Cocaine (and Crack) Neurobiology." In J. H. Lowinson, P. Ruiz, R. B. Millman, and J. G. Langrod (Eds.), *Substance Abuse: A Comprehensive Textbook.* 3rd edition. Baltimore: Williams and Wilkins.

Goldstein, P. J. 1985. "The Drugs/Violence Nexus: A Tripartite Conceptual Framework." *Journal of Drug Issues* 14:493–506.

Goldstein, P. J. 1998. "Drugs, Violence, and Federal Funding: A Research Odyssey." *Substance Use and Misuse* 33(9):1915–36.

Goldstein, P. J., H. H. Brownstein, P. J. Ryan, and P. A. Bellucci. 1997. "Crack and Homicide in New York City: A Case Study in the Epidemiology of Violence." In C. Reinarman and H. G. Levine (Eds.), *Crack in America: Demon Drugs and Social Justice.* Berkeley: University of California.

Goldstein, P. J., D. S. Lipton, E. Preble, I. Sobel, T. Miller, W. Abbott, W. Paige, and F. Soto. 1984. "The Marketing of Street Heroin in New York City." *Journal of Drug Issues* (Summer):553–66.

Golub, A., and B. D. Johnson. 1994a. "Cohort Differences in Drug Use Pathways to Crack Among Current Crack Abusers in New York City." *Criminal Justice and Behavior* 21(4):403–22.

Golub, A., and B. D. Johnson. 1994b. "A Recent Decline in Cocaine Use Among Youthful Arrestees in Manhattan (1987–1993)." *American Journal of Public Health* 84(8):1250–54.

Golub, A., and B. D. Johnson. 1996. "The Crack Epidemic: Empirical Findings Support a Hypothesized Diffusion of Innovation Process." *Socio-Economic Planning Sciences* 30(3):221–31.

Golub, A., and B. D. Johnson. 1997. "Crack's Decline: Some Surprises Across U.S. Cities." National Institute of Justice, *Research in Brief* NCJ 165707. Washington: U.S. Department of Justice.

Golub, A., and B. D. Johnson. 1999a. "Coerced Treatment for Drug-Abusing Criminal Offenders: A Referral Device for Use in New York City." *International Journal of Public Administration* 22(2):187–215.

Golub, A., and B. D. Johnson. 1999b. "From the Heroin Injection Generation to the Blunted Generation: Cohort Changes in Illegal Drug Use Among Arrestees in Manhattan." *Substance Use and Misuse* 34(13):1733–63.

Golub, A. and B. D. Johnson. 2000. "Monitoring the Marijuana Upsurge with DUF/ADAM Arrestees." Final Report to National Institute of Justice, Project 99-IJ-CX0020.

Golub, A. and B. D. Johnson. Forthcoming. "Substance Use Progression and Hard Drug Abuse in Inner-city New York." In Denise Kandel (Ed.), *Stages and Pathways of Drug Involvement: Examining the Gateway Hypothesis.* New York: Cambridge University Press.

Government Accounting Office (GAO) 1997. *Drug and Alcohol Abuse: Billions Spent Annually for Treatment and Prevention Activities.* HEHS-97-12. Washington.

Government Accounting Office (GAO). 1998a. *Emerging Drug Problems: Despite Changes in Detection and Response Capability, Concerns Remain.* HEHS-98-130. Washington.

Government Accounting Office (GAO). 1998b. *Drug Abuse: Studies Show Treatment Is Effective, but Benefits May Be Overstated.* T-HEHS-98-185. Washington.

Hamid, A. 1992a. "Drugs and Patterns of Opportunity in the Inner-City: The Case of Middle Aged, Middle Income Cocaine Smokers." In Adele Harrell and George Peterson (Eds.), *Drugs, Crime, and Social Isolation: Barriers to Urban Opportunity,* (pp. 209–239). Washington: Urban Institute Press.

Hamid, A. 1992b. "The Developmental Cycle of a Drug Epidemic: The Cocaine Smoking Epidemic of 1981–1991." *Journal of Psychoactive Drugs* 24:337–48.

Hamid, A., R. Curtis, K. McCoy, J. McGuire, A. Conde, W. Bushell, R. Lindenmayer, K. Brimberg, S. Maia, S. Abdur-Rashid, and J. Settembrino. 1997. "The Heroin Epidemic in New York City: Current Status and Prognoses." *Journal of Psychoactive Drugs* 29:375–91.

Hartman, D., and A. Golub. 1999. "The Social Construction of the Crack Epidemic in the Print Media." *Journal of Psychoactive Drugs* 31(4):423–33.

Hunt, L. G., and C. D. Chambers. 1976. *The Heroin Epidemic: A Study of Heroin Use in the U.S., 1965–1975.* Holliswood, NY: Spectrum.

Johnson, B. D. 1973. *Marihuana Users and Drug Subcultures.* New York: John Wiley.

Johnson, B. D. 1978. "Once an Addict, Seldom an Addict." *Contemporary Drug Problems* (Spring):35–53.

Johnson, B. D. 1980. "Towards a Theory of Drug Subcultures." In Dan Letteri et al. (Eds.), *Theories on Drug Abuse: Selected Contemporary Perspectives.* Research Monograph, No. 30. Rockville, MD: National Institute on Drug Abuse.

Johnson, B. D. 1984. "Empirical Patterns of Heroin Consumption Among Selected Street Heroin Users." In George Serban (Ed.), *Social and Medical Aspects of Drug Abuse.* Jamaica: Spectrum Publications, Inc.

Johnson, B. D., E. Dunlap, and Associates. 1998. *Natural History of Crack Distribution/Abuse.* Final Report. Washington, DC: National Institute on Drug Abuse.

Johnson, B. D., E. Dunlap, and L. Maher. 1998. "Nurturing for Careers in Drug Use and Crime: Conduct Norms for Children and Juveniles in Crack-Using Households." *Substance Use and Misuse* 33:1515–50.

Johnson, B. D., E. Dunlap, and S. C. Tourigny. 2000. "Crack Distribution and Abuse in New York City." In Mangai Natarajan and Michael Hough (Eds.), *Illegal Drug Markets: From Research to Prevention Policy. Crime Prevention Studies,* vol. 11. Monsey, NY: Criminal Justice Press.

Johnson, B. D., P. J. Goldstein, E. Preble, J. Schmeidler, D. S. Lipton, B. Spunt, and T. Miller. 1985. *Taking Care of Business: The Economics of Crime by Heroin Users.* Lexington, MA: Lexington Books.

Johnson, B. D., and A. L. Golub. Forthcoming. "Generational Trends in Heroin Use and Injection Among Arrestees in New York City." In D. Musto (Ed.), *One Hundred Years of Heroin: History, Medicine and Policy.* Westport, CT: Greenwood.

Johnson, B. D., A. Golub, and J. Fagan. 1995. "Careers in Crack, Drug Use, Drug Distribution and Nondrug Criminality." *Crime and Delinquency* 41(3):275–95.

Johnson, B. D., A. Hamid, and H. Sanabria. 1992. "Emerging Models of Crack Distribution." In T. Mieczkowksi (Ed.), *Drugs and Crime: A Reader*, (pp. 56–78). Boston: Allyn-Bacon.

Johnson, B. D., M. A. Kaplan, and J. Schmeidler. 1990. "Days with Drug Distribution: Which Drugs? How Many Transactions? With What Returns?" In Ralph A. Weischeit (Ed.), *Drugs, Crime, and the Criminal Justice System*, (pp. 193–214). Cincinnati, OH: Anderson Publishing Company.

Johnson, B. D., C. Lewis, and A. L. Golub. 1992. "Crack Onset in the 1980s in New York City." In P. Vamos and P. Corriveau (Eds.), *Drugs and Society to the Year 2000*, (pp. 365–369). Montreal: Portage Program for Drug Dependencies, Inc.

Johnson, B. D., M. Natarajan, E. Dunlap, E. Elmoghazy. 1994. "Crack Abusers and Noncrack Abusers: Profiles of Drug Use, Drug Sales, and Nondrug Criminality." *Journal of Drug Issues* 24(1–2):117–41.

Johnson, B. D., and A. Manwar. 1991. *Towards a Paradigm of Drug Eras*. Paper presented at the American Society of Criminology in San Francisco (Nov. 9).

Johnson, B. D., and J. Muffler. 1992. "Sociocultural." In J. H. Lowinson, P. Ruiz, R. B. Millman, and J. G. Langrod (Eds.), *Substance Abuse: A Comprehensive Textbook*, (pp. 118–135). 2nd edition. Baltimore: Williams and Wilkins.

Johnson, B. D., and J. Muffler. 1997. "Sociocultural." In J. H. Lowinson, P. Ruiz, R. B. Millman, and J. G. Langrod (Eds.), *Substance Abuse: A Comprehensive Textbook*. 3rd edition, (pp. 107–117). Baltimore: Williams and Wilkins.

Johnson, B. D., G. Thomas, and A. L. Golub. 1998. "Trends in Heroin Use Among Manhattan Arrestees from the Heroin and Crack Eras." In J. A. Inciardi and L. D. Harrison (Eds.), *Heroin in the Age of Crack-Cocaine*, (pp. 109–130). Beverly Hills: Sage.

Johnson, B. D., and G. Uppal. 1980. "Marijuana and Youth: A Generation Gone to Pot." In Frank Scarpitti and Susan Datesman (Eds.), *Drugs and the Youth Culture*, (pp. 81–108). Beverly Hills: Sage.

Johnson, B. D., T. Williams, K. Dei, and H. Sanabria. 1990. "Drug Abuse and the Inner City: Impact on Hard Drug Users and the Community." In Michael Tonry and James Q. Wilson (Eds.), *Drugs and Crime*, (pp. 9–67). *Crime and Justice*, vol. 13. Chicago: University of Chicago Press.

Johnston, L. D., P. M. O'Malley, and J. G. Bachman. 1998. "Drug Use by American Young People Begins to Turn Downward." Ann Arbor, MI: University of Michigan News and Information Service, December 18.

Kasarda, J. 1992. "The Severely Distressed in Economically Transforming Cities." In Adele Harrell and George Peterson (Eds.), *Drugs, Crime, and Social Isolation: Barriers to Urban Opportunity*, (pp. 45–98). Washington, DC: Urban Institute Press.

Kelling, G. L. and C. M. Coles. 1996. *Fixing Broken Windows: Restoring Order and Reducing Crime in Our Communities*. New York: Free Press.

Lipton, D. S. and B. D. Johnson. 1998. "Smack, Crack and Score: Two Decades of NIDA-Funded Drugs and Crime Research at NDRI 1974–1994." *Substance Use and Misuse* 33(9):1779–1815.

Maher, Lisa. 1997. *Sexed Work: Gender, Race and Resistance in a Brooklyn Drug Market.* Oxford UK: Oxford University Press.

Maher, L., E. Dunlap, B. D. Johnson, and A. Hamid. 1996. "Gender, Power, and Alternative Living Arrangements in the Inner-City Crack Culture." *Journal of Research on Crime and Delinquency* 33 (2):181–205.

Malcolm X, and A. Haley. 1965. *Autobiography of Malcolm X.* New York: Macmillan.

Massing, M. 1998. *The Fix.* New York: Simon and Schuster.

Mauer, M. 1995. *Young Black Men and the Criminal Justice System: Five Years Later.* Washington: The Sentencing Project.

Musto, D. 1973. *The American Disease: Origins of Narcotic Control.* New Haven, CT: Yale University Press.

Musto, D. (Ed.). Forthcoming. *One Hundred Years of Heroin: History, Medicine and Policy.* Westport, CT: Greenwood.

National Advisory Commission on Civil Disorders. 1968. *U.S. Riot Commission Report.* New York: Bantam Books.

National Institute of Justice (NIJ). 1998. *Arrestee Drug Abuse Monitoring Program: 1997 Annual Report on Adult and Juvenile Arrestees.* NCJ 171672. Washington: U.S. Government Printing Office.

New York Police Department (NYPD). 1998. "Persons booked in New York City." [unpublished figures]. New York: NYPD.

The New York Times. 1998a. "Changing the Drug Laws." August 8, p. A14.

The New York Times. 1998b. "As the City Grows Safer, Crime Loosens Its Grip on the News." September 6, p. A35–36.

The New York Times. 1998c. "Arrests Soar in Crackdown on Marijuana." November 17, p. B1, B13.

Nurco, D. N. 1998. "A Long-Term Program of Research on Drug Use and Crime." *Substance Use and Misuse* 33(9):1817–37.

O'Sullivan, C. 1999. *Monitoring Domestic Violence Among ADAM-NYC Arrestees.* Application to National Institutes of Justice. New York: Victim Services.

Preble, E. J. and J. J. Casey. 1969. "Taking Care of Business—The Heroin User's Life on the Street." *International Journal of Addictions* 4(1):1–24.

Randolph, D., E. Dunlap, and B. D. Johnson. 1998. *Blunted Youths: Three Case Studies.* Paper presented at the American Society of Criminology, November 16, Washington.

Reinarman, C. and H. G. Levine. 1997. *Crack in America: Demon Drugs and Social Justice.* Berkeley: University of California Press.

Reuter, P., R. MacCoun, and P. Murphy. 1990. *Money from Crime: A Study of the Economics of Drug Dealing in Washington, D.C.* Santa Monica, CA: Rand.

Sanchez, J. E., and B. D. Johnson. 1987. "Women and the Drug-Crime Connection: Crime Rates Among Drug-Abusing Women at Rikers Island." *Journal of Psychedelic Drugs* 19(2):200–16.

Sellin, T. 1938. *Culture, Conflict, and Crime.* New York: Social Science Research Council.

Sifaneck, S. J., and C. D. Kaplan. 1996. "New Rituals of Cannabis Preparation and Self-Regulation in Two Cultural Settings and Their Implications for Secondary Prevention." New York: National Development and Research Institutes. Working Manuscript.

Sifaneck, S. J., and C. Small. 1997. "Blunts and Forties: The Drugs of Choice for the New Generation." New York: National Development and Research Institutes. Working Manuscript.

Silverman, E. B., and P. E. O'Connell. 1999. "Organizational Change and Decision Making in the New York City Police Department: A Case Study." *International Journal of Public Administration* 22(2):217–59.

Sullivan, M. 1989. *Getting Paid.* New Brunswick, NJ: Rutgers University Press.

Sviridoff, M., S. Sadd, R. Curtis, and R. Grinc. 1992. "The Neighborhood Effects of New York City's Tactical Narcotics Teams on Three Brooklyn Precincts." New York: Vera Institute of Justice. Unpublished paper.

Taylor, Angela, B. D. Johnson, and Jonathan Caulkins. 1999. *Drug Sellers' Accounts Regarding Gun Possession and Nonuse During Episodes Involving Conflict or Violence.* New York: National Development and Research Institutes (Unpublished manuscript).

Tonry, M., and J. Q. Wilson (Eds.) 1990. *Drugs and Crime. Crime and Justice: A Review of Research,* vol.13. Chicago: University of Chicago Press.

Uniform Crime Reports. 1998. *Crime in the United States in 1997.* Washington: Federal Bureau of Investigation.

U.S. Department of Justice. 1998. "Criminal Victimization 1997: Changes 1996–97 with Trends 1993–97." Press release, December 27. Washington: U.S. Department of Justice.

Van Dyke C., and R. Byck. 1982. "Cocaine." *Scientific American* 246(3):128–41.

Waldorf, D. 1973. *Careers in Dope.* Englewood Cliffs, NJ: Prentice Hall.

Waldorf, D. 1998. "Misadventures in the Drug Trade." *Substance Use and Misuse* 33(9):1957–91.

Waldorf, D., C. Reinarman, and S. Murphy. 1991. *Cocaine Changes: The Experience of Using and Quitting.* Philadelphia: Temple University Press.

Waterston, A. 1993. *Street Addiction: The Political Economy.* Philadelphia: Temple University Press.

Williams, T. 1989. *The Cocaine Kids: The Inside Story of a Teenage Drug Ring.* Reading, MA: Addison-Wesley.

Williams, T. 1991. *Crackhouse.* Reading, MA: Addison-Wesley.

Wilson, J. Q., and G. L. Kelling. 1982. "The Police and Neighborhood Safety." *Atlantic Monthly* (March):29–38.

Wilson, O. W. 1963. *Police Administration.* 2nd edition. New York: McGraw Hill.

Wilson, W. J. 1987. *The Truly Disadvantaged: The Inner-city, the Underclass, and Public Policy.* Chicago: University of Chicago Press.

Wilson, W. J. 1993. *The New Urban Poverty and the Problem of Race: The Tanner Lecture.* Ann Arbor: University of Michigan.

Wilson, W. J. 1996. *When Work Disappears: The World of the New Urban Poor.* New York: Random House.

Wolfgang, M. F. 1967. "The Culture of Youth." In *President's Commission on Law Enforcement, Task Force Report: Juvenile Delinquency and Youth Crime.* Washington: Government Printing Office.

Wolfgang, M. F. and F. Ferracuti. 1967. *The Subculture of Violence.* London: Tavistock.

Zimmer, L. 1987. "Operation Pressure Point: The Disruption of Street-Level Drug Trade on New York's Lower East Side." Center for Research in Crime and Justice, New York University School of Law.

CHAPTER SEVEN

Have Changes in Policing Reduced Violent Crime?
An Assessment of the Evidence

John E. Eck and Edward R. Maguire

The police do not prevent crime. This is one of the best kept secrets of modern life. Experts know it, the police know it, but the public does not know it. Yet the police pretend that they are society's best defense against crime and continually argue that if they are given more resources, especially personnel, they will be able to protect communities against crime. This is a myth.

David Bayley, *Police for the Future*

The connection of policing to risk factors is the most powerful conclusion reached from three decades of research. Hiring more police to provide rapid 911 response, unfocused random patrol, and reactive arrests does not prevent serious crime. Community policing without a clear focus on crime risk factors generally shows no effect on crime. But direct patrols, proactive arrests, and problem-solving at high-crime "hot spots" has shown substantial evidence of crime prevention. Police can prevent robbery, disorder, gun violence, drunk driving and domestic violence, but only by using certain methods under certain conditions.

Lawrence Sherman, "Policing for Crime Prevention"

THESE STATEMENTS SUMMARIZE two popular perspectives held by social scientists on the effect of police on crime. Some believe that the police do not and probably cannot have a significant effect on crime rates (Gottfredson and Hirschi 1990; Klockars 1983; Moran 1995). This viewpoint was forged from a sociological tradition in which theories provide no role for police in their explanations of crime. It also stems from more than two decades of evaluation research showing that, within reasonable bounds, neither the level of police resources nor the core strategies of policing appear to have much effect on crime. Dramatic reductions in violent crime (particularly homicide) throughout the United States over the past seven years have led some social scientists to question this stance (DiIulio 1995; Kelling and Coles 1996). Sherman (1995, p. 330), for instance, suggests that "police presence can reduce or even increase the crime rate substantially in specific places at specific times, depending on what the police do." In this chapter, we examine the scientific evidence about the contributions of the police to recent reductions in violent crime in the United States.

American policing is in the midst of significant changes at multiple levels. Some changes are generic, implemented throughout the nation to improve the responses of police to general classes of problems such as crime, disorder, fear, and quality of life. Others are more specific, focusing instead on a particular geographic area, time, offense type, or some combination of these factors. In Part One, we examine three generic changes in American policing over the past decade that are frequently credited for recent reductions in violent crime. These include increases in the size of police agencies, a growing movement toward more aggressive order-maintenance policing strategies, and community policing. Part Two examines a number of more focused policing strategies, including those aimed at specific places, times, offenders, and offenses. In Part Three, we summarize our findings and describe their implications for future developments in policing and crime prevention.

Part One: Generic Changes in American Policing

Changing the Number of Police. Across time and place, one of the most common reactions to increases in crime is to hire more police officers. American police agencies have been increasing in size since their inception, and despite problems in estimating the number of police officers nationwide, it is fair to say that we now have more police officers per capita than ever (Maguire et al. 1998).[1] Recent research shows that both police executives and the public believe increasing the number of police to be an important and effective method for reducing crime (Maguire and Pastore 1995, p. 172; McEwen 1995; National Association of Police Organizations [NAPO] 1997, 1999). A key feature of President Clinton's 1992 presidential campaign was his promise to increase the number of police officers in the United States by 100,000. Once in office, Clinton successfully implemented plans to fulfill his campaign promise, enacting the Violent Crime

Control and Law Enforcement Act (the "Crime Act") on September 13, 1994 (U.S. Congress 1994). As of May 12, 1999, Crime Act funds had been awarded for hiring or redeploying 100,000 officers (though not all of them are trained and on the streets) (Office of Community Oriented Policing Services 1999). For one commentator, such increases are not nearly enough. In a 1995 *Atlantic Monthly* article, Adam Walinsky suggested that the United States needs at least 500,000 new police officers.

Has increasing the number of police officers affected rates of violent crime? As mentioned, some police and government officials have been quick to answer "yes" to this question. To date, however, we are not aware of a single empirical study that supports the claim that increases in the number of police officers are responsible for recent decreases in violent crime. Some of the cities experiencing the greatest reductions in crime did so without increasing the number of officers. For example, among the twenty-five largest cities in the United States, San Diego and New York experienced the greatest decreases in crime from 1990 to 1996 (more than 40 percent). During that same time, however, the number of police officers per capita grew by 18 percent in New York, but only one percent in San Diego (Cordner 1998; Independent Budget Office 1998, p. 5). Furthermore, Dallas's crime rate plummeted by 39 percent, while the number of officers per capita declined by almost 3 percent (Independent Budget Office 1998, p. 6). Seattle's crime rate dropped by 18 percent, despite a decrease of 6 percent in the number of officers per capita (Independent Budget Office 1998, p. 6). At this point, there is little evidence that changes in the number of police officers are responsible for recent changes (in either direction) in violent crime.

Although there is no reliable evidence to support the link between *recent* increases in the number of police officers and the drop in violent crime, there is a large body of existing research on the relationship between police strength and crime rates.[2] The most difficult problem facing researchers attempting to unravel the relationship between police and crime is to determine if more police reduce crime or if more crime increases police hiring. If deterrence theorists are correct, then increasing the number of police officers should produce decreases in crime. On the other hand, society's first reaction in the face of increasing crime rates is usually to hire more police officers. Like the fabled chicken and egg, it is extremely difficult to determine which came first (or which causes which). Social scientists describe relationships in which two variables are suspected to cause each other as simultaneous or reciprocal. The statistical methods used by social scientists to unravel simultaneous causal relationships are complex. Consequently, the literature on the relationship between police strength and crime is often difficult to understand. Further, the results of this research are thoroughly mixed, with studies confirming all possible relationships – that police strength increases crime, decreases crime, and has no effect on crime.

In this section, we review this body of research to determine if it is possible to distill any generalizations about the effect of police strength on violent crime. Table 7.1 lists twenty-seven studies that examined the effects of police strength on violent crimes.[3] Violent crimes include the four crimes classified by the FBI as violent: murder, rape, robbery, and aggravated assault.[4] Studies estimating bivariate or partial correlations between police and violent crime are excluded unless the authors interpret the findings as the effect of police on crime (and not crime on police).

Because a single study can use multiple samples, several different independent variables, different dependent variables, and very different analytical strategies, these twenty-seven studies contain forty-one separate sets of analysis, with eighty-nine separate estimates of the effect of police on violent crime (each with a different dependent variable). There is tremendous variation in the nature and quality of these studies. Of the forty-one analyses, twenty-three are cross-sectional, examining differences across cities, states, or other geographic areas at a single point in time. Ten are longitudinal, examining changes in police strength and violent crime in a single cross-section (such as a city, state, or nation) over time. The remaining eight combine these two approaches, analyzing data from multiple cross-sections at multiple times. Some are based on tiny samples (as small as 15), while others are based on very large samples of more than 1,000. The independent variables used to measure police strength vary, including the number of police officers (seven analyses), the number of police employees (fourteen), and police expenditures (twelve). An additional eight studies did not provide sufficient detail to know which measure of police strength was used. In nearly every instance, the measure of police strength was expressed as a rate per capita, though a small number of studies used either raw numbers or police strength per unit of territory (either per acre or per square mile). The crime types – the dependent variable – included aggregate violent crimes (usually the sum of murders, rapes, robberies, and aggravated assaults), individual violent-crime categories, and various combinations. All studies relied on crimes reported to police, with the exception of one that used victimization data (Humphries and Wallace 1980). Finally, the crime measures were nearly always expressed as rates per capita, though a small number of studies used either raw numbers of

Table 7.1. Empirical Studies on the Effect of Police Strength on Violent Crime

Study	Method[a]	Cross-Section	Time[b]	I.V.	Simultaneity[d]	Findings[e]
Morris & Tweeten (1971)	CS	754 Cities	1967 & 1968	Police Employees	2SLS	Violent Crime (+)
Greenwood & Wadycki (1973)	CS	199 SMSAs	1960	Police Employees	3SLS	Violent Crime (+)
Swimmer (1974a)	CS	119 Cities	1960	Police Expenditures	2SLS	Murder (−), Rape (−) Robbery (−), Assault (G)
Swimmer (1974b)	CS	119 Cities	1960	Police Expenditures	2SLS	Violent Crime (−)
Wellford (1974)	(a) CS	21 Cities	1960 & 1970	Police Expenditures	None	Violent Crime (0)
	(b) CS	21 Cities	1960 & 1970	Police Expenditures	None	Violent Crime (0)
Levine (1975)	(a) CS	26 Cities	1961	Police Employees	None	Murder (+), Robbery (+)
	(b) Panel	26 Cities	1961 & 1971	Change in Police Employees	None	Change in Murder (0), Change in Robbery (0)
Pogue (1975)	(a) CS	163 SMSAs	1962	Police Expenditures	2SLS	Murder (0), Rape (0), Robbery (0), Assault (0)
	(b) CS	163 SMSAs	1967	Police Expenditures	2SLS	Murder (0), Rape (+), Robbery (+), Assault (+)
	(c) CS	66 SMSAs	1968	Police Expenditures	2SLS	Murder (0), Rape (0), Robbery (0), Assault (0)
Land & Felson (1976)	TS	U.S. Aggregate	1947–1972	Police Expenditures	None	Violent Crime (−)
Mathieson & Passell (1976)	CS	65 NYPD Precincts	1971	Uniformed Patrolmen	2SLS	Robbery (−)
Hakim, Ovadia, & Weinblatt (1978)	CS	61 Philadelphia Suburbs	1970	Police Expenditures	None	Robberies per Acre (+)
Fujii & Mak (1980)	(a) CS	25 Districts in Oahu	1975	Police per Acre	2SLS	Murder (0), Rape (+), Robbery (+), Assault (+)
	(b) TS	State of Hawaii	1961–1975	Police	None	Murder (0), Rape (+), Robbery (0), Assault (0)

(continued)

Table 7.1 *(continued)*

Study	Method[a]	Cross-Section	Time[b]	I.V.	Simultaneity[d]	Findings[e]
Huff & Stahura (1980)	CS	252 Suburbs	1971	Police Employees	2SLS	Violent Crime (+)
Humphries & Wallace (1980)	(a) Panel	23 Cities	1950 & 1971	Change in Police, 1950–1970	None	Change in Homicide (+), Change in Robbery (0)
	(b) CS	23 Cities	1971	1970 Police	Difference Score	1971 Robberies (0)
Jacob & Rich (1980–81)	TS	9 Cities	1948–1978	Police Expenditures	Lag	Robbery (+)
Greenberg & Kessler (1982)	Panel	130 Cities	1960 & 1962	Police Expenditures	Lag	Violent Crime (+)
Loftin & McDowall (1982)	TS	Detroit	1926–1977	Police Employees	Granger	Violent Crime (0)
Greenberg, Kessler, & Loftin (1983)	(a) Panel	252 Suburbs	1960 & 1970	Police Employees	Lag	Violent Crime (0)
	(b) Panel	269 Cities	1960 & 1970	Police Employees	Lag	Violent Crime (+)
Belknap (1986)	CS	260 SMSAs	1980	Police Expenditures	2SLS	Violent Crime (0)
Howsen & Jarrell (1987)	CS	120 Kentucky Counties	1981	Police per Square Mile	2SLS	Robbery (–)
Corman & Joyce (1990)	TS	New York City	195 months	Police Officers (1970–1986)	Granger	Murder (0), Rape (0), Robbery (–), Assault (–)
van Tulder (1992)	(a) CS	40 large Dutch areas	1979 & 1980	Police Strength	None	Violent Crime (0)
	(b) CS	80 small Dutch areas	1979 & 1980	Police Strength	None	Violent Crime (+)
	(c) CS	805 Dutch municipalities	1979 & 1980	Police Strength	None	Violent Crime (+)
Niskanen (1994)	CS	50 States + Washington DC	1991	Police Employees	2SLS	Violent Crime (0)

Chamlin & Langworthy (1996)	TS	Milwaukee	1930–1987	(a) Police Employees	Granger	Personal Crime (0), Robbery (0)
				(b) Patrol Employees		Personal Crime (0), Robbery (0)
				(c) Detective Employees		Personal Crime (0), Robbery (+)
Corman and Mocan (1996)	TS	New York City (1970–1990)	252 months,	Police Officers	Granger	Murder (0), Rape (−), Robbery (−)
Marvell & Moody (1996)	(a) TSCS	49 States	1973–1993	Police Employees	Granger	Homicide (−), Robbery (−), Rape (0), Assault (0)
	(b) TSCS	56 Cities	1973–1993	Police Employees	Granger	Homicide (−), Robbery (−), Rape (0), Assault (0)
Levitt (1997)	TSCS	59 Cities	1970–1992	Police Officers	2SLS	Violent Crime (−), Murder (−), Robbery (0), Rape (0), Assault (0)
Lundman (1997)	(a) CS	50 Cities	1991	Police Officers	Lag	Murder (+), Robbery (+), Rape (−), Assault (0)
	(b) CS	50 States	1991	Police Officers	Lag	Murder (+), Robbery (+), Assault (+), Rape (0)
	(c) TS	United States	1960–1994	Police Officers	Lag	Murder (0), Rape (0), Robbery (+), Assault (+)

a CS = cross-sectional model, TS = time series model, Panel = two- or three-wave panel model, TSCS = pooled time series–cross-sectional model.

b All longitudinal data are yearly unless otherwise noted.

c Unless otherwise indicated, all police-strength measures are per capita except Mathieson and Passell (1976), Corman and Mocan (1996), and some estimates by Chamlin and Langworthy (1996).

d Procedures used for dealing with the simultaneity between police and crime: None = no attempt to deal with simultaneity, Lag = lag value of police strength is included in the violent-crime equation, 2SLS/3SLS = two- or three-stage least squares regression, Granger = Granger causality test (Granger 1968).

e Unless otherwise indicated, all violent-crime variables are expressed as rates except Corman and Mocan (1996) and some estimates by Chamlin and Langworthy (1996) and Wellford (1974).

crimes or crimes per unit of territory. This brief review illustrates that the methods used to assess the effects of police strength on violent crime vary tremendously across studies.

Overall, of the eighty-nine dependent variables listed in Table 7.1, forty-four (49.4 percent) found no effect of police on crime, twenty-seven equations (30.3 percent) found a positive effect of police strength on violent crime (i.e., more police results in more crime), and eighteen (20.2 percent) found a negative effect (i.e., more police results in less crime). Thus, after nearly three decades of research on the relationship between police strength and violent crime, there is not a consistent body of evidence supporting the assertion that hiring more police is an effective method for reducing violent crime. However, many of these studies suffer from flaws in design, analysis, or both, so aggregating the results in this fashion may be misleading. To examine this possibility, we briefly explore the quality of the studies in Table 7.1. The goal is to determine whether the same ambiguous pattern of results persists after eliminating some of the more problematic studies.

Model Identification Issues. More than twenty years ago, Fisher and Nagin (1978; Nagin 1978, 1998) found that one of the most serious problems in previous research on the deterrent effects of criminal sanctions was inadequate model identification. As mentioned earlier, there are good reasons to suspect that police (P) and crime (C) have a simultaneous causal effect on the other. Model identification is a technical matter beyond the scope of this chapter, but the following example illustrates the general concept. Suppose we were to collect data from fifty cities on the number of police and the number of violent crimes per capita. Given the results of previous research, we would most likely find that these two variables are highly (and positively) correlated. The problem is that, when using cross-sectional data (data collected from a single period in time), we would not know whether the correlation was due to the effect of P on C, C on P, the influence of a third variable on P and C, or the simultaneous effect of each one on the other. Thus, given only these two variables, we would not be able to estimate the effect of P on C because there is insufficient information to determine which of these alternative explanations is the most plausible.

Econometric methods have been devised to deal with the problem of simultaneous causal relationships. One frequently used solution is to add an outside variable to the model (known as an instrumental variable) that is a known cause of one variable (in this case P), but has no causal effect on the other (C). By providing this kind of "identification restriction," we provide sufficient information in the system of equations to obtain unique estimates of the effect of P on C. Fisher and Nagin (1978) and others have argued convincingly that most researchers have paid too little attention to these identification restrictions, choosing instrumental variables that are based on unrealistic assumptions. Nagin (1978, p. 118) showed that when the assumptions regarding identification restrictions are incorrect, the resulting analysis "can be completely misleading."[5] Unfortunately, many researchers have failed to heed Fisher and Nagin's advice. As a result, the findings of most cross-sectional studies in Table 7.1 are suspect. Others have ignored the simultaneity issue altogether: findings from those studies are even more suspect.

Measurement Error. Although nearly every study of the relationship between police strength and violent crime has acknowledged the well-known problems with Uniform Crime Reports (UCR) crime figures, none have acknowledged the problems of accurately measuring police strength. A recent study showed that much of the data used for "counting cops" in the United States has been egregiously inaccurate (Maguire et al. 1998). Only three decades ago, police scholars and government agencies were still estimating that there were approximately forty thousand separate police agencies in the nation. We now know that the true figure is about one-half that number.

Current data on police strength are probably the best yet, but there are still problems. To illustrate this, Table 7.2 shows the results of the last two censuses of state and local law enforcement agencies, conducted by the Bureau of Justice Statistics (BJS) in 1992 and 1996 (Reaves 1993; Reaves and Goldberg 1998). The total number of agencies listed grew by 1,411 over this four-year period although there is no other evidence that the number of police agencies in the nation is actually growing.[6] In fact, King (personal communication to Edward Maguire, March 30, 1999; King, Travis, and Langworthy 1997), applying a biological framework to the study of police organizations in three states, has found the number of agencies that have "died" is much greater than the number that have been born.[7] The increase in the number of agencies recorded in the 1996 census is due in large part to efforts by BJS to locate additional law enforcement agencies missing from the previous census. Yet, for some reason, BJS did not take these newly discovered agencies into account when reporting that "nationwide, the number of state and local full-time sworn personnel in June 1996 was 9 percent greater than in June 1992" (Reaves and Goldberg 1998, p. 1). Thus, even today, estimates of increases in police strength contain some (unknown) degree of measurement error.

Table 7.2. Estimates of the Number of U.S. Police Agencies, 1992 & 1996

Agency Type	1992	1996
Local	12,502	13,578
State	49	49
Sheriff	3,086	3,088
Special	1,721	2,054
Total Agencies	17,358	18,769

The size of police agencies in the United States is undoubtedly growing, however. Unfortunately, historically inaccurate methods of counting police make it difficult to know by how much.[8] We suggest the following set of strategies for assessing the degree of error in measures of police strength and evaluating the research presented in Table 7.1. First, the larger the aggregate, the greater the error. Because there is controversy about what counts as a police agency or officer (consider the numerous types of specialized police agencies), larger aggregates such as counties, states, and nations probably have much more measurement error than cities or precincts (Maguire et al. 1998). Second, there is less measurement error associated with counting police in city police departments than in specialized police and in county sheriffs' agencies. Because county sheriffs are responsible for a multitude of functions, the proportion of employees in these agencies with responsibility for law enforcement functions is much lower than in other agency types. Yet some measures of police strength include deputy sheriffs who work exclusively as jail guards, court guards, and process servers. In fact, there are several states in which sheriffs' agencies have no generalized law enforcement responsibilities. Including these measures in county, state, or national estimates of police strength (which was done in many of the studies in Table 7.1) introduces severe measurement error. Finally, some longitudinal data series change definitions and recording practices over time, so it is difficult to know whether apparent changes in police strength are real changes or simply the product of changes in recording. All of this points to the need to consider issues of measurement error in estimates of police strength.

Other Issues. There is tremendous inconsistency across studies in the methods and measures used. For instance, Chamlin and Langworthy (1996) were the only researchers to systematically examine the effect of expressing the police and crime measures as either raw numbers or rates per capita, and they found that it made a difference. They were also the only researchers to systematically examine the effect of disaggregating employment measures by assignment (patrol officers and detectives). Some of the studies had very low sample sizes (as few as fifteen), and probably should not be trusted. Many failed to identify their measures of police strength, while others proceed as if police expenditures, police employees, and police officers are interchangeable variables. Though these three variables are highly correlated, they are very different, and the failure of previous research to consider the implications of different measures of police strength is another probable reason for the mixed findings. Finally, it is time to systematically explore the differential effect of police strength on individual types of violent crime rather than overall rates of crime and violent crime.

Given these various issues in the research, is it possible to exclude some of the studies from consideration to get a "purer" picture of the effect of police strength on violent crime? We began by excluding all of the cross-sectional studies on the basis of inadequate identification restrictions. Next, among the remaining longitudinal studies, we excluded all of those based on an aggregate larger than a city. Finally, we excluded all studies that made no attempt to deal with the simultaneity between police and crime. After excluding all of these, we were left with nine studies containing twenty-seven separate dependent variables. Police strength has no effect on crime in fifteen equations (55 percent), a positive effect in four equations (15 percent), and a negative effect in eight equations (30 percent). Thus, even when we examined only the most rigorous studies, we could not find consistent evidence that increases in police strength produce decreases in violent crime. Overall, the research suggests that hiring more police officers did not play an independent or consistent role in reducing violent crime in the United States.

Community Policing. At least since the early 1980s, police agencies in the United States have been undergoing a host of reform efforts generally known as community policing. These reforms were undertaken to address a number of concerns including conflicts between racial minorities and the police, research suggesting that traditional police practices were ineffective at controlling crime, and to improve handling of noncriminal matters the public brings to police attention. There are no commonly accepted definitions of community policing (Eck and Rosenbaum 1994), but most serious efforts in this direction include changes in organizational structures to decentralize decision making and programs to stimulate and foster police-community partnerships (Kennedy and Moore 1995; Maguire and Uchida 1998). In this section we will examine whether these reform efforts could have reduced violent crime in the United States.

National surveys of police agencies continue to show that community-policing strategies are being implemented throughout the United States (Maguire et al. 1997; Wycoff 1994). Many advocates and other observers claim that community policing deserves much of the credit for recent reductions in violent crime. Others are skeptical or even doubt that the contributions of community policing can be assessed. Bayley (1994a, p. 278), for example, argues that "the success of community policing will never be evaluated ... [because it] means too many things to different people." Because community policing involves a wide array of fairly heterogeneous changes in policing, we find it necessary for organizational and analytical purposes to break it into smaller components. Following Maguire and Uchida (1998) and Maguire et al. (2000), we divide community policing into three dimensions: internal organizational changes, community partnerships, and problem solving. Because the first two of these strategies are more generic, we examine them here. Problem-solving strategies tend to be more focused, therefore we discuss them and related efforts in Part Two.

Organizational Change. Reformers suggest that in order to implement community policing, there must be fundamental changes in the management, structure, and culture of police organizations. Many of these recommendations entail changes that are similar to popular organizational-change strategies found in the private and public sectors (Das 1985; Mastrofski 1998; Moore and Stephens 1992; Moore and Trojanowicz 1988). Reformers give two very different reasons these changes are necessary: first, to stimulate and encourage officers to perform community-policing functions (Weisel and Eck 1994); second, to make the organization more flexible and amenable to developing community partnerships and creative problem-solving strategies (Bayley 1994b; Community Policing Consortium 1994; Mastrofski 1998; Moore 1994; Skolnick and Bayley 1986, 1988). The community-policing literature has clearly established the need for police agencies to respond to both of these organizational and managerial challenges. The effect of this one element of community policing on violent crime is presumably indirect, operating through community partnerships and problem solving. Nevertheless, given popular claims about the effectiveness of community policing, it is important to address the effectiveness of *each* of its dimensions. In this section, we discuss whether these diverse changes in organization and management might be responsible for recent drops in violent crime. Before exploring that causal link explicitly, we first examine the evidence that such changes are even taking place in American police agencies.

When community-policing reformers discuss organizational change, three elements appear over and over again: organizational structure, organizational culture, and managerial and leadership styles. Evidence of change in these three arenas is far from convincing, though relevant empirical research is sparse.[9] Maguire (1997) found that from 1987 to 1993, large police agencies had not significantly altered their structures in the directions urged by community-policing reformers. In fact, on one structural dimension (specialization), police agencies changed in the opposite direction. The most recent national data suggest that police agencies may just now be starting to alter some structural elements by flattening hierarchies, decentralizing, and adopting geographic command authority (Hassell et al. 1999). However, the magnitudes of these changes were small, and most occurred after the national decline in violent crime. Similarly, a recent study of Florida police agencies found that the "organizational impacts of community policing have been minimal" (Gianakis and Davis 1998, p. 496).

While the reform literature is full of prescriptions about the need to change organizational culture, empirical studies of such changes are rare. Zhao, He, and Lovrich (1998) argued that individual values and culture are inextricably linked, with each affecting the other. Their research suggested that the value orientations of American police officers have remained stable over the past twenty years. In a later study, Zhao, He, and Lovrich (1999) surveyed police officers from a department with a national reputation for community policing. Researchers found that from 1993 to 1996, officers' value orientations changed significantly. Priority ratings for values reflecting individual happiness, comfort, and security increased over the three-year period, while ratings for more social or collective values decreased. Alarmingly, the social value experiencing the greatest decline in importance among the officers was "equality." These findings were stable across all levels of education and experience. Zhao et al. (1999) conclude that the value-changes evident in this sample of officers are antithetical to the basic shifts in culture expected under community policing.

Research on police officers' attitudes might also be useful for drawing inferences about recent changes in organizational and occupational culture. For instance, studies examining attitudes about community policing have found a lack of understanding, acceptance, or both among police officers (Kratcoski and Noonan 1995; Lurigio and Skogan 1994; Sadd and Grinc 1994). Greene and Decker (1989) found that a classroom program in Philadelphia designed to improve relations between police officers and residents actually resulted in poorer officer attitudes toward the community. Wood's (1998) study of community policing in Albuquerque finds that changes in organizational culture are difficult to achieve in the face of the traditional police culture. Despite these frequent negative findings, some research has found that police agencies can change officers' attitudes. For instance, a longitudinal study in Joliet, Illinois, found that although "the absence of change was the norm rather than the exception," many officers showed favorable changes in attitudes toward and knowledge of community policing (Rosenbaum, Yeh, and Wilkinson 1994, p. 349). Other studies have also found evidence of positive changes in police officers' attitudes (McElroy, Cosgrove, and Sadd 1993; Wycoff and Skogan 1994). Overall, these studies of police attitudes and values generally suggest that the culture of a police organization can change, but such shifts are not likely to occur often or quickly.

Evidence of changes in styles of leadership and management is also sparse. Hoover and Mader (1990) found that Texas police chiefs generally supported the principles of excellence found in the private sector managerial-reform literature, though data were not available about whether the chiefs actually followed these principles. Witte, Travis, and Langworthy (1990) found that employees in fourteen Ohio police agencies generally agreed about the value of participatory management. Few, however, reported that such a management style existed within their own agency. Compelling evidence of changes in management style tends to come in the form of case studies, though it is impossible to draw general conclusions from this kind of design. The best-known recent case study of managerial change in policing occurred in Madison, Wisconsin. Wycoff and Skogan (1994) found that the Madison Police Department successfully implemented a participatory management style. Their evaluation showed that these organizational changes had significant effects inside and outside the department. Strangely, though residents perceived robberies and attacks to be less of a problem there was no significant change in actual robbery victimization rates. Though case studies can be valuable for understanding how organizational changes are implemented and some of their short-term consequences, they are not very useful for drawing broader conclusions about violent-crime trends.

Although some police organizations have undoubtedly changed their structures, cultures, and management styles, evidence suggests that overall, such shifts are occurring glacially. Changes in structure are just now starting to occur nationally. Evidence suggests that changes in culture, if they are occurring at all, are probably not widespread. There are no national data on changes in management styles, though the limited research suggests that they are probably no more prevalent than changes in structure and culture. Even if it could be demonstrated that organizational and managerial changes are occurring widely, there is little or no empirical evidence to support a claim that changing the management and organization of a police agency can lower crime. Overall, the causal connection between these internal reforms and violent crime is the weakest (and most indirect) of all those considered in this chapter. Given that police agencies nationwide have not experienced dramatic shifts in formal and informal organization, it is difficult to attribute recent declines in violent crime throughout the nation to such changes.

Community Partnerships. A core feature of the community-policing movement is forging better relationships between police and communities. Nearly every prescriptive discussion of community policing cites the need for the police and community to form coalitions or partnerships with one another. Reformers disagree about the extent of involvement that citizens should have in policing, with opinions ranging from no involvement or simply serving as the "eyes and ears" of the police to playing a direct role in the formulation of police policy (Bayley 1994b). Because the scope and depth of police-community partnerships is so broad, this is probably the hardest generic policing strategy to evaluate. The task is made more difficult because in many studies, community partnerships are implemented simultaneously with other strategies, such as increases in patrol strength, problem solving, and internal innovations. In this section, with these (and other) significant limitations in mind, we attempt to synthesize the findings from numerous evaluations of police-community partnerships in the United States.

Although community policing has swept through the nation over the past decade, there is surprisingly little evidence about its effect on violent crime. There are at least four reasons for this. First, most evaluations focus on the process, rather the impact, of implementing community policing. Second, even when evaluations do study impact, they sometimes focus on fear of crime or police and citizen attitudes, rather than on levels of crime and victimization. Third, some impact evaluations focus on nonviolent crimes such as burglary or "soft" crimes (Reiss 1985). Finally, some impact evaluations include violent crimes in their measures of total crime, but they do not disaggregate these composite measures (e.g., Lasley, Vernon, and Dery 1995; Trojanowicz 1986). Despite these limitations, there are patches of evidence on the effectiveness of various efforts by the police to improve relationships and form partnerships with communities.

One body of evaluation research has examined the impact of community-policing strategies on *perceptions* (i.e., do people believe crime is going up or down, regardless of its actual trend) of violent crime and other community conditions. We review just a handful of these studies here. Brown and Wycoff (1987) found that of five community-partnership strategies implemented in Houston, only storefront police stations and community contact patrols reduced perceptions of personal crime in the area. Williams and Pate (1987) found that none of the three community-partnership strategies implemented in Newark to reduce fear of crime had an effect on perceptions of personal crime. In the most recent study, Skogan and Hartnett (1997) examined the impact of Chicago's Alternative Policing Strategy (CAPS) on perceptions of the four most serious problems in each of five Chicago neighborhoods (as nominated by residents in each neighborhood). Of six problems involving violent crime (robbery, assault, or gang violence), residents of these neighborhoods thought that two of the problems decreased relative to resident perceptions in comparison neighborhoods. For two other problems, residents of comparison neighborhoods perceived significant decreases while residents in the experimental areas did not think their problems had declined. Unfortunately, as very little is known about the relationship between perceptions of violent crime and actual violent crime, we cannot be certain about the difference between the two measures. An earlier report from CAPS's evaluation found that although perceptions of crime had decreased significantly in all five prototype districts, official reports and victimization surveys showed that robberies had decreased in only three of the five districts (Skogan, 1995). It is difficult to know how much faith to place in the findings that community partnerships reduce *perceptions* of violent crime.[10] If people routinely overestimate the volume of violent crime, it might be easier to influence these perceptions of violence than the violence itself.

Several studies have examined the impact of community-partnership strategies on reported violent-crime rates or victimizations. For purposes of organization, we divide these evaluations into three groups according to the partnership strategies evaluated. We begin by reviewing the evidence on foot patrols. Next, we review evaluations of Neighborhood Watch and similar community crime-prevention strategies. Finally, we examine a host of other studies evaluating miscellaneous community-partnership strategies.

To some advocates, foot patrols are one of the cornerstones of community policing: a back-to-the-basics way to recharge the relationship between the police and the community.[11] Evaluations of foot-patrol strategies in Boston (Bowers and Hirsch 1987), Newark (Pate 1986), and an unidentified southeastern city (Esbensen 1987) have found no effect on rates of total or violent crime. Cordner and Jones (1995) found that after part-time foot patrols were instituted in a public housing project, "personal crime" victimization rates decreased among females and stayed about the same for males. These studies show that foot patrols can provide some benefits but overall reduction in violent crime does not appear to be one of them.

National studies of community policing routinely find that Neighborhood Watch is one of the most popular community-partnership strategies implemented by American police agencies (Maguire et al. 1997; Wycoff 1994). In a comprehensive review, Bennett (1990) notes that the most evaluations of Neighborhood Watch have been done by the police, and perhaps not surprisingly, these studies generally find it effective at reducing crime. On the other hand, studies conducted by researchers tend to conclude that "Neighborhood Watch is partly or wholly unsuccessful" (Bennett 1990, p. 45). Researchers have noted that the majority of these studies suffer from serious methodological problems (Bennett 1990; Kessler and Duncan 1996; Lurigio and Rosenbaum 1986). The most recent research in London (Bennett 1990) and Houston (Kessler and Duncan 1996) found that Neighborhood Watch was not effective at reducing reported crime.[12]

Several other community-partnership strategies have also been evaluated. One early national study found that cities with training programs in police-community relations experienced lower increases in crime than other cities (Lovrich 1978). In Baltimore, an experiment assessing the effect of foot-patrol and ombudsman policing together produced no significant effects on violent crime (Pate and Annan 1989). In Oakland and Birmingham, researchers found that beats in which police officers made door-to-door contacts with citizens experienced notable declines in reported violent crimes (Uchida, Forst, and Annan 1992). Skogan's (1994) cross-site analysis found that home visits reduced victimizations (robbery, burglary, and assault) in all three cities in which they were implemented. A number of other community-partnership strategies in six cities had no effect on victimizations.

Evidence on the effectiveness of community partnerships is thoroughly mixed. As we have noted in each section of this chapter, much of the research is flawed.[13] Perhaps the most optimistic lesson we can derive from this line of research is that it is possible for community partnerships, under some circumstances, to reduce violent crime. The conditions under which they serve as effective crime-prevention strategies remain unknown. Survey research continues to show that community-partnership strategies are being implemented widely in American police agencies, yet survey research does not allow us to evaluate the depth of these partnerships. Evidence from a recent national evaluation suggests that "true" community partnerships are rare (Koper et al. 1998), though the modest progress made so far represents an important breakthrough in police-community relations. Others have reviewed the efficacy of community organizing in reducing crime. These reviews are pessimistic about the ability of community organizing to reduce serious crime, particularly in the most crime-ridden neighborhoods (Hope 1995; Rosenbaum 1988; Sherman 1997a). Assembling these various research findings, we do not find compelling evidence that police-community partnerships are either prevalent enough or effective enough to be responsible for recent national reductions in violent crime.

Zero-Tolerance Policing. A third generic change that seems to be gaining momentum in police agencies includes a myriad of aggressive policing strategies, popularly known as "order maintenance," "broken windows," "quality-of-life," or "zero-tolerance" policing. In contrast to community policing, which attempts to produce order and reduce crime through cooperation with community members, zero-tolerance policing attempts to impose order through strict enforcement (Cordner 1998; Massing 1998). Much of the resurgence in this aggressive policing style can be traced to the "Broken Windows" thesis outlined by Wilson and Kelling in 1982. Wilson and Kelling used broken windows as a metaphor for neighborhood disorder, arguing that unchecked disorder is an open invitation to more serious crime. The implications for police strategy were clear: to reorient police resources toward maintaining order and preventing crime. The appearance of Wilson and Kelling's article launched a debate about the proper role of police in a democratic society, with some supporting a shift toward order-maintenance policing to clean up communities and prevent crime (Kelling 1985; Sykes 1986). Others expressed concerns about the potential of this form of policing for abuse, discrimination, and violations of civil liberties (Klockars 1985, 1986; Walker 1984).

The best-known application of the Broken Windows thesis to policing was undertaken in New York City in 1993 by former Police Commissioner William Bratton and continues today under Commissioner Howard Safir

(Harcourt, 1998). Bratton provides detailed descriptions of the changes he implemented in the New York City Police Department (NYPD) in his recent autobiography (1998). In short, he takes issue with the conventional view of many social scientists that crime is attributable to structural features of communities (e.g., poverty, inequality) that are largely outside the influence of the police. Using the Broken Windows thesis, Bratton and Mayor Rudolph Giuliani instituted a quality-of-life enforcement strategy in the NYPD that was designed to "reclaim the public spaces of New York" (Bratton 1998, p. 228). The crux of this strategy was a campaign to restore order in New York by making arrests for minor offenses such as approaching a vehicle in traffic to wash its windshield (the infamous "squeegee men"), littering, panhandling, prostitution, public intoxication, urinating in public, vandalism, and a variety of other misdemeanor public-order offenses. Many observers credit the quality-of-life initiative for New York's plummeting crime rates over the past seven years.

Evidence of the increase in proactive enforcement was dramatic. Misdemeanor arrests in the NYPD rose from 133,446 in 1993 to 205,277 in 1996, while misdemeanor complaints rose only slightly (Harcourt 1998, p. 340). In addition, due to procedural changes in the processing of arrestees, misdemeanor arrests increased in severity as well as volume (Harcourt 1998). For instance, Bratton curtailed the use of desk appearance tickets (DATs), in which people accused of minor offenses were given a court date and released: "No more DATs. If you peed in the street, you were going to jail. We were going to fix the broken windows and prevent anyone from breaking them again" (Bratton 1998, p. 229).[14]

The NYPD's aggressive order-maintenance strategy has inspired a rancorous debate among criminologists, journalists, police executives, and the public.[15] Bratton (1998, p. 289–90) decided "to take on the academics, to challenge conventional wisdom about crime in America and prove that effective policing can make a substantial impact on social change ... we lined up their alternate reasons like ducks in a row and shot them all down." Supporters echoed his message. DiIulio (1995), arguing that aggressive police efforts to take bad guys off the street are responsible (in part) for the recent decline in crime rates, calls this explanation "Bratton's Law." DiIulio praised Bratton for challenging the "criminologically correct." O'Hara (1998, p. 14) likens him to Bruce Springsteen, concluding his review of Bratton's autobiography with unfettered praise: "It is Bratton whom I'd like to see on stage leading the band – because he wrote the music. I have seen the future of public administration, and his name is William Bratton."

Critiques of the NYPD's quality-of-life initiative focus on several different themes. First, many claim that police tactics are not solely responsible for decreases in crime. One former police chief believes that Bratton was lucky to have held office while crime in New York City decreased for reasons other than police activity (Bouza 1997). Some note that crime rates have decreased rapidly in other large cities (such as Boston, San Diego, and Washington, DC) that used very different policing strategies (Cordner 1998; Greene 1999; Massing 1998; Shapiro 1997). Others point out that crime was already decreasing in New York City prior to Bratton's arrival (Karmen 1996; Muwakkil 1997). Fagan, Zimring, and Kim (1997, p. 13), for instance, observe that many forms of interpersonal violence were declining in New York by the late 1980s. Their analysis of homicide trends in New York City from 1985 to 1996 shows that nongun homicides declined steadily during this period, while gun-related homicides began declining in 1991 (with a sharper decline beginning in 1993). Fagan and his colleagues interpret the overall decline in gun crimes as more consistent with Bratton's focused efforts to rid the streets of guns than with his "indiscriminate quality of life interventions" (we will examine gun-enforcement strategies in Part Two). Harcourt (1998) challenges the very premise of the Broken Windows thesis, that disorder and serious crime are intertwined. Re-analyzing data used in Skogan's book *Disorder and Decline* (1990), Harcourt finds evidence that there is no causal relationship between disorder and more serious crime.[16] He concludes by suggesting that if Bratton's methods are responsible for reductions in crime, this is due not to the Broken Windows dynamic, but to the increased "surveillance" inherent in his strategies. That is, any reduction in crime is due to the increased concentration of police officers, not the increased police attention to quality-of-life concerns (i.e., any concentrated, aggressive enforcement campaign, regardless of the target, would be just as effective). Taylor (1998), although not addressing police tactics per se, provides additional evidence on the Broken Windows perspective, concluding that "grime" doesn't necessarily mean crime. When we examine directed patrol strategies later in this chapter, we will return to the question of whether New York's decline in homicides can be attributed to changes instituted following Bratton's appointment.

Other critics argue vociferously that the quality-of-life initiative created by Bratton and continued by Safir is simply "harassment policing" (Panzarella 1998). Furthermore, critics allege that minorities bear the brunt of this strategy (Harcourt 1998; Manning 1998). Minorities complain of being frequently and disproportionately subjected to arrest, stop-

and-frisk searches, disrespect, and brutality (Muwakkil 1997; Yardley 1999). A widely contested report by Human Rights Watch (1998) drew linkages between aggressive policing strategies and brutality in New York and other cities. A similar report by Amnesty International (1996) also found increases in reports of police brutality and excessive force in the NYPD. Several observers have noted the rise in civilian complaints and allegations of police brutality since 1993 (Davis and Mateu-Gelabert 1999; Greene 1999; Harcourt 1998; Manning 1998).[17] Critics point to another indicator of increasing police misbehavior: the amount of money paid out in civil settlements continues to rise (Harcourt 1998). To some critics, such problems are a predictable consequence of aggressive order-maintenance policing (Panzarella 1998). In contrast, a recent report by the Vera Institute highlights two NYPD precincts in which both crime and civilian complaints are down. The authors conclude that if police managers are serious about controlling police misbehavior, citizens don't necessarily need to choose between respectful and effective policing (Davis and Mateu-Gelabert 1999).

Finally, some critics have suggested that even if aggressive quality-of-life enforcement does produce declines in crime, it is a short-term strategy with little regard for longer-term implications. Goldstein warns that if aggressive police strategies generate hostility in the community, then at some point, police departments will need "to deal with the consequences of that hostility" (Rosen 1997, p. 9). Similarly, Shapiro (1997) notes that one dire consequence of overzealous enforcement in the NYPD may be the erosion of police legitimacy. Panzarella (1998, p. 15), playing off the title of Bratton's autobiography (*Turnaround*), suggests that in the aftermath of his "harassment strategy," it may take another generation for the NYPD "to turn around again." Sherman (1997b) argues that although such strategies may reduce crime in the short-term, they may actually be planting the seeds for increases in crime in the long-term. Based on research, Sherman identifies two avenues through which this might occur. First, tagging vast numbers of misdemeanor offenders with an arrest record might limit their future ability to participate in the legitimate labor market. Second, as Sherman (1993) found in his previous research on domestic-violence recidivism, arrest may have criminogenic effects on some offenders, leading them to become more angry and defiant. Another recent study shows that domestic-violence arrestees who thought they were treated fairly by police were least likely to reoffend (Paternoster et al. 1997). Further research is needed to determine whether this finding is robust across offense types, but it suggests another reason to be wary of police strategies that alienate substantial portions of the community.

Bratton's experience in New York is important for a number of reasons. He argues that his strategies offer a blueprint for reducing crime and disorder "that would work in any city in America – indeed, in any city in the world" (Bratton 1998, p. 309). Police agencies all over the world, in fact, are implementing similar strategies based on the New York experience, with many generating similar controversy (Burke 1998; Cordner 1998). Yet the strategy remains untested. Trying to disentangle the causal relationships responsible for the recent drop in New York's crime rate is a daunting task. Many strategies designed to lower the crime rate were implemented simultaneously, including: the quality-of-life initiative, hiring more officers, Compstat (which we will discuss shortly), and a variety of crime-specific efforts that we will discuss in Part Two. Although it is difficult to know for certain how much credit to give the quality-of-life initiative, we can say for certain that it: 1. has generated a substantial amount of criticism, and 2. has not been tested empirically.

Although there has been no evaluation of zero-tolerance policing per se, there are bits of evidence on the effectiveness of related generic order-maintenance strategies in reducing violent crime.[18] For instance, Sherman (1990) reports that although an areal crackdown on disorder in one section of Washington, DC, had an effect on perceptions of safety, it had an insignificant effect on street robberies. Reiss (1985) found that when Oakland police increased arrests and citations for misdemeanor "soft crimes," there was a small (but inconsistent) decrease in robbery and rape rates in the study beats. Sampson and Cohen (1988) found that in their sample of police agencies, police aggressiveness had an inverse effect on robbery rates. Echoing the concerns voiced by critics of order-maintenance policing, Sampson and Cohen found that aggressive policing styles had a disproportionate effect on black arrest rates (as compared to whites).[19] Overall, the evidence is mixed on the efficacy of generic zero-tolerance strategies in driving down rates of violent crime, though serious questions have been raised about their effects on police-community relations. In the next section, we consider crackdown strategies that focus attention on specific high crime locations and the offenders found there.

Part Two: Focusing Police on Repeat Places and People

Having found little evidence that generic changes in policing have contributed to recent drops in violent crime, we now turn to strategies that focus police efforts on concentrations of specific crimes. These concentrations stem from combinations of three "repeats:" repeat offenders, repeat places, and repeat victims (Eck, forthcoming). Unlike English police forces, the police in the United States have placed little emphasis on repeat victimization. Repeat-offender and place strategies have longer histories.

Focusing on these "repeats" varies from the simple to the complex. At one end of this spectrum is directed patrolling, and at the other extreme is problem-oriented policing. These efforts share two common features: the concentration of police resources on small geographic areas, and the use of information to determine when and where to concentrate these resources. Police agencies have conducted directed-patrol operations based on crime analysis for more than twenty-five years (Bieck, Spelman, and Sweeney 1991). The most recent manifestations of directed patrol are based on computer-generated maps of reported crimes rather than the pin maps of yesteryear. Problem-oriented policing has a much shorter history, but requires the use of a richer diversity of information from police and nonpolice sources to identify and resolve problems at their underlying sources. Also, problem-oriented policing shares with community policing a fundamental concern with police-public partnerships. Collaboration with community groups is not a typical feature of directed-patrol operations.

In this section, we examine four forms of focused interventions: 1. directed patrolling and its most recent incarnation, Compstat; 2. gun enforcement, a variant of directed patrolling that attempts to reduce firearm deaths and injuries; 3. retail drug enforcement; and 4. problem-oriented policing. We will demonstrate that the limited evidence currently available suggests that these efforts might have had an influence on violent-crime rates, though there is not an abundance of evidence to support any single type of focused policing. A stronger argument can be made that focused policing may have contributed to the decline in crime *in combination* with other forces outside the control of the police.

Compstat. In his review of directed-patrol studies, Sherman (1997b) concludes that there is reasonably solid evidence to believe that focusing patrol efforts on very small areas with high concentrations of crime can result in less crime in these areas. He reviewed eight studies, conducted from 1971 to 1995, and found that "the more precisely patrol presence is concentrated at the 'hot spots' and 'hot times' of criminal activity, the less crime there will be in those places and times" (pp. 8–14). The most rigorous test of this strategy was conducted in Minneapolis. One hundred ten very small geographic areas with disproportionately large numbers of crime and disorder – hot spots – were randomly divided between two groups. One group of fifty-five hot spots, the control sites, received the same form of police attention they would normally receive. The second group received intensive patrolling roughly 2.5 times greater than the control sites. The comparison of the crime changes in these two groups revealed a significant drop in serious crime in the hot spots that received the intensive patrolling (Sherman and Weisburd 1995).

Probably the best-known implementation of directed patrolling is the NYPD's Compstat process. Implemented in 1994, Compstat blends directed patrol, geographic accountability of precinct commanders, and the use of information and mapping technology. Under Compstat, police headquarters maintains statistical profiles for each precinct, including arrests, complaints, shooting incidents, and other information. Precinct commanders are expected to be vigilant about responding to shifting patterns of crime in their jurisdictions (Safir 1998). They are held accountable through frequent debriefings at police headquarters, where they are "grilled" about crime-reduction strategies and resource-allocation decisions. Commanders who don't measure up are reassigned to less-demanding tasks. Compstat won an Innovations in Government Award in 1996. Many claim that Compstat is responsible for the precipitous drop in New York's violent-crime rate, with particular attention paid to the drop in homicides. For instance, Dodenhoff (1996) wonders, "who could argue with a process that has driven murder rates down by more than 50 percent in a few short years, and has made similarly sharp cuts in other major crimes?" (p. 5). Based on its well-known success in New York, Compstat is now being implemented in other cities throughout the United States.[20]

Could the Compstat process be responsible for the reductions in homicides in New York City? Compstat was implemented along with a number of other changes in the NYPD, including zero-tolerance policing (discussed earlier), gun enforcement (discussed later), and a variety of other changes, including a dramatic increase in the number of officers. Consequently, it is difficult to attribute any reductions in crime to specific police changes. Nevertheless, Compstat is often considered the linchpin strategy that binds these other changes together (Silverman and O'Connell 1997). Further, as mentioned, many police agencies are adopting Compstat-like approaches. Could widespread adoption of Compstat have made a major contribution to the national reduction in homicides?

Four types of evidence are necessary to demonstrate convincingly that Compstat was a major contributor to the reduction in homicides. First, we would need a plausible theory linking the Compstat process to crime reductions in general, and homicide in particular. Because there is a consistent body of evidence that directed patrolling can reduce crimes in small areas and places with very high numbers of crimes, the basic notion behind Compstat is plausible. We do not know, however, whether this reduction is produced through general deterrence of all those who frequent hot spots, through specific deterrence of hot-spot offenders who come under closer scrutiny of the police, or through the incapacitation of repeat offenders following their arrest at these hot spots. So, there is an array of possible mechanisms through which directed patrol could reduce crime at hot spots.

In addition to a description of how Compstat would influence crime, we would need a statistical association between the implementation of Compstat and reductions in crime. A central feature of Compstat is accountability: precinct commanders are held accountable for crimes in their areas. This increases the possibility that reported crimes could be manipulated. Homicide counts are less likely to change based on either citizen reporting or police recording practices, so we will use homicide as an indicator of crime. To control for changes in the number of people at risk, we will use homicides per 100,000 population. Homicide rates have declined significantly from 1994 through 1997, following the implementation of Compstat. But a plausible explanation and a drop in homicides following implementation are not, by themselves, sufficient to demonstrate a causal connection between the drop in homicides and Compstat.

The third piece of evidence we would need is data showing that the drop in homicides came after the establishment of Compstat. If homicides per capita were stable or increasing in New York before 1994, then the decline after 1994 could be due to Compstat. However, if homicides per capita were declining prior to Compstat's introduction, then either other social processes caused the reduction, or changes in policing prior to the implementation of Compstat were responsible for the decline. Figure 7.1 shows homicides per 100,000 New Yorkers for the years 1986 through 1998. These data indicate that three years before the implementation of Compstat (or zero-tolerance policing) in 1994 homicides per capita had already peaked and had begun their decline. This does not support a claim that Compstat was the cause of the decline.

Could Compstat have accelerated the decline? If this occurred, then the speed of the decline in homicides per capita should be steeper after 1994. Table 7.3 shows the proportional change in the homicide rate for the three years before and after Compstat was instituted.[21] Following Compstat's

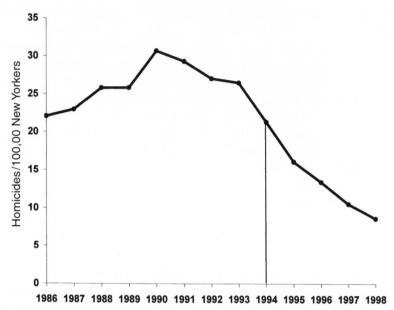

Figure 7.1. New York City homicides per 100,000 population from 1986–1998. Source FBI Uniform Crime Reports 1986 through 1998.

implementation, homicides per capita fell faster than they had been falling prior to Compstat. If this acceleration in the decline in homicides per capita were due to Compstat, then this acceleration would be unique to New York City. The table also shows changes in homicides per capita for the surrounding states. All these jurisdictions showed greater declines for the three years after 1993 than for the three years before Compstat. After Compstat, the rates of decline in Connecticut and New York (outside of New York City) were greater than the decline within New York City. New Jersey and Pennsylvania, and the United States as a whole, also showed greater declines in the second three-year period than in the first three years, though not as great as those shown in New York City. Overall, the claim that the decline in homicides accelerated due to Compstat, or other changes in New York policing implemented in 1994, is not supported by these findings.

The final piece of evidence we would need to support the claim that Compstat contributed to the decline in homicides is to eliminate rival explanations for the decline in homicides in New York City. If Compstat had been implemented as part of a randomized experiment, we might

Table 7.3. Average Yearly Changes in Homicides per Capita for New York City, Surrounding States, and the U.S. 1991–1996

	Before (1991–93)	After (1994–96)	After-Before
NY City	−.047	−.152	−.105
NY State (excluding NYC)	−.094	−.057	−.151
New Jersey	−.016	−.052	−.035
Connecticut	.086	−.051	−.137
Pennsylvania	.007	−.042	−.048
United States	.004	−.060	−.064

Source: FBI, Uniform Crime Reports 1991 through 1996.

have had strong evidence that it was the most likely cause of the decline. Although we cannot produce such strong evidence, we can examine some weaker evidence. We have already seen that changes in homicides per capita were not isolated to New York. This suggests that something other than Compstat was influencing homicides in New York City and surrounding jurisdictions. Further, evidence undermining the claim that Compstat created the decline in homicides can be seen if we look at other large cities. If Compstat was a major contributor to the decline in homicides in New York City, then the trend in homicides per capita for New York should be different from other large cities. Such a finding would indicate that there is something unique about New York City, such as Compstat, that caused the difference. Figure 7.2 shows trends in homicides per capita for the ten largest cities of the United States. Again, declines appeared in or before 1994 in all cities except Philadelphia. Further, the city with the highest murder rate, Detroit, shows obvious declines throughout the period of 1986–98. The same trend is evident in the city with the lowest murder rate, San Diego. Most of these cities have their peak homicide rate in 1990 or 1991. Further, the New York trend is almost indistinguishable from the cities in the middle of the chart. Clearly, we cannot eliminate rival explanations for the decline in New York's homicide rate.

On balance, these data do not support a strong argument for Compstat causing, contributing to, or accelerating the decline in homicides in New York City or elsewhere. Social forces other than Compstat were driving the homicide trend in New York City, and these forces were not peculiar to this one city. Around the same time that Compstat was implemented in New

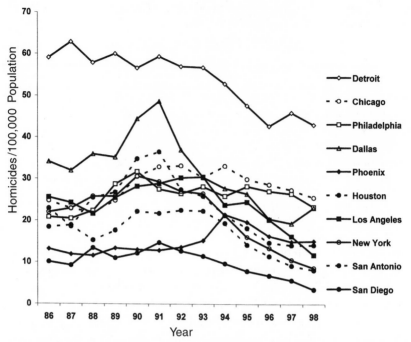

Figure 7.2. Homicides per 100,000 population for 10 largest cities from 1986–1998. Source FBI Uniform Crime Reports 1986 through 1998. Philadelphia homicide and population figures were not reported in the Uniform Crime Reports in 1997. The Pennsylvania homicide and population figures, which included Philadelphia numbers, were reported. The proportion of the state's homicides coming from Philadelphia has been relatively constant since 1986. To estimate the number of homicides for Philadelphia in 1997 we used the average proportion of Pennsylvania homicides that were from Philadelphia (.572) for the previous 11 years. Philadelphia's proportion of the state's population declined from 1986 through 1995 but increased from 1995 through 1996. So we used the average of the 1995 and 1996 proportions of the state's population that lived in Philadelphia to estimate the 1997 Philadelphia population.

York, the same downward trend in homicide was also occurring in the surrounding states and in other large cities.

This leads us to two conclusions. First, the implementation of Compstat in New York in 1994 cannot be credited independently with the decline in homicides in that city. Second, for the same reasons as the first conclusion, the other changes in New York City's policing practices implemented around the same time as Compstat (e.g., zero-tolerance policing) cannot be given credit for the decline in homicides in New York City. Third, the diffusion of the Compstat process to other cities throughout the United States came too late to have produced the national decline in homicides.

We do not wish to overstate these conclusions. Our analysis does not show that Compstat is ineffective. This exploration cannot be interpreted as a rigorous evaluation of Compstat. The narrow question we are addressing is whether Compstat may have had an impact on homicides in the United States. The data we have examined suggest that it did not. But Compstat was developed to address more than homicides. We add this cautionary note so that our findings do not become as exaggerated as some of the claims in favor of Compstat. It is possible, given the complexity of homicide patterns, that the Compstat process had a subtle and meaningful but difficult-to-detect effect on violent crime in New York. If this is the case, then the most plausible impact would be as an interaction of policing with other government and social changes. The data we have examined here are not sufficient to test this explanation.

Though there is little evidence to support the assertion that Compstat caused the decline in homicides, Compstat is only one manifestation of focused policing in general and directed patrolling in particular. If the NYPD and other departments around the country adopted directed patrolling and focused policing prior to 1991, then it is possible that these policing strategies did contribute to the decline in homicides and other violent crimes.

Gun Interdiction Patrols. In late 1992 and early 1993, the Kansas City, Missouri, Police Department experimented with gun-detection patrols. Police officers, working overtime, patrolled a small geographic area with many gun crimes, looking for people who they reasonably suspected to be carrying firearms. Offenses with firearms dropped by 49 percent after the patrols were begun, while in the comparison area, where no gun patrols were instituted, gun offenses increased slightly (Sherman and Rogan 1995b).

The findings from Kansas City have received support from a recent report on two gun-patrol efforts in another midwestern city, Indianapolis. McGarrell, Chermak, and Weiss (1999) report that in the two geographic areas with patrols directed at firearms (north and east), homicides declined. However, in only one of these areas (the north area) was the decline in other firearms-related crime significant. The authors speculate that the differences may be due to the manner in which the patrols were implemented. The north-area patrols were directed at potential offenders who might be carrying firearms and therefore constituted a form of special deterrence or incapacitation. The east-area patrols involved increasing the number of vehicle stops, a form of general deterrence.

The gun patrols in Kansas City have received a great deal of attention, but it is not clear how widely they have been implemented in other cities or whether they have been applied with the same rigor as in the original test sites. If they have been widely adopted with the same or greater levels of intensity than in Kansas City, then it is possible that this form of patrolling could have contributed to the decline in violence. Because gun patrols are a simple variant of directed patrols, it is not surprising that this tactic has been incorporated into many directed-patrol operations, including Compstat (Safir 1998). Because the national decline in homicides began at about the same time as the Kansas City gun experiment, it is tempting to give much of the credit for the drop to the widespread adoption of this strategy. Unfortunately, the only evidence of widespread adoption is sporadic news reports and occasional mentions by scholars. The Kansas City gun-patrol experiment expressly targeted areas with high volumes of gun crime and used specially trained officers. The variation in the Indianapolis results suggests that how one implements this type of patrol can make a difference in the outcomes. This implies that if other agencies adopted the idea of targeting firearms, but did not adopt the specific procedures used in Kansas City, then we cannot be sure that these other agencies achieved the same results as Kansas City.

This raises the question of the mechanism by which gun patrols reduce crime. Sherman and Rogan (1995b) suggest three plausible mechanisms. First, gun patrols could increase the chances that people carrying guns illegally in high gun-crime neighborhoods will be arrested and have their guns taken by the police. In response, they leave their firearms at home. This makes these firearms less available when disputes arise, so disputes (outside the home) are less likely to result in gunfire, injury, and death. This would explain why a small number of gun seizures (twenty-nine in the Kansas City neighborhood studied) could result in a large decline in gun related crimes (eighty-three fewer gun crimes in this neighborhood).

The second hypothesis suggested by Sherman and Rogan is that the arrest and incapacitation of people who might be high-rate gun users – seventeen repeat offenders, in the case of Kansas City – might be the causal mechanism. Gun removal, in other words, might have only a spurious relationship with the reduction in gun crime. If this hypothesis is correct, then would any police effort designed to focus attention on people with histories of violent behavior be fruitful, even if illegal firearms were not the targets?

Their third hypothesis is that the intensive patrolling of the area had a deterrent effect on people most likely to engage in gun crimes. The small number of gun seizures is dwarfed by the "1,434 traffic and pedestrian stops (and) the total of 3,186 arrests, traffic citations, and other police encounters" (Sherman and Rogan 1995b, p. 690). If this is the mechanism, then simple directed patrolling of small areas with high numbers of gun crimes is the appropriate strategy. Again, there is no need for guns to occupy the central focus of such patrols.

Neither the Kansas City nor the Indianapolis study provides sufficient information to select among these three alternative mechanisms. The Indianapolis study does suggest that the more the directed patrols focus on potential offenders (rather than on people driving poorly or with equipment damage to their automobiles), the fewer the vehicle stops required and the greater the impact on firearms crimes.

There have been a number of variations on the strategy to reduce gun-carrying by offenders. Recently, Richmond (Virginia), Philadelphia, and Rochester (New York) have adopted "Project Exile," a National Rifle Association endorsed program that couples long federal prison sentences for offenders caught with firearms with publicity warning offenders not to be caught carrying guns. Richmond police assert that the drop in homicides from 1997 to 1998 in their city is due to this effort and the public ad campaign surrounding it (Janofsky 1999). Again, it not clear if the reported decline in violent crime was due to the focus on guns, to the effect on repeat offenders, or to the effect on both guns and repeat offenders.

In Boston, a problem-solving effort to address homicides targeted gangs and their use of firearms (Kennedy 1997; Kennedy, Braga, and Piehl 1997). A direct message was sent to gangs in Boston that if they were caught carrying firearms, they would receive stiff prison sentences. Police collaborated with probation authorities to closely scrutinize known offenders already within the control of the criminal justice system. Boston officials claim that the dramatic decline in juvenile homicides was due to these efforts. Since attention to firearms was coupled with attention to individuals who had a history of involvement in violent crime, it is impossible to determine if illegal gun enforcement is effective, relative to close scrutiny of high-rate offenders in high-risk places and small areas.

The Boston and Richmond gun-enforcement efforts sound promising, but we must reserve judgment about their validity. In the absence of published scientific evaluations of their effectiveness our confidence in the claims for these efforts must be restrained. Homicides, even in moderate-size cities, can fluctuate considerably because they are relatively rare events, as compared to other crimes such as burglary. When examining a subset of homicides, such as juvenile killings (as was the case in Boston), these fluctuations are even greater. This means that it is extremely difficult to attribute short-term (e.g., year to year) changes in homicides to a single factor. Slight variations in many possible social processes could account for changes in homicides and many of these factors are not within the control of the police. After a number of years have passed, statistical analysis can be used to rule out random fluctuations and other possible explanations. The decline in Richmond is too recent to permit such analysis. However, an unpublished report on the Boston experience provides data that suggests that gun enforcement may have contributed to this decline (Braga et. al. 1999a). Nevertheless, homicides have been declining in many large cities across the United States during this same time period, and most of this decline was due to reductions in youth killings involving firearms (see Chapter 1). Therefore, it is possible that the declines in Boston and Richmond would have occurred without the interventions discussed or that the publicized interventions in these two cities, though effective, were not substantively different from less well known police interventions occurring throughout the United States.

This leaves us in a quandary. The question is whether firearms enforcement is a plausible reason for the decline in homicides throughout the United States, but little is known about how widely such enforcement strategies have been implemented. There is also no evidence that these strategies began early enough in the decade to have caused the decline in homicides. Two studies strongly suggest a link between firearms patrols and reductions in crime, but the authors of these studies are uncertain whether the effect was due to gun enforcement or directed patrolling. Finally, there is evidence that drops in violent crime have followed implementation of some form of gun enforcement, but we do not know if reported declines in homicides are significantly greater than those experienced by other jurisdictions. In a period of declining homicides, almost any intervention can appear successful, even if it is irrelevant. Like directed patrol in general, there is just enough evidence to suggest that gun-enforcement strategies contributed to the decline in homicides, but not enough evidence to be confident about such claims.

Retail Drug Enforcement. Police have made considerable changes in their tactics to combat drug dealing. Prior to the crack epidemic, drug enforcement was the special domain of plainclothes investigators in the drug squads of police agencies. The scale of the crack epidemic forced police agencies to consider a variety of other tactics, including enforcement by uniformed officers either as part of their patrol activities or as members of special tactical units (see Weisel 1996). Unlike the focused policing efforts we have examined to this point, drug enforcement clearly pre-dates the national decline in homicides and has been widely used throughout the United States. Consequently, there is more reason to believe drug enforcement may have contributed to the decline in violent crime than the other police strategies examined so far. Further, there is reasonable empirical support for the argument that the decline in crack markets is in large part responsible for the decline in homicides (Lattimore et al. 1997; Chapters 2 and 6). If police drug enforcement contributed to the decline in drug markets, then police antidrug efforts probably contributed to the decline in criminal violence.

Evidence for the effectiveness of police enforcement against drug markets is mixed, often depending on the police tactic being applied and the methods used to evaluate the tactics. Evaluations of police crackdowns on drug markets suggest that they sometimes suppress retail drug markets. This is not always the result (Sherman 1997b), and the effects of drug raids may be small and limited in duration (Sherman and Rogan 1995a; Weisburd and Green 1995). At first glance, these results suggest that police drug enforcement may have had only a minor impact on the collapse of the crack cocaine market. Nevertheless, there are two other possible mechanisms that might link police drug enforcement to the decline in retail drug markets: accelerating the "wearing down" of active drug-market participants, and denying drug-market participants access to places where they can conduct their business.

Tactical Drug Enforcement As a Hassle. Although the short-term effect of drug raids and other enforcement may be slight, the long-term impact of persistent drug enforcement may have contributed to the wearing down of drug-market participants. Drug dealing and using, even in the absence of police enforcement, is arduous (see Chapter 6 or Simon and Burns 1997). It is not difficult to conceive of drug epidemics as being self-limiting. Stepped-up street drug enforcement might contribute significantly to the fatiguing of drug-market participants, thus making these markets collapse earlier than they would have collapsed otherwise, and thereby reducing violence.

Although this argument is plausible, there are at least three counterarguments. First, there is no evidence to support it. It may be true, or it may be false: we just do not know. Second, some have argued that jailed drug users get an enforced break from the stresses of hustling, which prolongs their careers on the street (Simon and Burns 1997). According to this argument, even a miserable ninety days in jail is healthier for drug users than spending the same time on the street. If this is true, then a policy of arrest and short-term incarceration might have prolonged crack markets. Strong evidence for this effect is also lacking. Finally, enforcement that disrupts drug markets might create violence. Violence could increase as several dealers move onto the same turf, either to avoid the police or to fill market opportunities made available by the removal of other dealers. If this hypothesis is correct, then some of the violence that occurred in the latter half of the 1980s and early 1990s may have been an indirect result of police actions. According to this line of reasoning, police tactics wear down drug-market participants, but rather than reduce violence this increases violence (see Chapter 6). If this argument is correct, then not only was the increase in violence partially attributable to the police, but a decline in police enforcement of crack markets might reduce violence. Though there is anecdotal evidence that drug enforcement increases violence, systematic evidence is lacking.

Denying Places for Drug Dealing. The second way police actions may have contributed to the decline in crack markets pertains to the management of places. Drug dealing, especially retail dealing to strangers, requires dealers to find locations where property owners will not interfere with their behaviors. Such places are highly concentrated in economically depressed neighborhoods, where property owners have less incentive to maintain their properties. In extremely depressed neighborhoods, many landlords have defaulted on bank loans or on their local taxes. In these cases, lenders and cities hold property but they do very little to regulate the behavior of those who use or occupy these places, except, perhaps, to board up buildings. When such places are located on arterial routes or near concentrations of other activities, they become ideal for drug dealing (Eck 1995).

Police enforcement, coupled with civil action against landlords, appears to have a powerful impact on drug dealing (Green 1996; Mazerolle, Kadleck, and Roehl 1998; Eck 1997). The effectiveness of such "nuisance abatement" strategies as a threat to compel landlords to remove drug dealers from their property may hinge on the value of the property (Eck 1995; Eck and Wartell 1998). In neighborhoods where property values and the returns on landlords' property investments are high, police don't need to spend as much time encouraging landlords to maintain their properties. Landlords in these areas already have strong economic incentives to address drug problems (see, for example, Curtis 1998, p. 1248). At the other extreme, if landlords are on the verge of abandoning their properties, the threat of nuisance abatement is negligible because they have no incentive to make changes. Nuisance abatement may work the best between these two extremes.

This hypothesis suggests that the booming national economy since the early 1990s may have increased the effectiveness of focused police efforts to address drug problems in specific places. If the surge in the economy provided even small inducements to property owners in marginal neighborhoods to improve management of their places, then police threats of civil action might have had greater leverage. Nuisance abatement has been discussed in law enforcement circles since the early 1990s and has spread throughout the United States, along with police-sponsored courses for landlords on how to handle drug dealing on their properties. The extent to which these tactics have been implemented is unknown, however. Nevertheless, it seems plausible that the increased emphasis on place managers by the police, coupled with increased incentives for place managers to move against drug dealers, might have hastened the demise of drug dealing in many cities.

But place-based efforts by the police, some have argued, only displace drug dealers to other locations. The problem with this assertion is the "only." The evidence supporting this claim is limited at best (see Cornish and Clarke 1987; Eck 1993; Hesseling 1995). The most-cited and best-conducted study of drug enforcement and displacement is the Vera Institute's examination of New York City's Tactical Narcotics Teams (Sviridoff et al. 1992). Though this evaluation found some reduction in street dealing, it noted that dealers moved from the curbside to inside foyers of apartment buildings. Johnson, Golub, and Dunlap (Chapter 6) report that this has occurred throughout drug-dealing areas in New York City. This type of displacement would be a serious blow to the effectiveness of drug enforcement if drug dealers could maintain the same volume of trade from their new positions inside buildings as they enjoyed at the curb. Displacement would also be an extreme limitation on the reduction in violence through drug enforcement, if inside dealers have the same risk of being robbed or having violent encounters with rivals as curbside dealers.

The evidence for such displacement effects is limited. The Vera study did find displacement but did not measure its magnitude. Consequently, we know how some dealers were displaced but we do not know how many were displaced, the volume of their sales after their move, or their risks of violent encounters after displacement. If the dealers had to work harder to sell drugs from the new location, then the enforcement added to the difficulties dealers faced thus eroding the drug market. If dealers were safer inside buildings, this reduction in their risk might have translated into a small but meaningful decline in drug-related violence.

There is reason to believe that the dealers' level of activity probably declined, or that the effort needed to maintain a fixed level of dealing increased. Being inside offers distinct advantages over outside dealing: it is dry in wet weather, it is out of sight of passing police cars, and it offers some protection from rip-offs. If dealing from inside buildings were as lucrative as selling from the curbside, dealers would probably have preferred it; the fact that they didn't suggests that working outside is more profitable. This in turn suggests that displacing dealers inside locations reduces drug sales.

Moving drug dealers inside might also decrease their risk of violent encounters (there is no empirical research on this issue, unfortunately). Outside, someone interested in attacking a dealer can approach from a number of directions. Inside, the number of approaches is limited and more easily watched. Inside dealing may also decrease the likelihood of accidental but dangerous jostling and chance encounters between rivals, which could lead to violence.

The number of alternative dealing locations is severely limited for drug sellers who want to market to strangers (Eck 1994). The best locations will be on busy streets in poor neighborhoods and at places where the owner is not attentive, customers have easy access, and building features offer the dealer some form of security. If persistent police actions over several years slowly reduced the viable dealing locations, dealers would be likely to restrict their selling either to people they knew or to people who were vetted by people they knew or to take other actions to reduce their exposure to police tactics. These are forms of displacement, of course, but they are forms of displacement that come at the price of reduced drug sales and profits, and could result in less violence (Eck 1995).

To summarize, if antidrug enforcement directed at retail markets was somewhat effective (and we do not have to assume it was extremely effective), it may have contributed to the decline in crack markets. As mentioned, police efforts to curb crack markets pre-date 1991, so we do not have the problem here that attends analysis of other police efforts, in which the downward trend in homicides (and other violent crimes) started before the police actions. Police attention to crack markets was widespread, so it could have had a nationwide impact. In short, persistent police efforts against retail drug markets, in combination with other factors outside the control of the police (such as the natural wearing down of drug-market participants, an aging offender population, and increases in property values), may have had an important influence on the decline of such markets. The decline of these markets, in turn, may have had a substantial role in reducing homicides and other associated forms of violent crime. Any claim that police helped to reduce homicides through their attack on retail drug markets rests on the assumption that declining street drug markets led to a reduction in violent crime. In the absence of a link between the decline of retail drug markets and the decline in violence the conjecture that police drug enforcement helped reduce violence cannot be sustained.

Problem-Oriented Policing. None of the police strategies described so far was implemented alone. Police agencies often adopted several strategies simultaneously or through sequential experimentation. In addition to forms of directed patrolling, gun enforcement, and street-level drug enforcement, police agencies since the late 1980s have increasingly adopted aspects of problem-oriented policing, frequently to address problems of violence, public disorder, firearms, or drugs.

Problem-oriented policing is one of the most important innovations in policing this century (Goldstein 1990). Problem-oriented policing focuses police attention on the problems faced by the community rather than on the administration of the police agency. Problem-oriented policing puts considerable emphasis on analyzing the nature of problems, searching through a wide range of potential solutions, and implementing responses to problems in collaboration with others outside of policing. Problem-solving efforts have been directed against a host of persistent concerns, from loitering youths to homicides. Though it is often confused with community policing or implemented along with community policing, it is distinguished from community policing by its emphasis on the ends of policing rather than on the means of policing (Eck and Spelman 1987a; Goldstein 1990). Simply put, in community policing the goal is to build a strong positive relationship between the public and the police. Addressing problems is secondary. Whereas in problem-oriented policing the goal is to reduce problems of concern to the public. Close community partnerships are often important elements in addressing problems, but they are not the final objective.

There have been a large number of attempts to apply problem-oriented policing to violent crime, though most of these efforts have not been thoroughly evaluated. In 1985, the Newport News, Virginia, Police Department used a problem-oriented approach to reduce prostitution-related robberies and domestic violence. The first of these efforts was thoroughly evaluated. Eck and Spelman, using an interrupted time-series design, reported a 43 percent decline in robberies in the target area as a result of the prevention measures that were implemented (1987b, p. 80). The domestic-violence effort was not evaluated, though police department data showed that domestic-violence deaths had declined substantially (Eck and Spelman 1987b). The Boston effort, described earlier, was an outgrowth of a problem-solving effort (Braga et al. 1999a), and so was the attempt to reduce homicides in Richmond, California (Fyfe, Goldkamp, and White 1997). To their credit, authors of the report on the Richmond (California) problem-solving effort did not make claims that the effort reduced homicides, despite declines in killings following implementation. The absence of published impact evaluations provides no sound basis for assessing whether such efforts work. Finally, an experiment in the Jersey City Police Department found significant reductions in reported robberies and calls about street fighting due to problem solving.[22] This study is particularly notable since it was conducted using a randomized treatment design (Braga et al. 1999b).

Claims that problem-oriented policing contributed substantially to the reduction in violent crime confront some of the same difficulties we have seen with other strategies. Chronological precedence is not one of them. Problem-oriented policing was first implemented in the United States around 1984 in Baltimore County (Maryland) and Newport News. By 1988, it was becoming established in the San Diego Police Department; by 1990 it was frequently combined with community policing. Thus, it precedes the fall in violent crime.

Two other issues, though, need to be answered before problem-oriented policing can be credited with a significant contribution to the decline in criminal violence. The first is how widely problem-oriented policing had been implemented before homicides began to decline. Some aspects of this strategy were built into New York City's Community Police Officer Program in the early 1990s. The Office of Community Oriented Policing Services, part of the U.S. Department of Justice, attempted to institutionalize problem solving in their community-policing efforts starting in late 1994 (Maguire et al. 1997; Office of Community Oriented Policing Services [COPS], 1998).[23] It is possible, therefore, that problem-oriented policing reached enough police agencies in the beginning of the 1990s that it contributed to the decline in violence. By 1997, a national survey found that 55 percent of large local law enforcement agencies reported that they actively encouraged patrol officers to participate in problem-solving projects on their beats (Reaves and Goldberg 1999). The second

issue is more difficult to resolve: Was problem-oriented policing implemented with sufficient rigor in enough departments that it could have had
an appreciable effect on violent crime? There is little evidence for a positive answer; in fact, some scholars have pointed to the weak application of
problem-oriented policing (Buerger 1994; Capowich, Roehl, and Andrews
1995; Eck and Spelman 1987b). In summary, there is little evidence to suggest that problem-oriented policing reduced serious violent crime
throughout the United States. It may have had an impact, but we simply do
not know.

Each of the focused policing strategies we have discussed – directed
patrolling, gun patrols, retail drug enforcement, and problem-oriented
policing – has generated some solid evaluation evidence that it works, at
least on a limited scale. With one exception, we lack convincing evidence
that police agencies implemented the strategy on a wide scale and prior to
the time homicides began to decline. Policing is replete with superficial
adoption of carefully crafted programs, so simply counting the number of
agencies that claim to be using strategy X is a poor indicator of the diffusion of the innovation. The possible exception to this pessimistic conclusion is drug enforcement. It was both widely used and deployed before the
crime drop commenced.

Part Three: Lessons for Policing

American police agencies are growing, adopting new strategies, and experimenting with new techniques for reducing violent crime. Throughout this
chapter, we have assessed the research evidence on whether these changes
are responsible for recent drops in violent crime. We have explored a number of popular hypotheses about the role of the police in producing these
reductions. Table 7.4 provides a brief summary of our findings. In general,
there is little evidence that generic changes in policing are responsible for
reducing violent crime. There is greater evidence for focused policing
strategies contributing to the drop in violent crime, though there is still a
great deal of uncertainty about these strategies' effectiveness. Overall,
police agencies might have had an impact on violent crime – there is too
much supportive evidence to assert that the effect of police on crime is a
myth. Nevertheless, most of the claims about the police contribution overstate the available evidence. Some of the policing strategies that have
received the most attention (for example, Compstat and zero-tolerance
policing) are the least plausible candidates for contributing to the reduction in violent crime. Much remains to be learned about the impact of the

Table 7.4. *The Effect of the Police on Violent Crime. A Summary of Findings*

Strategy	Empirical Support	Implemented Before or Around 1991	Evidence for National Implementation	Other Comments	Conclusions
Increase in Number of Police Officers	Mixed, with most studies finding either no effect on crime or an association with increases in crime.	Police agencies have been steadily growing, but major federal funding for police hiring began after the decline in violent crime began.	Nationwide.		Probably had no influence on national rates of violent crime.
Community Policing	Weak to no evidence.	Community policing emerged well before 1990s, but the strength of implementation is unknown.	Nationwide.	May be too vague a concept to draw a conclusion.	Probably had no influence on national rates of violent crime.
Zero-Tolerance Policing	Has not been evaluated. Empirical support for underlying theory is weak. May have perilous side effects.	Began after violent crime began dropping in New York and the rest of the nation.	Probably not.	May be restricted to New York. Implemented together with other changes in policing in NYC, so its efficacy is difficult to determine.	Little evidence of an effect on violent crime in New York, and no evidence nationwide.
Directed Patrols in Hot Spots	Reasonably strong experimental and quasi-experimental support.	Compstat version emerged after the drop in violent crime. Other versions might pre-date the beginning of the national drop in crime	Uncertain. Possibility that it was widely used.		Plausible hypothesis in general, but implausible for Compstat specifically.

Strategy					
Firearms Enforcement	Moderate quasi-experimental evidence.	Unknown.	Unknown.	Not clear whether crime reductions were due to targeting of illegal forearms or of repeat offenders.	Though a plausible hypothesis, the evidence is weak due to uncertainty over what types of gun enforcement work well and how widely these tactics were applied.
Retail Drug Market Enforcement	Moderate evidence, particularly when coupled with the threat of civil action against drug property owners.	Concentrated enforcement against retail drug markets began long before national crime drop began.	Retail drug enforcement was implemented nationally.	This strategy's effectiveness may be dependent on other trends affecting drug markets and crime.	A plausible explanation, if the decline in crack markets was a principle reason for the decline in violent crime.
Problem-Oriented Policing (POP)	Some empirical evidence that this strategy can reduce violent crime.	Some agencies implemented POP well before the national drop in crime, but there is little evidence of widespread adoption until the drop was well underway.	Now implemented throughout the United States, often as part of community policing.	There is uncertainty about the rigor of implementation and scale of application to violent crime. This strategy is often coupled with other strategies listed above.	Though a plausible hypothesis, the evidence is weak due to an absence of information about widespread adoption.

police on violent crime, the conditions under which the impact is greater or lesser and how much of an impact it is realistic to expect.

What can we learn from these findings? Since the late 1970s, police agencies in the United States have experimented with methods of focusing their activities where they can have the greatest impact. We have seen that this has taken a number of paths. Most of these innovations preceded the crack epidemic of the 1980s and the decline in violence beginning in the early 1990s. Directed patrolling, attention to disorderly situations, problem-oriented policing, and crackdowns on drug markets had been underway for some time before homicide rates began to drop and had been attempted in a wide variety of police agencies throughout the United States. These may have contributed to the decline in violent crime.

We are not claiming that the entire reduction in violent crime is due to the diffusion of focused policing across the largest cities. We are not even claiming that most of the reduction is due to these changes. Rather, the limited evidence available suggests that it is possible that focused attention on small areas with very high numbers of crimes contributed to the overall reduction in violent crime. The most plausible hypothesis is that these police actions interacted with other criminal justice policies (such as imprisonment, see Chapter 4) and social forces (such as the aging of the population, see Chapter 9; or the decline of outside retail drug markets, see Chapter 6). Interactions between external processes and police reforms may have initiated the decline in violent crime, or changes in policing may have hastened an existing downward trend. However this interaction occurred, some form of interaction is more plausible than a claim that changes in policing were the sole or greatest contributor to the drop in violent crime.

Let us return to the patterns of change in homicides per capita in the United States, but rather than looking back a decade, we will look back to 1960. The line in Figure 7.3 shows changes in the number of homicides per 100,000 population. The bars show proportionate rates of change from one year to the next. Rising bars represent year-to-year increases, and falling bars show year-to-year declines in homicides per capita. The longer the bar, the bigger the increase or decrease. Beginning in 1964, we see more than a decade of rising homicide rates. After 1976, the bars cluster in groups of three or four upward years or three or four downward years. Between spurts of upward or downward changes, there are often one or two years in which no change takes place or the change is unstable.

Is the downward trend we currently observe like the downward trend in the early 1980s? Will we see an upturn in homicides after two or three years

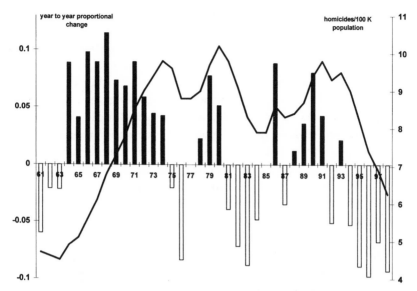

Figure 7.3. National trends and changes in homicides per 100,000 population from 1961–1998. Source FBI Uniform Crime Reports 1961 through 1998.

of instability? Or, are we seeing a descent from the plateau to which the United States climbed from 1964 through 1974? If we are seeing the downside of a short-term oscillation, then we must be extremely cautious about any claim that some specific change in policing in the last decade explains the recent decrease in violent crime (as measured by homicides). Downturns of nearly this magnitude have occurred before, and before any of the recent developments in policing. The oscillations since 1976 appear to suggest that we should consider the police contributions to crime increases as well. But there is no obvious reason to expect that there is symmetry between crime increases and decreases, i.e., that the factors we seek to explain one trend are the same factors we seek to explain the other (Lieberson 1985; Uggen and Piliavin 1998). The fluctuations in crime trends do suggest that we should consider the police influence on crime in a larger context.

There is one thing that is a myth: The police have a substantial, broad, and *independent* impact on the nation's crime rate. Rather than thinking of the police as an isolated institution that has a distinctive impact on crime, perhaps we should think of the police as part of a network of institutions, some of them formal (e.g., courts and schools) and some of them informal (e.g., families and churches), that respond to crime. When violent crime grows into a serious social concern, it is not just the police that focus more attention on the problem. Schools, community groups, businesses, health officials, and many other organizations and individuals also respond to crime.[24] Such a response might be likened to a regional reaction to a natural disaster, except it would be spread out over a longer period. The public response to AIDS also shows that, faced with a new medical threat, it was not just medical institutions that responded – education, criminal justice, business, and other organizations also developed responses. In fact, new institutions sprung out of the response to AIDS, just as there are government, private, and nonprofit institutions involved in crime prevention that were not present two decades ago. In summary, as the police mobilize to address crime more effectively, so do many other institutions.

When considered in isolation, the effectiveness of any one element of this diverse array of people and organizations may be slight. But collectively, the response might be more dramatic. Because it takes time to mobilize a diverse group of institutions, their collective impact will lag behind rising crime rates. Over time, however, the cumulative effect of these forces becomes more apparent. When crime ceases to be a major concern, all of these institutions, including the police, reallocate their scarce resources to other concerns. This reallocation is seldom coordinated; rather, each institution focuses on other pressing matters – literacy, traffic congestion, welfare, and infrastructure development – that may have been neglected while crime was the primary focus. If there is any truth to this speculation, then this change in focus and reallocation of resources away from violent crime might set the stage for another surge in crime.

Each surge in crime may have separate causes. The most recent increase in homicide may have been due to the onset of crack cocaine. Before that, it might have been something else, and in the next cycle, it may be something else again. Each time, the police and other institutions mobilize in response to the surge. It takes time to spread the word, figure out what to do, and put in place various strategies to suppress the surge. In each crime surge, the institutions involved, including the police, will find a portfolio of strategies that seem to address the peculiarities of the current crime wave.[25] And, while they are doing this, other social needs will be neglected and new ones will emerge.

In hindsight, we can speculate about plausible causes of any increase or decrease in crime. These may not be the same causes important to the previous increase or decrease, and they may not be the same causes that produce the next oscillation. In fact, the lessons that such short-term explanations provide may not be all that helpful. Not only might the next surge in violent crime have a different cause, the decision makers who address it will be different from those who addressed the prior crisis. If any lessons were learned from the prior surge, they are likely to have been forgotten.

On the other hand, perhaps the recent decline in violence is not like that of the early 1980s. Perhaps it is the undoing of the increase from the mid-1960s to the mid-1970s and the United States is recovering from a three-decade epidemic of killings. In this context it might be worth examining the history of changes in policing over the last third of this century. If the explanations for rising crime trends are symmetrical with explanations for declining crime trends, we need to ask whether changes in policing during the 1960s and 1970s allowed crime to rise during that period.

If police became less effective in the 1960s and 1970s, it may have been in response to public perceptions that police leaders and elected officials encouraged officers to abuse their authority, particularly against racial minorities. If this is true, then whatever contribution the police have made to reductions in crime over the last few years may be in jeopardy. Recent public protests against police use of force in New York City, Los Angeles, and other cities could be the beginning of the end of police effectiveness, unless police agencies find methods of being effective that are perceived to be fair and constitutional by all segments of society. This will be a much more difficult undertaking than intensively patrolling hot spots of crime and stopping suspicious young men in these areas. It will require the police, and criminologists, to carefully examine these hot spots, and the troublesome behaviors that occur within these areas, to find minimally coercive methods for addressing these problems. If the police continue to apply generic coercive measures, we may continue to oscillate between unfair but marginally effective police practices, and marginally fair but ineffective policing. Rather than looking for a single strategy that reduces crime, wherever and whenever it is applied, we should attempt to craft crime-reduction tactics that are effective and yet do not rely heavily on the application of force.

Acknowledgments

We could not have written this paper without the help of colleagues. Particularly we must thank Joel Wallman and Al Blumstein, who put us together, read early drafts, and provided thoughtful and insightful comments. Herman Goldstein and Stephen Mastrofski provided encouragement and valuable suggestions. We owe a special thanks to Kimberly

Hassell, who read and carefully edited several earlier drafts. We alone are responsible for any deficiencies in this paper.

Notes

1. Problems in estimating the number of police officers stem from at least three major sources. First, many police agencies are tiny, employing only one or two officers (sometimes only part-time). These agencies float in and out of existence based on local economic and political issues. Second, the proliferation of special police agencies sometimes makes it difficult to define a police officer. Third, sheriffs' agencies employ officers to guard jails and courts or serve civil process. Some efforts to enumerate American police count these employees as police officers, and others do not.
2. The term "police strength" has been used frequently in this line of research. As we will discuss later, it is an imprecise term that has been used to refer to the number of police officers, the number of police employees (including civilians), the amount of police expenditures, or all three.
3. The structure of this table was adapted from Marvell and Moody (1996). Unlike their review, ours includes only those studies that assess the effect of police on violent crime. This excludes studies that examine the effect of police on property crime and studies that examine the effect of crime on police. In addition, this table includes nine studies not covered by Marvell and Moody.
4. Although economists frequently classify robbery as a property crime because it produces economic benefits, we treat it here as a violent crime even when the original researchers did not.
5. More specifically, when weak instruments are used, parameter estimates will be inconsistent (and frequently biased).
6. Recent federal funding opportunities have provided grants to start new police agencies. However, as of July 1, 1996, the Office of Community Oriented Policing Services had only provided funding to eighty-four startup agencies (COPS Management System, 1999).
7. The most frequent reason cited for the death of a police organization is consolidation with other agencies to take advantage of the cost savings associated with economies of scale.
8. Maguire and colleagues (1998) criticized several official methods of counting cops for either overcounting or undercounting, thus making it difficult to adjust estimates.
9. A great deal of the research on community policing is cross-sectional, which limits our ability to draw inferences about change. Longitudinal studies of community-policing trends across the nation are fairly rare.
10. In fact, there is evidence that some types of partnership activities may increase the perceived amount of crime. Lavrakas (1986) found that Houston residents perceived more local crime after receiving an anticrime newsletter listing neighborhood offenses by time, date, and location.
11. Cordner (1995) points out that foot patrols can also be implemented without a focus on community- or problem-oriented policing.
12. Houston's BOND program (Neighborhood Watch augmented with several other community-partnership strategies) had no effect on reported serious crimes in one area and increased the number of reported serious crimes in another area.
13. Comprehensive critiques of evaluation research on community crime prevention and community policing can be found in Greene and Taylor (1988) and Lurigio and Rosenbaum (1986).
14. Commissioner Safir announced another procedural change, in which "anyone arrested for even minor offenses, such as fare beating or drinking in public, must now remain in police custody until a computerized fingerprint check can verify the person's identity" (Kocieniewski and Cooper, 1998).
15. In fact, it is difficult to find published opinions in which the author has mixed feelings: most appear to be either loyal fans or staunch foes of Bratton and his approaches.
16. Harcourt's (1998) analysis is not entirely convincing. After removing several neighbor-

hoods from Skogan's sample, he finds that the relationship between disorder and crime disappears. Information presented in his article suggests, however, that if had he removed other neighborhoods from the sample, the relationship would have been strengthened. What this indicates, however, is that Skogan's results are extremely sensitive to outliers and therefore do not provide a sound basis for policy. Rather, they suggest possible relationships that deserve further inquiry.

17. However, as Walker (1998) points out, police-complaint data are notoriously unreliable. In some instances, a rise in citizen complaints may be a signal of a healthy police organization with fair and open complaint procedures.

18. Because our interest is violent crime, this section excludes a number of studies that examine the effect of aggressive order-maintenance strategies on property crimes or visible nonviolent offenses that are thought to be more "suppressible" by police (e.g., Boydstun 1975).

19. Sampson and Cohen measured police aggressiveness by computing the number of DUI and disorderly conduct arrests per officer. We included this study here because disorderly conduct arrests are related to the notion of aggressive order-maintenance policing. For the same reason, we excluded other well-known studies in which the measure of police aggressiveness is the number of traffic citations issued (Wilson and Boland 1978).

20. Compstat is a comprehensive reform strategy with elements that are appropriate for discussion in several sections of this chapter. Elements of Compstat are related to organizational change, retail drug enforcement, and gun enforcement. However, we chose to discuss it in one place rather than breaking it up into components and discussing each separately.

21. The proportional change was calculated by subtracting the homicides per capita for a given year from the homicides per capita for the previous year, and then dividing the difference by the homicides per capita from the previous year.

22. The robbery results are a bit ambiguous. Two types of robbery data were reported. The first was based on incident reports completed by police officers responding to calls from the public (the original call may or may not have mentioned a robbery). These robbery reports declined significantly in the treatment areas relative to the control areas. The second measure of robbery was based on the calls to the Jersey City Police Department in which the caller asserted a robbery had taken place (though a subsequent investigation may not have substantiated the claim). Though there was a decline in robbery calls in the treatment areas compared to the control areas, the decline was not significant. The authors of this study suggest the discrepancy may have been due to the police encouraging reporting of violence as part of problem-solving efforts (Braga et al. 1999b).

23. More intensive efforts by COPS to institutionalize problem solving in American police agencies were not initiated until 1996, long after violent crime rates began dropping.

24. Interestingly, there is no body of theory or research on the relationship between police responses to crime and the responses of other institutions. Though it appears quite plausible that public and private institutions would join the police in a response to crime, this has been given little attention. Among the useful questions that need to be answered are: Do the police react to crime along with other institutions? With which institutions are the police most closely associated? Do the police respond first or do they lag behind other institutions? And to what degree are these responses coordinated, uncoordinated, or contradictory?

25. Much of what the police and other institutions do in response to a crime surge may be ineffective, irrelevant, and occasionally counterproductive. The efficiency of the mobilization may be low. Still, the collective response involving the police may be effective over time.

References

Amnesty International. 1996. "Police Brutality and Excessive Force in the New York City Police Department." (June).

Bayley, David H. 1994a. "International Differences in Community Policing." In Dennis P. Rosenbaum (Ed.), *The Challenge of Community Policing* (pp. 278–81). Thousand Oaks, CA: Sage.

Bayley, David H. 1994b. *Police for the Future.* New York: Oxford University Press.

Belknap, Joanne E. 1986. *The Effects of Poverty, Income Inequality, and Unemployment on Crime Rates.* Doctoral Dissertation, Michigan State University.

Bennett, Trevor. 1990. *Evaluating Neighbourhood Watch.* Aldershot, UK: Gower.

Bieck, William H., William Spelman, and Thomas J. Sweeney. 1991. "The Patrol Function." In William Geller (Ed.), *Local Government Police Management* (pp. 59–95). Washington: International City Management Association.

Bouza, Tony. 1997. "NYPD Blues: Good, Lucky, or Both?" *Law Enforcement News,* January 31, 8–10.

Boydstun, John E. 1975. *San Diego Field Interrogation: Final Report.* Washington: Police Foundation.

Bowers, William J., and Jon H. Hirsch. 1987. "The Impact of Foot Patrol Staffing on Crime and Disorder in Boston: An Unmet Promise." *American Journal of Police* 6(1):17–44.

Braga, Anthony, David M. Kennedy, Elin J. Waring, and Anne M. Piehl. 1999a. *Problem-Oriented Policing, Deterrence and Youth Violence: An Evaluation of Boston's Operation Ceasefire.* Unpublished paper, John F. Kennedy School of Government, Harvard University.

Braga, Anthony A., David L. Weisburd, Elin J. Waring, Lorraine Green Mazerolle, William Spelman, and Francis Gajewski. 1999b. "Problem-Oriented Policing in Violent Crime Places: A Randomized Controlled Experiment." *Criminology* 37:541–80.

Bratton, William, with Peter Knobler. 1998. *Turnaround: How America's Top Cop Reversed the Crime Epidemic.* New York: Random House.

Brown, Lee P., and Mary Ann Wycoff. 1987. "Policing Houston: Reducing Fear and Improving Service." *Crime and Delinquency* 33(1):71–89.

Buerger, Michael. 1994. "The Problems of Problem-Solving." *American Journal of Police* 13:1–36.

Burke, Roger Hopkins (Ed.). 1998. *Zero Tolerance Policing.* Leicester, UK: Perpetuity Press.

Capowich, George E., Janice E. Roehl, and Christine M. Andrews. 1995. "Final Report to the National Institute of Justice Evaluating Problem-Oriented Policing: Process and Outcomes in Tulsa and San Diego." Alexandria, VA: Institute for Social Analysis.

Chamlin, Mitchell B., and Robert H. Langworthy. 1996. "The Police, Crime, and Economic Theory: A Replication and Extension." *American Journal of Criminal Justice* 20:165–82.

Community Policing Consortium. 1994. *Understanding Community Policing: A Framework for Action.* Washington: U.S. Bureau of Justice Assistance.

COPS Management System. 1999. Data extracted from COPS Management System databases on May 12, 1999.

Cordner, Gary W. 1995. "Foot Patrol Without Community Policing: Law and Order in Public Housing." In Dennis P. Rosenbaum (Ed.), *The Challenge of Community Policing* (pp. 182–91). Thousand Oaks, CA: Sage.

Cordner, Gary W. 1998. "Problem-Oriented Policing Vs. Zero Tolerance." In Tara O'Connor Shelley and Anne C. Grant (Eds.), *Problem Oriented Policing* (pp. 303–14). Washington: Police Executive Research Forum.

Cordner, Gary W., and Michael A. Jones. 1995. "The Effects of Supplementary Foot Patrol on Fear of Crime and Attitudes Toward the Police." In Peter C. Kratcoski and Duane Dukes (Eds.), *Issues in Community Policing* (pp. 189–98) Cincinnati, OH: Anderson.

Corman, Hope, and Theodore Joyce. 1990. "Urban Crime Control: Violent Crimes in New York City." *Social Science Quarterly* 71:567–84.

Corman, Hope, and H. Naci Mocan. 1996. "A Time Series Analysis of Crime and Drug Use in New York City." National Bureau of Economic Research, Cambridge, MA, Working Paper 5463.

Cornish, D. and R. V. Clarke. 1987. "Understanding Crime Displacement: An Application of Rational Choice Theory." *Criminology* 25:933–47.

Curtis, Richard. 1998. "The Improbable Transformation of Inner-City Neighborhoods: Crime, Violence, Drugs, and Youth in the 1990s." *Journal of Criminal Law and Criminology* 88(4):1233–76.

Das, Dilip K. 1985. "What Can the Police Learn From 'Excellent Companies'?" *Journal of Criminal Justice* 13:381–85.

Davis, Robert C., and Pedro Mateu-Gelabert. 1999. *Respectful and Effective Policing: Two Examples in the South Bronx.* New York: Vera Institute of Justice.

DiIulio, John J. 1995. "Arresting Ideas: Tougher Law Enforcement is Driving Down Urban Crime." *Policy Review* 74:12–16.

Dodenhoff, Peter C. 1996. "LEN Salutes its 1996 People of the Year, the NYPD and its Compstat Process." *Law Enforcement News* XXII(458):1–5, December 31.

Eck, John E. 1993. "The Threat of Crime Displacement." *Criminal Justice Abstracts* 25:527–46.

Eck, John E. 1994. "Drug Markets and Drug Places: A Case-Control Study of the Spatial Structure of Illicit Drug Dealing." Doctoral dissertation. University of Maryland, College Park, MD: Department of Criminology and Criminal Justice.

Eck, John E. 1995. "A General Model of the Geography of Illicit Retail Market Places." In John E. Eck and David Weisburd (Eds.), *Crime and Place.* Monsey, NY: Criminal Justice Press.

Eck, John E. 1997. "Preventing Crime at Places." In Lawrence W. Sherman, Denise Gottfredson, Doris MacKenzie, John Eck, Peter Reuter, and Shawn Bushway (Eds.), *Preventing Crime: What Works, What Doesn't, What's Promising – A Report to the Attorney General of the United States.* (pp. 7–1 to 7–62).

Washington: U.S. Department of Justice, Office of Justice Programs, NCJ 165366.

Eck, John E. Forthcoming. "Policing and Crime Event Concentration." In Leslie Kennedy, Vincent Sacco, and Robert Meier (Eds.), *The Criminal Event Perspective*. New Brunswick, NJ: Transaction Press.

Eck, John E., and Dennis Rosenbaum. 1994. "The New Police Order: Effectiveness, Equity and Efficiency in Community Policing." In Dennis Rosenbaum (Ed.), *Community Policing: Testing the Promises* (pp. 3–23). Newbury Park, CA: Sage.

Eck, John E., and William Spelman. 1987a. "Who Ya Gonna Call: The Police as Problem-Busters." *Crime and Delinquency* 33:31–52.

Eck, John E., and William Spelman. 1987b. *Problem-Solving: Problem-Oriented Policing In Newport News*. Washington: Police Executive Research Forum.

Eck, John E., and Julie Wartell. 1998. "Improving the Management of Rental Properties with Drug Problems: A Randomized Experiment." In Lorraine Mazerolle and Jan Roehl (Eds.), *Civil Remedies and Crime Prevention. Crime Prevention Studies*, Vol 9, (pp. 161–186). Monsey, NY: Criminal Justice Press.

Esbensen, Finn-Aage. 1987. "Foot Patrols: Of What Value?" *American Journal of Police* 6(1):45–65.

Fagan, Jeffrey, Franklin E. Zimring, and June Kim. 1998. "Declining Homicide in New York City: A Tale of Two Trends." *National Institute of Justice Journal* 237:12–13.

Federal Bureau of Investigation. 19xx. *Crime in the United States: Uniform Crime Reports, 19xx.* Washington: USGPO.

Fisher, Franklin M., and Daniel Nagin. 1978. "On the Feasibility of Identifying the Crime Function in a Simultaneous Model of Crime Rates and Sanction Levels." In Alfred Blumstein, Jacqueline Cohen, and Daniel Nagin (Eds.), *Deterrence and Incapacitation: Estimating the Effects of Criminal Sanctions on Crime Rates* (pp. 361–99). Washington: National Academy of Sciences.

Fujii, Edwin, and James Mak. 1980. "Tourism and Crime: Implications for Regional Development Policy." *Regional Studies* 14:27–36.

Fyfe, James J., John S. Goldkamp, and Michael D. White. 1997. *Strategies for Reducing Homicide: The Comprehensive Homicide Initiative in Richmond, California.* Washington: U.S. Bureau of Justice Assistance, NCJ 168100.

Gianakis, Gerasimos A., and G. John Davis, III. 1998. "Reinventing or Repackaging Public Services? The Case of Community-Oriented Policing." *Public Administration Review* 58(6):485–98.

Goldstein, Herman. 1990. *Problem-Oriented Policing.* New York: McGraw-Hill.

Gottfredson, Michael R., and Travis Hirschi. 1990. *A General Theory of Crime.* Stanford, CA: Stanford University Press.

Granger, Clive W. J. 1968. "Investigating Causal Relations by Econometric Models and Cross-Spectral Methods." *Econometrica* 37:424–38.

Green, Lorraine. 1996. *Policing Places with Drug Problems.* Thousand Oaks, CA: Sage.

Greenberg, David F., and Ronald C. Kessler. 1982. "Model Specification in Dynamic Analyses of Crime Deterrence." In John Hagan (Ed.), *Deterrence Reconsidered: Methodological Innovations* (pp. 15–32). Beverly Hills, CA: Sage.

Greenberg, David F., Ronald C. Kessler, and Colin Loftin. 1983. "The Effect of Police Employment on Crime." *Criminology* 21:375–94.

Greene, Jack R., and Scott H. Decker. 1989. "Police and Community Perceptions of the Community Role in Policing: The Philadelphia Experience." *The Howard Journal* 28(2):105–23.

Greene, Jack R., and Ralph B. Taylor. 1988. "Community-Based Policing and Foot Patrol: Issues of Theory and Evaluation." In Jack R. Greene and Stephen D. Mastrofski (Eds.), *Community Policing: Rhetoric or Reality* (pp. 198–223). New York: Praeger.

Greene, Judith A. 1999. "Zero Tolerance: A Case Study of Police Policies and Practices in New York City." *Crime & Delinquency* 45(2) (June 28):171–87.

Greenwood, Michael J., and Walter J. Wadycki. 1973. "Crime Rates and Public Expenditures for Police Protection: Their Interaction." *Review of Social Economy* 31:138–52.

Hakim, Simon, Aric Ovadia, and J. Weinblatt. 1978. "Crime Attraction and Deterrence in Small Communities: Theory and Results." *International Regional Science Review* 3(2):153–63.

Harcourt, Bernard E. 1998. "Reflecting on the Subject: A Critique of the Social Influence Conception of Deterrence, the Broken-Windows Theory, and Order Maintenance Policing New York Style." *Michigan Law Review* 97:291–389.

Hassell, Kimberly, Johnette Peyton, Jihong Zhao, and Edward R. Maguire. 1999. *Structural Change in Large Municipal Police Organizations: Evidence From a National Study.* Presentation delivered at the annual meeting of the Academy of Criminal Justice Sciences, (March 12). Orlando, Florida.

Hesseling, Rene B. P. 1995. "Displacement: A Review of the Empirical Literature." In Ronald V. Clarke (Ed.), *Crime Prevention Studies.* Vol. 3. Monsey, NY: Criminal Justice Press.

Hoover, Larry T., and Edward T. Mader. 1990. "Attitudes of Police Chiefs Toward Private Sector Management Principles." *American Journal of Police* 9:25–35.

Hope, Tim. 1995. "Community Crime Prevention." In Michael Tonry and David P. Farrington (Eds.), *Building a Safer Society. Crime and Justice: A Review of Research,* Vol. 19. Chicago: University of Chicago Press.

Howsen, Roy M., and Stephen B. Jarrell. 1987. "Some Determinants of Property Crime: Economic Factors Influence Criminal Behavior but Cannot Completely Explain the Syndrome." *American Journal of Economics and Sociology* 46:445–57.

Huff, C. Ronald, and John M. Stahura. 1980. "Police Employment and Suburban Crime." *Criminology* 17:461–70.

Human Rights Watch. 1998. *Shielded From Justice: Police Brutality and Accountability in the United States.* New York: Human Rights Watch.

Humphries, Drew, and Don Wallace. 1980. "Capitalist Accumulation and Urban Crime, 1950–1971." *Social Problems* 28(2):179–93.

Independent Budget Office. 1998. "Police Staffing Levels and Reported Crime Rates in America's Largest Cities: Results of Preliminary Analysis." New York: Independent Budget Office. Available at: http://www.ibo.nyc.ny.us/crimerep.html. Access date, 5/1/99.

Jacob, Herbert, and Michael J. Rich. 1980–81. "The Effects of the Police on Crime: A Second Look." *Law and Society Review* 15(1):109–22.

Janofsky, Michael. 1999. "New Program in Richmond is Credited for Getting Handguns off Streets." *The New York Times,* February 10, p. A1.

Karmen, Andrew. 1996. "What's Driving New York's Crime Rate Down? Is Improved Policing Responsible for the Sharp Drop in Murder Rates?" *Law Enforcement News,* November 30, 8–10.

Kelling, George L. 1985. "Order Maintenance, the Quality of Urban Life, and the Police: A Line of Argument." In William A. Geller (Ed.), *Police Leadership in America: Crisis and Opportunity* (pp. 296–308). New York: Praeger.

Kelling, George L., and Catherine Coles. 1996. *Fixing Broken Windows: Restoring Order and Reducing Crime in our Communities.* New York: The Free Press.

Kennedy, David M. 1997. *Juvenile Gun Violence and Gun Markets in Boston. Research Preview.* Washington: National Institute of Justice.

Kennedy, David M., Anthony A. Braga, and Anne M. Piehl. 1997. "The (Un)Known Universe: Mapping Gangs and Gang Violence in Boston." In David Weisburd and Thomas McEwen (Eds.), *Crime Mapping and Crime Prevention. Crime Prevention Studies,* Vol 8. Monsey, NY: Criminal Justice Press.

Kennedy, David M., and Mark Moore. 1995. "Underwriting the Risky Investment in Community Policing: What Social Science Should be Doing to Evaluate Community Policing." *The Justice System Journal* 17(3):271–89.

Kessler, David A., and Sheila Duncan. 1996. "The Impact of Community Policing in Four Houston Neighborhoods." *Evaluation Review* 20(6):627–69.

King, William R., Lawrence F. Travis, III, and Robert H. Langworthy. 1997. *Police Organizational Death.* Paper presented at the annual meeting of the American Society of Criminology (November 22), San Diego.

Klockars, Carl, Ed. 1983. *Thinking About Police.* New York: McGraw Hill.

Klockars, Carl. 1985. "Order Maintenance, the Quality of Urban Life, and Police: A Different Line of Argument." In William A. Geller (Ed.), *Police Leadership in America: Crisis and Opportunity* (pp. 309–21). New York: Praeger.

Klockars, Carl. 1986. "Street Justice: Some Micro-Moral Reservations: Comment on Sykes." *Justice Quarterly* 3(4):513–16.

Kocieniewski, David, and Michael Cooper. 1998. "Police to Tighten the Scrutiny of All Suspects Under Arrest." *The New York Times,* May 28:p. A1.

Koper, Christopher S., Jan Roehl, Jeffrey Roth, and Joseph Ryan. 1998. *Return on Investment: A National Evaluation of the COPS Program.* Paper presented at the National Conference on Community Policing, November 9, Alexandria, VA.

Kratcoski, Peter C., and Susan B. Noonan. 1995. "An Assessment of Police Officers' Acceptance of Community Policing." In Peter C. Kratcoski and Duane Dukes (Eds.), *Issues in Community Policing* (pp. 169–86). Cincinnati, OH: Anderson.

Land, Kenneth C., and Marcus Felson. 1976. "A General Framework for Building Dynamic Macro Social Indicator Models: Including an Analysis of Changes in Crime Rates and Police Expenditures." *American Journal of Sociology* 82(3):565–604.

Lasley, James R., Robert L. Vernon, and George M. Dery, III. 1995. "Operation Cul-de-Sac: LAPD's 'Total Community' Policing Program." In Peter C. Kratcoski and Duane Dukes (Eds.), *Issues in Community Policing* (pp. 51–68). Cincinnati, OH: Anderson.

Lattimore, Pamela K., James Trudeau, K. Jack Riley, Jordan Leiter, and Steven Edwards. 1997. *A Study of Homicide in Eight U.S. Cities: An Intramural Research Project.* Washington: National Institute of Justice, NCJ 167263.

Lavrakas, Paul J. 1986. "Evaluating Police-Community Anti-Crime Newsletters: The Evanston, Houston, and Newark Field Studies." In Dennis P. Rosenbaum (Ed.), *Community Crime Prevention: Does It Work?* (pp. 269–291). Newbury Park, CA: Sage.

Lieberson, Stanley. 1985. *Making it Count: The Improvement of Social Research and Theory.* Berkeley: University of California Press.

Levine, James P. 1975. "The Ineffectiveness of Adding Police to Prevent Crime." *Public Policy* 23(4):523–45.

Levitt, Steven D. 1997. "Using Electoral Cycles in Police Hiring to Estimate the Effect of Police on Crime." *American Economic Review* 87(3):270–91.

Loftin, Colin, and David McDowall. 1982. "The Police, Crime, and Economic Theory: An Assessment." *American Sociological Review* 47:393–401.

Lovrich, Nicholas P., Jr. 1978. "Reducing Crime Through Police-Community Relations: Evidence of the Effectiveness of Police-Community Relations Training from a Study of 161 Cities." *The Policy Studies Journal* 7:505–12.

Lundman, Richard. 1997. *Police Levels and Crime: Additional Evidence.* Paper presented at the annual meeting of the American Society of Criminology, November 22, San Diego.

Lurigio, Arthur J., and Dennis P. Rosenbaum. 1986. "Evaluation Research in Community Crime Prevention: A Critical Look at the Field." In Dennis P. Rosenbaum (Ed.), *Community Crime Prevention: Does It Work?* (pp. 19–45). Newbury Park, CA: Sage.

Lurigio, Arthur J., and Wesley G. Skogan. 1994. "Winning the Hearts and Minds of Police Officers: An Assessment of Staff Perceptions of Community Policing in Chicago." *Crime & Delinquency* 40(3):315–30.

Maguire, Edward R. 1997. "Structural Change in Large Municipal Police Organizations During the Community Policing Era." *Justice Quarterly* 14(3):701–30.

Maguire, Edward R., Joseph B. Kuhns, Craig D. Uchida, and Stephen M. Cox. 1997. "Patterns of Community Policing in Non-Urban America." *Journal of Research in Crime and Delinquency* 34:368–94.

———. 2000. "Measuring Community Policing at the Agency Level." Unpublished manuscript, George Mason University.

Maguire, Edward R., Jeffrey B. Snipes, Craig D. Uchida, and Margaret Townsend. 1998. "Counting Cops: Estimating the Number of Police Officers and Police Agencies in the USA." *Policing: An International Journal of Police Strategies and Management* 21(1):97–120.

Maguire, Edward R., and Craig D. Uchida. 1998. *Measuring Community Policing at the Precinct and Agency Levels.* Paper presented at the annual meeting of the American Society of Criminology, Washington, DC, Nov 14, 1998.

Maguire, Kathleen, and Anne L. Pastore. 1995. *1994 Sourcebook of Criminal Justice Statistics.* Washington: U.S. Bureau of Justice Statistics. NCJ 154591.

Manning, Peter K. 1998. Review of *Fixing Broken Windows: Restoring Order and Reducing Crime in our Communities,* by George Kelling and Catherine Coles (1997). *Social Pathology* 4(1):68–71.

Marvell, Thomas B., and Carlisle E. Moody. 1996. "Specification Problems, Police Levels, and Crime Rates." *Criminology* 34(4):609–46.

Massing, Michael. 1998. "The Blue Revolution." *The New York Review of Books* XLV(18): (November 19):32–36.

Mastrofski, Stephen D. 1998. "Community Policing and Police Organization Structure." In Jean-Paul Brodeur (Ed.), *How to Recognize Good Policing: Problems and Issues* (pp. 161–89). Newbury Park, CA: Sage.

Mathieson, Donald, and Peter Passell. 1976. "Homicide and Robbery in New York City: An Economic Model." *The Journal of Legal Studies* 5(1):83–98.

Mazerolle, Lorraine Green, Colleen Kadleck, and Jan Roehl. 1998. "Controlling Drug and Disorder Problems: The Role of Place Managers." *Criminology* 36(2):371–403.

McElroy, Jerome E., Colleen Cosgrove, and Susan Sadd. 1993. *Community Policing: The CPOP in New York.* Newbury Park, CA: Sage.

McEwen, Tom. 1995. "National Assessment Program: 1994 Survey Results." Washington: National Institute of Justice.

McGarrell, Edmund, Steven Chermak, and Alexander Weiss. 1999. *Reducing Firearms Violence Through Directed Police Patrol: Final Report on the Evaluation of the Indianapolis Police Department's Direct Patrol Project.* Report to the National Institute of Justice. Indianapolis, IN: Crime Control Policy Center.

Moore, Mark H., and Darrell Stephens. 1992. "Organization and Management." In William A. Geller (Ed.), *Local Government Police Management* (pp. 22–55). Washington: International City Managers Association.

Moore, Mark H. 1994. "Research Synthesis and Policy Implications." In Dennis P. Rosenbaum (Ed.), *The Challenge of Community Policing* (pp. 285–99). Thousand Oaks, CA: Sage.

Moore, Mark H., and Robert C. Trojanowicz. 1988. "Corporate Strategies for Policing." *Perspectives on Policing,* No. 6. Washington: National Institute of Justice.

Moran, Richard. 1995. "More Police, Less Crime, Right? Wrong." *The New York Times,* February 27, p. A15.

Morris, Douglas, and Luther Tweeten. 1971. "The Cost of Controlling Crime: A Study in Economics of City Life." *The Annals of Regional Science* 5(1):33–49.

Muwakkil, Salim. 1997. "The Other Side of Zero Tolerance." *In These Times,* October 5.

Nagin, Daniel S. 1978. "General Deterrence: A Review of the Empirical Evidence." In Alfred Blumstein, Jacqueline Cohen, and Daniel Nagin (Eds.), *Deterrence and Incapacitation,* (pp. 95–139). Washington: National Academy of Sciences.

Nagin, Daniel S. 1998. "Criminal Deterrence Research at the Outset of the Twenty-first Century." In Michael Tonry (Ed.), *Crime and Justice: A Review of Research,* Vol. 23 (pp. 1–42). Chicago: University of Chicago Press.

National Association of Police Organizations (NAPO). 1997. "Press Release: NAPO Releases Results of 1997 Survey on Crime and Public Safety," August 28. Washington: NAPO.

National Association of Police Organizations (NAPO). 1999. "Press Release: NAPO Releases Results of 1999 Survey on Crime and Public Safety," February 3. Washington: NAPO.

Niskanen, William A. 1994. "Crime, Police, and Root Causes." *Policy Analysis* 218 (November 14th), Cato Institute. Washington, DC.

O'Hara, Patrick. 1998. "Bratton's 'Turnaround': Glimpse of the Future or Reinvention of the Past?" *Law Enforcement News* June 15–30, 13–14.

Office of Community Oriented Policing Services (COPS). 1998. *Problem-Solving Tips: A Guide to Reducing Crime and Disorder Through Problem-Solving Partnerships.* Washington: U.S. Department of Justice.

Office of Community Oriented Policing Services (COPS). 1999. "COPS Home Page." Available at http://www.usdoj.gov/cops/. Accessed March 1.

Panzarella, Robert. 1998. "Bratton Reinvents 'Harassment Model' of Policing." *Law Enforcement News* June 15–30, 13–15.

Pate, Anthony M. 1986. "Experimenting with Foot Patrol: The Newark Experience." In Dennis P. Rosenbaum (Ed.), *Community Crime Prevention: Does It Work?* (pp. 137–156). Newbury Park, CA: Sage.

Pate, Antony M., and Sampson O. Annan. 1989. "Baltimore Community Policing Experiment: Summary Report." Washington: Police Foundation.

Paternoster, Raymond, Bobby Brame, Ronet Bachman, and Lawrence W. Sherman. 1997. "Do Fair Procedures Matter? The Effect of Procedural Justice on Spouse Assault." *Law and Society Review* 31(1):163–204.

Pogue, Thomas F. 1975. "Effect of Police Expenditures on Crime Rates: Some Evidence." *Public Finance Quarterly* 3(1):14–44.

Reaves, Brian A. 1993. *Census of State and Local Law Enforcement Agencies, 1992.* Washington: U.S. Bureau of Justice Statistics, NCJ 142972.

Reaves, Brian A., and Andrew L. Goldberg. 1998. *Census of State and Local Law Enforcement Agencies, 1996.* Washington: U.S. Bureau of Justice Statistics, NCJ 142972.

Reaves, Brian A., and Andrew L. Goldberg. 1999. *Law Enforcement Management and Administrative Statistics, 1997: Data for Individual State and Local Agencies with 100 or More Officers.* Washington: U.S. Bureau of Justice Statistics, NCJ 171681.

Reiss, Albert J., Jr. 1985. "Policing a City's Central District: The Oakland Story." *National Institute of Justice Research Report* (April). Washington: U.S. Government Printing Office.

Rosen, Marie Simonetti. 1997. "LEN Interview with Professor Herman Goldstein, the 'Father' of Problem-Oriented Policing." *Law Enforcement News* February 14, 8–11.

Rosenbaum, Dennis P. 1988. "Community Crime Prevention: A Review and Synthesis of the Literature." *Justice Quarterly* 5(2):323–95.

Rosenbaum, Dennis P., Sandy Yeh, and Deanna L. Wilkinson. 1994. "Impact of Community Policing on Police Personnel: A Quasi-Experimental Test." *Crime & Delinquency* 40(3):331–53.

Sadd, Susan, and Randolph Grinc. 1994. "Innovative Neighborhood Oriented Policing: An Evaluation of Community Policing Programs in Eight Cities." In Dennis P. Rosenbaum (Ed.), *The Challenge of Community Policing: Testing the Promises* (pp. 27–52). Thousand Oaks, CA: Sage.

Safir, Howard. 1998. *The Compstat Process.* New York: New York City Police Department, Office of Management Analysis and Planning.

Sampson, Robert J., and Jacqueline Cohen. 1988. "Deterrent Effects of the Police on Crime: A Replication and Theoretical Extension." *Law and Society Review* 22(1):163–89.

Shapiro, Bruce. 1997. "Zero Tolerance Gospel." *Index on Censorship,* April.

Sherman, Lawrence W. 1990. "Police Crackdowns: Initial and Residual Deterrence." In Michael Tonry and Norval Morris (Eds.), *Crime and Justice: A Review of Research,* Vol. 12 (pp. 1–48). Chicago: University of Chicago Press.

Sherman, Lawrence W. 1993. "Defiance, Deterrence, and Irrelevance: A Theory of the Criminal Sanction." *Journal of Research in Crime and Delinquency* 30:445–73.

Sherman, Lawrence W. 1995. "The Police." In James Q. Wilson and Joan Petersilia (Eds.), *Crime* (pp. 327–48). San Francisco: ICS Press.

Sherman, Lawrence W. 1997a. "Communities and Crime Prevention." In Lawrence W. Sherman, Denise Gottfredson, Doris MacKenzie, John Eck, Peter Reuter, and Shawn Bushway (Eds.), *Preventing Crime: What Works, What*

Doesn't, What's Promising – A Report to the Attorney General of the United States (pp. 3–1 to 3–49). Washington: U.S. Department of Justice, Office of Justice Programs, NCJ 165366.

Sherman, Lawrence W. 1997b. "Policing for Crime Prevention." In *Preventing Crime: What Works, What Doesn't, What's Promising – A Report to the Attorney General of the United States* (pp. 8–1 to 8–58). Washington: U.S. Department of Justice, Office of Justice Programs, NCJ 165366.

Sherman, Lawrence, and Dennis Rogan. 1995a. "Deterrent Effects of Police Raids on Crack Houses: A Randomized Controlled Experiment." *Justice Quarterly* 12:755–82.

Sherman, Lawrence, and Dennis Rogan. 1995b. "Effects of Gun Seizures on Gun Violence: Hot Spot Patrol in Kansas City." *Justice Quarterly* 12:673–94.

Sherman, Lawrence, and David Weisburd. 1995. "General Deterrent Effects of Police Patrol in Crime 'Hot Spots': A Randomized, Controlled Trial." *Justice Quarterly* 12:625–48.

Silverman, Eli B., and Paul E. O'Connell. 1997. "Revolutionizing the Police: Fighting Crime in New York City." *Security Journal* 9:101–4.

Simon, David, and Edward Burns. 1997. *The Corner: A Year in the Life of an Inner-City Neighborhood.* Broadway Books: New York.

Skogan, Wesley G. 1990. *Disorder and Decline: Crime and the Spiral of Decay in American Neighborhoods.* New York: The Free Press.

Skogan, Wesley G. 1994. "The Impact of Community Policing on Neighborhood Residents: A Cross-Site Analysis." In Dennis P. Rosenbaum (Ed.), *The Challenge of Community Policing* (pp. 167–81). Thousand Oaks, CA: Sage.

Skogan, Wesley G. 1995. "Community Policing in Chicago: Year Two." *National Institute of Justice Research Preview* (October), Washington, DC.

Skogan, Wesley G., and Susan M. Hartnett. 1997. *Community Policing, Chicago Style.* New York: Oxford University Press.

Skolnick, Jerome H., and David H. Bayley. 1986. *The New Blue Line: Police Innovation in Six American Cities.* New York: The Free Press.

Skolnick, Jerome H., and David H. Bayley. 1988. "Theme and Variation in Community Policing." In Michael Tonry and Norval Morris (Eds.), *Crime and Justice: A Review of Research,* Vol. 10. (pp. 1–37). Chicago: University of Chicago Press.

Sviridoff, Michele, Susan Sadd, Richard Curtis, and Randolph Grinc. 1992. *The Neighborhood Effects of Street-Level Drug Enforcement: Tactical Narcotics Teams in New York.* New York: Vera Institute of Justice.

Sykes, Gary W. 1986. "Street Justice: A Moral Defense of Order Maintenance Policing." *Justice Quarterly* 3(4):497–512.

Swimmer, Eugene. 1974a. "Measurement of the Effectiveness of Urban Law Enforcement – A Simultaneous Approach." *Southern Economic Journal* 40:618–30.

Swimmer, Eugene. 1974b. "The Relationship of Police and Crime: Some Methodological and Empirical Results." *Criminology* 12:293–314.

Taylor, Ralph B. 1998. *Orienting Overview on the Incivilities Thesis.* Paper presented at the National Conference on Community Policing, November 9, Alexandria, VA.

Trojanowicz, Robert C. 1986. "Evaluating a Neighborhood Foot Patrol Program: The Flint, Michigan Project." In Dennis P. Rosenbaum (Ed.), *Community Crime Prevention: Does It Work?* (pp. 157–78). Newbury Park, CA: Sage.

Uchida, Craig, Brian Forst, and Sampson Annan. 1992. "Modern Policing and the Control of Illegal Drugs: Testing New Strategies in Two American Cities." Final Technical Report. Washington: Police Foundation.

Uggen, Christopher, and Irving Piliavin. 1998. "Asymmetrical Causation and Criminal Desistance." *Journal of Criminal Law and Criminology* 88(4):1399–1422.

U.S. Congress. 1994. *Congressional Record: Proceedings and Debates. 103rd Cong. 2nd sess.* 140(120):H8772–H8878.

van Tulder, Frank. 1992. "Crime, Detection Rate, and the Police: A Macro Approach." *Journal of Quantitative Criminology* 8(1):113–31.

Walinsky, Adam. 1995. "The Crisis of Public Order." *Atlantic Monthly* 276(1):39–54.

Walker, Samuel. 1984. "Broken Windows and Fractured History: The Use and Misuse of History in Recent Police Patrol Analysis." *Justice Quarterly* 1:57–90.

Walker, Samuel. 1998. "A Primer on Police Complaint Data." *Subject to Debate* 12(1,2):6–7.

Weisburd, David, and Lorraine Green. 1995. "Policing Drug Hot Spots: The Jersey City Drug Market Analysis Experiment." *Justice Quarterly* 12:711–36.

Weisel, Deborah L. 1996. *Police Anti-Drug Tactics: New Approaches and Applications.* Washington: Police Executive Research Forum.

Weisel, Deborah L., and John E. Eck. 1994. "Toward a Practical Approach to Organizational Change: Community Policing Initiatives in Six Cities." In Dennis P. Rosenbaum (Ed.), *The Challenge of Community Policing* (pp. 53–72). Thousand Oaks, CA: Sage.

Wellford, Charles R. 1974. "Crime and the Police: A Multivariate Analysis." *Criminology* 12:195–213.

Williams, Hubert, and Antony M. Pate. 1987. "Returning to First Principles: Reducing the Fear of Crime in Newark." *Crime and Delinquency* 33(1):53–70.

Wilson, James Q., and Barbara Boland. 1978. "The Effect of the Police on Crime." *Law and Society Review* 12:367–90.

Wilson, James Q., and George L. Kelling. 1982. "Broken Windows: Police and Neighborhood Safety." *Atlantic Monthly* 249 (March):29–38.

Witte, Jeffrey H., Lawrence F. Travis, III, and Robert H. Langworthy. 1990. "Participatory Management in Law Enforcement: Police Officer, Supervisor and Administrator Perceptions." *American Journal of Police* 9:1–23.

Wood, Richard L. 1998. *Creating a Culture of Community Policing: Police Cultures and Organizational Independence.* Paper presented at the National Conference on Community Policing, November 9, Alexandria, VA.

Wycoff, Mary Ann. 1994. *Community Policing Strategies.* Final report. Washington: National Institute of Justice, NCJ 159603.

Wycoff, Mary Ann, and Wesley G. Skogan. 1994. "The Effect of a Community Policing Management Style on Officers' Attitudes." *Crime & Delinquency* 40(3):371–83.

Yardley, Jim. 1999. "In Two Minority Neighborhoods, Residents See a Pattern of Hostile Street Searches." *The New York Times,* March 29, p. B3.

Zhao, Jihong, Ni He, and Nicholas Lovrich. 1998. "Individual Value Preferences Among American Police Officers: The Rokeach Theory of Human Values Revisited." *Policing: An International Journal of Police Strategies and Management* 21:22–37.

Zhao, Jihong, Ni He, and Nicholas Lovrich. 1999. "Value Change Among Police Officers at a Time of Organizational Reform: A Follow-Up Study Using Rokeach Values." *Policing: An International Journal of Police Strategies and Management* 22(2):152–170.

An Economic Model of Recent Trends in Violence

Jeff Grogger

BETWEEN THE MID-1980s AND THE EARLY 1990s, violent crime in the United States rose by 41 percent, from 538 to 758 such crimes per 100,000 residents. As great as this increase was, it masked even sharper increases in particular crimes in particular areas. In Washington, D.C., for example, the number of murders climbed from 147 in 1985 to 482 in 1991, an increase of 328 percent during a period when the D.C. population was declining. In the early 1990s, much of the United States was in the midst of a violent crime epidemic.

By 1997, the violent crime rate had dropped to 611 per 100,000 residents, down 15 percent from its peak in 1991. The murder rate was 6.8 per 100,000 residents, down from 9.8 at its 1991 high. Just a few years after its peak, violent crime generally stood at its lowest level in a decade. The murder rate was lower than at any time since 1967.

What explains the rise and fall of violence over this period? A number of hypotheses have been offered to explain the increase in violent crime during the late 1980s and early 1990s. These explanations range from the "super-predator" hypothesis (Bennett, DiIulio, and Walters 1996) to the proliferation of guns to the emergence of crack cocaine (Blumstein 1995; Blumstein and Cork 1996; Cook and Laub 1998; Grogger and Willis forthcoming).

The decline in violence since the early 1990s has received less research attention, presumably because it is so recent. Blumstein and Rosenfeld (1998) have suggested that the link between crack cocaine and violence explains both the rise and the fall of violent crime: as crack use rose, so did violent crime, and as crack use and handgun availability declined, violent crime fell with it. This explanation raises two important questions, however. First, why did the crack market cause violence to rise? Second, why did the crack market decline?

In this chapter I offer an explanation of the rise in violence and discuss a number of economic factors that may explain its fall. The explanation of the rise in violence is based on two hypotheses. The first is that an individual's choice to engage in some types of violence can be described by a model similar to that used to explain the choice to engage in property crime. The second is that crack cocaine was the catalyst for the initial increase in crime.

The link between property crime and violence exists for a simple reason: Violence, or at least a willingness to commit violence, may be an effective instrument in carrying out crimes of acquisition. This is true for many types of traditional property crime, such as robbery, but may be particularly true in the case of illegal markets. In illegal markets, traders have none of the legal property rights enjoyed by participants in legal markets. Thus violence is used as a means of enforcing agreements, disciplining subordinates, protecting profits, and expanding one's market share. All else equal, the more violence a criminal commits, the greater the income from crime.

The introduction of crack cocaine, as I have argued elsewhere (Grogger and Willis forthcoming), expanded the market for cocaine intoxication and made drug dealing more attractive. As markets and profit opportunities expanded, the number of market participants rose. Because violence plays an instrumental role in the conduct of illegal markets, the initial expansion of drug markets that resulted from the emergence of crack cocaine led to an increase in violence.

This initial increase in the level of violence subsequently had effects of its own on the market for cocaine intoxication. First, high levels of violence raised the effective price of obtaining crack. Even if the dollar price of crack remains unchanged, an increase in violence raises the risk associated with obtaining the drug, reducing demand on the part of some users. At the same time, high levels of violence may act as a barrier to entry, dissuading some would-be sellers from entering the market. I elaborate on these issues later. I also consider two other factors as explanations for the recent decline in violence: recent wage growth in low-skill labor markets and the role of increased cooperation among drug dealers.

In addition to providing an explanation of the rise and fall in violence, this model explains two other important phenomena as well. The crack-as-catalyst hypothesis explains why violence peaked in larger cities before it peaked in smaller cities, and the labor-market model explains why the increase in violence was concentrated among disadvantaged youths.

The Model

A Labor-Market Model of Property Crime. It may surprise the reader that the labor market would play a central role in a theory of violent crime. One might anticipate more readily that the labor market would be linked to property crime, and indeed the model I propose to analyze violence is an extension of a model I first proposed to study property crime (Grogger 1998). I therefore offer a digression on the basic labor-market model of property crime. Once it is spelled out and its results understood, the extension from property crime to violent crime is easier to make. In fact, many of the predictions from this model about property crime carry over to the extended model as predictions about violence.

As with all economic models, the operative assumption is that individual agents seek to maximize their utility. In the context of a labor-market model, utility is generally taken to be a function of consumption and leisure. Consumption can be thought of as expenditures on all consumption goods. Leisure is defined as time spent neither working nor committing crime, thereby including some tasks, such as household work, that fall beyond the vernacular definition of the term. Utility increases at a decreasing rate in consumption and leisure. This means that more leisure is preferred to less, all else equal, and likewise for consumption, but that the 24th hour of leisure in a day generates less utility than the 23rd, and so on.

The need to work, or otherwise generate income, leads to a trade-off between consumption and leisure: Agents have only so much time at their disposal, and each hour of leisure reduces time spent earning income by one hour, which in turn reduces consumption. I assume that the agent can generate income in one of two ways, either by working or by committing property crime. When working, the agent earns the going wage commanded by someone with the agent's skills. When committing crime, the agent's efforts are subject to diminishing returns, which arise because moral hazard prevents criminals from reaping the benefits of specialization and division of labor that are available to other sectors of the economy. This is essentially a problem of poorly defined property rights. In an environment that lacks legal recourse for disputes, criminals face limits on how much hired help they can profitably employ. The possibility of employee theft, the costliness of extralegal means of preventing it, and the possibility that an employee someday might provide incriminating evidence to authorities, all limit the size of criminal "firms" and with it criminals' ability to achieve the scale economies available to legal enterprises.

One feature of this model that distinguishes it from other economic models of crime is that I largely abstain from analyzing issues of risk. The reason for this is simple: Accounting for behavior toward risk complicates the model substantially. My exclusion of such issues should not be taken to suggest that rising incarceration risk has played no role in the recent decline in violence. Indeed it may have had an important, independent effect (see Chapter 4). Rather, in abstracting from issues of risk, I focus on the labor market, and ask whether labor-market mechanisms could explain recent violence trends even in the absence of any changes in incarceration rates.

Formally, the agent's problem can be stated as choosing the amount of time to devote to the labor market (h_m) and the amount of time to devote to crime (h_c) to solve:

$$\begin{aligned} &\underset{h_m,\ \mathrm{h_c}}{\text{maximize}} \quad U(c,\ L) \\ &\text{subject to} \quad c = w\,h_m + r(h_c;\ \pi) + A \\ &\qquad\qquad\quad T = L + h_m + h_c \end{aligned}$$

where $U()$ is the utility function, c is consumption, L is leisure, w is the market wage, and $r()$ is the criminal production function, which gives the amount of income that results from spending h_c hours committing crime. As noted above, $r()$ is assumed to increase at a decreasing rate in h_c. The variable A is nonlabor income, and T is the total amount of time at the agent's disposal.

The term π in the criminal production function is a productivity parameter that cannot be directly manipulated by the agent. The greater is π, the more productive is the criminal at any level of h_c. This parameter can be thought of in a couple of different ways. First, one can think of different individuals as having different values of π, so that across the entire population, π follows some sort of distribution function. In this case, individuals with higher values of π are more productive in crime than those with lower values, and one might expect agents with high values of π to be more likely to commit crime than those with low values.

Alternatively, one can think of a given agent as having different values of π at different times. The value of π could change for reasons beyond the agent's immediate control, owing to a change in law enforcement budgets or a change in the market for illegal drugs, for example. It could also change endogenously. If there is a learning-by-doing aspect to crime, then π grows over time as the criminal gains experience committing crime. This productivity parameter, and the notion of its distribution across the population, will play an important role below when I analyze the effects of the crack market.

As shown in Grogger (1998), this model has a particularly simple crime-participation rule: The agent will work if the wage is high enough, and a worker will commit crime if the returns to crime exceed the wage. As simple as this rule may be, it nevertheless represents an important difference between this model and many other models of crime and the labor market. In many models, the focus is on a relationship between unemployment and crime. In this model, the focus is on the relationship between *wages* and crime. In fact, in the context of this model, the question of how unemployment affects crime is ill-posed: In this model, employment and crime both are determined by wages and the returns to crime. Considering that employment and crime are both endogenous outcomes of the model, neither can be said to cause the other.

The empirical importance of this distinction can be seen in Table 8.1. There I tabulate responses to questions about wages, work, and income from crime from a subsample of young men who participated in the 1980 wave of the National Longitudinal Survey of Youth (NLSY). The NLSY began in 1979 as a national probability-sample of youths between the ages of 14 and 22. Because of the respondents' ages, because the survey oversampled disadvantaged groups, and because I required sample members to be finished with their schooling in order to be drawn into my analysis, the result is a fairly at-risk group.[1]

The top row of Table 8.1 shows that 24 percent of the sample indicated that they had earned some income from crime in the previous year. The next row shows that nearly 95 percent had worked in the previous year,

Table 8.1. Employment and Participation in Property Crime Among At-Risk NLSY Youth (N = 1,075)

	Any Income from Crime?	
Variable	Yes (24%)	No (76%)
Employed in 1979	94.5%	94.9%
Hourly Wage	$4.34	$4.97
Annual Hours of Work	1,500	1,755

irrespective of whether they had earned any income from crime. Thus a model focusing on a relationship between employment and crime would have no explanatory power and lead one to conclude, as many previous researchers have concluded, that employment has no effect on crime.

The model yields the intuitive predictions that an increase in the wage will lead to less crime, whereas an increase in criminal productivity will result in more crime. In other words, for a given wage, a higher value of π leads to more crime, and for a given level of π, higher wages lead to less crime. The second row of Table 8.1 provides evidence that is consistent with this prediction. On average, wages are 15 percent higher among non-criminals than among criminals. The final row shows that criminals work less than their law-abiding counterparts, which is consistent with another prediction of the model. Focusing on a link between wages and crime, rather than employment and crime, pays off in terms of power to explain the data.

The prediction that higher wages lead to lower crime has other implications as well. First, it suggests that minorities will be more likely to commit crime than whites, because minorities earn less than whites even after controlling for broad determinants of workplace productivity. Second, it suggests that the young will commit more crime than the old. Younger workers have less workplace experience than older workers, and wages grow rapidly with experience during the early part of one's career.

After fitting a simultaneous-equations model of the determinants of wages, work, and crime to the NLSY sample, I found support for all of these predictions. First, the data reveal a high degree of responsiveness to wages: On average, a 10-percent increase in wages leads to a 10-percent decrease in the crime participation rate. Second, the wage gap between black and white men explains roughly one-fourth of the race difference in crime-participation rates. In other words, the model offers a partial explanation for the racial distribution of property crime. Finally, the fact that young workers earn less than older workers explains entirely why property crime is concentrated among youths. In other words, the model explains the downward-sloping portion of the age-offending profile, at least for property crimes.

Figures 8.1 and 8.2 illustrate this last finding graphically. The downward-sloping lines in Figure 8.1 are age-offending profiles from the NLSY sample. The circle symbols mark the actual age-offending profile; the square symbols mark the age-offending profile predicted by the estimated model. The fit is not exact, but the predicted profile tracks the general downward trend of the actual profile fairly well.

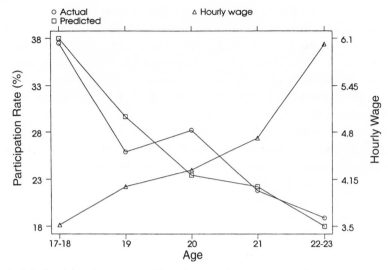

Figure 8.1. Participation rates and hourly wages by age.

The upward-sloping line is the age-wage profile. The negative relationship between the age-wage and age-offending profiles is striking. When wages are low, crime is high, and when wages are high, crime is low.

What would the age-offending profile look like if wages were constant rather than rising with age? To answer this question, I used the estimated

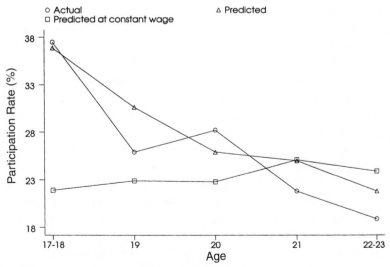

Figure 8.2. Property crime participation rates by age.

model to construct another predicted age-offending profile, this time holding wages fixed at their mean value. The resulting relationship is plotted in Figure 8.2 along with the actual age-offending curves from Figure 8.1.

The figure shows that when wages are constant, so too is participation in property crime. At constant wages, predicted participation rates range only from 22 percent to 25 percent, with no downward trend. In other words, wages explain why property offending falls with age after peaking in the late teens.

There are several conclusions worth taking from the model. First, it may be more fruitful to characterize the link between the labor market and crime in terms of a relationship between wages and crime rather than in terms of a relationship between employment and crime. Second, participation in property crime is responsive to wage incentives. Finally, because of this responsiveness, wages explain important components of the racial distribution of crime and the age distribution of crime.

This summary of the basic labor-market model of property crime is offered for two reasons: to familiarize the reader with its workings and to demonstrate its power in explaining important facts about property crime. If the basic model can be extended to apply to important types of violence, then the extended model might inherit much of the explanatory power of the basic model. The next task is to ask how the model might be extended to offer an explanation of violent crime as well.

A Labor-Market Model of Instrumental Violence. One implicit assumption of the basic model is that the agent's time is the only input to generating income from crime. Clearly this is unrealistic, as other inputs, such as violence, also play a role in income-generating crimes. This is true not only for traditional property crimes such as robberies but also for drug dealing, which provides another criminal alternative to the labor market, particularly for unskilled workers. Thus by recognizing that violence may be instrumental in committing some types of economically motivated crimes, the labor-market model of property crime can be extended to become a labor-market model of instrumental violence.

Of course, such an extension is interesting only to the extent that the recent changes in aggregate violence stem from changes in instrumental violence. Some evidence suggests that this is the case. First, most of the increase in homicides in the late 1980s and early 1990s was driven by an increase in gun homicides (Cook and Laub 1998). Second, most of the increase in homicides resulted from an increase in stranger-homicides, and in fact, homicides arising from domestic violence fell (Cook and Laub

1998, Rosenfeld 1997, Chapter 5). Although neither of these facts provides conclusive evidence that changes in instrumental violence underlie changes in the overall violence statistics, both point in that direction. Guns probably provide the most effective threat for settling disputes in illegal markets, and when such threats fail, the murders that result are most likely to be classified as stranger-homicides. Thus it seems likely that extending the labor-market model to account for instrumental violence may contribute to the understanding of recent violence trends.

Extending the model requires relatively few changes. The agent is still assumed to derive utility from consumption and leisure, and consumption is still financed by some combination of work and crime. Although crime technically could include any type of crime that yields income, it is useful to think of crime here as drug dealing, because the drug market will play an important role in my explanation of recent crime trends.

The changes to the model have to do with making the criminal-production function more realistic by allowing not only the agent's time, but also the amount of violence the agent commits, to affect the income from crime. In the context of drug dealing, it is particularly easy to see why violence would be instrumental in carrying out what are essentially economically motivated crimes. Participants in illegal markets lack the property rights enjoyed by participants in regular markets. As a result, explicit contracts are impossible to make and implicit contracts are impossible to enforce. Disputes with suppliers, employees, and other firms cannot be taken to the courts as they can in legal markets. One's market share cannot be expanded by buying out the competition, because the target of the buy-out could renege after taking the payment. Finally, drug dealers make attractive robbery targets, as they have no recourse to the police to recover their stolen drug profits. As noted by many researchers, violence, or even the threat of violence, may be an effective if costly means of enforcing agreements, expanding one's operations, and protecting one's profits in an environment where legal protections are unavailable (Fagan and Chin 1990; Goldstein 1985; Grogger and Willis forthcoming; Johnson et al. 1990).

Formally, allowing for the fact that violence may be instrumental to the commission of some types of economically motivated crimes amounts to rewriting the criminal-production function as $r(h_c, v; \pi)$, where v is the amount of violence the agent commits. The variable v now becomes another choice variable for the agent in pursuing illegal income. A technical issue that has to be resolved is whether h_c and v are substitutes or complements in the production of income from crime. If time and violence are complements, then a greater level of violence will raise the marginal productivity of the time one devotes to crime, and the agent will tend to raise v when raising h_c and lower v when lowering h_c. If time and violence are substitutes, then greater levels of violence lower the marginal productivity of the time one devotes to crime, and the criminal may choose to reduce the amount of violence committed even as more time is devoted to crime.

Of the two possibilities, it seems more plausible that time and violence would be complements rather than substitutes. It seems unlikely that a criminal, upon deciding to devote more effort to the drug trade, for example, could decide explicitly or implicitly to simultaneously reduce the amount of violence committed. For this reason I explicitly assume that h_c and v are complements in the production of income from crime.

Having extended the basic labor market model to allow for complementary instrumental violence, many of the predictions from the basic model regarding the factors that influence crime carry over directly, yielding predictions regarding the factors that influence violence. For example, considering that the basic model predicts that higher wages result in less crime, the extended model predicts that higher wages will result in less instrumental violence. Likewise, predictions about the effects of criminal productivity carry over as well. Because the basic model predicts that increases in criminal productivity increase crime, the extended model predicts that increases in criminal productivity result in higher levels of violence. By the same token, the extended model offers at least a partial explanation for the observed distributions of instrumental violence by race and age.

Explaining the Rise in Violence

In terms of the model, there are two things that could have precipitated the increase in violence that began in the mid-1980s: declining wages or an increase in criminal productivity. Real wages, particularly those paid to young men, indeed were falling in the mid-1980s, but they had been falling steadily since the mid-1970s, and the decrease over the entire period was steadily trending without any abrupt changes (Bound and Johnson 1992; Murphy and Welch 1992). Because violent crime rose abruptly, it is unlikely that gradually declining wages are the explanation. In the context of the model, that leaves an increase in criminal productivity.

What could have caused criminal productivity to rise? By most accounts, crack cocaine first emerged in the early to mid-1980s (Kozel 1997). Crack is the result of a simple chemical process by which cocaine hydrochloride is converted to cocaine base, with the result that the active cocaine alkaloid can be ingested by smoking rather than by "snorting" or injection. Smoking delivers the cocaine molecules to the brain much more quickly than snorting, allowing them to concentrate more rapidly. Because the euphoric effects of cocaine result more from the speed at which the alkaloid concentrates in the brain than with the level of the drug in the bloodstream (Jones 1990; Schuster 1986), smoking crack is more intoxicating than snorting cocaine powder. It therefore seems reasonable to think of crack as a technology shock, or technological innovation, that ultimately lowers the price of cocaine intoxication (Grogger and Willis forthcoming).

In terms of the model, the emergence of crack leads to an increase in π for virtually the entire population. In other words, the entire distribution of π shifts to the right. Viewed from the perspective of a potential criminal, this means that the arrival of crack makes crime – in the form of drug dealing – more productive. Given the negative correspondence between productivity and costs, this means that it becomes less costly to supply any given amount of cocaine intoxication. As a result, a greater number of individuals find it worthwhile to participate in the crack market, and the drug trade expands. Because violence is instrumental to drug dealing, violence rises too.

The actions of the various individuals affected by the emergence of crack can be aggregated in the form of a supply-and-demand diagram of the market for cocaine intoxication. The demand function, given by the line labeled DD in Figure 8.3, shows the quantity of cocaine intoxication that buyers are willing to consume at each possible price. The initial supply function, given by the line labeled SS, shows the quantity of cocaine intoxication that sellers are willing to provide at each possible price. It reflects sellers' costs of doing business. When costs are higher, the supply curve shifts up; when costs are lower, it shifts down. At the initial equilibrium, prior to the emergence of crack, the equilibrium price is p and equilibrium consumption is q.

With the emergence of crack, a given amount of time devoted to crime yields greater income than before. Put differently, the emergence of crack reduces the cost of supplying any given amount of cocaine intoxication. As a result, the supply function shifts down to S'S'. At the initial price p, profits are now substantially higher than they were prior to the introduction of crack. As profits rise as a result of the technology shock, increasing numbers of individuals enter the market to take advantage of those opportunities. This expansion in the market occurs until a new equilibrium is

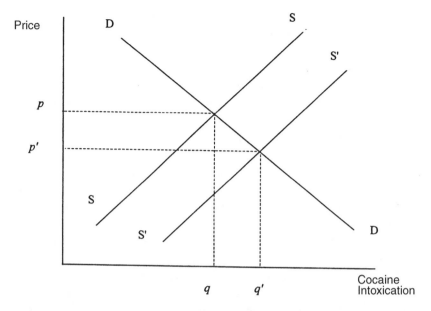

Figure 8.3. The initial effect of the emergence of crack on the market for cocaine intoxication.

reached at price p' and consumption level q'. The expansion in the market is accompanied by a corresponding increase in violence.

Explaining the Fall in Violence

Having offered an explanation for the rise in violence, I now turn to a discussion of its decline. I consider a number of factors. The first two could be considered endogenous to the model, because they arise from the effects of violence on the demand for and supply of illegal goods. We will see that the model offers a common rationale for two apparently disparate explanations offered by other analysts. I also consider two exogenous factors, including recent trends in wages and greater cooperation among drug dealers in the conduct of their business.

Instrumental Violence and the Supply of Illegal Goods. The initial increase of violence brought about by the introduction of crack may have had subsequent effects of its own on the supply side of the market for cocaine intoxication. The model predicts that, as the crack market expands, violence rises also. As an extension to the model, one could allow for sellers to choose not only the amount of violence they employ, but also the lethality of their weapons. An intuitive result is that an expanding illegal market would lead to increasingly large numbers of increasingly lethal weapons as each drug seller sought an advantage over rivals. Thus this extension of the model provides an economic rationale for Blumstein's (1995) hypothesis that crack led to a proliferation of guns in the hands of young urban males.

The virtue of the economic explanation, however, is that it also provides a rationale for how violence could have fallen even after weapons had proliferated. Indeed, it points to the proliferation of weapons as one of the principal reasons for the reduction in violence. As the arms race among drug sellers escalates, the cost of entering the drug market rises. This raises barriers to entry, as entry requires greater quantities of increasingly expensive armaments and entails greater risks of injury or death. Put differently, an arms race raises the costs of supplying goods to the market. Because the supply curve represents the cost of bringing any given quantity of goods to the market, increased costs due to arms races and increased proliferation of weapons shift the supply curve upward. This is depicted in Panel A of Figure 8.4 in the movement of the supply curve from S'S' to S"S". The result is that after expanding in response to the emergence of crack cocaine, the market subsequently contracts due to the increase in violence that accompanied that initial expansion. Subsequently, violence falls as well.

Instrumental Violence and the Demand for Illegal Goods. Although violence in illegal markets arises largely from interactions between sellers, it also can affect demand for the product on the part of buyers. To see this, it is useful to distinguish between the nominal and effective price of the good traded on the illegal market. The nominal price is the stated dollar price, represented by p in Figure 8.3 and Figure 8.4. The effective price consists of the nominal price plus additional costs associated with obtaining the good. These additional costs are not unique to markets for illegal goods; for example, the effective price of obtaining a legal good would consist of the nominal price plus the costs of transportation to reach the store and return.

Unique to illegal markets, however, is the cost imposed by violence. Presumably, the demand for an illegal drug is a function of the nominal price and the risk of violence incurred in obtaining the drug. Thus as violence rises, the effective price of the drug rises even if the nominal price stays constant. As the effective price of cocaine intoxication rises, less of

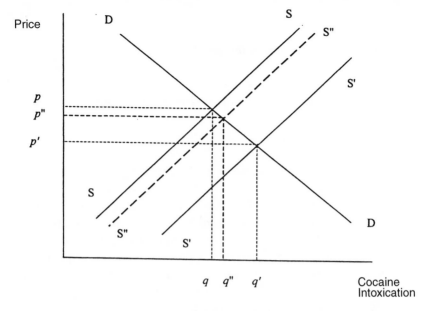

Panel A: Supply-side Effect

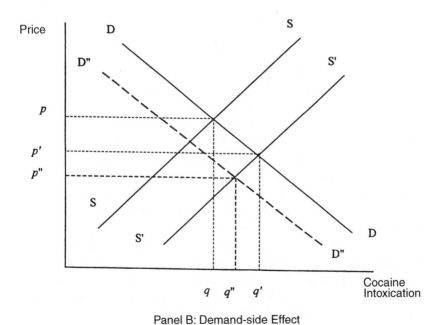

Panel B: Demand-side Effect

Figure 8.4. The subsequent effects of the initial rise in violence on the market for cocaine intoxication.

the drug is purchased at any nominal price. This is depicted in panel B of Figure 8.4 as a shift in the demand curve from DD to D″D″. Thus the initial increase in the level of violence may eventually lead to a reduced demand for the drug, which in turn causes the market, and the level of violence, to decline.

This approach to analyzing drug markets offers an economic alternative to what heretofore have been offered as culture-based explanations for the decline in violence. Whereas other analysts have suggested that cultural responses to rising levels of violence eventually turned consumers away from crack (see Chapter 6), the economic approach explains declining crack consumption as an endogenous response to the violence that is instrumental to illegal markets. Once market-related violence rises in response to the initial technology shock, it raises the effective price of the drug. As a result, demand and consumption subsequently fall, and violence declines.

Of course, the effects of violence need not have been restricted to either the demand side or the supply side of the market; in all probability, both responded to the rise in violence that followed the initial introduction of crack. Nevertheless, it seems doubtful that market forces alone could have led to reductions in violence below the levels observed immediately prior to the emergence of crack. In all likelihood, other factors contributed to the downturn as well.

The Role of Market Wages. Given the important role played by wages in the theory developed here, it is natural to ask what role they might have played in recent violence trends, and whether they might help explain why violence has fallen below its immediate pre-crack levels. Figure 8.5 plots median real wages for males ages 16 to 24 from 1979 to 1997. Nominal hourly wages were taken from the Bureau of Labor Statistics' Annual Earnings Files and have been deflated by the Consumer Price Index for Urban Consumers. Real hourly wages are reported in 1997 dollars.

The most notable feature of the graph is the sharp drop in real wages from 1979 to 1993. This is actually a continuation of a decline that began about 1973 and affected all but the highest paid workers. The overall decline in wages has been attributed to an increase in the demand for skill (Bound and Johnson 1992; Murphy and Welch 1992); because young workers as a group tend to have little experience and low education levels, their wages have fallen by a particularly large amount.

Calculations by Grogger (1998) suggest that the decline in youth wages may have played an important role in the rise in youth property crime that

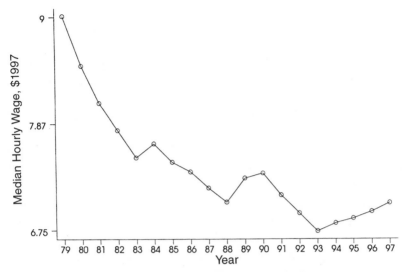

Figure 8.5. Median hourly wages for 16-to-24 year old males by year.

took place during most of the 1980s. Between 1979 and 1988, real wages paid to young men fell 22 percent. Grogger (1998) estimates that the elasticity of crime participation with respect to the wage is about −1.0, suggesting that a 22 percent decrease in wages should give rise to a 22 percent increase in youth property crime. Age-specific arrest data show that the property arrest rate for 16- to 24-year-old males rose 18 percent over that period. Taken literally, the calculation indicates that, in the absence of other factors working to decrease crime over this period, the decline in real wages would have caused property crimes to rise by an even greater amount than they did.

The question here, however, concerns the role that wages might have played in recent violence trends. Clearly, the decline of the labor market during the 1980s and early 1990s may have contributed to the appeal of the crack market as a source of income for young, unskilled men. Table 8.3 shows that crack first began appearing in large U.S. cities in 1984. Between 1984 and 1988, when crack was spreading most rapidly, youth wages fell from $7.66 to $7.04, a decline of more than 8 percent. Although wages rose a bit for the next two years, by 1993 they stood at $6.74, down another 4 percent from where they were in 1988. It seems safe to say that such a deteriorating labor market provided little outside impetus for young unskilled men to leave the crack trade.

Starting in 1993, however, the downward trend in wages started to reverse as the overall economic picture brightened. By 1997, median youth wages were $7.03, up 4 percent from their 1993 low. For a couple of reasons, though, it seems unlikely that wages played the leading role in reversing the rise in violence. First, murder peaked in 1991, whereas wages first started rising two years later.[2] Second, a 4-percent rise in wages is not enough to explain the magnitude of the reduction in violence since the early 1990s.

Even if wages did not play the leading role in reducing violence, however, they may have played an important supporting role. Particularly as the dangers of the drug trade grew, even modest improvement in the youth labor market may have made it easier for some dealers to leave the drug market behind. Equally important, improving legal job prospects may have been enough to dissuade some potential new recruits – such as youngsters just leaving school – from entering the drug trade to begin with.

Cooperation Between Drug Sellers. Finally, I consider the notion that violence may have fallen because, over time, drug sellers came to an understanding to resolve disputes among them using less costly means than violence. This is an appealing notion because it is based on the logical premise that the common interests of the sellers would be best served if indeed they could agree to some alternative method of resolving disputes and allocating market share. The problem with this explanation is that, even though the common interests of drug sellers may be served by reaching such an agreement, in all likelihood it would be in the interests of each individual to break such an agreement if in fact it could ever be reached.

The problem is analogous to that of cartels in traditional models of market structure. In cartel theory, the firms in the market recognize that their total profits would be maximized if they each agreed to reduce their output and charge the monopoly price for their product. The problem is that each firm has an incentive to deviate from this agreement if they expect the other firms to abide by it. By lowering its price slightly, each firm can capture a greater share of the market and expand its profits, provided that the other firms keep their output and prices at the agreed-upon level. The agreement to fix prices is thus unstable, with the result that cartels tend to be short lived.

In the case of drug markets, dealers face decisions not only about how to price their product but also about how much violence to employ in maintaining their market share. As in the case of conventional cartels, dealers would benefit collectively by agreeing to limit the amount of violence that they employ. The problem is that each dealer would then stand to gain by breaking the agreement, provided that the other dealers could be expected to abide by it. For this reason, violence-limiting drug cartels are likely to be as unstable as output-limiting conventional cartels, and one would expect any such cartel to be short lived.

Thus the hypothesis that drug dealers have "learned to get along" is unlikely to explain the decline in violence. The notion that drug dealers' collective interests would be best served by agreeing to reduce violence is intuitive, but incomplete. Once any such collective agreement were reached, the drug dealers' individual interests would best be served by breaking it.

The Distribution of Violence by Age, Race, and Space

The labor-market model of instrumental violence, in conjunction with the crack-as-catalyst hypothesis, provides an explanation for the rise and fall of violence over the last fifteen years or so. As in all social science research, however, the real power of a model is revealed not by its ability to explain just the phenomenon that it was designed to explain but rather by its ability to explain important related phenomena. I consider two such related phenomena in this section.

First, as indicated previously, the model offers a ready explanation for why the increase in violence was concentrated among minority youths. Just as in the simple model, the extended model predicts that crime will be most attractive to those with the lowest wages. As criminal earnings opportunities improve, the workers drawn to them will be predominantly those with weak conventional opportunities, that is, those with low wages. Young workers earn less than older workers because they have less experience; minority members are paid less on average than whites, even after accounting for observable measures of workplace productivity. Considering that those involved in the illegal market will be the primary perpetrators (and victims) of the resulting violence, the predictions of the model are consistent with Blumstein and Rosenfeld's (1998) findings that the greatest increases in homicide occurred among young minority men. To the extent that young minority men are clustered geographically within central cities, the model also explains why crack markets were largely an urban phenomenon: agents for whom the crack trade is relatively more rewarding than work are disproportionately located in central cities.

Next, the hypothesis that the emergence of crack was the catalyst for the increase in violence helps explain why crime peaked earlier in big cities and later in smaller cities. This was first noted by Blumstein and Rosenfeld (1998), who report that violence-peaks differ by about three years between the two groups of cities. Table 8.2 provides data on crack cocaine introduction dates for nineteen cities. The data are taken from Grogger and Willis (forthcoming), who used two approaches to determine the introduction dates. First, in 1991 they surveyed chiefs of police in twenty-seven cities, asking when crack first became known to their force. Second, they used data from the Drug Abuse Warning Network (DAWN), which provides information on drug-related emergency room visits. Introduction dates are determined on the basis of the proportion of visits caused by cocaine smoking; see Grogger and Willis (forthcoming) for more details. The cities included are those that provided crime reports to the FBI throughout the 1979–96 period. Eight cities in the original sample provided incomplete data and had to be dropped from this analysis.

The first two columns of the table provide introduction dates from both sources. The third and fourth columns display the same dates, but ordered by time rather than by source. The next column shows the year in which UCR murder counts peaked in each city. Finally, the last column ranks the cities by the population of their metropolitan statistical area.

These data exhibit patterns similar to those reported by Blumstein and Rosenfeld (1998). The average of the peak year for murders in the largest nine cities is 1990.1, whereas the average among the smallest ten cities is 1991.4. In other words, murders peaked in the larger cities about 1.3 years before they peaked in the smaller cities. This is a smaller gap than that reported by Blumstein and Rosenfeld (1998); the difference presumably has to do with differences in geographic coverage between their data-set and mine.

Table 8.3 reports mean crack introduction dates by city size. These data suggest strongly that differences in the introduction of crack explain the difference in peak murders. The DAWN data suggest that crack arrived in the larger cities about three-tenths of a year earlier than in the smaller cities. The police-chief survey, in contrast, shows a difference of over two years. Among the cities with introduction dates from both sources, the earlier introduction date shows crack arriving in the larger cities roughly 1.13 years before it arrived in the smaller cities, whereas the later introduction date shows a difference of 1.25 years. Thus the difference in introduction dates by city size corresponds closely to the difference in peak murder dates by city size.

Table 8.2.   Crack Cocaine Introduction Dates and Peak Murder Dates

City	DAWN Data (1)	Police Survey (3)	Earlier Introduction Date (4)	Later Introduction Date (4)	Peak Murder Year (5)	Population Rank (6)
Atlanta, GA	1984	1981	1981	1984	1989	8
Baltimore, MD	1986	1988	1986	1988	1993	10
Boston, MA	1986	n/a	n/a	n/a	1990	7
Columbus, OH	n/a	1986	n/a	n/a	1991	18
Dallas/Fort Worth, TX	1987	1986	1986	1987	1991	6
Denver, CO	1986	1986	1986	1986	1992	14
Detroit, MI	1984	1986	1984	1986	1987	4
Los Angeles, CA	1984	1984	1984	1984	1992	1
Miami, FL	1984	n/a	n/a	n/a	1986	12
Milwaukee, WI	n/a	1991	n/a	n/a	1993	16
New Orleans, LA	1987	1986	1986	1987	1994	19
New York, NY	1986	1985	1985	1986	1990	2
Newark, NJ	1985	1985	1985	1985	1988	13
Norfolk, VA	1985	1988	1985	1988	1991	17
Philadelphia, PA	1985	1985	1985	1985	1990	3
Pittsburgh, PA	n/a	1987	n/a	n/a	1993	11
San Diego, CA	1984	1984	1984	1984	1991	9
San Francisco, CA	1985	1985	1985	1985	1993	15
Washington, DC	1986	1986	1986	1986	1991	5
Average	1985.25	1985.82	1984.86	1985.79	1990.79	10

Source: Columns 1–4: Grogger and Willis forthcoming; 5–6: FBI, *Crime in the United States: Uniform Crime Reports,* annual.

Table 8.3.   Mean Peak Murder Dates and Crack Introduction Dates, by City Size

Variable	Large Cities	Small Cities	Difference
Peak Murder Date (n = 19)	1990.1	1991.4	−1.3
DAWN Introduction Date (n = 16)	1985.1	1985.4	−0.3
Police Survey Introduction Date (n = 17)	1984.6	1986.9	−2.3
Earlier Introduction Date (n = 14)	1984.4	1985.5	−1.1
Later Introduction Date (n = 14)	1985.3	1986.5	−1.2

Source: Author's tabulations of data from Grogger and Willis forthcoming and FBI, *Crime in the United States: Uniform Crime Reports,* annual.

Conclusion

At first glance, the notion that violence may be linked to labor-market conditions may seem far-fetched. When one realizes that much violence is carried out in the course of economically motivated crimes, however, the notion that wage trends could influence violence trends becomes more sensible. Most important, a labor-market model of violence, coupled with the hypothesis that the introduction of crack led to an expansion of drug markets, is capable of explaining the recent rise and fall of instrumental violence.

The rise in violent crime is fairly straightforward to explain. The emergence of crack expanded the size of illegal drug markets, making them profitable for a greater number of participants. Deteriorating youth wages probably exacerbated the movement of young, unskilled men into the drug trade. Because violence is instrumental to trade in illegal markets, violence rose as well.

As violence rose, however, the productivity of individual dealers fell. Violence is most effective when it is least likely to be met with violence; conversely, violence is least effective when it is most likely to be met with violence. In other words, drug dealers impose an external cost on one another, giving rise to a feedback mechanism whereby violence eventually subsides again. With violence near record levels, some market participants no longer found the drug trade worth their while, and some potential participants declined to enter the market. The improvement in youth wages, which began in 1993, reinforced this process.

There are doubtless other factors that contributed to the recent rise and fall in violence. An important exercise for future work will be to quantify the effects of these various influences on the violence trends of recent years. In particular, it is important to explain why violence in the post-crack era has fallen so far below its immediate pre-crack levels.

Notes

1. Grogger (1998) provides more details about the sample.
2. Youth murders did peak in 1993, however.

References

Bennett, William, John DiIulio, and John P. Walters. 1996. *Body Count: Moral Poverty and How to Win America's War against Crime and Drugs.* New York: Simon and Schuster.

Blumstein, Alfred. 1995. "Youth Violence, Guns, and the Illicit Drug Industry." *Journal of Criminal Law and Criminology* 86:10–36.

Blumstein, Alfred, and Daniel Cork. 1996. "Linking Gun Availability to Youth Gun Violence." *Law and Contemporary Problems* 59:5–24.

Blumstein, Alfred, and Richard Rosenfeld. 1998. "Exploring Recent Trends in U.S. Homicide Rates." *Journal of Criminal Law and Criminology* 88:1175–1216.

Bound, John and George Johnson. 1992. "Changes in the Structure of Wages in the 1980s: An Evaluation of Alternative Explanations." *American Economic Review* 82:371–92.

Cook, Philip J. and John H. Laub. 1998. "The Unprecedented Epidemic in Youth Violence." In M. Tonry and M. H. Moore (Eds.), Volume 24, *Crime and Justice: A Review of Research* (pp. 27–64). Chicago: University of Chicago Press.

Fagan J., and K. L. Chin. 1990. *Violence as Regulation and Social Control in the Distribution of Crack*, Volume 103, National Institute on Drug Abuse Research Monograph Series 8–43, Rockville, Maryland.

Goldstein, Paul J. 1985. "The Drugs/Violence Nexus: A Tripartite Conceptual Framework." *Journal of Drug Issues* 14 (Fall):493–506.

Grogger, Jeffrey. 1998. "Market Wages and Youth Crime." *Journal of Labor Economics* 16 (October): 756–91.

Grogger, Jeffrey and Michael Willis. Forthcoming. "The Emergence of Crack Cocaine and the Rise in Urban Crime Rates." *Review of Economics and Statistics*.

Johnson, Bruce D., Terry Williams, Kojo A. Dei, and Harry Sanabria. 1990. "Drug Abuse in the Inner City: Impact on Hard-Drug Users and the Community." In J. Q. Wilson and M. Tonry (Eds.), Volume 13, *Crime and Justice: A Review of Research* (pp. 9–67). Chicago: University of Chicago Press.

Jones, R. T. 1990. "The Pharmacology of Cocaine Smoking in Humans." National Institute on Drug Abuse Research Monograph Series 30–41.

Kozel, Nicholas. 1997. "Identifying and Monitoring Emerging Drug Abuse Problems." Washington, DC: National Institute on Drug Abuse.

Murphy, Kevin M., and Finis Welch. 1992. "The Structure of Wages." *Quarterly Journal of Economics* 107:285–326.

Rosenfeld, Richard. 1997. "Changing Relationships between Men and Women: A Note on the Decline in Intimate Partner Homicide." *Homicide Studies* 1:72–83.

Schuster, Charles R. 1986. Testimony in "'Crack' Cocaine." Hearing before the Permanent Subcommittee on Investigations of the Committee on Governmental Affairs, United States Senate, July 15.

Demographics and U.S. Homicide

James Alan Fox

THE RELEASE OF THE FBI'S 1998 UNIFORM CRIME REPORTS (Federal Bureau of Investigation, 1999) was met with a mix of celebration and skepticism. Lawmakers and public officials were quick to credit a variety of local, state, and federal crime-control initiatives (from community policing to "three-strikes" sentencing laws) for the seventh straight annual drop in crime rates, but many journalists and citizens remained somewhat incredulous. Questions about crime-data reliability and accuracy have been raised for such locales as Washington and Philadelphia (see Fazlollah, Matza, and McCoy 1998). At the same time, the public appears to be far more persuaded by the often sensational images contained in media crime reports (e.g., the recent string of school shootings) than by the somewhat understated figures contained in the Uniform Crime Reports. An October 1998 Gallup survey of over one thousand Americans found, for example, that a slight majority of respondents still maintain that crime is on the rise, despite the compelling statistics showing otherwise (O'Driscoll 1998).

The widespread skepticism surrounding reported crime trends may also stem in part from an increased level of quantitative sophistication among nonprofessional audiences, which have grown accustomed to *USA Today* style statistics and graphics. Both the public and the press may have come to understand what criminologists have known for some time – that year-to-year changes in aggregate crime levels, the usual method of FBI reporting, can obfuscate more than illuminate. Regardless of data source or collection strategy, moreover, crime statistics that overlook differences by demography can easily lead to misinterpretation.

Violent Crime Trends and Demography

A medical researcher would find it quite absurd to measure and track birth rates without adjusting for the population of women within child-bearing age groups, just as an epidemiologist would pay little attention to calculated rates of mortality that failed to take into account differences by age, sex, race, or ethnicity. Similarly, the usual strategy of measuring rates of violent crime at the national, state, or local level, which are adjusted for the size of resident population, can lead to erroneous conclusions when no attempt is made to distinguish among demographic subgroups of the population.

As early as the first half of the nineteenth century, French mathematician and astronomer Lambert-Aldolphe-Jacques Quetelet, in applying his principle of "social physics," observed that criminality varied according to age, sex, and other demographic and social factors (see Radzinowicz 1966). Still, it was not until the 1960s – after decades of searching for individual differences between criminals and noncriminals – that criminologists focused to any significant degree on the demographic characteristics related to crime patterns and trends in the aggregate.

In the early 1960s, levels of violence in America increased sharply, inspiring a wide range of sociological and cultural explanations for this frightening surge in street violence. Several researchers attempted to account for the rising crime levels by pointing to some rather significant shifts in the age, race, and sex composition of the U.S. population as well as to the progress of urban migration (see Blumstein and Nagin 1975; Chilton 1986, 1987, 1991; Chilton and Spielberger 1971; Ferdinand 1970; President's Commission on Law Enforcement and the Administration of Justice 1967; Sagl and Wellford 1968). Although the methods of demographic decomposition employed in these studies varied, as did the time periods and geographic areas used to assess the impact of population shifts, the demographic hypothesis was largely confirmed: All else equal, violent-crime rates rise as the percentage of the population in the more violence-prone age-race-sex groups (that is, young adult males, especially minorities) expands.

The explosion in crime during the 1960s and 1970s was seen partly as the result of major demographic shifts in the U.S. population. The post-World War II boom in births had created by the 1960s an escalation in the relative size of the population most at risk for violence. The post-World War II baby boomers had then reached their late adolescence and early twenties, the age at which aggressive tendencies tend to be the strongest.

The demographic explanation was also applied in reverse, to anticipate decreases in violence that were likely to occur once the baby-boom generation matured past their violence-prone years. As the baby-boom cohort aged deeper into adulthood during the 1980s, taking on families, jobs, and other responsibilities, it was expected that the violent-crime rate would subside. More to the point, the projected decline in the size of the population most prone to violence would probably translate into a reduced level of crime, violence, and disorder.

Using an econometric model relating crime trends to demographic factors as well as to socioeconomic and criminal justice variables, Fox (1978) forecasted that the rate of violence would peak in 1980, decline throughout the 1980s, and then rise once again in the 1990s, when the "baby-boomerang" generation (the offspring of the baby boomers) came of age. Blumstein, Cohen, and Miller (1980) made a similar forecast based on demographic factors alone.

As it happened, the rate of violent crime did peak in 1980. For example, the murder rate decreased by nearly one-fourth from 1980 to 1985, apparently giving support to the demographic hypothesis. In addition, several researchers found that the decline in violence at the start of the 1980s was at least partly explained by changes in age structure (see Cohen and Land 1987; Steffensmeier and Harer 1991), although others suggested that the age-crime nexus was more coincidental than causal (see Barnett and Goranson 1996; Farrington and Langan 1992).

Demographic Analysis of Homicide. For both substantive and methodological reasons, this demographic analysis of crime trends will focus exclusively on the most serious form of violence – murder and nonnegligent manslaughter, using the FBI's Supplementary Homicide Reports (SHR). Not only is homicide, because of its severity, of greatest concern to lay persons and experts alike, but available data on this offense are unmatched in terms of quality, consistency, and coverage. At a national level, no other crime is measured as accurately and precisely. Although other valuable data-series exist – specifically the National Crime Victim Survey (NCVS) and the National Incident-Based Reporting System (NIBRS) – neither is as long-term, nationally representative, or complete as the SHR. Thus, although homicide is not the only available measure of violent-crime patterns and trends, it is a fairly reliable barometer, relatively unaffected by nonuniformity in law enforcement definition and processing.

Homicide counts suffer from a minimal level of underreporting, and the clearance rate for this crime category is the highest among the FBI's featured list of serious violent offenses. In addition, while other index offenses are available only in summary-count form, homicides, through the SHR data, are available in incident form with detail on location, victim, and offender characteristics. These reports include information on the month and year of an offense; the reporting agency and its resident population, county and Metropolitan Statistical Area (MSA) codes, geographic division, and population group; the age, race, and sex of victims and offenders; and the victim-offender relationship, weapon use, and circumstance of the crime.

The SHR data are not, however, without their limitations (see Fox 1997a). Although national coverage is quite high (over 92 percent of homicides are included in the SHR), missing reports can be corrected using weights to match national and state estimates prepared by the FBI. The most significant problem in using SHR data to analyze offender characteristics, however, is the sizable and growing number of unsolved homicides contained in the data file. To the extent that the missing offender data is associated with certain offender characteristics, ignoring unsolved homicides would seriously underestimate rates of offending by particular subgroups of the population, distort trends over time among these same subgroups, and bias observed patterns of offending. To adjust for unsolved homicides, a method for offender imputation has been devised, using available information about the victims murdered in both solved and unsolved homicides (Fox 1997a). Through this imputation algorithm, the demographic characteristics of unidentified offenders are inferred on the basis of similar homicide cases – similar in terms of the victim profile and state and year of the offense – that had been solved. In other words, offender profiles for unsolved crimes are estimated based on the offender profiles in solved cases matched on victim age, sex, and race as well as year and state.[1]

The Importance of Demographic Disaggregation in Homicide. The 1990s may long be known as the decade when the crime rate fell sharply. Since 1991, the rate of homicide in the United States – the number of victims murdered per 100,000 population – has declined sharply, by about one-third. Specifically, the murder rate dropped from 9.8 in 1991 to 6.3 in 1998, down to a level last experienced some thirty years earlier.

A long-term view provides a fuller perspective on homicide trends (see Figure 9.1). After doubling during the late 1960s and 1970s, the U.S. homicide rate has fluctuated around a flat trend over most of the past fifteen years. Tempered by short-term upward and downward cycles, the rate has hovered over the past twenty-five years around the 9 victims per 100,000 population mark, that is, before the recent nosedive.

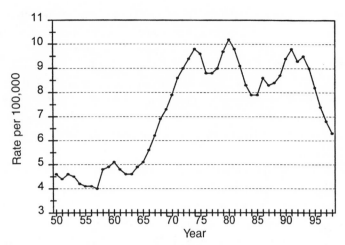

Figure 9.1. U.S. homicide rate from 1950–1998.

A very different picture of trends in homicide victimization and offending emerges when age differences are examined, however (see Chapter 5). While aggregate homicide rates have dropped to the lowest point in nearly thirty years, this is not nearly the case for all age groups. Actually, rates of victimization among adults over age 25 are much lower than in the 1970s, while those for younger groups – teens and young adults – are considerably elevated. Thus, there are two different crime patterns in America – one for the young and one for the mature – and they've moved in somewhat different directions. Moreover, age patterns are similar for victims and offenders, as most killings are intragenerational. Specifically, 42 percent of victims are killed by someone within five years of the victim's age, and 61 percent by someone within ten years.

Demographic Structure and Homicide Patterns. To return to the demographic hypothesis, Figure 9.2 shows the historically close connection between the rate of homicide and the percentage of the population in the most violence-prone age group, 18- to 24-year-olds. For two decades, aside from some fluctuation from year to year, the rate of murder closely tracked the percentage of the young adult population – both rising during the 1960s and 1970s, peaking in 1980, and then falling for the first half of the 1980s.

Then in 1986, quite unexpectedly, the rate of homicide began to change for the worse. The demographic dividend was discouragingly brief, as the rate of lethal violence began to rebound despite continued shrinkage in the population of young adults.

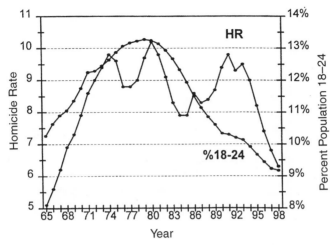

Figure 9.2. Homicide rate for ages 18–24.

Figures 9.3 and 9.4 show age-specific rates of homicide victimization and offending since 1976 (see also Tables 9.1 and 9.2).[2] Clearly, a pronounced change occurred in the mid-1980s in terms of the involvement of teenagers as victims and especially as offenders. Like never before, partly related to the spread of crack cocaine, guns, and gangs in large U.S. cities (see Blumstein 1995a, 1995b, and Chapter 2), teens began to expand their repertoire of offending to include murder. Research has suggested, moreover, that even though the percentage of teens involved in violence did not expand, the severity of crime committed by offending youth increased (see Cook and Laub 1998; Snyder and Sickmund 1995; Snyder, Sickmund, and Poe-Yamagata 1996, 1997).

These results show clearly the necessity of "unpacking" the varying contributions of different age groups to the overall violent-crime rate. Over the past two decades, the rate of victimization and offending involving young children (under age 14) has been low and fairly stable. Despite the massive publicity afforded cases of very young perpetrators, these crimes remain quite rare, numbering a few dozen per year and averaging only about two offenders per million.

At the other age extreme, murders involving adult victims or offenders (age groups 25 and above) have declined fairly steadily over the past two decades. From 1980 to 1998, for example, the rate of killing committed by adults, ages 25 and over, declined by about one-half, as the baby boomers matured and mellowed into their middle-aged years.[3] In addition, much of the decline in adult murder involves huge downturns in killings among

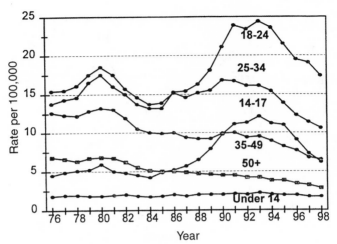

Figure 9.3. Homicide victimization by age.

spouses and ex-spouses owing to increased efforts to intervene in violent relationships before they lead to murder (see Greenfeld et al., 1998).[4]

At the same time that adult homicide progressed downward, rates of homicides involving young adults (18- to 24-years olds) as victims or perpetrators have grown. From 1985 to 1993, the victimization rate nearly doubled (from 13.2 to 24.4 per 100,000) before declining in recent years. The rate of murder committed at the hands of young adults also multiplied, from 21.4 in 1985 to 41.3 in 1993, before slipping back to 31.0 per 100,000 more recently.

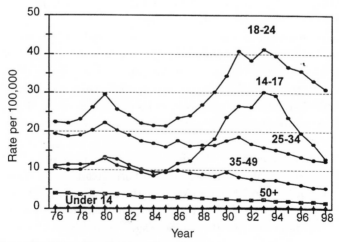

Figure 9.4. Homicide offending rates by age.

Table 9.1. Homicide Victimization Rates per 100,000 Population

Year	Total	< 14	14–17	18–24	25–34	35–49	50+	Male	Female	White	Black
1976	8.7	1.8	4.5	13.8	15.4	12.6	6.8	13.6	4.2	5.1	37.1
1977	8.8	1.9	4.9	14.3	15.5	12.3	6.6	13.7	4.2	5.4	36.2
1978	9.0	1.9	5.1	14.6	16.1	12.2	6.3	14.0	4.1	5.6	35.1
1979	9.8	1.8	5.2	16.5	17.5	12.8	6.7	15.4	4.4	6.1	37.5
1980	10.2	1.8	5.9	17.5	18.5	13.2	6.8	16.2	4.5	6.3	37.7
1981	9.8	1.9	5.0	16.0	17.5	13.0	6.7	15.6	4.3	6.2	36.4
1982	9.1	2.0	4.8	15.0	15.7	11.9	6.2	14.1	4.3	5.9	32.3
1983	8.3	1.8	4.5	13.7	14.6	10.5	5.5	12.8	3.9	5.3	29.4
1984	7.9	1.7	4.2	13.2	13.7	10.0	5.1	12.1	3.9	5.2	27.2
1985	8.0	1.8	4.9	13.2	13.9	9.9	5.0	12.1	4.0	5.2	27.5
1986	8.5	2.0	5.2	15.3	15.2	10.0	5.0	13.2	4.1	5.3	31.3
1987	8.3	1.8	5.7	15.4	14.6	9.4	4.9	12.5	4.2	5.1	30.6
1988	8.4	2.0	6.5	16.3	15.2	9.2	4.7	12.9	4.2	4.9	33.3
1989	8.7	2.0	7.9	18.1	15.5	9.2	4.6	13.6	4.0	4.9	34.9
1990	9.4	2.0	9.8	21.1	16.8	9.9	4.5	15.1	4.0	5.4	37.7
1991	9.8	2.1	11.1	23.9	16.7	10.0	4.5	15.7	4.2	5.5	39.3
1992	9.3	2.0	11.3	23.4	16.1	9.4	4.2	14.9	4.0	5.3	37.2
1993	9.5	2.2	12.1	24.4	16.1	9.5	4.2	15.0	4.2	5.3	38.7
1994	9.0	2.0	11.2	23.6	15.4	8.9	3.8	14.4	3.8	5.0	36.4
1995	8.2	1.9	11.0	21.5	13.9	8.2	3.8	12.9	3.7	4.8	31.6
1996	7.4	1.9	9.1	19.5	12.3	7.7	3.4	11.7	3.3	4.3	28.3
1997	6.8	1.7	7.3	19.1	11.4	6.8	3.2	10.7	3.0	3.9	26.1
1998	6.3	1.7	6.2	17.4	10.6	6.5	2.8	9.6	3.0	3.8	23.0

Even more alarming and tragic, homicide reaches down as never before to a much younger age group – children as young as 14 to 17 years old. Over the past decade, the rate of homicide committed by and against teenagers rose sharply. Victimization rates increased from 4.9 in 1985 to 12.1 in 1993 before dropping off to 6.2 by 1998. For offending, the rate swelled from 9.8 per 100,000 in 1985 to 30.2 in 1993 before falling back to 12.9 by 1998. This sudden and unprecedented rise in teen killing was, without a doubt, the most noteworthy feature of the 1980s surge in homicide. Juvenile crime has traditionally been characterized by mischief and mayhem, but not murder.

Recent trends in homicide are further clarified by disaggregating according to race and sex. Across all age groups, blacks are 7 times more likely to be murdered and 8 times more likely to commit homicide than are whites. The racial disproportionality is especially pronounced, however, among teen and young-adult offenders. As shown in Figures 9.5–9.12

Table 9.2. Homicide Offending Rates per 100,000 Population

Year	Total	< 14	14–17	18–24	25–34	35–49	50+	Male	Female	White	Black
1976	9.5	.2	10.6	22.4	19.4	11.1	4.0	16.3	3.1	5.1	44.7
1977	9.4	.2	10.0	22.1	18.7	11.4	4.0	16.2	3.0	5.3	42.3
1978	9.6	.3	10.1	23.1	19.0	11.4	3.7	16.8	2.8	5.5	42.3
1979	10.5	.2	11.7	26.2	20.3	11.6	4.1	18.6	2.9	6.0	45.2
1980	11.6	.2	12.9	29.5	22.2	13.3	3.8	20.6	3.1	6.7	49.9
1981	10.7	.2	11.2	25.7	20.3	12.8	3.8	18.9	2.9	6.1	44.8
1982	9.9	.2	10.4	24.2	19.0	11.3	3.5	17.4	2.8	5.8	39.8
1983	9.0	.2	9.4	22.1	17.5	10.2	3.0	15.8	2.6	5.3	35.6
1984	8.6	.2	8.5	21.5	16.9	9.5	3.0	15.2	2.3	5.3	32.8
1985	8.5	.2	9.8	21.4	16.0	9.4	3.0	15.2	2.2	5.1	33.3
1986	9.2	.2	11.7	23.4	17.6	9.9	2.9	16.5	2.3	5.4	36.8
1987	8.9	.2	12.3	24.1	16.2	9.2	2.9	16.0	2.2	5.3	35.6
1988	9.3	.2	15.5	26.9	16.5	8.9	2.7	16.8	2.2	5.0	40.3
1989	9.5	.3	18.1	30.2	16.4	8.4	2.5	17.4	2.1	5.1	41.9
1990	10.6	.2	23.7	34.4	17.6	9.5	2.5	19.6	2.2	5.6	46.9
1991	11.2	.3	26.6	40.8	18.6	8.2	2.3	20.7	2.2	5.7	50.4
1992	10.4	.3	26.3	38.4	16.8	7.7	2.3	19.3	1.9	5.2	46.8
1993	10.7	.3	30.2	41.3	15.9	7.4	2.4	19.9	2.0	5.2	49.3
1994	10.2	.3	29.3	39.6	15.2	7.4	2.0	18.8	1.9	5.0	46.1
1995	9.2	.3	23.6	36.7	14.4	6.7	2.0	17.2	1.6	4.9	39.1
1996	8.4	.2	19.6	35.7	13.4	6.2	1.8	15.5	1.7	4.5	35.8
1997	7.7	.2	16.7	33.1	12.6	5.5	1.8	14.2	1.5	4.1	32.4
1998	7.1	.2	12.9	31.0	12.3	5.4	1.6	13.0	1.5	4.1	28.3

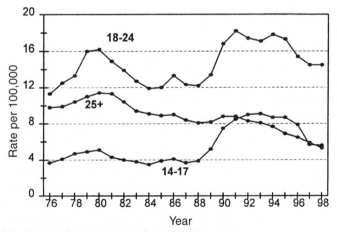

Figure 9.5. Homicide victimization by age. White males.

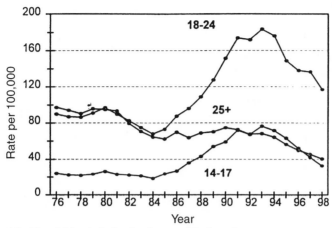

Figure 9.6. Homicide victimization by age. Black males.

(and Tables 9.3 and 9.4), trends in homicide victimization and offending are similar for whites and blacks but markedly different for males and females. Although at very different levels (note the magnified scale for blacks as compared with whites), in both victimization and offending the persistent declines for adults and the increase and subsequent decrease for teens and young adults hold for males of both races. For the most part, the rate of victimization and offending for adult females has declined over the past two decades for both races, whereas the shifts for younger females have been somewhat inconsistent and modest.[5]

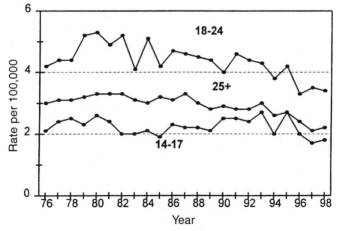

Figure 9.7. Homicide victimization by age. White females.

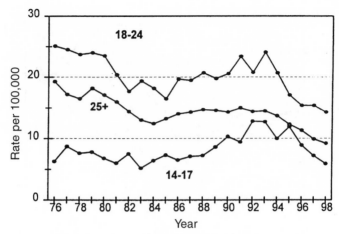

Figure 9.8. Homicide victimization by age. Black females.

The increased disproportionality of young males – white and especially black – has reaffirmed the importance of the demographic hypothesis. Males ages 14 to 24 are less than 8 percent of the U.S. population yet commit nearly one-half of the murders. They are also more than one-fourth of the victims of homicide. Isolating these trends by race (see Figures 9.13 to 9.14 and Table 9.5) shows that young white males, ages 14 to 24, have diminished in relative size to less than 7 percent of the population but have remained 10 percent of the homicide victims and nearly 20 percent of the perpetrators. More striking, however, is that over the past decade,

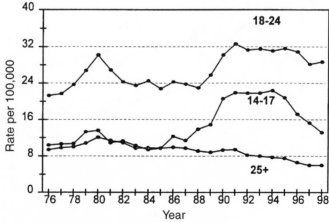

Figure 9.9. Homicide offending by age. White males.

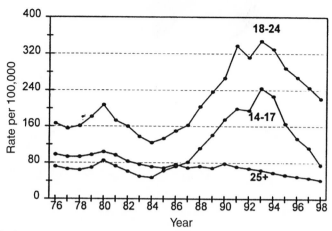

Figure 9.10. Homicide offending by age. Black males.

black males ages 14 to 24 have remained just above one percent of the population yet have expanded from 9 to 17 percent of the victims and from 17 to 30 percent of the offenders.

Thus, although the percentage of 18- to 24-year-olds has declined overall in recent years, younger teens have become more involved in serious violent crime, particularly homicide, thereby expanding the age limits of the most violence-prone group to those as young as 14 years. This new and major wrinkle hardly invalidates the demographic hypothesis, but rather updates it. Specifically, it was the age range of the most violence-prone age

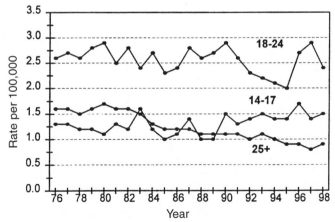

Figure 9.11. Homicide offending by age. White females.

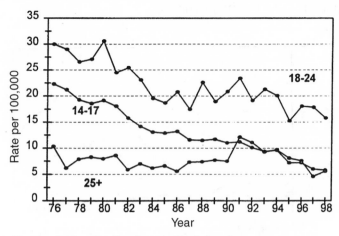

Figure 9.12. Homicide offending by age. Black females.

Table 9.3. *Homicide Victimization Rates per 100,000 by Sex, Race, and Age*

	Male						Female					
	White			Black			White			Black		
	14–17	18–24	25+	14–17	18–24	25+	14–17	18–24	25+	14–17	18–24	25+
1976	3.7	11.3	9.8	24.2	89.8	97.2	2.1	4.2	3.0	6.3	25.1	19.3
1977	4.1	12.5	9.9	22.4	86.9	94.1	2.4	4.4	3.1	8.7	24.5	17.2
1978	4.7	13.3	10.4	21.9	86.4	90.3	2.5	4.4	3.1	7.6	23.7	16.5
1979	4.9	16.0	11.0	23.2	90.9	95.7	2.3	5.2	3.2	7.8	24.0	18.2
1980	5.1	16.2	11.4	26.3	96.7	94.8	2.6	5.3	3.3	6.8	23.5	17.1
1981	4.3	14.9	11.3	23.0	89.7	93.2	2.4	4.9	3.3	6.0	20.4	16.0
1982	4.0	13.9	10.4	22.3	82.6	79.5	2.0	5.2	3.3	7.5	17.7	14.4
1983	3.8	12.7	9.4	21.3	75.0	70.6	2.0	4.1	3.1	5.2	19.4	13.0
1984	3.5	11.9	9.1	18.4	67.9	64.5	2.1	5.1	3.0	6.4	18.2	12.4
1985	3.9	12.0	8.9	23.6	73.1	62.2	1.9	4.2	3.2	7.3	16.5	13.2
1986	4.1	13.3	9.0	26.7	87.5	69.9	2.3	4.7	3.1	6.5	19.7	14.0
1987	3.7	12.3	8.4	36.0	95.9	63.7	2.2	4.6	3.3	7.1	19.5	14.3
1988	3.9	12.2	8.1	43.1	108.9	68.9	2.2	4.5	3.0	7.2	20.7	14.7
1989	5.2	13.4	8.2	54.0	127.6	70.1	2.1	4.4	2.8	8.6	19.8	14.6
1990	7.5	16.8	8.8	59.1	151.5	74.6	2.5	4.0	2.9	10.3	20.6	14.3
1991	8.5	18.2	8.8	71.9	173.7	72.6	2.5	4.6	2.8	9.4	23.4	15.0
1992	9.0	17.4	8.3	67.3	171.7	67.6	2.4	4.4	2.8	12.8	20.8	14.4
1993	9.1	17.1	8.1	76.4	183.4	68.2	2.7	4.3	3.0	12.7	24.1	14.5
1994	8.7	17.8	7.7	71.6	176.2	64.3	2.0	3.8	2.6	10.0	20.7	13.7
1995	8.7	17.3	6.9	63.2	148.8	56.4	2.7	4.2	2.7	11.9	17.1	12.3
1996	7.9	15.4	6.5	52.2	138.2	50.0	2.0	3.3	2.4	8.9	15.4	11.3
1997	5.7	14.5	5.9	42.1	136.6	45.5	1.7	3.5	2.1	7.2	15.4	9.9
1998	5.6	14.5	5.3	32.7	117.1	40.5	1.8	3.4	2.2	5.9	14.3	9.2

Table 9.4. Homicide Offending Rates per 100,000 by Sex, Race, and Age

| | Male | | | | | | Female | | | | | |
| | White | | | Black | | | White | | | Black | | |
	14–17	18–24	25+	14–17	18–24	25+	14–17	18–24	25+	14–17	18–24	25+
1976	10.4	21.3	9.4	72.4	166.4	98.3	1.3	2.6	1.6	10.3	30.0	22.3
1977	10.6	21.7	9.8	66.6	155.4	93.3	1.3	2.7	1.6	6.2	29.0	21.2
1978	10.7	23.7	10.0	64.5	161.2	93.1	1.2	2.6	1.5	7.9	26.6	19.3
1979	13.3	26.8	10.8	70.0	181.5	97.7	1.2	2.8	1.6	8.3	27.1	18.6
1980	13.6	30.2	12.1	85.2	207.9	104.1	1.1	2.9	1.7	8.0	30.6	19.2
1981	10.9	26.9	11.4	73.1	173.1	97.1	1.3	2.5	1.6	8.6	24.5	18.1
1982	11.3	24.3	10.9	61.6	160.2	83.6	1.2	2.8	1.6	5.9	25.5	15.8
1983	10.3	23.5	9.7	50.5	137.7	76.9	1.6	2.4	1.5	7.0	23.1	14.2
1984	9.4	24.5	9.8	47.6	124.2	71.6	1.2	2.7	1.3	6.2	19.6	13.1
1985	9.7	22.8	9.7	62.7	133.7	68.6	1.0	2.3	1.2	6.6	18.7	12.9
1986	12.3	24.3	9.9	72.2	149.9	76.5	1.1	2.4	1.2	5.6	20.8	13.2
1987	11.4	23.8	9.7	81.7	163.0	69.3	1.4	2.8	1.2	7.3	17.5	11.6
1988	13.9	23.0	9.1	111.9	204.0	72.7	1.0	2.6	1.1	7.4	22.6	11.5
1989	14.9	25.8	8.8	141.0	236.9	68.7	1.0	2.7	1.1	7.7	19.0	11.7
1990	20.6	30.2	9.3	175.3	266.7	78.4	1.5	2.9	1.1	7.5	20.9	11.0
1991	21.9	32.6	9.4	199.1	337.5	71.7	1.3	2.6	1.1	12.1	23.4	11.2
1992	21.8	31.3	8.2	195.2	312.0	67.9	1.4	2.3	1.0	11.1	19.2	10.1
1993	21.8	31.5	8.0	244.1	347.6	63.8	1.5	2.2	1.1	9.3	21.3	9.4
1994	22.4	31.1	7.7	226.7	329.8	58.5	1.4	2.1	1.0	9.7	20.1	9.6
1995	20.8	31.6	7.5	165.8	288.3	53.6	1.4	2.0	0.9	8.1	15.3	7.2
1996	17.2	30.9	6.6	133.5	268.0	49.9	1.7	2.7	0.9	7.6	18.1	7.2
1997	15.3	28.2	6.0	113.0	245.8	46.9	1.4	2.9	0.8	4.6	17.9	6.0
1998	13.2	28.7	6.0	75.5	221.6	41.8	1.5	2.4	0.9	5.6	15.8	5.8

group that changed, not the connection between the size of this group and the rate of homicide. Thus, even though the population of 18- to 24-year-olds was contracting, younger offenders more than picked up the slack. More precisely, teenagers began to mirror homicide patterns of their older brothers' generation (18- to 24-year-olds) more than they did that of their parents.

The presumed connection between the relative size of the at-risk population and the crime rate led economists Donohue and Levitt (1999) to a rather novel and controversial hypothesis, namely that the 1990s crime drop was in large part a result of abortion legalization in the early 1970s. They suggested that by the 1990s, abortion availability had not only

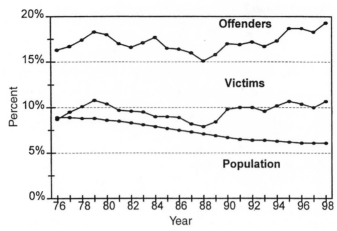

Figure 9.13. Victims and offenders as percentage of the population for 14–24-year-old white males.

reduced the overall size of the age group most prone to crime but had done so selectively – more for black and for single mothers, for example, whose offspring were particularly at risk.

Curiously, Donohue and Levitt failed to show a direct link between abortion legalization and subsequent birth rates or population counts. Rather, they considered the more indirect correlation, lagged some two decades, between abortion availability and utilization in the 1970s and crime drops in the 1990s.[6]

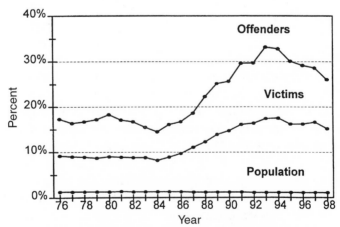

Figure 9.14. Victims and offenders as percentage of the population for 14–24-year-old black males.

Table 9.5. Population, Victims, and Offenders by Demographic Group

	14–24 White Males			14–24 Black Males			All Others		
	Population %	Victims %	Offenders %	Population %	Victims %	Offenders %	Population %	Victims %	Offenders %
1976	8.9	8.7	16.3	1.3	9.2	17.3	89.8	82.1	66.5
1977	8.9	9.5	16.7	1.3	9.0	16.4	89.8	81.6	66.9
1978	8.8	10.1	17.4	1.3	8.9	16.7	89.9	81.1	65.9
1979	8.8	10.8	18.3	1.3	8.7	17.2	89.9	80.5	64.6
1980	8.6	10.4	18.0	1.3	9.0	18.3	90.1	80.6	63.7
1981	8.5	9.7	17.0	1.4	8.9	17.1	90.2	81.4	65.9
1982	8.3	9.6	16.6	1.3	8.8	16.7	90.4	81.6	66.7
1983	8.1	9.5	17.1	1.3	8.8	15.5	90.6	81.7	67.5
1984	7.9	9.0	17.7	1.3	8.2	14.5	90.9	82.8	67.8
1985	7.7	9.0	16.5	1.3	8.9	16.1	91.1	82.2	67.3
1986	7.5	8.9	16.4	1.3	9.7	16.7	91.3	81.4	66.9
1987	7.3	8.2	16.0	1.2	11.1	18.6	91.5	80.6	65.5
1988	7.1	7.9	15.1	1.2	12.3	22.3	91.7	79.9	62.5
1989	6.9	8.4	15.8	1.2	13.9	25.2	91.9	77.8	59.0
1990	6.7	9.8	17.0	1.2	14.7	25.7	92.1	75.6	57.3
1991	6.5	10.0	16.9	1.2	16.1	29.6	92.3	73.9	53.5
1992	6.4	10.0	17.2	1.1	16.4	29.7	92.5	73.6	53.1
1993	6.4	9.6	16.7	1.1	17.4	33.2	92.5	73.0	50.1
1994	6.3	10.2	17.3	1.1	17.5	32.8	92.6	72.3	49.9
1995	6.2	10.7	18.7	1.1	16.2	30.1	92.6	73.1	51.2
1996	6.1	10.4	18.7	1.1	16.2	29.2	92.7	73.4	52.1
1997	6.1	10.0	18.3	1.1	16.6	28.6	92.8	73.5	53.1
1998	6.1	10.7	19.3	1.1	15.2	26.1	92.8	74.1	54.6

According to Donohue and Levitt, the most compelling evidence of the impact of abortion legalization comes from a regression analysis of post-legalization abortion rates in each state and its change in crime levels for the period 1985 to 1997, controlling for a variety of crime-related variables. By employing a single statistic summarizing change over this twelve-year span, however, they miss most of the shifts in crime during this period – the upward trend during the late 1980s crack era and the downward correction in the post-crack years. This is something like studying the effects of moon phases on ocean tides but only recording data for periods of low tide.

It is especially surprising that Donohue and Levitt did not examine the 1991–97 change, since much of their discussion concerns the extent to which this drop is attributable to abortion legalization. They conclude that as much as one-half the decline in crime during the 1990s stemmed from abortion availability. This assertion is rather difficult to accept, considering that so much of the drop was among age groups born before 1973.

In sum, the abortion-crime-drop hypothesis is an interesting one. However, far more analysis is needed to assess this connection adequately.

Juvenilization of Murder. The diverging rates of victimization and offending between older and younger groups have lowered the average age of murder victims and offenders, changing much about the way we think about murder and murderers. As shown in Figure 9.15, between the mid-1980s and early 1990s, the average age of victims and of offenders dropped by about four years (from 35 to 32 for victims and from 31 to 28 for offenders) before creeping back up slightly in recent years (as the rate of homicide has dropped fastest among teens).

The "youth movement" among victims and perpetrators of murder has altered not only the rate and volume of homicide, nor just the mean ages, but also the overall nature of homicide in America. As the age mix of perpetrators has shifted (more younger offenders and fewer older ones), many of the traditional patterns of homicide have changed. With gun use among youthful killers near 80 percent, the overall dominance of guns in homicide has increased (see Figure 9.16). Driven by the surge in gun killings by younger groups, the percentage of all offenders using a firearm rose from less than 60 percent in the mid-1980s to nearly 70 percent by 1990.

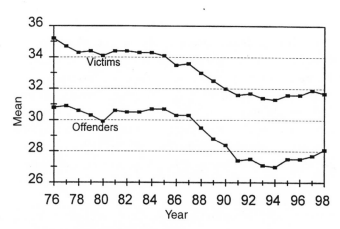

Figure 9.15. Mean victim and offender age.

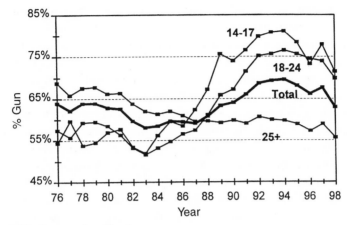

Figure 9.16. Gun use by offender age.

A younger mix of offenders has also boosted the overall percentage of killings by teams or groups (see Figure 9.17). In addition, because younger offenders tend to target strangers or acquaintances much more than older offenders do, the percentage of victims who know their assailants well has dropped. This change prompted the FBI (1994) to assert boldly (and somewhat inaccurately) that "every American now has a realistic chance of murder victimization in view of the random nature the crime has assumed" (p. 287). Regardless of the spin given to the flux in victim-offender relationships, much of what criminologists have long believed about homicide needs to be revisited (see Heide 1998).

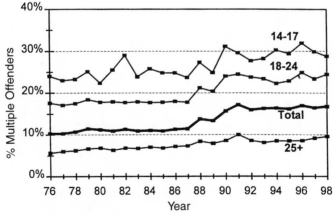

Figure 9.17. Multiple offenders by age.

Urban Differences. Several analysts have attributed the significant rise in youth violence from the mid-1980s to the early 1990s to the emergence of the volatile drug market surrounding crack cocaine (see Blumstein 1995b; Blumstein and Rosenfeld 1998; Chapters 2 and 8). It has also been noted that the timing and acceleration of violent-crime upturns can be traced to the spread of crack and guns first within the largest American cities and then out to smaller municipalities. This lag effect from larger cities to smaller can be seen quite clearly in the trends in gun-homicide offending by city size shown in Figure 9.18. The timing of the upturn, from start to peak, is associated with city size: from 1987 to 1991 for cities with populations over one million, from 1988 to 1993 for cities with populations between 250,000 and one million, from about 1988 to 1994 for cities with populations under 250,000, and little if any effect in nonurban areas. The slopes of increase and eventual decrease also appear to be related to city size, with sharper effects in larger cities, but a slower rise and fall in smaller cities.

Another approach to these data focuses on birth cohorts. Figure 9.19 displays the cumulative gun-homicide offender count during the 1976–97 crime-window period for cohorts born since 1945. Were it not for the impact of crack markets and the diffusion of guns among younger age groups, the peak for all city-size groups would likely have been around the 1960 birth cohort (who ranged in age from 16 to 37 during the 1976–97 window period). But a second bulge around the 1972 birth cohort (who ranged in age between 4 and 25 during the window period) appears to have altered the otherwise unimodal pattern. Moreover, the exposure to the impact of crack markets was largely invariant by city size (the 1969–78 cohorts were affected

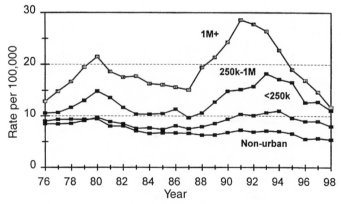

Figure 9.18. Gun-homicide offender rates by city size.

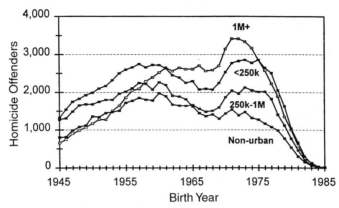

Figure 9.19. Gun offender birth cohorts by city size.

in all areas), with one notable exception: the level, rather than downward, pattern for the 1963–68 birth cohorts in the largest cities. The 1963–68 birth cohort was still young enough during the mid-1980s to have been affected by the early introduction of crack in major urban centers, while in smaller cities this cohort may have been sufficiently mature to be relatively immune to the effects of the delayed arrival of this drug market at the end of the 1980s.

Down But Not Out. This demographic analysis of homicide patterns has shown that for the most part the nation's widely reported surge in killing during the late 1980s and early 1990s can be traced exclusively to elevated rates among young adults and especially teenagers. The recent downturn in youth violence – and youth killing in particular – has been much heralded (see Reno 1998). Furthermore, a comparison of various age-race-sex combinations finds the largest drop to be among young black males, especially in large urban centers, such as Boston, New York, and Chicago, which directed intensive enforcement efforts against guns, gangs, and crack (see Blumstein and Rosenfeld 1998; Butterfield 1997).

In light of the 1990s drop in homicide, several authorities have questioned the role of demographics (see Krauss 1995). No one can reasonably assert that all – or even most – of the sharp decline in homicide since 1991 could be linked to demographic change. Although some decline could have been anticipated based on demographic shifts, this would hardly have been of the magnitude that has brought homicide rates to a thirty-year low.

Table 9.6 examines the precise issue of the extent to which the 1990s decline in murder can be traced to demographics. The first two columns of the table show the actual homicide rate for each year and the percentage

Table 9.6. 1990s Crime Drop Due to Demographics

Year	Offending Rate Per 100,000	% Change in Offending Rate	Offending Rate Predicted from Demographics	% Change Predicted from Demographics	% Change from Demographics
1991	11.21	—	11.21	—	—
1992	10.41	–.80	11.13	–.07	9.35
1993	10.72	–.49	11.13	–.08	16.31
1994	10.18	–1.03	11.05	–.16	15.76
1995	9.21	–2.00	10.99	–.22	11.12
1996	8.45	–2.76	10.92	–.29	10.51
1997	7.70	–3.51	10.86	–.35	9.88
1998	7.12	–4.09	10.81	–.40	9.69

change in these rates over the 1991 base year. The third column provides "predicted" rates, based on demographic change alone. Specifically, using 1991 age-race-sex-specific rates of offending, population counts for these demographic combinations are used to estimate what the aggregate rate would have been were only demographic change to have occurred. The fourth column gives the percentage change in predicted aggregate rates based on demographic change in column 3. Finally, the fifth column shows the percentage of the actual change that is explained by demographics (that is, column 4 as a percentage of column 2).

Had we asked the question about the role of demographics following the publication of the 1993 or 1994 crime rates – just prior to the sharp downturn in youth offending – the contribution of demographics would have appeared to be slightly more than 15 percent. With the post-crack plunge in youth homicide since 1993, the role of demographics would appear to have diminished to about 10 percent. Thus, demographics did play a role in the 1990s crime rate decline, albeit a modest one.[7]

Although the conditions associated with the emerging crack market may have been fleeting, we must still confront longer-term adverse influences on youth, from insufficient supervision to excess television, from anger and alienation to access to guns and ammunition. Not only are levels of youth homicide still well above those of the mid-1980s, but it appears that among certain groups the rates may have plateaued at a level higher than in earlier years. Thus, there is little time or reason for complacency, especially in light of what demographics holds for the future.

All Else Assumed Equal. The study of demographic correlates of crime naturally invites researchers to consider forecasting the future. Unlike changes in economy or legislation, demography can be predicted with a high level of certainty, suggesting future changes in crime that might occur with the rather bold assumption that all else remains equal. Absent major epidemics and catastrophes or significant shifts in immigration policy, the age-race-sex structure of the U.S. population can be projected with relative ease – especially for groups already born. That is, while future birth rates may shift unpredictably because of social or cultural change (as happened with baby boomers, who delayed or decided against childbirth far more than earlier generations), by contrast, we know that the existing population ages one year every year. Thus, demographic forecasts extending one or possibly two decades into the future can project with a high degree of accuracy the population in crime-prone age groups.

The assumption of "all else equal" is a rather problematic one, of course, particularly with longer-range forecasts. For example, Fox's (1978) forecast of the violent-crime rate for the last quarter of the twentieth century was remarkably accurate in anticipating the 1980 peak and early 1980s downturn in violent crime but failed to anticipate the (unpredictable) impact that crack, guns, and gangs would have on the rate of youthful offending beginning in the mid-1980s (see Fox 1996a).

As the late 1980s surge in youth crime unfolded, moreover, there was great temptation to ponder the future. Snyder, Sickmund, and Poe-Yamagata (1996, p. 15) asserted that "if trends continue as they have over the past 10 years, juvenile arrests for violent crime will more than double by the year 2010." In projecting more than a quarter-billion juvenile violent arrests annually, Snyder et al. assumed that the ongoing increase in rates would persist and would combine with the expected increase in youth population. Fox (1996a, 1997b) also projected the possible impact that population shifts could have, although he assumed no increase in rates within any population group.

No sooner had the Fox and Snyder et al. projections been set in print that the first signs of moderation in youth crime began to emerge. Fortunately, the youth-crime bubble burst – not because the demography was wrong, but because all else was far from equal.[8]

Staying Focused on the Horizon. Despite the encouraging downturn since 1993, the rates of youth homicide remain intolerably high and far above levels of previous eras. What makes the late 1980s surge in the volume of youth crime particularly noteworthy is that it occurred while the size of the most violence-prone age group (18- to 24-year-olds) was on the decline. Despite the demographic shrinkage, this age group increased their rate of involvement in homicide, as did their younger counterparts.

The decrease in the size of the young adult population is now over, however, and the number of 18- to 24-year-olds is beginning to rebound. As shown in Figure 9.20, the population of young adults is expected to expand in proportionate size over the next decade (as is the population of teenagers), as the offspring of the baby boomers mature into and past their adolescence.[9]

This demographic turnaround is precisely what prompted several observers to predict a future wave of youth violence (Bennett, DiIulio, and Walters 1996; DiIulio 1995; Fox 1995, 1996a). In reaction to these bleak and worrisome projections, critics questioned the size and significance of the expected demographic shift (see Austin and Cohen 1996; Murphy 1996). Murphy (1996, p. 4), for example, argued:

> The male "at risk" population is expected to increase over the next decade, and this trend has led some to conclude that we need to brace ourselves for a new crime wave of juvenile violent crime that may well negate recent declines in violent crime rates. *However, a closer look at population projections shows that while the numbers of youth age 15–24 will increase, this increase will not exceed that for the 1980s.* [Emphasis in the original]

In an overall sense, Murphy and other critics are quite correct. The population count of teens and young adults, though expected to increase, will

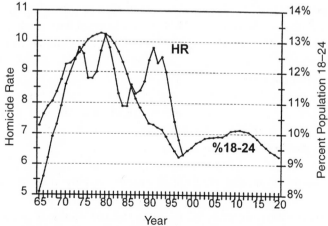

Figure 9.20. Projected aggregate homicide rates and percentage of 18–24-year-olds.

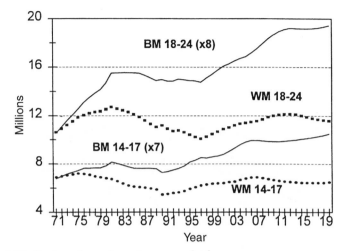

Figure 9.21. Projected number of young males by race.

not even achieve the level reached in the late 1970s, prior to the 1980s shrinkage in the at-risk population. What Murphy and others overlook, however, is that the race-specific age curves, although similar, also differ in rather important ways.

Figure 9.21 displays population projections separately for white and black youth (with the black population counts magnified by factors of 7 and 8 for 14- to 17-year-olds and 18- to 24-year-olds, respectively, to aid in making race comparisons). Although the overall pattern – downturn during the 1980s, a trough at or near 1990, and an increase thereafter – holds for both races, the slopes for the black populations are noticeably steeper. The projected rise in the white youth population is indeed modest, and the numbers are expected to plateau around the year 2010 at a level below that of the late 1970s. For black youth, however, the population has already exceeded that of the late 1970s, and it will continue to rise sharply for at least the next two decades.[10] Given the higher rates of violence perpetrated by black youth as compared with white youth, the disproportionate increase in the number of black teenagers and young adults could have a significant impact on the overall volume of youth violence in the years ahead.

It is important to place these somber projections into a larger demographic context. Figure 9.22 displays population projections for five different age groups – the "high risk" group of 14- to 24-year-olds, along with children under 14 and various subpopulations of adults. The younger age groups will expand, while the number of 25- to 34-year-olds will decline. For older groups, the population 35 to 49 will increase and then level,

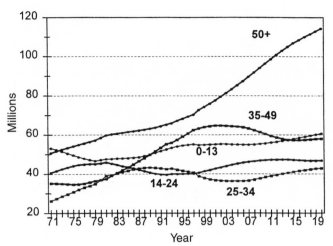

Figure 9.22. Demographic trends by age.

while the population 50 and over – the aging baby-boom cohort – will swell more than any other group. In fact, by the middle of the next decade, the population 50 and over will constitute nearly one-third of the U.S. population. Given the rather low proclivity of this elder group towards violence, the aggregate rate of violent crime in America, including homicide, may continue to fall. That is, the declining level of violence perpetrated by a greatly expanded elder population will more than balance any likely increase in the level of violence from a modestly growing teen population.

Considering the volatility of recent homicide rates, especially for younger age groups, it is rather difficult to produce with any degree of confidence precise numerical forecasts of homicide. Indeed, the variability over time in the rates of offending within any demographic group greatly dwarfs expected changes in the population composition. That is, for example, whereas the youth population is expected to expand by almost 2 percent per year, usual fluctuations in offending rates (be they upward or downward) can easily outweigh small increases in population. In general terms, however, even if rates of youth murder stabilize (or even approach the lower levels of the mid-1980s), the number of youth killings could once again rebound if only because of an expanded population at risk.

For the purposes of illustration – and only illustration – we can generate a projection of the number of homicide offenders by age category, with certain assumptions about future age-race-sex-specific rates of offending. In particular, we might assume that offending rates for age groups under

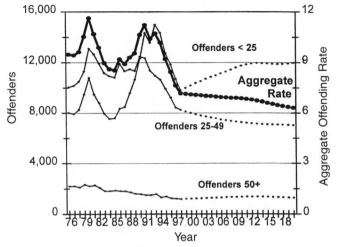

Figure 9.23. Projected rate of offenders.

25 remain unchanged from their current levels, while rates for older groups decline (as they have for nearly two decades) at small and progressive rates (one percent per year for 25- to 49-year-olds and 2 percent per year for the 50-and-over age group). As shown in Figure 9.23, the number of homicide offenders, ages 14 to 24, would rebound as a result of population expansion within this age group, and would also increase their representation among the overall pool of perpetrators. By contrast, the unprecedented growth in the older population (those ages 50 and over) would not have any major effect on the overall volume of homicide.

As noted at the outset, it is important not to be misled by aggregates. As shown also in Figure 9.23, the projected youth-offender counts may increase in the years ahead, but the aggregate rate of offending (which by nature of population composition is heavily weighted toward older age groups) would still decline. Thus, even if the FBI announces further declines in violent crime in future data and press releases, we must look closely within the overall figures to identify particular trends in youth violence. The long-term future and health of our nation depends on our ability to control youthful offending, even if it is overshadowed by the graying of America.

Notes

1. The imputation algorithm uses a weighting approach to allow solved cases to serve as proxies for unsolved ones. Unsolved cases are assigned zero weights, whereas solved cases

are weighted inversely proportional to the percentage of matched cases that are solved and thus receive weights of at least one. In terms of numerical value, 30.7 percent of the cases are unsolved and have zero weights, 61.9 percent of the cases have weights of at least one but less than two, another 6.0 percent have weights less than three, an additional 1.0 percent have weights less than four, and only about 0.4 percent have weights over four. As evidence that this weighting process does not distort the results, homicide trends with and without weighting are similar (in overall pattern, although not level).

2. Because multiple-offender homicides are more common than multiple-victim homicides, the offending rate exceeds the victimization rate.

3. Some baby boomers, of course, did their mellowing within the confines of a prison cell. The largest growth in prison populations since 1990 has been with violent offenders (see Darrell K. Gilliard and Allen J. Beck 1998), thereby increasing the suppression of adult violence through incapacitation.

4. The conventional wisdom used to be that the home was the most likely place for murder to occur. In recent years, we have apparently taken the "home" out of "homeicide." Thanks to a full range of legal and social interventions (from shelters for battered women to temporary restraining orders, from mandatory arrest procedures for domestic incidents to liberalized divorce laws), disputes are now far less likely to turn fatal. Curiously, the biggest drop has come among women killing their abusive mates – victims of domestic violence have some alternatives to picking up a loaded gun to protect against a loaded husband. In the past few years, however, the number of women killed by their intimates has decreased as well, but to a much smaller degree.

5. The recent increase observed in violent arrests for young women does not extend to murder. Apparently, homicide remains a male-dominated crime, among both victims and offenders.

6. Although the authors presented data on the rise in abortion per number of live births, no information was provided regarding whether there was an impact upon births themselves. It is possible, for example, that abortion availability could even have yielded an *increase* in the birth rate through increased sexual activity. Or it could have simply resulted in a net delay in child bearing for high-risk groups.

7. Regrettably, the discussion over those factors responsible for producing the drop in violent crime has sometimes become polarized. For example, a *New York Times* story regarding then New York City Police Commissioner William Bratton reported, "Perhaps the most popular theory, and the one most disdained by Mr. Bratton, argues that the crime rate is determined by the number of youths in society at any given time. At a news conference ... Mr. Bratton disparaged the major proponent of demographic criminology, James Alan Fox of Northeastern University, as well as the journalists who go to him for his opinions" (Krauss 1995, p. 1). The demographic hypothesis suggests, however, that population composition is but one explanation for changes in crime rates, not the only (or even the most important) explanation.

8. Fox and Dilulio were criticized for their unabashedly alarmist predictions and sensationalistic language (see Blumstein and Rosenfeld 1998; Zimring 1998). Neither intended the "coming crime storm" notion to be anything more than metaphorical. More important, the decidedly grim prophecy may very well have encouraged policy responses designed to avert the predicted youth crime wave.

9. This U.S. Bureau of the Census projection is produced by aging forward various existing birth cohorts while assuming stable levels of mortality and immigration.

10. Many white females of the baby boom postponed childbirth (often indefinitely) as they pursued expanded career options. This apparently was not so much the case for their black counterparts.

References

Austin, J. and R. L., Cohen. 1996. "Why are Crime Rates Declining: An NCCD Briefing Report" March 1. San Francisco: National Council on Crime and Delinquency.

Barnett, A. and J. Goranson. 1996. "Misapplications and Reviews: Good News Is No News?" *Interfaces* 26(3):35–39.

Bennett, W. J., J. J. DiIulio, and J. P. Walters. 1996. *Body Count: Moral Poverty and How to Win America's War Against Crime and Drugs.* New York: Simon and Schuster.

Blumstein, A. 1995a. "Violence by Young People: Why the Deadly Nexus?" *National Institute of Justice Journal*, August, 2–9.

Blumstein, A. 1995b. "Youth Violence, Guns, and the Illicit Drug Industry." *Journal of Criminal Law and Criminology* 86(1):10–36.

Blumstein, A., J. Cohen, and H. Miller. 1980. "Demographically Disaggregated Projections of Prison Populations." *Journal of Criminal Justice* 8:1–25.

Blumstein, A. and R. Rosenfeld. 1998. "Explaining Recent Trends in U.S. Homicide Rates." *Journal of Criminal Law and Criminology* 88(4):1175–1216.

Blumstein, A. and D. Nagin. 1975. "Analysis of Arrest Rates for Trends in Criminality." *Socio-Economic Planning Sciences* 9:221–27.

Butterfield, F. 1997. "Drop in Homicide Rates Linked to Decline in Crack Epidemic." *The New York Times*, October 27, p. A12.

Chilton, R. 1986. "Age, Sex, Race, and Arrest Trends for 12 of the Nation's Largest Central Cities." In J. M. Byrne and R. J. Sampson (Eds.), *The Social Ecology of Crime* (pp. 102–15). New York: Springer-Verlag.

Chilton, R. 1987. "Twenty Years of Homicide and Robbery in Chicago: The Impact of the City's Changing Racial and Age Composition." *Journal of Quantitative Criminology* 3(3):195–224.

Chilton, R. 1991. "Urban Crime Trends and Criminological Theory." *Criminal Justice Research Bulletin* 6. Huntsville, TX: Sam Houston State University.

Chilton, R., and A. Spielberger. 1971. "Is Delinquency Increasing? Age Structure and Crime Rate." *Social Forces* 49(3):487–93.

Cohen, L. E., and K. C. Land. 1987. "Age Structure and Crime: Symmetry Versus Asymmetry and the Projection of Crime Rates through The 1990s." *American Sociological Review* 52:170–83.

Cook, P. J., and J. H. Laub. 1998. "The Unprecedented Epidemic in Youth Violence," in M. Tonry (Ed.), *Crime and Justice: A Review of Research*, vol. 24. Chicago: University of Chicago Press.

Donohue, J. J., and S. D. Levitt. 1999. "Legalized Abortion and Crime," Unpublished manuscript, University of Chicago, Department of Economics.

DiIulio, J. J. 1995. "The Coming of the Super-Predators." *The Weekly Standard*, November 27, 23–28.

Farrington, D., and P. Langan. 1992. "Changes in Crime and Punishment in England and America in the 1980s." *Justice Quarterly* 9(1):5–46.

Fazlollah, M., M. Matza, and C. R. McCoy. 1998. "How to Cut City's Crime Rate: Don't Report It." *The Philadelphia Inquirer*, November 1, p. A1.

Federal Bureau of Investigation. 1999. *Crime in the United States 1998.* Washington: U.S. Government Printing Office.

Federal Bureau of Investigation. 1994. *Crime in the United States 1993.* Washington: U.S. Government Printing Office.

Ferdinand, T. N. 1970. "Demographic Shifts and Criminality: An Inquiry." *British Journal of Criminology* 10(2):169–175.

Fox, J. A. 1978. *Forecasting Crime Data: An Econometric Analysis.* Lexington, MA: Lexington Books.

Fox, J. A. 1995. *Homicide Offending Patterns, 1976–1993.* Paper presented at the annual meeting of the American Academy for the Advancement of Science, February 18. Atlanta, GA.

Fox, J. A. 1996a. "Trends in Youth Violence: A Report to the United States Attorney General on Current and Future Rates of Juvenile Offending." Northeastern University, Boston, Massachusetts. Available at: www.ojp.usdoj.gov/bjs/abstract/tjvfox.htm.

Fox, J. A. 1996b. "The Calm Before the Juvenile Crime Storm." *Population Today,* September, 4–5.

Fox, J. A. 1997a. "Missing Data Problems in the Supplementary Homicide Reports: An Offender Imputation Strategy Based on Victim Characteristics." Washington: U.S. Bureau of Justice Statistics, Workshop of Crime Imputation.

Fox, J. A. 1997b. "Trends in Juvenile Homicide, 1976–1999: An Update of the March 1996 Report to the U.S. Attorney General on Current and Future Rates of Juvenile Violence." Northeastern University, Boston, MA.

Gilliard, D. K., and A. J. Beck. 1998. *Prisoners-1998.* Washington: U.S. Bureau of Justice Statistics, NCJ 175687.

Greenfeld, L. A., M. R. Rand, D. Craven, P. A. Klaus, C. A. Perkins, C. Ringel, G. Warchol, C. Maston, and J. A. Fox. 1998. *Violence by Intimates: Analysis of Data on Crimes by Current or Former Spouses, Boyfriends, and Girlfriends.* Washington: U.S. Bureau of Justice Statistics, NCJ 167237.

Heide, K. 1998. *Young Killers.* Newbury Park, CA: Sage.

Krauss, C. 1995. "Crime Lab: Mystery of New York, the Suddenly Safer City." *The New York Times,* July 23 (Sec. 4, p. 1).

Murphy, L. 1996. "Statement before the Congressional Black Caucus Brain Trust on Juvenile Justice," May 14. Washington.

O'Driscoll P. 1998. "Crime Rate Recedes, But Wariness Remains." *USA Today,* November 20, p. 11A.

President's Commission on Law Enforcement and the Administration of Justice. 1967. *Task Force Report: Crime and its Impact—An Assessment.* Washington: U.S. Government Printing Office.

Radzinowicz, L. 1966. *Ideology and Crime.* New York: Columbia University Press.

Reno J. 1998. "Press Conference Comments," November 19. Washington: U.S. Department of Justice.

Sagi, P., and C. Wellford. 1968. "Age Composition and Patterns of Change in Criminal Statistics." *Journal of Criminal Law, Criminology, and Police Science* 59(1):29–36.

Snyder, H. N., and M. Sickmund. 1995. "Juvenile Offenders and Victims: A National Report." Washington: Office of Juvenile Justice and Delinquency Prevention.

Snyder, H. N., M. Sickmund, and E. Poe-Yamagata. 1996. "Juvenile Offenders and Victims: 1996 Update on Violence." Washington: Office of Juvenile Justice and Delinquency Prevention.

Snyder, H. N., M. Sickmund, and E. Poe-Yamagata. 1997. "Juvenile Offenders and Victims: 1997 Update on Violence." Washington: Office of Juvenile Justice and Delinquency Prevention.

Steffensmeier, D. J., and M. D. Harer. 1991. "Did Crime Rise or Fall during The Reagan Presidency? The Effects of an Aging U.S. Population on the Nation's Crime Rate." *Journal of Research in Crime and Delinquency* 28(3):330–59.

Zimring, F. 1998. *American Youth Violence.* New York: Oxford University Press.

Index

Page numbers followed by *f* indicate figures; page numbers followed by *t* indicate tables; page numbers followed by *n* indicate notes.